THE LIVING WORD COMMENTARY
ON THE OLD TESTAMENT

Editor
John T. Willis

Genesis

Genesis

John T. Willis

ABILENE CHRISTIAN UNIVERSITY
Abilene, Texas

A·C·U PRESS

LIBRARY OF CONGRESS CATALOG CARD NUMBER 78-52455
ISBN 0-915547-15-5
PRINTED IN U.S.A.

Writers in *The Living Word Commentary* series have been given freedom to develop their own understanding of the biblical text. As long as a fair statement is given to alternative interpretations, each writer has been permitted to state his own conclusions. Beyond the general editorial policies, the editors have sought no artificial uniformity, and differences are allowed free expression. A writer is responsible for his contribution alone, and the views expressed are not necessarily the views of the editors or publisher.

3 4 5

Contents

Preface

Beginning in 1974 and throughout subsequent years, some twenty thousand cuneiform tablets have been discovered at Tell Mardikh (ancient Ebla) in northern Syria by archaeologists working under the direction of Professor Paolo Matthiae of the University of Rome. These tablets date from about 2400–2250 B. C. Undoubtedly, in time their contents will shed much light on the world of the patriarchs. At the present time (1979), however, it is much too early to include any information gleaned from these discoveries in a work on Genesis. Leading scholars cannot agree on what is there at this point. Persons interested in this material are directed to the following works, where more extensive bibliographical material and information may be found:

I. J. Gelb, "Thoughts about Ibla: A Preliminary Evaluation, March 1977," *Syro-Mesopotamian Studies* 1, no. 1 (May 1977).

P. Matthiae, "Ebla in the Late Early Syrian Period: The Royal Palace and the State Archives," *Biblical Archaeologist* 39 (1976), pp. 94–113.

P. Matthiae, "Preliminary Remarks on the Royal Palace of Ebla," *Syro-Mesopotamian Studies* 2, no.2 (February 1978).

G. Pettinato, "The Royal Archives of Tell Mardikh-Ebla," *Biblical Archaeologist* 39 (1976), pp. 44–52.

Reports in recent issues of *Biblical Archaeology Review*.

My wife, Evelyn, and I would like to dedicate this volume to three gospel preachers and their wives and families, with whom we attended Abilene Christian University, and who have been faithful and dear fellow Christians and very close friends over a quarter of a century: Robert and Willora Oglesby of Richardson, Texas; Jim and Nona Sue Sheerer of Chickasha, Oklahoma; and Bob and Doris Vance of Nashville, Tennessee. With men and women and families the quality of these, the church has a bright future.

Acknowledgments

Unless otherwise indicated, scripture quotations are from the Revised Standard Version of the Bible, copyright 1946, 1952, and 1971 by the Division of Christian Education, National Council of Churches of Christ in the U.S.A. Used by permission.

Grateful acknowledgment is also made to the publishers of the following works for permission to quote material:

From *A Survey of Old Testament Introduction*, by G.L.Archer, Jr. Copyright 1964, 1974 by Moody Press, Moody Bible Institute of Chicago.

From *The Jerome Biblical Commentary,* by Brown, Fitzmyer and Murphy. Latest copyright 1973 by Prentice-Hall, Inc., Englewood Cliffs, N.J.

From *Genesis 1-11,* by Alan Richardson, Torch Bible Commentary. Copyright 1971 by SCM Press Ltd., London.

From *Genesis,* by Derek Kidner, The Tyndale Old Testament Commentary. Copyright 1973 by Tyndale Press, London. Used by permission of InterVarsity Press, Downers Grove, Ill.

From *A Critical and Exegetical Commentary on Genesis,* The International Critical Commentary. Copyright by Charles Scribner's Sons, New York, N.Y.

From *The Interpreter's Bible* and *The Interpreter's Dictionary of the Bible.* Copyright by Abingdon Press, Nashville, Tenn.

From *Genesis, A Commentary,* by Gerhard von Rad, translated by John H. Marks. Westminster Press, Philadelphia, Pa. Copyright 1961 by W. L. Jenkins.

From *Genesis,* The Anchor Bible, edited by E. A. Speiser. Copyright 1965 by Doubleday & Company, New York, N.Y.

From "The Tale of the Two Brothers," by J. M. Plumley, *Documents from Old Testament Times,* D. Winton Thomas, ed. Copyright 1961 by Harper & Row, Scranton, Pa.

From "Genesis," by W. Möller, *The International Standard Bible Encyclopedia,* vol. 2, copyright 1947; *Introduction to the Old Testament,* by R. K. Harrison, copyright 1971; and "St. Matthew," by A. L. Williams, *The Pulpit Commentary,* copyright 1950 by William B. Eerdmans Publishing Co., Grand Rapids, Michigan.

Abbreviations

AB	Anchor Bible
ASV	American Standard Version
BDB	F. Brown, S. R. Driver, and C. A. Briggs, *A Hebrew and English Lexicon of the Old Testament*. Oxford: Clarendon Press, 1957.
CB	Century Bible
CBQ	Catholic Biblical Quarterly
GHG	E. Kautzsch and A. E. Cowley, eds., *Gesenius' Hebrew Grammar*. Oxford: Clarendon Press, 1946.
IB	Interpreter's Bible
ICC	International Critical Commentary
IDB	Interpreter's Dictionary of the Bible
IOVC	Interpreter's One-Volume Commentary
ISBE	International Standard Bible Encyclopedia
JBC	Jerome Biblical Commentary
JBL	Journal of Biblical Literature
KJV	King James Version
LWC-OT	Living Word Commentary—Old Testament
LXX	The Septuagint
MT	Massoretic Text
NEB	New English Bible
NT	New Testament
OT	Old Testament
OTL	Old Testament Library
PC	Pulpit Commentary
PCB	Peake's Commentary on the Bible
RSV	Revised Standard Version
TDOT	Theological Dictionary of the Old Testament
TOTC	Tyndale Old Testament Commentary

I
Introduction

The Jews named the books of the OT after the first word in each book. So the Jewish name for the first book of the OT is *Bere'shith*, "In the beginning." The modern English name "Genesis" originated with the Greek translation (the Septuagint [LXX]) about 280–250 B.C., where the genitive form of the Greek word *genesis* (*geneseōs*) actually occurs in Genesis 2:4a, which reads, "This is the book of the genesis of heaven and earth." In the early fifth century A.D., this name was adopted in the Latin Vulgate by Jerome and from the Vulgate has come into English.

The book of Genesis records and gives divinely inspired evaluations of selected events extending from the creation of the world to the death of Joseph in Egypt, which signaled the beginning of Israel's 430-year sojourn in Egypt (cf. Gen. 15:13; Exod. 12:40-41). This material may be subdivided in several ways. For example, after the Introduction (1:1-2:3), there are ten (actually eleven if one includes 36:9) sections beginning with the Hebrew word *toledhoth* (which may be translated "generations" or "descendants" as the context requires):

Introduction—Creation of the heavens and the earth—1:1–2:3

Generations of the heavens and the earth—2:4–4:26

Generations of Adam—5:1–6:8

Generations of Noah—6:9–9:29

Generations (Descendants) of the Sons of Noah—10:1–11:9

Descendants of Shem—11:10-26
Descendants of Terah—11:27–25:11
Descendants of Ishmael—25:12-18
Descendants of Isaac—25:19–35:29
Descendants of Esau—36:1–37:1
Descendants of Jacob—37:2–50:26

It is also possible, however, to analyze the contents in the book of Genesis along the lines of great themes and people selected for inclusion and special attention by the writer. Then the broad outline would appear something like this:

Creation—1–2
Four accounts of sin and punishment, grace and renewal (linked together by genealogies)—3:1–11:26
Abraham—11:27–25:18
Jacob—25:19–36:43
Joseph—37–50

The present commentary attempts to combine these two schemes, placing special emphasis on the latter because it appears to bring out the religious message of the book more vividly.

TEXT, VERSIONS, AND TRANSLATION

The reader should keep in mind that this commentary is not scholarly, but popular; yet the author has based his comments and conclusions on his own research in the original languages and context, and has endeavored to a limited extent to fairly represent leading views of a passage, especially in instances where there have been significant varying positions. This means two things: (1) The nature of this work and its projected audience make it impossible to detail the evidence and arguments lying behind many conclusions. For this, the reader who knows the original languages and is concerned to delve more deeply into scholarly debate on a specific point will find ample discussion in the commentaries, journal articles, and monographs or special studies listed on pages 74–77. (2) One just beginning a serious study of the book of Genesis will encounter new ideas. In such cases, the author urges comparison with well-researched works on Genesis.

The extant copies of the book of Genesis in Hebrew are very late. The Codex Leningradensis, on which the third edition of Kittel's *Biblia Hebraica* depends, dates from the early eleventh century A.D. Only scattered fragments of Genesis have been discovered at Qumran. In fact, the most notable find at Qumran pertaining to Genesis is the Aramaic Genesis Apocryphon, which was published in 1956.

Four translations were made into Greek: the Septuagint (third century B.C.—our most trustworthy manuscripts date from the fourth and fifth centuries A.D.), Aquila, Symmachus, and Theodotion (all second century A.D.; only portions of these translations are extant today). The Samaritan Pentateuch originated about 400 B.C. (again, our manuscripts are relatively late).

In the late fourth and early fifth centuries A.D., Jerome translated the OT from Hebrew into Latin (the Vulgate), using the Old Latin, Origen's Hexapla, and the LXX to aid in interpreting obscure and difficult passages. Also in the fifth century A.D. the OT was translated into Syriac to produce a version called the Peshitta. The translators of this version depended heavily on the LXX. From the second century A.D. following, Palestinian rabbis produced Aramaic translations and paraphrases of the OT called Targums. The most important of these are the Targum Onkelos and the Targum Pseudo-Jonathan. These ancient versions have been taken into consideration in the present commentary, and significant variants are noted and evaluated at the appropriate places.

The commentary takes into account the MT and the ancient versions and includes a careful comparison of the KJV, ASV, RSV, and NEB. In isolated passages throughout the book of Genesis, sometimes one English translation is superior and sometimes another. However, on the whole it is quite clear that of these four versions the RSV is closest to the original text, and it is this text which appears in boldface type as the commentary's primary reference.

The translation of ideas from one language into another is always a difficult task. Space does not allow an extensive treatment of the problems involved, either here or at appropriate points in the commentary. However, certain suggestions and observations may be helpful.

(1) A literal, word-for-word rendering from Hebrew (or Aramaic or Greek) into English frequently does not capture the thought of the original. Thus, often it is best to translate clusters of words idiomatically than to give a literal translation (e.g., see comments on 14:15; 30:8, 23-24). On this point, the RSV is generally more accurate than the KJV or ASV.

(2) The same word or phrase means one thing in one context and another thing in another. Therefore, in the final analysis, the context must be the major criterion for determining the meaning of a difficult word or thought. Along this same line, there are often several possible literal renderings from which the translator must choose, and frequently such a choice is very difficult to make. In the book of Genesis, this is especially true of Hebrew phrases using *'elohim*, as is recognized by all modern English versions. The issue is whether this word in a given context should be interpreted as a divine name, "God," or as a noun of quality, "divine, awesome, mighty" (see the notes on 1:2; 23:6; 30:8). The verb *yadha'* varies in sense from passage to passage. For example, it means "to have direct cognition of" in 4:9, "to be certain of" in 12:11, and "to have sexual intercourse with" in 19:8 and 24:16. The noun *zera'*, literally "seed," differs in meaning from text to text. It can be used of plants (1:11, 12, 29), animals (3:15), and man (12:7). As elsewhere in the Bible, it usually has the collective meaning in Genesis, and in most cases it is best to translate it by "descendants" or "offspring," as in the RSV and NEB.

(3) Varying translations in modern English versions are frequently due to the translators' decision to follow a par-

ticular reading in an ancient version. For example, the translators of the KJV follow the Targum Onkelos in reading "the plain of Moreh" in 12:6, while the ASV, RSV, and NEB follow the MT and all the other ancient versions in reading "the oak (terebinth) of Moreh." The present writer believes that the MT should be followed unless there is strong evidence from the ancient versions and/or the context to do otherwise. Again, the RSV proves to be the strongest modern version.

(4) A correct rendering into English by no means solves all the problems involved in interpreting a biblical passage. For example, "for ever" is a correct rendering of the Hebrew expressions *'adh 'olam* and *le'olam*, but one must still decide whether this means "endless time," "a relatively long time," "a lifetime," or something else in each text. For example, God promises Abram that he will give to him and to his descendants the land of Canaan "for ever" (13:15). If this means "throughout endless time" or "as long as the earth shall stand," the claims of Christianity that God's relationship with Israel is superseded by his relationship with the church through Christ are invalid. Surely the meaning is something like "a long period of time."

(5) As words in the English language change meaning, it continues to be necessary to produce new versions of the Bible. In many cases, it is necessary for one to be schooled not only in the biblical languages but also in early English in order to correctly comprehend the KJV. For example, he must learn that the word "earing" in the KJV of Genesis 45:6 comes from the Latin *arare*, "to plow"; or that "wotteth" in the KJV of 39:8 is the third person present singular of the archaic English verb *wit*, which is derived from the Anglo-Saxon verb *witan*, meaning "to know."

(6) Sometimes translations are quite ambiguous. For example, the statement "my wrong be (is) upon you" (16:5) can mean "the wrong that I have done be upon you" or "the wrong done to me be upon you."

(7) In interpreting the Bible, it is most important to understand whether the subject of a verb, an adjective, or a

pronoun is singular or plural. Since the RSV and NEB use "you" throughout, it is often impossible to make this distinction in these versions. On this item, the KJV and ASV are superior because they consistently use "thou, thy, thine, thee" for the singular and "you, your, yours, ye" for the plural. Thus, the text of 17:10 reads: "This is my covenant, which you [plural] shall keep, between me and you [plural] and your [singular] descendants after you [singular]: Every male among you [plural] shall be circumcised."

(8) There are many important Hebrew wordplays throughout the book of Genesis. It is virtually impossible to render these into English, since English does not have words of equivalent force on which puns can be made as they are in Hebrew. One value of a commentary is to call attention to and to explain such wordplays. For example, God tells Abraham to call his son "Isaac" (Heb. *yitschaq*) because Abraham and Sarah "laughed" (Heb. *tsachaq*) when God announced that Sarah would bear a child (17:17, 19; 18:12-14; 21:3, 6). It is a mistake to think that such paronomasias are attempts to explain the etymology of a Hebrew word. Instead, they are plays on words, as one might make plays in English on words like "blue" and "blew" or "lead" (the mineral) and "led."

Appraisals of the Book of Genesis

Scholars of all persuasions are generally agreed on a number of matters pertaining to the book of Genesis. (1) Most of the stories, customs, language, and religious concepts reflected in the book are very ancient. In fact, they go back to the period prior to Israel's conquest of Canaan. (2) The author (or authors) responsible for the present form of the book made use of several earlier oral and/or written sources of some sort. In this particular, Genesis is like the OT books of Samuel, Kings, and Chronicles, and the four Gospels of the NT. (3) Some of the accounts in Genesis have to do with individuals and some with tribes or clans. As might be expected, there is great divergence of opinion over which specific sections should be ascribed to each.

(4) While there are (sometimes striking) parallels between ancient Mesopotamian and Egyptian accounts and the OT narrative (e.g., in the stories of creation, the flood, the tower of Babel, etc.), the author (or authors) of Genesis did not borrow these accounts indiscriminately but reflected a much nobler view of God (e.g., monotheism rather than polytheism), a much higher ethical standard, and a much more realistic view of life (e.g., history rather than mythology).

Broadly speaking, scholars hold one of three different views on the Pentateuch, of which Genesis is the first book. An exhaustive presentation of these opinions would require a large volume of very technical argumentation and is therefore out of the question. However, some of the major defenses and weaknesses of each view may be explored in the brief appraisal which follows.

The Documentary Hypothesis

The widely espoused "documentary hypothesis" of the Pentateuch is the end-product of a long history of Pentateuchal study and interpretation. As early as the second century A.D., the Talmud (Baba Bathra 14b) affirmed that Joshua (and not Moses) must have written the account of Moses' death and burial in Deuteronomy 34:5-12. In the twelfth century, the Jewish Rabbi Ibn Ezra (died 1167) observed that Genesis 12:6 must have come from a time when the Canaanites were no longer in the land of Palestine, and thus long after the time of Moses. In 1520, Carlstadt took the position that Moses could not have compiled Genesis–Deuteronomy because it does not make sense that he wrote the account of his own death in Deuteronomy 34:5-12, a passage which has the same style as that which precedes. Masius (1574), de la Peyrère (1655), and Simon (1685) concluded that an author later than Moses compiled the Pentateuch, using the notes of Moses. Hobbes (1651) and Spinoza (1670) argued that Moses did not write the entire Pentateuch but is responsible for those passages explicitly ascribed to him (e.g., Exod. 24:4; 34:28; etc.). Witter (1711) and Astruc (1753) believed that there were two main sources in Genesis because two different divine names are used in the book. Astruc also found ten additional fragmentary sources in the book but argued that Moses was the compiler. This was the "older documentary hypothesis." Geddes (1792), Vater (1802), and de Wette (1805) explained the Pentateuch as a collection of larger and smaller fragments; and their view is appropriately labeled the "fragmentary hypothesis." Ewald (1831) and Schrader (1869) championed the view that originally there was an E (Elohistic) document (Schrader thinks there were two), to which a later J (J[Y]ahwist) editor added supplementary material. This is the "supplementary hypothesis."

All these views were destined to give way to the "new documentary hypothesis." This view began with Hupfeld (1853), Dillmann (1875), and Delitzsch (1880), who found four sources in the Pentateuch, arranged chronologically as P (Priestly Code), E (Elohist), J (Yahwist), and D (Deuteronomy). It remained only for Reuss (1833), Graf (1866), Kuenen (1870), and Wellhausen (beginning in 1876) to carry the day for modern scholarship by rearranging the chronological order of these documents into J (850 B.C. in Judah), E (750 B.C. in North Israel), D (650 B.C.), and P (400 B.C.).

Since their work, scholars have modified their view in minor ways, but by and large this theory holds major respect in contemporary critical circles. Modifications include R. H. Pfeiffer's S (Seir, i.e., Edomite) source, Morgenstern's K (Kenite), Simpson's J¹ and J², Eissfeldt's L (Lay), Fohrer's N (Nomadic), etc. Some of the supports for this hypothesis may now be discussed and evaluated.

Different divine names. The divine name *Yahweh* (the Lord) is predominant in some passages (cf. Gen. 7:1ff.; 11:1ff.; 18:1–19:28), and the divine name *Elohim* (God) is predominant in others (cf. 1:1–2:3; 6:9ff.; 17:2ff.). Furthermore, Exodus 3:14 and 6:2-3 state that God did not reveal himself as "Yahweh" until the time of Moses, and yet "Yahweh" occurs often in Genesis (cf. 4:26; 6:5; etc.). Most critical scholars explain this by theorizing that two originally independent sources lie behind the book of Genesis: J (which uses Yahweh) and E (which uses Elohim).

On the other hand, the Islamic Koran has two divine names—Allah and Rab, Ugaritic sources use both Baal and Haddu of the same deity, and Egyptian combines Amon and Re into one god; yet experts do not assign passages in which these varying names occur to different independent sources. There is another way to explain these varying names. Elohim is the universal name for God, while Yahweh is the name by which he reveals himself as the God of his people. The same writer could have used these two terms in connection with different works or functions of the deity or simply to avoid monotony. E. A. Speiser, who champions the documentary hypothesis, repeatedly denies that an earlier source can be determined on the basis of different divine names (see his remarks in *Genesis*, AB, pp. 260, 322, 330, 338, etc.). Exodus 6:1-9 does not necessarily mean that the name "Yahweh" had never been used before, but only that its full significance had not yet been revealed or emphasized to man as God revealed it to Moses.

Different names or terms for the same person, groups, and places. The pre-Israelite inhabitants of Canaan are called "Canaanites" in Genesis 12:6 and 50:11 but "Amorites" in 15:16 and 48:22. The home of the patriarchs is termed "Paddan-aram" in 25:20; 37:2, 5, 6, and 7 but "Aram-naharaim" (RSV "Mesopotamia") in 24:10. The Hebrew word for a female slave is *shiphchah* in 16:5 and 32:22 (Hebrew 23) but *'amah* in 21:12 and 30:3. Isaac's son is called "Jacob" in 25:26-34; 27:6, 11; etc. (E) but "Israel" in 32:28, 32 (Hebrew 29, 33), etc. (J). Many other examples in Genesis and throughout the Pentateuch could be cited. Again, however, this can be explained by an author's natural inclination to avoid monotony. For example, the Tell el-Amarna tablets (fourteenth century B.C.) use "Canaan" for Syria and Palestine in a general sense, but a stele from the period of Amenophis II (ca. 1440 B.C.) uses the same word in the narrower sense of "merchant." "Amorite" can also be used in a broad sense for the inhabitants of Syria and Palestine (Josh. 24:15, 18), or in a narrower sense for part of the inhabitants of the hill country of Palestine (Num. 13:29; Josh. 5:1). Accordingly, "Canaanite" and "Amorite" can be used interchangeably by the same speaker or writer. It is noteworthy that many critics assign Genesis 16:5 to J (note "Yahweh" here) and 16:3 to P, and yet *shiphchah*, "maid," appears in both verses. Furthermore, it seems rather strange to insist that "Israel" is peculiar to J, but "children of Israel" can occur in any source (see Speiser, *Genesis*, p. 321, on 42:5).

Two or more accounts of the same event. Abraham lies about his relationship to his wife twice (12:10-20; 20), and Isaac does the same (26:6-11). Jacob twice changes the name of Luz to Bethel (28:19; 35:6, 15). God twice changes Jacob's name to Israel (32:28; 35:10). Numerous other examples could be given. Now, with regard to Abraham's lying about his wife, circumstances provided such dangerous situations for seminomads in the ancient world that it would not be unthinkable at all for Abraham to use this expedient to spare his household at two different places, spaced several years apart, and before two kings in two different countries. Genesis 20:13 states that Abraham told Sarah to lie about their relationship "every place" they went. The similarities of storytelling and language can easily be attributed to the fact that the same person tells similar stories in similar (though not exact) ways. Genesis 26:1 refers back to 12:10. Furthermore, if Jesus changed Simon's name to Peter on two different occasions (John 1:42; Matt. 16:17-18), and if Peter kept wearing his name Simon after this change took place (Acts 10:5, 18; 11:13), there is no reason why God could not have changed Jacob's name to Israel on two different occasions, especially since a change of name was intended to encourage a person to alter his life (see notes on 35:10).

Discrepancies. According to the creation story in Genesis 1, God created vegetation, then fish, then birds, then animals, and finally man and woman; but in Genesis 2 he created man, then vegetation, then animals, and finally woman. God commanded Noah to take two of each kind of animal into the ark in 6:19-20, while 7:2-3 says he commanded him to take two of each kind of unclean animal and seven (or seven pair) of each kind of clean animal. It rained on the earth for forty days according to 7:12, but 7:24 says the waters prevailed on the earth 150 days. Many additional examples might be cited.

In the opinion of the present writer, this is one of the weakest points in the critical position. It amounts to superimposing modern canons of handing down traditions and of writing on the ancient mind. For example, there is no reason why the same ancient traditionist or writer cannot first state or sketch a general truth to place a panoramic picture before the eyes of his readers and then come back over the same material in order to emphasize certain things he wants to stand out in their minds. It is *only* if one takes both Genesis 1:1–2:3 and 2:4-25 *chronologically* that a discrepancy can be demonstrated. But if either section is not chronological, the alleged discrepancies disappear. Evidently 2:4-25 expands on and elaborates the work of God on the third and sixth days and especially on the sixth day because his main concern is man. Furthermore, there is no reason why the same writer could not make the general statement that Noah took two of all kinds of animals into the ark, and then modify this slightly by adding that the only exception was that he took seven (or seven pair) of clean beasts into it. Again, the length of time that it rained on the earth during the flood can be explained in two ways. Either it rained 40 days, and the waters stayed on the earth 150, or it rained 40 days until the water bore up the ark (cf. 7:17) and continued to rain another 110 days. (See the chart with notes on 7:11.)

Chronological problems. In Genesis 12:11, Abram describes Sarai as "a woman beautiful to behold"; however, she was sixty-five at the time, because 17:17 shows that she was ten years younger than Abraham and 12:4 states that Abraham was seventy-five when he and his household came into Canaan. Again, 25:26 says that Isaac was sixty when Jacob and Esau were born; 26:34 says he was 100

when he blessed them on his deathbed (see 27:2, 4); yet
35:28 states that he did not die until he was 180. Several
other similar chronological difficulties appear in Genesis.

To keep matters in perspective, it should be remembered
that all historical records from all countries in all ages contain chronological problems. The veracity of a text cannot
be impugned on the basis of such problems. The biblical
writers were selective, and often problems that arise are
due to a lack of detailed information. By now, however,
sufficient archeological discoveries have been made which
illuminate previously misunderstood biblical statements
that scholars have come to view the biblical text with much
greater respect than was the case several decades ago. At
the same time, tentatively, there are logical explanations
for the problems stated above. In ancient times, men and
women lived longer than they do today, and thus the aging
process was slower. Since Sarah lived to age 127 (23:1), she
had lived approximately half her total years at sixty-five.
Just as many women today are beautiful at half their life-
span (35-40), the same could certainly have been true of
Sarah. Further, the situation with Isaac was not much different from that of Abraham. Abraham considered himself
to be an old man at 100 (17:17), yet he did not die until he
was 175 (25:7). Isaac was old at 100 but did not die until he
was 180.

Discordant views of God and religion. According to expo-
nents of the documentary hypothesis, the most striking difference between J and E is that J presents God in bold
anthropomorphic terms (he forms man from the dust of the
ground as a potter would make a vessel out of clay, 2:7; he
walks in the garden in the cool of the day, 3:8; etc.), while
E describes God as standing aloof from man and revealing
himself to him by dreams (20:3, 6; 28:10-17; etc.) or night
visions (15:1; 21:12-14; etc.) or an angel speaking from
heaven (21:17). It is also argued that P does not mention
sacrifices until Exodus 6.

This approach is based on the Hegelian view that the OT
reflects an evolution from a lower to a higher level of religion and thought. For example, to the early period belong

animism, polytheism, sacrifices at any number of places in a family context; this gradually evolved into henotheism or monolatry (the belief that each nation has its own god), and then with the eighth century B.C. prophets, into ethical monotheism. History, however, has shown that man can deteriorate from a higher to a lower form of religious and ethical standards. Even if one adopts the generally accepted division of the material in Genesis into sources, he finds that an angel mediates God's message to man not only in E (21:17), but also in J (16:7, 9-11), and that God reveals himself in dreams and night visions in J (15:12ff.; 26:24; 28:13-16; 32:27) as well as in E. According to this division, J speaks of Yahweh smelling the "pleasing odor" of Noah's sacrifice (Gen. 8:21), yet this phrase is said to occur often in P (Num. 15:3, 7, 10, 13-14, 24; 18:17).

When proponents of the documentary hypothesis find difficulty in maintaining a consistent view, they often resort to two expedients: either (1) the redactor omitted important material, or (2) he felt constrained to preserve material because it had already gained wide popular acceptance as a part of the tradition which he inherited from the former generation. It should be evident that these two explanations, which in reality mutually exclude each other, are nothing but "escape valves" to be used whenever the biblical text does not support the critical theory.

The more arbitrarily and carelessly the redactors are thought to have gone to work in many places in removing contradictions, the more incomprehensible it becomes that they at other places report faithfully such contradictions and permit these to stand side by side, or, rather, have placed them thus. And even if they are thought not to have smoothed over the difficulties anywhere, and out of reverence for their sources, not to have omitted or changed any of these reports, we certainly would have a right to think, that even if they would have perchance placed side by side narratives with such enormous contradictions as there are claimed to be, e.g., in the story of the Deluge in P and J, they certainly would not have woven these together. If, notwithstanding, they still did this without harmonizing them, why are we asked to believe that other places they omitted matters of the greatest importance?

W. Möller, "Genesis," ISBE, vol. 2, p. 1203

Three other particulars demonstrate the weak foundation on which the documentary hypothesis rests.

(1) Since its beginning, this approach has led to a great proliferation of sources by those who have attempted to demonstrate its validity. Different critics have championed two J sources, two or three E sources, two P sources, L, K, S, and N. Such conclusions raise serious doubts as to the ability of modern man to successfully separate out sources lying behind finished ancient documents. To be sure, comparisons of Samuel and Chronicles, Kings and Chronicles, Samuel and Psalms, Chronicles and Psalms, as well as biblical statements such as those found in Luke 1:1-4 and John 20:30-31 show that the biblical writers used sources. But this does not suggest that they used them indiscriminantly or incoherently or without divine guidance. It is hardly scientific to apply modern Western canons of thought and structure to ancient literature, or to assume that because supernatural occurrences and/or inspiration do not come within the scope of one's own personal experience, such cannot happen elsewhere.

Recent studies of smaller portions of the book of Genesis have led certain scholars to express a deeper appreciation for the coherence of this material. In a study of Genesis 2-3, R. Gordis writes:

The assumption made a generation ago that the alleged biblical redactor operated mechanically with his sources and could not be expected to have had any intelligent view of the material he used is now rightly rejected by contemporary research. Even if "sources" were to be assumed, we still must come to grips with the conception underlying the "finished product" that we find in Genesis.

"The Knowledge of Good and Evil in the Old Testament and the Qumran Scrolls," JBL 76 (1957), p. 129

In his widely heralded comparison of the Gilgamesh

Epic and Genesis 6–8, Heidel says:

> I am not at all convinced that the biblical material can be resolved into its constituent elements with any degree of certainty. Moreover, I am not in sympathy with the common practice of treating the alleged remnants of each supposed document as if it constituted the whole, with the result that the Genesis account of the deluge . . . fairly teems with discrepancies.
>
> A. Heidel, *The Gilgamesh Epic and Old Testament Parallels*, p. 245

Whatever the sources lying behind the present final form of the book of Genesis may have been or may have meant to those who handed them down, the primary task of the serious Bible student is to attempt to understand the text as it now stands and to determine the meaning which the inspired biblical author had in mind for his audience.

(2) Although the book of Genesis is large, as biblical books go, the language, customs, thought patterns, syntax, psychological presuppositions, and religious insights are so few in comparison with all that was said and done by the people living in the time covered in its pages that it would be very presumptuous for men several thousand years removed to think that they knew everything that an author could have said or reported. The book of Genesis itself covers such a wide range of human history that it would be amazing indeed if different words and phrases from different places and periods did not appear within it. Over a period of months and years, one person's vocabulary, manner of speaking, and insights change radically. It would be rather shortsighted to think that the same could not have happened in ancient times, especially when large numbers of people were involved.

(3) Champions of the documentary hypothesis express appreciation for the coherence of the biblical material, even while they are engaged in the process of trying to show its disparity. They seem to walk a tightrope between homogeneity and heterogeneity in evaluating and analyzing various passages. At the beginning of his treatment of the

Joseph story, for example, Speiser writes: "The casual reader is hardly aware that he has a composite story before him; and even the trained analyst is sometimes baffled when it comes to separating the parallel accounts" (*Genesis*, p. 294). One frequently gets the distinct feeling that critics of this persuasion approach the text in search of sources rather than permitting the text to speak for itself.

One Conservative View

Two views of the authorship and composition of the book of Genesis have been held by conservative scholars. One is that Moses is the author of the whole book. This position is based on five major arguments.

Jewish and Christian tradition. The Jewish Mishna (Pirqe Aboth I, 1) and Talmud (Baba Bathra 14b) attribute the Pentateuch to Moses, except that the Talmud states that Joshua wrote the account of Moses' death in Deuteronomy 34:5-12. Similarly, Philo (*Vita Mosis* III, 39) and Josephus (*Antiquities* IV, 8, 48) declare that Moses wrote the entire Pentateuch, including the account of his own death. Most of the early church fathers concur in expressing belief in the Mosaic authorship of the Pentateuch. At the same time, there are other traditions espoused by these same groups of Jews and Christians which modern conservatives have come to reject, and one must decide whether to build his case for Mosaic authorship on human traditions.

The unity of the Pentateuch. There are numerous statements in Exodus–Deuteronomy which assume a knowledge of events and statements now recorded in the book of Genesis. For example, the statement that seventy persons went with Jacob into Egypt in Exodus 1:5 concurs with the similar statement in Genesis 46:27; the mention of a new king that knew not Joseph in Exodus 1:8 presupposes a knowledge of Joseph's death, which is related in Genesis 50:24-26; the sabbath law in Exodus 20:8-11 assumes that the hearers or readers are already aware of God's having rested on the seventh day of creation, which is recorded in Genesis 2:2-3. Many other examples could be given. The point is that if a unity can be demonstrated between Genesis and Exodus – Deuteronomy, since the Bible often claims the Mosaic authorship of at least portions of the latter, he must also be the author of Genesis.

However, it is also true that other books in the OT assume a knowledge of what is recorded in Genesis. Joshua 21:43-45 is very important here because it states that the Lord gave Israel the land he had sworn to give to their fathers, which clearly presupposes the readers know of such promises as those found in Genesis 12:1-3; 13:14-17; 15:18-21; 26:2-5; 28:13-15; and 35:10-12. This and similar considerations have led some scholars to argue that the first book of the OT was the Hexateuch (Genesis – Joshua), not the Pentateuch. Here one must decide whether dependence on another biblical book indicates that the author referring to or assuming an acquaintance with that book is its author. When one remembers that NT writers often refer to events recorded in Genesis (cf. Acts 7:2-16; Heb. 11:3-22), this argument turns out to be inconclusive.

Biblical claims of the Mosaic authorship. Exodus – Deuteronomy contain several claims that Moses wrote certain records now contained in these books (cf. Exod. 17:14; 24:4; 34:27; Num. 33:1-2; Deut. 31:9). Outside the Pentateuch in the OT, several passages state that Moses wrote the book of the law or in some way connect his name with the law (Josh. 1:7-8; 8:31, 35; 23:6; 1 Kings 2:3; 8:53, 56; Ezra 6:18; 7:6; Neh. 9:14; 13:1; Dan. 9:11-13; Mal. 4:4). The NT does the same (Luke 16:29, 31; 24:27, 44; John 5:46-47; 7:19, 22; Acts 3:22; Rom. 10:5; etc.). A closer examination of these passages indicates that many of them are ambiguous on the question of authorship. If Moses wrote the entire Pentateuch, why is it necessary for him to state several times in Exodus – Deuteronomy that he wrote down this item or that item now related in the Pentateuch? The meaning of the word "law" in the phrase "law of Moses" or in a statement like "Moses gave you the law" is problematic, because it could mean "the Pentateuch" (as seems to be the case when it is used alongside "the prophets and the psalms" as in Luke 24:44) or "the legal material that God gave Moses on Sinai" (as seems to be the case in John 7:22, where a distinction is made between Moses' giving the law of circumcision [Lev. 12:1-3] and this law having originated with the fathers [Gen. 17:1-14]).

It is difficult to tell whether the biblical writers are affirming that Moses wrote the whole Pentateuch or whether they are declaring that he wrote the law at Sinai. It is true that "the book of the law" in Nehemiah 9:3 includes events found in the book of Genesis (as vss. 6-8 show), but it is called "the book of the law of the Lord" and embraces the "law" made known by Moses in verse 14, so that in this passage the "law" connected with Moses in verse 14 is a smaller part of "the book of the law of the Lord" mentioned in verse 3. The same could be true of the "law" attributed to Moses in other texts listed above. Furthermore, it must be decided whether the expression "law of Moses" represents a claim for Mosaic authorship of the Pentateuch or whether it is simply an ancient means of identifying the block of material under consideration. In Hebrews 4:7 "David" apparently is a term used for the Psalms without any necessary claim to authorship. There is no heading over Psalm 95 (which is the psalm to which reference is made in this verse in Hebrews), and while David wrote some of the Psalms, he did not write all of them, for example, those which refer to the temple as already being in existence (cf. 42:4; 84:1-4; 127:1; etc.) or those which presuppose that the Babylonian exile has already taken place (cf. 137; etc.). Apparently, then, his name is used in connection with that body of literature, not as a claim of Davidic authorship but to identify the mass of biblical material under consideration. The same may be true of the terms "Moses" and "law of Moses."

Familiarity with details. There are details relating to the lifetime of Moses which only an eyewitness could have known, such as that there were twelve springs of water and seventy palm trees at Elim (Exod. 15:27) or that manna looked like coriander seed and bdellium and tasted like cakes baked with oil (Num. 11:7-8). The author of Genesis and Exodus used Egyptian names (as Zaphenath-paneah, Asenath, and Potiphera, Gen. 41:45, 50), words (as *'abhrekh*, "Bow the knee," Gen. 41:43—see notes on this text), weather (as the reference to the crop sequence in connection with the plague of hail, Exod. 9:31-32), flora and fauna (as the *shiṭṭim* or acacia wood and the *tachash* or "tanned rams'" skins used in the making of the tent of meeting, Exod. 25:5; 36:19), and geographical allusions (as his comparison of the Jordan plain with "the land of Egypt, in the direction of Zoar," Gen. 13:10).

The whole setting assumed in the books of Exodus–Numbers is that of the desert. The tabernacle fits a desert milieu of people who wander about from place to place. The goat on which the lot falls for Azazel is to be sent away into the wilderness (Lev. 16:10). The sanitary instructions given in Deuteronomy 23:12-13 do not fit a settled society, but wanderers in the desert. The customs reflected in the book of Genesis (such as a barren wife providing a handmaid for her husband to bear legitimate children by her, Gen. 16:2 [see more details below and the note on this verse]) belong to the second millennium B.C., and many words in the Pentateuch are spelled archaically, indicating an early date.

Now all this evidence is certainly sound. However, is it not possible that a later writer could have used earlier material which contained all these particulars, just as a modern historian can use earlier sources in writing his book? If Luke was not an eyewitness of the events and sayings in the life of Jesus which he relates but himself used earlier oral and written accounts that had already been preserved by eyewitnesses and ministers of the word (Luke 1:1-4), the same could have happened in the writing of any other biblical book. God is not restricted to one certain way of preserving the truths that he wishes to make known to man. He works in and with man to relate his will, not against his nature as a thinking and acting being.

Moses' qualifications. Moses was eminently qualified to write the Pentateuch. He "was instructed in all the wisdom of the Egyptians, and he was mighty in his words and deeds" (Acts 7:22). His forebears handed down memories, records, and laws which they had preserved from the time that Abram had lived in Mesopotamia and even before. He had a firsthand knowledge of the geography, customs, agricultural practices, and climate of Egypt and the Sinai Peninsula. Since Moses was aware that one of his major tasks was to weld the Israelites into a nation and to prepare them to enter the land that God had promised to their ancestors, he would have had proper motivation and divine guidance to write a history of the patriarchs and to record the laws which were to be Israel's guide in Canaan. During the forty years in the wilderness, he would have had the time necessary for such a challenging task.

While all this is true, it leave some unanswered questions about certain passages in the book of Genesis. (1) Genesis 10—This list of nations that ultimately arose from the sons of Noah extends chronologically much later than the time of Moses, as the references to the Cimmerians ("Gomer," vs. 2), Medes ("Madai," vs. 2), and Scythians ("Ashkenaz," vs. 3) indicate (see notes on these names), because there are no allusions to them in written records before the first millennium B.C. In response to this, some conservative scholars conjecture that these peoples existed as tribal or clan groups much earlier. (2) Genesis 14:14—This verse mentions "Dan" by name as a city in northern Canaan in the days of Abraham. But Joshua 19:47 and Judges 18:27-29 make it clear that this city did not receive the name "Dan" until the end of the period of the Judges and that previously it was called "Leshem" or "Laish." Some conservative critics argue that a later scribe changed the original text to the name of the place that was current in his time, but there is no proof for this in the ancient manuscripts or versions, and if this is the case in this verse it might be the case in other verses. Were both Moses and scribal redactors inspired? (3) Genesis 31:47—This verse contains an Aramaic word—"Jegar-sahadutha"—and Aramaic represents a later state in the development of the Hebrew language. Some conservative scholars seek to solve this problem by conjecturing that there were Aramaic influences in Hebrew from the very beginning and contend that this is indicated by similarities between Aramaic and Ugaritic. (4) Genesis 36:31—In historical retrospect, the author of this verse informs his readers that he will now give a list of Edomite kings who ruled "before any king reigned over Israel." Such a statement "dates itself, on any normal understanding, in or after the time of Saul" (D. Kidner, *Genesis*, TOTC, p. 16). Yet there are some conservative critics who insist that this verse was written by Moses. G.L. Archer, Jr., argues·

> The appointment of a Hebrew king is regarded as a mere possibility, at best a remote future eventuality that would furnish a fulfillment of the promise made to Abraham in Genesis 17:6 (P): ". . . and kings shall come out of thee." In view of the fact that only the secondary line of Esau had achieved royal status, it was appropriate for a covenant-conscious author in the fifteenth century to note the fact that the posterity of Jacob had not yet attained to that dignity.
>
> *A Survey of Old Testament Introduction*, p. 146, n.11

Another Conservative View

Other conservative scholars believe that it is necessary to attribute to Moses only those portions of the Pentateuch which the Bible itself attributes to him. They contend that the Bible alone is final authority in such matters and thus put no stock in Jewish or early Christian tradition. It is generally agreed that many such traditions are unreliable, for example, when one Talmudic tradition says that Moses wrote the book of Job about 2100 B.C.! They believe that the expressions "law of Moses," "law given by Moses," and the like do not necessarily refer to the whole Pentateuch but apply only to those portions which contain legal material that the Lord handed down to Israel through Moses. If Baruch wrote sections of the book of Jeremiah (cf. Jer. 36), a successor of Moses could have written sections of the Pentateuch. It is most natural to believe that the account of Moses' death and succeeding events recorded in Deuteronomy 34:5-12 come from a hand much later than the time of Moses; but if this section of the Pentateuch is not from him, one does not detract from the biblical teaching on inspiration or authority by thinking that certain other parts of the Pentateuch are not from Moses. One's inability to discover the name of the author of the book of Hebrews in the NT does not undermine its credibility for Christian doctrine and life. The most natural explanation of the references to Moses in the third person in Exodus–Deuteronomy is that someone other than Moses wrote these lines, while what follows in each case is genuinely Mosaic. The most natural interpretation of Genesis 10:2-3, 14:14, 31:47, and 36:31 is that these verses or portions thereof are the work of a later hand.

This view is adopted by a number of conservative scholars, including Derek Kidner and R. K. Harrison. Kidner contends that "the material [in the book of Genesis] is from Moses, whoever was his biographer and editor" (*Genesis,* p. 15). Then, taking a cue from E. Robertson, he suggests that Samuel may have been that biographer and editor:

> Certainly the spiritual stature of Samuel, and his experience of the realms of government, priesthood and prophecy, make him as likely a final architect of the Pentateuch as any of whom we know before Ezra; and if he was the narrator who told of Moses and edited his writings, the occasional references to post-Mosaic names and situations . . . would be fully in keeping with the fact.
>
> Ibid., p. 25

Harrison acknowledges the existence of post-Mosaic additions throughout the Pentateuch, including Exodus 11:3 (R. K. Harrison, *Introduction to the Old Testament*, p. 573); 12:42 (p. 570); Numbers 12:3; 15:22-23; 32:34 (pp. 616–17); Deuteronomy 1:1-2; 3:14-17 (pp. 637–38); 10:6-7 (pp. 639–40); etc. As to the book of Genesis, he writes:

> While Genesis is an anonymous work, . . . its attributive author is Moses. However, to what extent he wrote any of its contents . . . is unknown. In attributing Mosaic author-

ship to the Pentateuch as a whole, conservative scholars have pointed out that the Torah in its entirety must not necessarily be assumed to have been the work of his own hands, any more than any of the *stelae* of antiquity were the product of direct activity on the part of their attributive authors. Some writers, such as Young, have not precluded the possibility that the writer drew on earlier written sources, but in general the ascription of Mosaicity to the Pentateuch implies its historicity and its foundation by Moses under divine inspiration, with the supposition that later editors may have revised the contents somewhat in accord with the traditions of the ancient Near Eastern scribes.

Harrison, *Introduction*, p. 542

Harrison believes that Genesis 36:31 (p. 550) and portions of 10:2-3 (p. 559) are post-Mosaic scribal or editorial additions. According to this view, it is possible that Moses wrote or dictated or had written the Pentateuch in its final form and that later scribes or editors made a few explanatory and transitional additions to clarify obscure matters for their readers, or that Moses was responsible for preserving earlier material handed down to him by his ancestors (in the case of Genesis) and for saying and writing the things attributed to him (in the case of Exodus–Deuteronomy), and that later scribes or editors collected and arranged this material in its final form. The latter would correspond to the way in which the four gospels were composed (see Luke 1:1-4; John 20:30-31; 21:25).

The present commentary assumes that the book of Genesis was arranged in its present final form for a specific reason and that the scholar's first task is to deal with the text as it now stands. Neither space nor purpose allows much room for treatment of documentary, traditio-historical, or form-critical matters. While it is therefore limited in many ways, perhaps the emphasis chosen will allow for a deeper appreciation of the coherence of the book of Genesis in its present form, and accordingly, for a more profound understanding of its divinely inspired religious message. Surely this was the main concern of its author.

ANCIENT NEAR EASTERN HISTORY AND
THOUGHT CONCURRENT WITH GENESIS

Archeological research, linguistic studies, and a continually increasing understanding of ancient Near Eastern beliefs, laws, and customs have greatly advanced man's understanding of the OT world and consequently of the OT itself. Using the book of Genesis as a control, we sketch here some of the major points of interest pertaining to a study of the contents of this book.

Mesopotamia

The geographical location of the incidents related in the earlier chapters of the book of Genesis is Mesopotamia. Two of the rivers connected with the garden of Eden are the Tigris and the Euphrates (Gen. 2:14). The ark landed on one of the mountains of Ararat (8:4) in Armenia. The list of nations in Genesis 10 includes a reference to Nimrod, who began his royal tasks in Babel, Erech, and Accad, all of which are in the land of Shinar (i.e., Babylon), and who later went north to Assyria and built great cities (10:8-12). Ancient mankind built a city and a tower in the land of Shinar and called it Babel (Babylon; 11:1-9). Abram came from Ur of the Chaldeans (11:28, 31; Acts 7:2, 4) in the southern part of the Fertile Crescent of Mesopotamia and moved to Haran (Gen. 11:31; Acts 7:2) in the north. While Abram was living in Hebron and Lot in Sodom in the land of Canaan, kings from the Mesopotamian region attacked Sodom and the cities of the valley (Gen. 14:1-12). When Abraham thought it time to select a wife for Isaac, he sent his servant back to the city of Nahor in Mesopotamia (24:10). Similarly, Isaac later sent his son Jacob to Haran in Paddan-aram to find a wife from among his own people (28:6, 7, 10; etc.), and Jacob lived there twenty years (31:38, 41). Since there are so many references to Mesopotamia in the book of Genesis, it stands to reason that the more one can learn about this region in ancient times, the better he can interpret this book.

The Sumerians. As early as 4000 B.C. a people called the Ubaidians lived in southern Mesopotamia and founded villages which were destined to become the great cities of the Sumerians. About 3300 B.C. the Sumerians began to pour into this region, probably from the Caucasus Mountains. By the beginning of the third millennium B.C. they began to establish strong city-states, including Ur (Abram's early home), Erech (Uruk, Warka) about fifty miles northwest of Ur, and Lagash about fifty miles north of Ur. Sumerian poets wrote epic tales about two of the kings of Erech (viz., Enmerkar and Lugalbanda). Four of these epics have been unearthed. One of the kings of Nippur, Enmebaraggesi, built a temple to the Sumerian air-god Enlil, called "father of all the gods," and Nippur became Sumer's leading religious and cultural center. One of the most famous rulers of Erech was Gilgamesh, concerning whom a long epic was written. Tablet XI of this epic contains the celebrated Babylonian account of the Flood. (For a discussion of the content of this account and its relationship to the Genesis flood story, see Excursus, "The Genesis Flood and Babylonian Parallels," p.184, below.)

Toward the close of the Sumerian period (ca. 2400–2300 B.C.), the city-state of Lagash replaced Erech as the ruling city in Sumer. Its last ruler, Urukagina, was the first known social reformer, for he restricted the oppression of the rich and powerful, lowered taxes, halted injustice and exploitation, and took measures to help the poor, the widow, and the orphan. In the early years of Sumerian control, the city-states were ruled democratically by an assembly of freemen and a governor (called an *ensi*). As time went on, a king (called a *lugal*) seems to have been appointed for limited times of military crisis, but ultimately this gave way to an ongoing dynastic arrangement. The Sumerians developed very advanced social, economic, legal, and educational systems. Tens of thousands of clay tablets with cuneiform writing have been uncovered in the ancient cities of Sumer. They include governmental, legal, and economic documents, as well as myths, epics, hymns, laments, proverbs, fables, and essays. The school offered professional and academic training. Teachers prepared advanced grammatical texts, dictionaries, complicated mathematical problems and tables, and poetic and prose writings.

About 2360 B.C., Sargon, king of Agade (Akkad), invaded Sumer from the north, conquered it, and replaced the Sumerian language with the Semitic Akkadian language. Agade became a major trading center in the ancient world. Sargon's dynasty lasted through the reign of his grandson Naram-Sin (ca. 2180 B.C.), when it was overthrown by Gutian invaders from the mountains in the northeast. This opened the door for a Sumerian revival, and the city of Lagash was the first to gain control in the southern region under its governor and king, Gudea. In time, however, Ur gained the upper hand under a powerful king named Ur-Nammu, who established the Third Dynasty of Ur (ca. 2060–1950 B.C.). Ur-Nammu was responsible for the oldest law code thus far unearthed by archeologists. It forbade chiselers and grafters to work in the land, required just weights and measures, protected the poor, the widow, and the orphan, and exacted a fine on one who injured his fellow man. Akkadian continued to be the spoken language in this period, but Sumerian was still used among the academicians. In time the population became chiefly Semitic.

The religion of the Sumerians was built around the phenomena of nature, particularly the seasons. The Sumerians thought that the universe originated from the primeval sea that completely surrounded it. It was composed of a vaulted heaven placed upon a flat earth, and from this atmosphere came all life. This universe was controlled by a pantheon, the four main deities of which were An (heaven), Ki (earth), Enlil (air), and Enki (water), the four creating gods. Man was formed out of clay for the sole purpose of providing the gods with food, drink, and shelter so they would have sufficient time for their divine activities. The fate of each individual was determined by the arbitrary will of the gods and was to be accepted without question. Public worship at the temple was very important.

The annual highlight of Sumerian religion was the New Year celebration, which reached its climax in the holy marriage (*hieros gamos*) between the ruling king and Inanna, the goddess of love and reproduction, represented by the queen. It was thought that the death of all plant life during the hot summer months was due to the death of the god of vegetation, represented by the king. He went down into the netherworld until autumn; then he was raised from the dead, came back to earth, and had sexual relations with his wife, thus causing vegetation to spring forth again.

The Amorites. The Amorites ("Westerners") were so called because they lived in the land of Amurru (the territory "west" of Mesopotamia), which includes the northwest portion of the Fertile Crescent, Syria, and Palestine. About 2000 B.C. they invaded the northern part of the Fertile Crescent from the west, and established the powerful city of Mari (the modern Tell Hariri) on the Euphrates. The ruins of Mari were first excavated by A. Parrot in 1933–1939 and then again in 1951–1956. Among other things, archeologists unearthed a temple to the goddess Ishtar, a temple tower (ziggurat) and sanctuary, a huge palace with almost three hundred rooms, and approximately twenty thousand cuneiform tablets dating form the time of Iasmah-Adad (ca. 1739–1730 B.C. or ca. 1789–1780 B.C.) and Zimri-Lim (ca. 1730–1700 B.C. or ca. 1780–1745 B.C.). These tablets include administrative, economic, and juridical documents and royal correspondence written to Zimri-Lim from a wide variety of individuals ranging all the way from foreign kings to the common people. Many scholars link a tribe often mentioned in the Mari texts with the OT tribe of Benjamin because of similarities in the names and descriptions of the two groups.

Amorites were rather widespread in the ancient Near East. Shortly after 2000 B.C., one group of Amorites overran the Third Dynasty of Ur to the southeast and brought an end to the last Sumerian kingdom. Others established strong city-states in Palestine, including Kadesh. By the time the Israelites invaded Canaan in the thirteenth century B.C., they lived east of the Jordan (Num. 21:13, 21,

29, 31; Josh. 2:10; 9:10; 24:8; Judg. 10:8; 11:19-23), in the southern territory that later became the territory of Judah (Deut. 1:19-20, 27, 44; Josh 10:5, 6, 12), and throughout the land of Canaan (Gen. 15:16; Josh. 24:11, 12, 15, 18). Ultimately, the Amorites at Mari were defeated by the powerful Babylonian King Hammurabi (ca. 1728–1686 B.C. or ca. 1792–1750 B.C.), who was responsible for a famous ancient law code and during whose reign copies of earlier Babylonian accounts of creation and the flood were made.

The Hurrians. The Hurrians were an ancient people that originally came from Armenia and surrounding regions and spread throughout the ancient Near East from about 2500 to about 1000 B.C. They founded the mighty Mitanni empire and made Haran the center of their political and economic life. The moon-god Sin was worshiped in both Ur and Haran, which may have provided a strong inducement for Terah and his family to stay in Haran (Gen. 11:31; Acts 7:2, 4) instead of going on to Canaan. Hurrians are called Horites, Hivites (cf. Gen. 36:2, 20 with notes on these verses), and Jebusites (Araunah [2 Sam. 24:16] is a Hurrian name) in the OT.

Several thousand cuneiform (Akkadian) tablets were unearthed at the Hurrian city of Nuzi (the modern Yoghlan Tepe, located ca. one hundred fifty miles north of Baghdad) by a joint expedition of the American School of Oriental Research in Baghdad and Harvard University in 1925–1931. The tablets date from the fifteenth and fourteenth centuries B.C. and have shed a great deal of light on previously puzzling customs found in the book of Genesis. Specific examples are noted at appropriate places throughout the commentary, but some may be mentioned briefly here. Nuzi custom dictated that if a man and wife had no child, their chief servant would inherit their possessions; this would explain why Abram concluded that Eliezer of Damascus was to be his heir (15:2). Sometimes the father of a bride would give her a slave girl at the time of her marriage; this may clarify the reason Laban gave Zilpah to Leah and Bilhah to Rachel (29:24, 29). The slave girl was to bear children to the husband of her mistress in case her mistress was barren; this would indicate why Sarai offered Hagar to Abram (16:2). In such a case, the child born to the slave girl was legally considered to be the wife's child; perhaps this is why Abraham thought Ishmael was the son that God had promised him (17:15-18).

Hurrian customs declared that a birthright was handed down from father to son, not on the basis of the order of birth but on the basis of the father's decree. Such a proclamation was most binding when the father issued it on his deathbed; this helps one understand why several individuals in the book of Genesis receive the patriarch's birthright and blessing in his old age, in spite of the fact that they are not the oldest son or grandson (as Jacob—27:1-41; Ephraim—48:1-20; and Judah—49:1-28). Nuzi law stated that if a man desired to deed his property over to his son-in-law, he had to give him his household gods; this would explain why Laban was so distraught when Jacob and his family left Mesopotamia, and he could not find the *teraphim* or household gods (31:14-21, 30-35). In addition to these particulars, Speiser argues that in the Hurrian culture often a man's wife was also given the legal status of sister, and that this helps explain why Abraham (12:13; 20:2, 5, 12-13) and Isaac (26:6, 9) said that their wives were their sisters (*Genesis*, pp. 91–94, 151–52).*

The Canaanites. The word "Canaanites" is used in the OT alongside "Amorites" (see above) to describe the pre-Israelite inhabitants of the region west of the Jordan (cf. Gen. 12:5-6; 13:7, 12; 50:11; Num. 33:50-53; Josh. 7:9; 11:3). Some scholars think that this word may be Hurrian in origin and that it originally denoted "merchants." This view receives some support from the use of the Hebrew

* This has been challenged by D. Freedman, "A New Approach to the Nuzi Sistership Contract," *The Journal of the Ancient Near Eastern Society of Columbia University* 2 (1970), p. 80; S. Greengus, "Sisterhood Adoption at Nuzi and the 'Wife-Sister' in Genesis," *Hebrew Union College Annual* 46 (1975), pp. 5–31; and H. Shanks, "The Patriarchs' Wives and Sisters—Is the Anchor Bible Wrong?" *The Biblical Archaeology Review* 1 (1975), pp. 22–26, because of the slim and subjective evidence on which Speiser builds his case.

word *kena'an* (in varying forms) with the meaning "trade" in Isaiah 23:8; Ezekiel 17:4; Hosea 12:7 (Hebrew 8); Zephaniah 1:11; and Zechariah 11:7, 11. Semitic-speaking peoples settled in the area west of the Jordan as early as 3000 B.C. Hittites and Amorites moved into this region in the early part of the second millenium B.C., and the Amorites established some strong city-states here. During most of this period, the land was under Egyptian control.

The Canaanites were a very mixed and heterogeneous people, who isolated themselves from each other in a number of fortified city-states, each of which was governed by a "king." Immigrants that moved into the region from other areas were regarded as "sojourners," which was a social rank between "native citizen" and foreigner." The sojourner sought the protection of the city-state or region to which he attached himself (cf. Gen. 12:10; 20:1), but he was expected to be loyal to his protector (21:23). Normally he was not allowed to own land (23:4) and could not question the rights of the native citizens (19:9). Such was the situation when Abram brought his household into this territory and when Isaac and Jacob lived there. This made it possible for these men and their families to survive in a country not their own.

Brief attention should be given to the cities and towns in Canaan which played a prominent role during the period of the patriarchs. Shechem (the modern Tell Balatah, about one and one-half miles east of Nablus) is located between Mount Gerizim and Mount Ebal. This site began to be inhabited about 4000 B.C. It is mentioned in Egyptian texts as early as the nineteenth century B.C. and in the Tell el-Amarna Tablets about 1375–1366 B.C. Its population, occupation, and significance differed with the times and circumstances. Shechem was the first place that Abram came in the land of Canaan (12:6). On their return from Paddan-aram, Jacob and his household tarried here for a while, during which time Jacob purchased a piece of land from the sons of Hamor and built an altar (33:18-20). At this place, Shechem the son of Hamor raped Jacob's daughter Dinah, and her brothers Simeon and Levi slaughtered the men of the city while they were healing from circumcision (34:1-31). Joseph's brothers were pasturing their flocks near Shechem when Jacob sent him to check on their safety (37:12-14).

When Abram moved on south from Shechem, he next built an altar between Bethel (modern Beitin) on the west and Ai (modern et-Tell) on the east (12:8; 18:3-4). Bethel was inhabited at least as early as 2000 B.C. and was important during the period of the patriarchs. At an earlier time it was called Luz (28:19; 35:6). It was here that Jacob saw the vision of angels ascending and descending on the stairs and gave it the name "Beth-el" (house of God; 28:10-22; 31:13) and some twenty years later built an altar and reemphasized that the name of the site was Bethel (or El-Bethel; 35:1-15).

Abram moved farther south to Kiriath-arba or Hebron (Gen. 13:18; cf. 23:2; 35:27; Josh. 15:13, 54; 20:7; 21:11; Neh. 11:25), the modern el-Khalil (er-Rahman), which is located about nineteen miles south of Jerusalem. It was here by the oaks of Mamre that he was destined to spend most of his time in the land of Canaan (cf. Gen. 14:13; 18:1; 23:2, 17-20; 35:27; 49:29-32). During this period there seems to have been a mixture of peoples in this region, who were probably suspicious of and hostile to one another, for the Bible speaks of Amorites (who were Abram's allies, 14:13, 24) and Hittites (from whom Abram bought a field and cave, 23:3-20) as inhabitants of this area.

Sodom and Gomorrah (along with Admah and Zeboiim, cf. Gen. 10:19; Hos. 11:8) played a major role in the story of Abram and Lot. In their day, these cities were located in a fertile valley (13:10) southeast of Hebron. When strife arose between Abram's herdsmen and Lot's herdsmen, Lot chose to take up his abode in this region (13:11-12). Sodom and the other cities of the Valley of Siddim were subject to Mesopotamian rulers when Lot and his household moved there. When these cities rebelled against their overlords, Lot and his family were carried off as prisoners of war. Abram and his men rescued them from their captors in northern Palestine (14:1-16). Because of the horrible sins of the cities of the valley, God destroyed them, and only Lot and his two daughters escaped (18:22–19:38). Evidently Sodom and her sister cities were located under what is now the southern tongue of the Dead Sea (cf. 14:3), whose maximum depth is about eighteen feet in modern times. Just to the west of this portion of the Dead Sea lies Jebel Usdum, a mountain about seven hundred feet high and five miles long, which is largely a mass of crystalline salt (which calls to mind Lot's wife, who looked back and became a pillar of salt, 19:26) and whose modern Arabic name means "Mount of Sodom." The biblical text does not give enough evidence to indicate exactly how God destroyed the cities of the valley. However, biblical and extrabiblical sources as well as modern investigations suggest that bitumen (asphalt), oil, and gases seeped out of the ground in ancient times. The fire mentioned in 19:24 may be lightning, which ignited the gases and oil and caused a great explosion (or a series of explosions), and the brimstone may refer to heated rocks and debris flying through the air. Heavy black smoke from the ensuing fire (or fires) could be seen miles away (cf. 19:28). The date at which this happened is uncertain. Nevertheless, archeologists have discovered that pilgrimages to the nearby site called Bab edh-Dhra', which began about 2300 B.C., suddenly stopped about 1900 B.C.; and it has been conjectured that the destruction of the cities of the valley took place about this time.

Genesis 14:17-20 tells of a meeting between Abram and Melchizedek, king of Salem. Salem has been variously identified with Shalem (four to five miles east of Shechem; cf. the LXX, Vulgate, and Syriac of Gen. 33:18, followed by the KJV), Salim (located near Aenon, where John the Baptist was baptizing; cf. John 3:23), and Jerusalem (cf. Ps. 76:2 [Hebrew 3]). The reference to Melchizedek in Psalm 110:4 seems to support its identification with Jerusalem (cf. vs. 2).

Both Abraham (Gen. 21:25-34) and Isaac (26:26-33) spent a great deal of time in the region around Beer-sheba, which is located about twenty-five miles southwest of Hebron. Here there was much underground water, and they dug wells to procure water for their flocks and herds. Abraham called the place Beer-sheba because he gave Abimelech seven (*shebha'*) ewe lambs as a witness to the fact that he had dug the wells and because the two of them swore an oath (*shabha'*) there that Abraham's rights would be respected (21:28-31). Here he worshiped God as "the Everlasting God" (21:33). Several years later, Isaac reasserted this name for the place for similar reasons (26:32-33; see notes on 21:25-34 and 26:26-33). At a later period, God appeared to Jacob at Beersheba and told him to go with his family into Egypt (46:1-5).

On his return from Paddan-aram to Canaan, Jacob spent the night east of the Jordan at Peniel on the River Jabbok. Here he struggled with a "man" (32:24, 25, 28 [Hebrew vss. 25, 26, 29]), who is also identified as an "angel" (Hos. 12:4 [Hebrew 5]) and as "God" (Gen. 32:28, 30 [Hebrew 29, 31]; Hos. 12:3 [Hebrew 4]). Peniel is located east of Succoth and east of the modern Tulul edh-Dhahab.

When Joseph went to search for his brothers at his father's bidding, he found them at Dothan, the modern Tell Dotha, about ten miles north of Shechem. This was an important trade route in ancient times for merchants going from Mesopotamia to the Mediterranean Sea on their way to Egypt. Archeologists have found that this site was inhabited as early as 3000 B.C. Here the brothers of Joseph cast him into a pit and later sold him to Ishmaelite or Midianite traders going to Egypt (Gen. 37:17-36).

The Hittites. In the patriarchal age, Hittites lived in southern Palestine alongside Amorites as part of the native population (Num. 13:29). In some way, the Hittites and Amorites were ancient ancestors of the Israelites (Ezek. 26:3, 45). At Hebron, Abraham purchased a field including the cave of Machpelah from Ephron the Hittite and his associates (Gen. 23:1-20; 25:8-10; 49:29-32; 50:12-13). Esau married some Hittite women (26:34; 36:2), apparently at Beer-sheba (cf. 26:23). They made life so bitter for Isaac and Rebekah that they urged Jacob not to do likewise but to go to Haran in Mesopotamia to find a wife (26:34; 27:46–28:2).

The Hittites can be traced back to Anatolia (modern Turkey) as early as about 2000 B.C. Between 1600 and 1200 B.C., they had a strong empire extending eastward into northern Syria and at one point as far as Babylon, with its capital at Hattusas (modern Boghazköy in Turkey; cf. Josh. 1:4). Evidently groups or clans of Hittites moved farther south into Palestine and settled there, since Hittites are frequently listed as one of the seven peoples living in Palestine at the time of the Israelite conquest (Deut. 7:1; Josh. 9:1; Judg. 3:5). Two ancient extrabiblical sources (the Annals of Sargon II and a cuneiform Hittite tablet from Boghazköy) confirm the presence of Hittites in Palestine at an early period.

The Hebrews. In the book of Genesis, both Abram (14:13) and Joseph (39:14, 17) are called "Hebrews." Recent archeological and linguistic studies have led scholars to relate the Hebrews to the Habiru or Hapiru in some way. The earliest reference to the Habiru is in texts dating from the Third Dynasty of Ur (ca. 2050 B.C.). Then they appear in texts from Mesopotamia, Mari, Alalakh, Nuzi, Boghazköy, Tell el-Amarna, and Ras Shamra. In all this material, they are mercenary soldiers or a social class between free citizens and slaves. If the Habiru and Hebrews are to be connected, it seems best to suppose that the Hebrews were a smaller part of the larger ethnic or social group called the Habiru.

Egypt

The Egyptians. About 2100 B.C. internal strife between two powerful city-states (Herakleopolis and Thebes) broke out in Egypt. In time Thebes gained the upper hand, and from about 1991 to 1778 B.C. the powerful Twelfth Dynasty ruled Egypt. It was during this time that Abram and his family migrated into Egypt to secure food, water, and resources during a severe famine in Canaan (Gen. 12:10). The Egyptians were accustomed to foreigners coming into their land during times of famine and thus welcomed them as long as they remained peaceful. Egyptian wall paintings and reliefs from the last half of the third millennium and the first half of the second millennium B.C. depict starving herdsmen. Asiastics often came into Egypt for relief in times of famine. Genesis 12:16 lists a number of Abram's possessions, some of which apparently were given to him by the Pharaoh. Sarah's Egyptian handmaid Hagar (16:1, 3) may have been among the maidservants he procured. Included among the animals are camels, which many scholars consider to be out of place in ancient Egypt. However, two small statues of camels have been found in Egypt, one at Abusir el Melek dating from the First Dynasty, and one at Tanis dating from the Ptolemaic period, indicating the presence of camels in certain regions of Egypt at a rather early age. An ancient Egyptian story (ca. 1900 B.C.) tells how an Egyptian official named Sinuhe left Egypt because of political pressures and fled to Mesopotamia, where he learned to live a seminomadic life raising flocks and herds like the patriarchs (cf. Gen. 13:2-12; 30:14-43). Beginning about 1850 B.C., the Egyptians began composing execration texts, which were magical formulas designed to place curses on the enemies of the Pharaoh. A stereotyped formula was inscribed on a pottery bowl or clay figurine with the enemy's name, and then the object was smashed, symbolizing by sympathetic magic what would happen to that enemy.

The Hyksos. About 1720 B.C. peoples from Asia Minor called the Hyksos ("Rulers of Foreign Countries") overran Egypt and set up their capital at Avaris (Tanis; OT Zoan, cf. Ps. 78:12, 43; the modern San el-Hagar), a city dedicated to the worship of the god Seth. They introduced the horse, the chariot, the composite bow, a heavier sword, body armor, and the rectangular fortress of beaten earth as military components into Syria, Palestine, and Egypt. In their attempt to unite Egypt under their control, they welcomed foreigners into the land; therefore, this would have been an ideal time for Jacob's family to come into Egypt (Gen. 46) and for Joseph to attain a high position in government (41:38-46; 45:8-9), since the Egyptians would hardly have allowed a foreigner to hold such a high office. If the Israelite exodus from Egypt took place about 1290

B.C. (as many scholars think), Jacob's family must have gone into Egypt about 1720 B.C. since 430 years separated the two events (Exod. 12:40-41; cf. Gen. 15:13).

The Egyptian Pharaoh had kitchen officials, brewers, bakers, and candymakers, as well as a special "cupbearer" (Egyptian *wdpw*) who stood behind him while he ate and waited on him. These details fit the story of Joseph's imprisonment with the chief butler and the chief baker (40:1-23). Joseph was called "overseer of the house" of Potiphar (39:4) and of the Pharaoh (41:40), which is an official Egyptian title. An ancient Egyptian text tells how Ramses II gave his second gold ring and his golden cane to a certain Nebunnef when he made him the first prophet of Amon. Similarly, the Pharaoh of Joseph's day gave him fine gifts when he made him second-in-command in Egypt (41:42-43). It seems to have been customary for the Pharaoh to release a prisoner each year on his birthday, which would corroborate the account of the release of the chief butler on the Pharaoh's birthday (40:20).

Egyptian texts also tell of dreams and their interpretation. These include the dreams of Prince Thut-mose, the Ethiopian Pharaoh Ta-nut-Amon, and a number of commoners. The dreams of the Pharaoh (41:1-8) and of the chief butler and chief baker (40:1-23) certainly fit into this ancient outlook. Joseph died when he was 110 (50:22), which the Egyptians regarded as the ideal age. It is well known that Egyptians mummified or embalmed important people, and both Jacob (50:2) and Joseph (50:26) were embalmed. One Egyptian text states that a certain Abdu was placed in a coffin in Egypt, and the same is said of Joseph (50:26; cf. Exod. 13:19; Josh. 24:32).

Several Egyptian stelae and the Brooklyn Papyrus tell how Asiatic immigrants came to Egypt and took Egyptian names. The Pharaoh Merneptah gave the foreigner Ben-Ozen two Egyptian names when he elevated him to a high governmental position. Accordingly, the Pharaoh of Joseph's time gave him the name Zaphenath-paneah (which probably means something like "the god says he lives") when he raised him to the position of second-in-command

(41:45). The Egyptian name Potiphar (37:36; 39:1) or Potiphera (41:45, 50) means "the one whom (the god) Re has given." According to Egyptian religion, shepherds were an abomination (43:32; 46:34). The book of Genesis, and especially the story of Joseph (37–50), contains a number of Egyptian customs, words, names, and geographical allusions which support the authenticity of this material.

Jacob and his family (45:10; 46:28; 47:1) and their descendants the Israelites (Exod. 8:22 [Hebrew 18]; 9:26) lived in that part of Egypt called the land of Goshen (and at the time of Ramses II [1290–1224 B.C.] and following, the land of Rameses, Gen. 47:11). The land of Goshen, which is often mentioned in Egyptian texts, is located near Avaris in the northeastern portion of the Nile Delta. It was especially good for shepherds and herdsmen because it had excellent grazing land (47:6, 11). The city of On (Heliopolis, Gen. 41:45, 50; 46:20), where Joseph's father-in-law Potiphera functioned as a priest, is located just northeast of modern Cairo near the village of Matariyah by Tell Hisn. It was long famous in ancient times as a cult center with numerous objects of worship.

After controlling Egypt for about one hundred seventy years, the Hyksos were driven out in a series of military campaigns by the Egyptian Pharaohs Ka-mose and Ahmose I (ending ca. 1550 B.C.). In time there grew up an Egyptian Pharaoh who did not know Joseph (Exod. 1:8), probably Seti I (1308–1290 B.C.) or Ramses II (1290–1224 B.C.).

THE RELIGIOUS TEACHING
OF THE BOOK OF GENESIS

Paul writes to Timothy:

> But as for you, continue in what you have learned and have firmly believed, knowing from whom you learned it and how from childhood you have been acquainted with the sacred writings which are able to instruct you for salvation through faith in Christ Jesus. All scripture is inspired by God and profitable for teaching, for reproof, for correction, and for training in righteousness, that the

man of God may be complete, equipped for every good
work.

2 Timothy 3:14-17

And to the Roman Christians Paul says, "For whatever
was written in former days was written for our instruction,
that by steadfastness and by the encouragement of the
scriptures we might have hope" (Rom. 15:4). Thus, like
Jesus and other leaders in the early church, Paul viewed
the OT primarily as a book of religious teaching or instruction. Since it is "inspired by God," the book of Genesis
does not simply relate a series of ancient historical events,
and its author does not merely write to his readers interesting information. Rather, God is at work with him to interpret the events he records and thereby to teach his audience great truths which transcend the time, customs, and
human limitations of those who were involved in them.
Thus they are just as applicable and indispensable to the
NT Christian as they were to the first readers of this book.

God

The main character in the book of Genesis (as in the
entire Bible) is God. He is the prime mover in human life
and history. He reveals his nature to man through his deeds
and words.

Creator. The book of Genesis declares God to be creator
of the heavens, the earth, and everything in the universe
(the sun, moon, and stars—chs. 1–2). Melchizedek (14:19)
and Abram (14:22) confess him as "maker of heaven and
earth." Accordingly, the OT view is not that God is limited
to the land of Canaan but that he functions with equal
power and wisdom in Ur of the Chaldees and Haran, in
Hebron and Egypt, in Shechem and Bethel, in Dothan and
Sodom and Gomorrah, on earth and throughout the vast
universe. The OT, like the NT, declares that "the God who
made the world and everything in it, being Lord of heaven
and earth, does not live in shrines made by man, nor is he
served by human hands, as though he needed anything,
since he himself gives to all men life and breath and every-

thing" (Acts 17:24-25). It declares that God is "the God of heaven and of the earth" (Gen. 24:3, 7), "the Lord of all the earth" (Josh. 3:11, 13), that "the earth is the Lord's and the fulness thereof, the world and those who dwell therein" (Ps. 24:1), and that God's "glory is above earth and heaven" (Ps. 148:13). When Solomon gave his speech at the dedication of the temple, he said: "Will God indeed dwell on the earth? Behold, heaven and the highest heaven cannot contain thee; how much less this house which I have built!" (1 Kings 8:27).

Genesis 1–2 emphasizes that in creation God provided for the needs of all his creatures. He made water for fish, air for birds, dry land for land animals and man, vegetation for food, and woman for man. Through creation God reveals his basic nature. He is incomparable. King Hezekiah once prayed: "Thou art the God, thou alone, of all the kingdoms of the earth; thou hast made heaven and earth" (2 Kings 19:15; cf. Isa. 40:25-26; Neh. 9:6). He is all wise.

> The Lord by wisdom founded the earth;
> by understanding he established the heavens.
>
> Proverbs 3:19

(Cf. Ps. 104:24; Jer. 10:12-13.) God is all-powerful. "Ever since the creation of the world his invisible nature, namely, his eternal power and deity, has been clearly perceived in the things that have been made" (Rom. 1:20). And, as a great umbrella covering all his other qualities, he demonstrates his steadfast love in creation.

> To him who alone does great wonders,
> for his steadfast love endures for ever;
> to him who by understanding made the heavens,
> for his steadfast love endures for ever;
> to him who spread out the earth upon the waters,
> for his steadfast love endures for ever;
> to him who made the great lights,
> for his steadfast love endures for ever;
> the sun to rule over the day,
> for his steadfast love endures for ever;
> the moon and stars to rule over the night,

> for his steadfast love endures for ever.
>
> Psalm 136:4-9

Sustainer. In a very real sense, the Bible acknowledges a certain continuing order in the natural world. In the process of creation, God decreed that the sun, moon, and stars "be for signs and for seasons and for days and years" (Gen. 1:14). And after the flood, God promised: "While the earth remains, seedtime and harvest, cold and heat, summer and winter, day and night, shall not cease" (8:22; cf. Job 38:33; Pss. 104:9; 148:6; Jer. 31:36). Yet, this does not mean that the universe is self-sustaining, that is, that God wound up nature as one would wind up a clock and abandoned it to its own self-preservation. On the contrary, God himself continues to sustain the fundamental principles that he built into his world. Ezra declares not only that God "made heaven, the heaven of heavens, with all their host, the earth and all that is on it" but also that he "*preserves* all of them" (Neh. 9:6). Similarly, Paul declares that "in him [Christ] all things *hold together*" (Col. 1:17). And the author of Hebrews affirms that Christ "*upholds* the universe by his word of power" (Heb. 1:3).

Furthermore, God is active in all natural and human life. The primary way in which he differs from false gods is that he is a living God (Deut. 5:26; Josh. 3:10; Jer. 10:10; Hos. 1:10), who works continually in his world. Against the Jews who argued that God ceased working on the seventh day of creation, Jesus declared: "My Father is working still, and I am working" (John 5:17).

The scriptures do not represent God's working in his world as isolated, infrequent, irregular occurrences but as recurring, continuing, regular actions of a sovereign Lord. He "brings clouds over the earth" (Gen. 9:14), "withholds rain" and "sends rain" (Deut. 11:17; 1 Kings 17:14; 2 Chron. 7:13; Amos 4:7; Matt. 5:45), "causes grass and plants to grow" (Ps. 104:14), "opens" and "closes" wombs (Gen. 20:17-18; 1 Sam. 1:5-6, 19-20), "gives" parents children (Gen. 4:1, 25; 18:9-14; 21:1-2; 33:5; 48:9; Ps. 127:3; etc.), "sends" armies to punish the wicked (Isa. 10:5-6;

13:17; Jer. 25:9; Amos 6:14; etc.), gives food to all his creatures (Ps. 104:27-28), takes away the breath from his creatures so that they die (Ps. 104:29), etc.

Jesus promised to be with us *"always, to the close of the age"* (Matt. 28:20). The author of Hebrews affirms that "Christ *always* lives to make intercession" for those who draw near to God through him (Heb. 7:25). Paul repeatedly speaks of Christ as personally living or dwelling in the Christian (Gal. 2:20; Eph. 3:17; etc.). It would be diametrically opposed to the teaching of the Bible, therefore, to believe or teach that God and Christ do not work actively in nature, history, and individual lives. Jesus' illustration of God's love toward his enemies (Matt. 5:45) is not valid unless God actively *"makes* his sun *rise* on the evil and the good, and *sends* rain on the just and on the unjust," because we are challenged to act toward our enemies as God acts toward his, so we can be "sons" of our Father who is in heaven. In this text, "Jesus assumes that God is completely omnipotent and *cares directly and personally* for all that he has made" (S.E. Johnson, "The Gospel according to St. Matthew," IB, vol. 7, p. 303; cf. 1 Pet. 5:7). "Our Lord here brings out *God's active love* as seen in nature, nourishing and maintaining men, irrespective of the qualities of individuals and of their treatment of him and his laws" (A.L. Williams, *St. Matthew*, PC, vol. 15, p. 168; italics in both quotations mine—JTW).

Companion. As creator and sustainer of the universe, God is not a part of the world or in any way limited by it. And yet, he is always present in each person's life (Ps. 139:7-12) and near everything and everyone he has made (Jer. 23:23; Acts 17:27-28; Phil. 4:5). The book of Genesis emphasizes that he is "with" man (26:3, 24; 28:15; 35:3; 29:2, 3, 21, 23; 46:4), as does the rest of the OT (Isa. 7:14; Hos. 11:9; Joel 2:27; Amos 5:14; Zech. 8:23; etc.). Jesus promised that he would be with his people always (Matt. 28:20). It is in this particular that the true and living God is different from all false gods. If God were not living and active personally in the world and in men's lives, it would be futile to pray for him to do anything or to praise and thank him for having done something. "For what great nation is there that has a god so *near* to it as the Lord our God is to us, *whenever we call* upon him?" (Deut. 4:7). "By *the power at work within us* [God] is able to do far more abundantly than all that we *ask* or think" (Eph. 3:20). And again:

> The Lord is at hand. Have no anxiety about anything, but in everything by prayer and supplication with thanksgiving let your requests be made known to God. And the peace of God, which passes all understanding, will keep your hearts and your minds in Christ Jesus.
>
> Philippians 4:5-7

Judge and Redeemer. The Bible declares that Yahweh is a God of wrath. Yet this does not mean that by nature God loses control of himself and flies into a wild rage or that anger is the fundamental quality of his character. On the contrary, the basic attitude from which he works is steadfast love, and his wrath is fatherly punishment evoked by that love, the purpose of which is to correct and improve man, to keep him from destroying himself, and to redeem him from ruin and failure.

> For his anger is but for a moment,
>   and his favor is for a lifetime.
>
> Psalm 30:5 (Hebrew 6)

Again,

> For a brief moment I forsook you,
>   but with great compassion I will gather you.
> In overflowing wrath for a moment
>   I hid my face from you,
> but with everlasting love I will have
>   compassion on you,
>   says the Lord, your Redeemer.
>
> Isaiah 54:7-8

The OT repeatedly describes God as "merciful and gracious, slow to anger, and abounding in steadfast love" (Exod. 34:6; Num. 14:18; Neh. 9:17, 31; Pss. 86:15; 103:8; 145:8; Joel 2:13; Jonah 4:2). On the basis of this understanding of God, Abraham urges him as "the Judge of all the earth" (Gen. 18:25) to spare Sodom and Gomorrah if ten righteous people could be found within the city (18:22-33). It is God's "steadfast love" that motivates him to guide Abraham's servant to find a wife for Isaac (24:12, 27), and to bless Jacob's household (32:10 [Hebrew 11]). When man sins, God punishes him to show him the seriousness of his rebellion and to correct his wrongdoing, as when he pronounces the curses on Adam and Eve (3:16-19) and on Cain (4:11-12), sends the flood (6:17), scatters men abroad on the face of the earth when they try to make a name for themselves by building a city and a tower at Babel (11:7-9), closes the wombs of the house of Abimelech (20:3, 7, 17-18), etc. He does this out of love for man, as a concerned father chastens his rebellious child (cf. Prov. 3:11-12; Heb. 12:3-11).

That God's main concern is man's improvement is emphasized powerfully in the book of Genesis by the recurring rhetorical question, "What have you done?" (3:13; 4:10; 12:18; 20:9; 26:10; 29:25; 31:26; 42:28; 44:15). Such a question requires the sinner to reflect on the seriousness of his wrong and hopefully leads him to repent.

The author of the book of Genesis consistently depicts man as a sinner. This is true not only of Adam and Eve, Cain, the "sons of God," and the builders at Babel, but also of Abraham and Sarah, who laughed in unbelief when God promised them a son in their old age and who agreed that they would lie about their relationship to each other (20:13); Jacob, who obtained his brother's birthright by taking advantage of his circumstances (25:29-34), and who, in collusion with his mother Rebekah, received his father's birthright by lying and deceit (27:1-29); Reuben, who committed adultery with his father's concubine (35:22; 49:4); Simeon and Levi, who had the men of Shechem circumcised and then killed them while they were healing (34:13-31); and Joseph, who had money and his royal cup put in his brothers' bags so that he could charge them with theft and put them in prison (chs. 42, 44).

No man is able to restore the broken relationship with God which is caused by sin. It is only by God's forgiveness that that relationship can be restored. That God blesses sinful man even while he punishes him is possible because he forgives him. The OT repeatedly states that God forgives the sinner (Exod. 34:7, 9; Lev. 4:26, 31, 35; 5:10, 13, 16; Num. 14:18; 2 Sam. 12:13; 1 Kings 8:30, 34, 36, 39, 50; Pss. 103:3; 130:3-4; Isa. 6:7; 38:17; Mic. 7:18-19; etc.). The very nature of man's rebellion against God and his inability to heal the broken relationship between himself and God demand that he throw himself upon God's mercy and forgiveness through faith. And God declares that he reckons that faith to man as righteousness (Gen. 15:6). Man cannot approach God with sufficient gifts to atone for his sin (cf. Ps. 50:7-15; Mic. 6:6-8) or with adequate works of righteousness to justify himself. "No man living is righteous before thee" (Ps. 143:2). "There is none that does good, no, not one" (Pss. 14:3; 53:3 [Hebrew 4]). Accordingly, the altars that the patriarchs built and the animal sacrifices that they offered (cf. Gen. 4:3-5; 8:20-21; 12:7-8; 13:4, 18; 15:9-21; 22:3-14; 26:24-25; 35:1-4) were not legal acts of obedience or religious good works calculated to earn God's favor. An altar designated that God had appeared and been present at a specific locality on earth (cf. 26:24-25). An animal sacrifice was not a gift growing out of human fear to appease the wrath of an angry God but an acknowledgment that all things on earth are the Lord's as Creator and a petition that God grant man the privilege of using God's creatures to meet his needs. It was not an act of magic which automatically assured man of God's favor but a plea for God's intervention and fellowship. A sacrifice was not an external act intended to test man's willingness to keep God's commandments but an outward expression of man's genuine inner submission to God as a way of life.

> Because he [God] was personal, he called for a response on the part of his people. The response had to be correspondingly personal, rational. Sacrifice, then, was the external expression of man's personal response to a personal

God. It was not a mechanical, magic gesture with an effi-
cacy unrelated to the interior dispositions of the one offering it. If sacrifice was not motivated by sincere interior
dispositions, it was empty formalism, a mocking of true
divine-human relationship.

> J. Castelot, "Religious Institutions of
> Israel," JBC, vol. 2, p. 724

It was because of God's "grace" (RSV "favor"; Heb.
chen) that Noah and his family were spared from the flood
(Gen. 6:8) and that Lot and his family were delivered from
the destruction of Sodom (19:19). Their own "righteousness" (Noah—6:9; Lot—2 Pet. 2:7) was a grateful response to God's salvation, not a legalistic cause or requirement that was necessary to receive it. The principle is the
same as that which permeates and governs all divine-
human relationships. Paul states this very clearly and succinctly when he writes:

> But when the goodness and loving kindness of God our
> Savior appeared, *he* saved us, *not because of deeds done
> by us in righteousness, but in virtue of his own mercy*, by
> the washing of regeneration and renewal in the Holy
> Spirit, which he poured out upon us richly through Jesus
> Christ our Savior, so that we might be *justified by his
> grace* and become heirs in hope of eternal life.

> Titus 3:4-7

Names of God. The book of Genesis (like the rest of the
Bible) uses a wide variety of names in speaking of God.
These names describe and reveal his character and thus
correspond to the fundamental emphases suggested above.
The name *Yahweh* (translated "the Lord" in the RSV and
most English versions) occurs frequently in the book of
Genesis (2:4, 5, 7, 8, 9, etc.). Some scholars think that this
name should be read actively as "he who is," emphasizing
his *presence* with man and particularly with his people
(i.e., "he who is present"), in which case his companion-
ship with man is stressed. Others are convinced that it
should be read causatively as "he who causes to be," emphasizing his creative power manifested in his mighty acts

in nature and history. The contexts in which this name is explained in Exodus 3:13-17 and 6:2-9 seem to favor the first view, but this is by no means certain.

El, Eloah, and *Elohim* (the plural in form) are often used as generic terms for God in the OT, and cognates of these terms occur in many ancient Near Eastern religious texts. In the book of Genesis, sometimes *El* is connected with some other word in speaking of God, as *El Elyon* ("God Most High," Gen. 14:18, 19, 22; cf. Num. 24:16; Deut. 32:8; 2 Sam. 22:14; etc.), *El Shadday* ("God Almighty," literally, "God, the one of the mountain," Gen. 17:1; 28:3; 35:11; 43:14; 48:3; 49:25; cf. Num. 24:4, 16; Ruth 1:20, 21; etc.), *El Olam* ("the Everlasting God," Gen. 21:33; cf. Isa. 40:28), *El Bethel* ("the God of Bethel," Gen. 31:13; 35:7), *El Roi* ("God of seeing," Gen. 16:13), and *El Elohe Israel* ("God, the God of Israel," Gen. 33:20). These terms point to God's power, everlastingness, and presence with man.

In connection with patriarchs, God is called "the God of my [their, your] father" (Gen. 26:24; 28:13; 31:42, 53; 32:9 [Hebrew 10]; 43:23; 46:3; 49:25; 50:17), "the God of Nahor" (31:53), "the God" (28:18; 31:42) or "Shield of Abraham" (15:1), "the God" (28:13; 32:9 [Hebrew 10]) or "Fear of Isaac" (31:42, 53), "the Mighty One of Jacob" (49:24; cf. Isa. 1:24—"the Mighty One of Israel"), "the Shepherd" (49:24), and "the Rock of Israel" (49:24). These expressions reflect the intimate, personal relationship between God and the patriarchs, his protection of them, and their reverence for him.

Man

A created being. Man is not God (Isa. 31:3; Hos. 11:9), but a being "created" (Gen. 1:27), "made" (1:26), "formed" (2:7, 8), or "built" (2:22) by God. Therefore, he is "little less than God" (Ps. 8:5 [Hebrew 6]). He is not "from everlasting to everlasting" like God (Ps. 90:2), that is, he is not an incarnate soul but an animated body. In other words, no man exists until he is created by God to live on earth. Any attempt on man's part to be "like God" (cf. Gen. 3:5, 22) is doomed to failure, for he is only a creature.

Made in God's image. The literary sequence of Genesis 1 indicates that man is the climax and zenith of God's creation, and this is confirmed by the affirmation that he is made "in the image," "after the likeness," of God (1:26, 27; 5:1; 9:6). This expression has been interpreted in many ways (see notes on 1:26, 27), but it seems most likely that the author has in mind two major thoughts: (1) man is not God but at best only "the image of God"; (2) man is a creature of dignity and thus deserves the respect and admiration of his fellowman. This second emphasis is delineated especially in Genesis 9:6, where man is forbidden to kill his fellowman because "God made man in his own image," and in James 3:9, where man is condemned for cursing his fellowmen "who are made in the likeness of God." It lies at the very root of the Christian principle that calls on one to love, honor, and respect black and white, old and young, Jew and Greek, male and female, master and slave.

A weak being. God made man "of dust from the ground" (Gen. 2:7). Thus, he is "but dust and ashes" (18:27; cf. Ps. 103:14) and in due time shall return to dust (Gen. 3:19). The book of Genesis is filled with records of the deaths of its characters, not only minor figures (cf. the list in 5:4-31) but also major ones, including Adam (5:5), Noah (9:29), Abraham (25:7-11), Isaac (35:29), Jacob (49:33), and Joseph (50:26). Furthermore, while living on earth, man is compassed about with fear, anxieties, conflicts, and afflictions. Cain kills his own brother (4:8). Yahweh afflicts the Pharaoh of Egypt and his household with great plagues when he takes Sarai as his wife (12:17). Abram's and Lot's herdsmen strive with one another because the land is not able to support their flocks and herds (13:5-7). An army from the Fertile Crescent overruns the cities of the Valley of Siddim (including Sodom) and carries off their inhabitants (including Lot and his family) as prisoners of war (14:1-12). Abraham and Sarah are unable to have a child of their own (11:30; 15:2). Lot strives against the men of

Sodom when they determine to abuse homosexually the two angels that have come to stay with him (19:5-7). Abraham feuds with Abimelech of Gerar over the possession of a well of water (21:22-34), etc. It seems that mankind moves from one crisis to another.

A creature of free will. God did not create man to be a robot and to do everything God wishes regardless of his own desires. When God placed man in the garden of Eden, he intended for man "to till it and keep it" (2:15), but man could choose whether he would do this or not. God commanded man not to eat of the tree of the knowledge of good and evil (2:16-17; 3:3), but man had the God-given ability and prerogative to decide whether he would obey this command (3:6). God brought the woman to the man when he had created her (2:22), but man had to decide whether to take her as his mate (2:23-25). This ability to make such decisions did not come as a curse on man as a result of his sin but was a central feature of his nature from the very beginning. If this were not the case, God would be the author of sin (which contradicts passages like James 1:13), and man could not be held responsible for his thoughts, words, or actions (which contradicts passages like Rom. 2:26; 2 Cor. 5:10).

An individual created for family life. God created man to live in a family, not to be a hermit or a recluse or an unsocial or antisocial being. He declared: "It is not good that the man should be alone" (Gen. 2:18). And then he made a woman for the man and brought her to him to be his wife (2:21-24). Accordingly, the primary human relationship is not that which exists between friends or between parent and child but that which exists between husband and wife. The sexual relationship between man and wife is good in and of itself irrespective of its fruits in reproduction. It is in no sense a curse that God placed on man as a result of the first sin. Furthermore, God charged man to "be fruitful and multiply, and fill the earth and subdue it" (1:28) *before* the fall, which demonstrates that conception and birth are good in the sight of God. The curse that God placed on the woman was that he would greatly multiply her *pain* in childbearing (3:16) and not that she would bear children.

Children are God's gifts to parents (4:1, 25; 18:10; 21:1-2; 29:31-35; 33:4-5; 48:8-9). Since both parent and child are made in the image of God, each deserves the respect of the other. By virtue of age and maturity, it is the parent's responsibility to initiate a healthy relationship with his child by demonstrating his respect for him. Abraham's deep concern for Ishmael when God told him to send him away with Hagar (21:9-14) and his love for Isaac (22:2) provide good examples of this important trait. Paul sums up this point when he says: "Fathers, do not provoke your children to anger, but bring them up in the discipline and instruction of the Lord" (Eph. 6:4); and again, "Fathers, do not provoke your children, lest they become discouraged" (Col. 3:21). Since Abraham had such a wholesome attitude toward his children, it is little wonder that God said concerning him: "I have chosen him, that he may charge his children and his household after him to keep the way of the Lord by doing righteousness and justice" (Gen. 18:19).

The book of Genesis describes family life as it really was in the patriarchal age. Therefore, it depicts the bad along with the good. Lamech (4:23), Abraham (16:2; 21:9), Jacob (29:21-30), and Esau (26:34; 36:2-3) were polygamists, that is, they were married to more than one wife at the same time. Lot (19:30-38) and Judah (38:12-26) had sexual relations with their own daughters. The men of Sodom were homosexuals (19:4-11). Rebekah and Jacob deliberately deceived Isaac in order to secure the birthright that belonged to Esau (27:1-40). Shechem raped Dinah, the daughter of Jacob (34:1-2). The author of the book of Genesis does not condone these practices any more than the author of 2 Samuel 11-12 approves of David's adultery with Bathsheba and murder of Uriah, but he describes family life as it really was in patriarchal society.

An economic, social, and political being. In the patriarchal period, men were engaged in economic pursuits. When Abram moved from Haran to Canaan, he had many possessions and servants (12:5). Later, in Egypt, he procured even more from the Pharaoh (12:16). "Abram was very rich in cattle, in silver, and in gold" (13:2). Lot also had many possessions (13:6; 14:16), and when he got the opportunity to do so, he moved into the region of Sodom because the land looked promising to him for agricultural pursuits (13:10-11). Abimelech gave Abraham possessions and money in an attempt to rectify the wrong done to him by taking his wife into his harem (20:14, 16). Abraham purchased a field and the cave of Machpelah from Ephron and his fellow-Hittites for 400 shekels of silver (23:3-20). Abraham's servant gave Rebekah and Laban rich gifts to indicate Isaac's ability to care for Rebekah, to express his love for her, and to persuade her and her family to consent to the marriage proposal (24:53). Isaac grew very wealthy in Gerar (26:12-14). Jacob worked seven years for Leah, another seven years for Rachel (29:15-30), and then six more years for flocks and herds (31:41), as a result of which he became very rich in Haran (30:43; 32:5 [Hebrew 6]). He increased his wealth in Canaan (45:10; 46:6-7; 47:1), and later in Egypt (47:27). On his return from Haran to Canaan, he bought a piece of land near Shechem from Hamor for 100 pieces of money (33:19). Joseph's brothers sold him to Midianite or Ishmaelite traders going to Egypt for twenty shekels of silver (37:28, 36). Judah gave Tamar his signet and cord and staff as a pledge that he would give her a kid from his flock as a harlot's hire (38:16-18, 25). During the seven years of plenty, Joseph taxed the people of Egypt one-fifth of their grain harvest to store up for the years of famine (41:34-36, 47-49), then when the famine came charged a certain price for the grain from foreigners (42:7, 10, 25-28, 35; 43:2, 4, 18-24; 44:1-13) and Egyptians (47:14-26).

The book of Genesis also depicts man as involved in social and political activities. Cain and his descendants built cities, made musical instruments and played on them, and forged weapons and agricultural implements from bronze and iron (4:17-22). The men of Babel built a city and a tower (11:3-5). The patriarchs settled in populated areas and established friendly relationships with the inhabitants of the land (13:12, 18; 14:12-13, 24; 19:1; 21:25-34; 26:27-33; 33:18-20; 47:4-12; 50:7-11). Their social and political status was neither that of a native citizen nor that of a slave but that of a "sojourner" (12:10; 15:13; 19:9; 20:1; 21:23, 34; 26:3; 32:4 [Hebrew 5]; 35:27; 47:4), which means that they had no real voice in local government or in making important decisions affecting the peoples already inhabiting the land. Both Abraham (18:1-8) and Lot (19:1-3) entertained guests in their dwellings (cf. Heb. 13:2). Joseph was the only patriarch mentioned in the book of Genesis who attained a high governmental position. This was possible because God was with him, and probably also because he lived in Egypt when foreigners (the Hyksos) were in control of the land. Politically speaking, he was second-in-command (41:39-45) over the Pharaoh's house (41:40) and a "father" to the Pharaoh (45:8).

A ruler over the rest of creation. Ultimately, God made everything in creation for man's benefit. He gave man dominion over the fish, the birds, the cattle, the creeping things, and all the earth (1:26, 28; 9:2; cf. Ps. 8:6-8 [Hebrew 7-9]). He gave him vegetation and, later, meat as food (Gen. 1:29; 9:3). Before God, therefore, man is responsible to preserve and promote the well-being of the flora and fauna in the world. To fail to practice wholesome ecological principles is to fail to discharge the responsibility which God himself has placed in man's care.

Sin and Punishment

God created man with the potential of becoming a specific kind of spiritual being. He placed him in an environment that was conducive to this goal and provided him opportunities for advancement toward it. Sin is man's rejection of God's intention for his life.

Outward expressions of sin. Man's sin expresses itself in a variety of ways. The book of Genesis mentions eating forbidden fruit (3:6), murder (4:8; 34:25), marriages between good and bad people (6:2), excessive and self-centered involvement in earthly pursuits such as building cities, making cultural advancements, etc. (4:17-22; 10:8-12; 11:3-5; 13:10-13), drunkenness (9:21; 19:32-35), apathy (11:31), lying (12:13; 20:2-13; 26:7, 9; 27:1-40; 39:13-20), strife (13:7-8), thoughtless association with sinners (13:11-13), war (14:1-12), polygamy (4:23-24; 16:2-6; 21:8-13; 25:1-4; 29:15-30), doubting God's motives, promises, and warnings (3:1-6; 17:15-18; 18:10-15; 21:7), homosexuality (19:4-11), taking advantage of one in destitute circumstances (25:29-34), dishonesty in business and personal dealings (29:15-30; 31:7, 38-42), rape (34:2), adultery and incest (19:30-38; 38:12-30), partiality (37:3), etc. Surely, all these acts and many others like them (cf. the lists of Paul in Rom. 1:28-32; Gal. 5:19-21; Eph. 4:25-31; 1 Tim. 1:8-11) are "sins." Yet they arise from a deeper human problem and to try to deal with these "expressions" of that deeper problem without attempting to cope with that problem itself is like a doctor treating the symptoms of a disease without attacking the disease itself.

The core of the problem. According to the book of Genesis (and, indeed, the entire Bible), sin is fundamentally a heart problem. Eve ate of the forbidden fruit because she began doubting God's motives in commanding man not to eat of it (Gen. 3:1-6) and because she "saw" (thought she realized [this word does not refer to the physical act of "seeing" here]) that it was good for food, a delight to the eyes, and to be desired to make one wise (3:6). Cain killed his brother because he was "very angry" with him because God had accepted Abel's sacrifice but had rejected his own (4:5-7). The sons of God married the daughters of men because "every imagination of the thoughts of (man's) heart was only evil continually" (6:5). The people at Babel built a city and a tower because they had the ambition of making a name for themselves (of becoming famous; 11:4). Abraham lied about his wife because he was afraid that the Pharaoh of Egypt might kill him to get his wife (12:11-12). Joseph's brothers sold him to Midianite merchants because they "hated" him (37:4, 8) and "were jealous" of him (37:11; cf. 50:20).

But what is there about man's inner drives and motivations that produce these attitudes? All the contexts which describe sin in the book of Genesis indicate that it is self-centeredness, selfishness, pride; and this agrees with the analysis of sin throughout the Bible. Eve ate the forbidden fruit to satisfy her own desires and to become like God (3:6). Cain killed Abel because God complimented Abel for his sacrifice but denounced Cain (4:3-8). The people of Babel built a city and a tower to receive praise from their fellowmen (11:4). Abraham lied about his wife to save his own life (12:12-13). Lot chose to live at Sodom because the land appeared to be especially suited to his own advancement in the sheep- and cattle-raising business (13:11-13). Lot's daughters got their father drunk and had sexual relations with him because they thought if they did not do so they would never have children of their own (19:31-38).

Consequently, *pride* —arrogance, haughtiness, presumptuousness, boasting in oneself or one's accomplishments— is the fundamental attitude in man's inner being that is wrong, and from this distorted nature of the heart all sins come. Through Ezekiel God says to Jerusalem:

> Behold, this was the guilt of your sister Sodom: she and her daughters had *pride*, surfeit of food, and prosperous ease, but did not aid the poor and needy. They were *haughty*, and did abominable things before me; therefore I removed them, when I saw it.
>
> Ezekiel 16:49-50

Over 100 years before this, Isaiah announced to Jerusalem:

> For the Lord of hosts has a day
> against all that is *proud and lofty*,
> against all that is *lifted up and high*;
> against all the cedars of Lebanon,
> *lofty and lifted up*;
> and against all the oaks of Bashan;
> against all the *high* mountains,
> and against all the *lofty* hills;
> against every *high* tower,
> and against every fortified wall;

> against all the ships of Tarshish,
>   and against all the beautiful craft.
> And the *haughtiness* of men shall be humbled,
>   and the *pride* of men shall be brought low;
>   and the Lord alone will be exalted in that day.
>
> Isaiah 2:12-17

Self-centeredness lies at the very heart of worldliness, "for all that is in the world, the lust of the flesh and the lust of the eyes and the pride of life, is not of the Father but is of the world" (1 John 2:16). The lust of the flesh, the lust of the eyes, and the pride of life all stem from man's self-centeredness (cf. also 2 Chron. 26:16; 32:25; Prov. 15:25; 16:18; 27:1-2; Isa. 10:12-14; Amos 6:8; Obad. 3-4; Zeph. 3:11-13; Luke 18:9-14; 1 Pet. 5:5-7).

Man's efforts to cope with sin and guilt. When man sins, he seeks an easy solution to his problem. Instead of dealing with the attitude of his *heart* and allowing God to transform his *thoughts* to noble motivations (cf. Rom. 12:2; 2 Cor. 11:2-3; Eph. 4:17-24), he brings some external gift, such as an animal sacrifice (cf. Isa. 1:10-17; Hos. 6:4-6; Amos 5:21-24; Mic. 6:6-8; Pss. 50:7-23; 51:15-17 [Hebrew 17-19]), words of flattery (Ps. 73:32-39, especially vs. 36) or penitence (Isa. 29:13; Jer. 3:22–4:4; 12:1-2; 14:7-10; 14:19–15:4; Titus 1:16), loud or beautifully articulated songs (Amos 5:23), long and eloquent prayers (Isa. 1:15; Matt. 6:5-7), a host of good works (Matt. 19:16-22; Luke 18:9-14; Phil. 3:4-7), large monetary contributions (Acts 5:1-11), etc. It is significant that God accepted first Abel and then his offering (Gen. 4:4) and that he rejected first Cain and then his offering (4:5). First a person must give himself to the Lord, and then he is in a proper relationship to offer his possessions (cf. 2 Cor. 8:1-9, especially vs. 5).

The OT, and particularly the book of Genesis, is replete with examples of man's attempts to evade the responsibility for his sin on the deepest level (viz., in his heart). When Adam and Eve ate the forbidden fruit, they immediately tried to cover up their sin: they sewed fig leaves together to make themselves aprons to cover their nakedness

(Gen. 3:7); they hid from God among the trees of the garden (3:8); Adam blamed both Eve ("the woman") and God ("whom *thou* gavest to be with me") for his sin (3:12); and the woman blamed the serpent (3:13). Cain tried to cover up his sin of murdering Abel by burying him (4:10) and by lying to God about his knowledge of his brother's whereabouts (4:9). Abraham tried to avoid the responsibility of lying about his relationship to his wife Sarah by blaming it on the circumstances (he was afraid that if he did not lie about her he would be killed—12:12-13; 20:11) and on her willingness to participate in the lie (20:5, 13). Aaron tried to excuse himself of the guilt of making the golden calf by arguing that he did it only because the people would have it no other way and that the product of his work was purely accidental (Exod. 32:21-24; cf. also vss. 1-4). Saul defended his offering of the sacrifice at Gilgal by pointing out that his soldiers were abandoning him; Samuel did not come within the agreed time; the Philistines were preparing to attack; he dared not enter the battle without entreating the favor of the Lord; and he had to force himself (against his will!) to offer the sacrifice (1 Sam. 13:11-12). On another occasion, when Samuel rebuked him for not utterly destroying the Amalekites like God had commanded, Saul excused himself by contending that the people had spared the best of the Amalekites' sheep and oxen to sacrifice to the Lord (1 Sam. 15:15, 20-21, 24). These excuses and others like them are typical of man's efforts to cope with sin on the deepest level.

Punishment—God's means of redemption. Since God created man in his own image, he loves man and is deeply concerned with his well-being (cf. Pss. 8:3-4 [Hebrew 4-5]; 139:1-18). Accordingly, he uses every conceivable means to prevent man from destroying himself and to redeem man so that he can accomplish the purposes for which God placed him on earth. It is significant that often in the book of Genesis the first thing God does when man sins is to ask him (or to have someone ask him), "What have you done?" (cf. Gen. 3:13; 4:10; 12:18; 20:9; 26:10; 29:25; 31:26; 44:15; see also Josh. 7:19; 1 Sam. 13:11). The purpose of this question is not to secure information (God already knows the answer) but to force the sinner to look within his heart and to realize that he (and no one else and nothing else) is responsible for his sin.

Then God punishes the sinner to bring him to his senses in order that he might repent and be saved and to show others the seriousness of sin in an attempt to prevent them from committing the same crimes. Moses declared to Israel: "Know then in your heart that, as a man disciplines his son, the Lord your God disciplines you" (Deut. 8:5). A psalmist says:

> Blessed is the man whom thou dost
> chasten, O Lord,
> and whom thou dost teach out of thy law
> to give him respite from days of trouble,
> until a pit is dug for the wicked.
>
> Psalm 94:12-13

The wise man instructs his student:

> My son, do not despise the Lord's discipline
> or be weary of his reproof,
> for the Lord reproves him whom he loves,
> as a father the son in whom he delights.
>
> Proverbs 3:11-12

(See also Job 5:17-18; Heb. 12:4-11.)

The law stated that if a malicious witness falsely accused someone of a crime, "then you shall do to him as he had meant to do to his brother . . . and the rest shall hear, and fear, and shall never again commit any such evil among you" (Deut. 19:15-21, especially vss. 19-20). The sin and punishment of Sodom and Gomorrah (Gen. 19:1-29) became an object lesson for mankind throughout the rest of biblical history (cf. Deut. 29:23 [Hebrew 22]; 32:32; Isa. 1:9-10; 3:9; 13:19; Jer. 23:14; 49:18; 50:40; Amos 4:11; Zeph. 2:9; Matt. 10:15; Rom. 9:29; 2 Pet. 2:6-7; Jude 7).

Universal Redemption and Election

The Bible does not begin with God's election of a special people to save but with the creation of man. God's main concern is all mankind, and his ultimate goal has always been to save all mankind. As creator of all mankind, by his very nature he is "not wishing that any should perish, but that all should reach repentance" (2 Pet. 3:9). The ideas that God learned from Jesus how to love mankind or that Jesus must soothe God's anger toward man or that God made no attempts to redeem mankind before Jesus came are wholly foreign and contrary to biblical teaching. From the very first chapters of the Bible, God makes it clear that he "is the Creator and Father of all men, and all men are equally His children" (J. Morgenstern, *The Book of Genesis*, p. 22). Paul emphasizes this in his sermon in Athens (cf. Acts 17:26-29).

Now in order to reach mankind, God, in his infinite wisdom, did not speak directly out of heaven, or force all men to do his will whether they liked it or not, or send an army of heavenly angels to overpower man in some miraculous way to coerce or persuade him to repent. Rather, he determined to choose a certain people to be an influence on the rest of mankind, to teach the nations God's ways and will, and to plead with the nations to turn to him. The only reason for the existence of Israel and the church of Christ is to bring the nations of the world back to God.

In this light, God's election of Israel is totally arbitrary on his part. He does not choose them because they outnumber other nations (Deut. 7:7), or because they are stronger than all other peoples (Deut. 8:17), or because they are more righteous than the rest of mankind (Deut. 9:4-6), but simply because he has made a decision to use them as his missionaries to reach the nations. Paul explains this clearly when he writes:

> When Rebecca had conceived children by one man, our forefather Isaac, though they were not yet born *and had done nothing either good or bad,* in order that God's purpose of election might continue, *not because of works but because of his call,* she was told, "The elder shall serve

the younger." As it is written, "Jacob I loved, but Esau I hated."

Romans 9:10-13

This is exemplified in the story of Abraham and Abimelech. Abraham lies about his relationship to Sarah, and Abimelech takes her into his harem in all good conscience. God himself praises Abimelech because of the integrity of his heart (Gen. 20:6). Yet it was Abraham, and not Abimelech, whom God chose to bless the nations. God's intention in electing a people (be it Israel or the church) is not fundamentally that they might be saved, but that they might serve. It is true that the elect are the saved, but their election is for the purpose of proclaiming God's saving message to mankind. Consequently, election is an occasion for humility and service, not for pride and boasting. Paul says to Christians:

> Consider your call, brethren; not many of you were wise according to worldly standards, not many were powerful, not many were of noble birth; but God *chose* what is foolish in the world to shame the wise, God *chose* what is weak in the world to shame the strong, God *chose* what is low and despised in the world, even things that are not, to bring to nothing things that are, *so that no human being might boast in the presence of God.*

1 Corinthians 1:26-29; cf. James 2:5

To put it another way, election is an "in-house" divine teaching designed for the saved to encourage and motivate them to strive to save the rest of mankind and is not a legalistic doctrine designed for the saved to use in self-justifying harangues against the lost. Anyone who realizes truly that he is saved understands that God has saved him *in spite of* his own thoughts and works and *not because of* them (Eph. 2:8-10; Phil. 3:3-11; 1 Tim. 1:12-16; Titus 3:4-7). "Election is an act of God, not based on any inherent superiority of those elected, but grounded in the love and grace of God" (G. E. Mendenhall, "Election," IDB, vol. 2, p. 81). The call of Abraham at Haran (Gen. 12:1-3) lies at the end of a long period of human history, not

Israelite history. The Israelites were not a "pure people" but had Amorite and Hittite blood coursing through their veins (Ezek. 16:3, 45). And the church is not a "pure people" but is composed of Jew and Gentile, slave and free, circumcised and uncircumcised, barbarian and Scythian (1 Cor. 12:13; Gal. 3:28; Col. 3:11). It is impossible to believe genuinely that "the earth is the Lord's and the fulness thereof" (Ps. 24:1) without believing that he wants all mankind to recognize and accept his lordship over them. Whereas many Israelites had the attitude of Jonah and did not want God to save other nations (cf. Jonah 3:10-4:3), those who took God's universal lordship seriously endeavored to bring the nations back to God and encouraged their fellow-Israelites to do likewise. Several hundred years before Christ, God pleaded through his servant:

> Turn to me and be saved,
>   all the ends of the earth!
> For I am God, and there is no other.
> By myself I have sworn,
>   from my mouth has gone forth in righteousness
>   a word that shall not return:
> "To me every knee shall bow,
>   every tongue shall swear."
>
> Isaiah 45:22-23

One psalmist pleads with his fellow-Israelites:

> O give thanks to the Lord,
>   call on his name,
>   make known his deeds among the peoples!
> Sing to him, sing praises to him,
>   tell of all his wonderful works!
>
> Psalm 105:1-2

The book of Jonah is pointless unless its author intends to encourage his fellow-Israelites not to feel and act toward the nations as Jonah had felt and acted toward Nineveh. The prophetic oracles addressed to foreign nations (Isa. 13-23; Jer. 46-51; Ezek. 25-32; Amos 1-2; Obadiah; Nahum) indicate that God is as concerned to bring them to repentance as he is to bring Israel or Judah to repentance. Just as the Israelite high priests mediated between God and Israel, God charged the nation of Israel as a kingdom of priests to mediate between him and the rest of mankind: "Now therefore, if you will obey my voice and keep my covenant, you shall be my own possession among all peoples; *for all the earth is mine, and you shall be to me a kingdom of priests* and a holy nation" (Exod. 19:5-6). The same God who gave Israel the land of Canaan gave Mount Seir to the Edomites (Deut. 2:4-5), Ar to the Moabites (Deut. 2:9), and Ammon to the Ammonites (Deut. 2:19). And the same God who brought Israel out of Egypt also brought the Philistines out of Caphtor and the Syrians out of Kir (Amos 9:7). God loves and desires to save all mankind. This is the way he has always felt. And the means he has chosen to use to accomplish this is a people that he elects for the task.

It might be said that God uses two logical steps to reach lost mankind. First, he saves or redeems a people and blesses them abundantly. Various forms of the word "bless" are found throughout the book of Genesis referring to God's "blessings" on those whom he had chosen (cf. Gen. 1:28; 5:2; 9:1, 26), especially Abraham and his descendants (12:2-3; 17:16, 20; 22:17; 26:3; 32:26, 29 [Hebrew 27, 30]; 48:3; 49:25-26). By and large, these blessings consisted of God's promises that Abraham's descendants would become a mighty nation (cf. 13:16; 15:5; 17:16; 18:18; 28:14; 35:11; 46:3; 48:4; etc.) and that they would receive the land of Canaan as a possession or inheritance (cf. 13:17; 15:7, 18-21; 22:17; 26:3; 28:13, 15; 35:12; 50:24). It seems that one purpose of the altars and pillars which the patriarchs built in Canaan (cf. 12:7, 8; 13:4, 18; 22:9; 26:25; 28:18, 22; 35:3, 14) was to claim the land as Yahweh's.

But God's blessings are too great to be limited to a single people. Therefore, second, he calls on the elect to share their blessings with the rest of mankind, to do unto others as God has done unto them. One of the psalmists captures the thought beautifully:

May God be gracious to us and *bless us*
   and make his face to shine upon us,
that thy way may be known *upon earth*,
   thy saving power *among all nations*.
Let *the peoples* praise thee, O God;
   let *all the peoples* praise thee!
Let *the nations* be glad and sing for joy,
   for thou dost judge *the peoples* with equity
   and guide *the nations* upon earth.
Let *the peoples* praise thee, O God;
   let *all the peoples* praise thee!
The earth has yielded its increase;
   God, our God, has *blessed us*.
God has *blessed us*;
   let *all the ends of the earth* fear him!

Psalm 67

"Thus Israel appears as the bearer of the great invitation to
the peoples to turn to Yahweh for salvation" (E. J. Hamlin,
"Nations," IDB, vol. 3, p. 516). God repeatedly tells Abraham (Gen. 12:3; 18:18; 22:18), Isaac (26:4), and Jacob
(28:14), "By you and your descendants shall all the nations
[families] of the earth be blessed." (See notes on all these
passages.)

> Though the introduction [i.e., to the book of Genesis],
> chs. 1-11, with its universal character, includes all man-
> kind in the promise given at the beginning of the history of
> Abraham (12:1-3), it is from the outset distinctly declared
> that God, even if He did originally set apart one man and
> his family (Gen. 12–50), and after that a single nation
> (Exod. 1ff.), nevertheless intends that this particularistic
> development of the plan of salvation is eventually to in-
> clude all mankind. The manner in which salvation is de-
> veloped historically is particularistic, but its purposes are
> universal.

Möller, "Genesis," p. 1200

Again:

> One central theme gives [the book of Genesis] distinct
> unity of thought and purpose. This central theme is God's
> selection of Israel to be the witness and messenger of His

truth and His law unto all the peoples of the earth, and
His testing and preparation of Israel for this arduous and
sacred task.

Morgenstern, *Genesis,* p. 20

And, as J. L. McKenzie says, "The function of Israel in
history then becomes the function of mediating the knowledge of Yahweh to the nations" ("Aspects of Old Testament
Thought," *Jerome Biblical Commentary,* vol. 2, p. 756).
Tragically, Israel failed in her mission. Consequently, God
sent his only Son to do what Israel had failed to do. In
turn, he commissioned his people (the church) to go into all
the world and preach the gospel to every creature, to all
nations (Matt. 28:18-20; Mark 16:15-16; Luke 24:46-47).

BIBLIOGRAPHY

Of the thousands of commentaries, books, monographs,
and journal articles on various aspects of the book of
Genesis, only a selected list can be offered here. In addi-
tion to these references, see the bibliographies in
O. Eissfeldt, *The Old Testament: An Introduction* (New
York: Harper and Row, Publishers, 1965), C. Westermann,
Genesis, in *Biblischer Kommentar Altes Testament*
(Neukirchen-Vluyn: Neukirchener Verlag des Erziehungs-
vereins, 1974); the *Elenchus Bibliographicus Biblicus*
published annually by the Pontifical Biblical Institute in
Rome; and the *Index to Religious Periodicals.*

The following list includes representative liberal and
conservative introductions, commentaries, Bible dictionaries, studies in special areas, and works in comparative
literature and religion. The list is limited to works in English. No journal articles are included, because the number
dealing with each issue in Genesis studies is so great. (A
few key articles are mentioned in the commentary.)

Archer, G. L., Jr. *A Survey of Old Testament Introduction.* 4th printing.
Chicago: Moody Press, 1968. Pp. 73-208.

Avi-Yonah, M. *Encyclopedia of Archaeological Excavations in the Holy
Land.* 4 vols. London: Oxford University Press, 1975.

Bennett, W. H. *Genesis.* The Century Bible. Edinburgh: T. C. & E. C. Jack, 1905.

Davies, G. H. *Genesis.* The Broadman Bible Commentary. Nashville: Broadman Press, 1969. Pp. 101–304.

Eissfeldt, O. *The Old Testament: An Introduction.* New York: Harper and Row, 1965. Pp. 155–241.

Harrison, R. K. *Introduction to the Old Testament.* 2nd printing. Grand Rapids, Michigan: William B. Eerdmans Publishing Company, 1971. Pp. 1–168, 495–565.

Heidel, A. *The Babylonian Genesis.* 7th impression. Chicago: University of Chicago Press, 1972.

Heidel, A. *The Gilgamesh Epic and Old Testament Parallels.* 9th impression. Chicago: University of Chicago Press, 1973.

Hooke, S. H. "Introduction to the Pentateuch" and "Genesis," *Peake's Commentary on the Bible.* 4th reprint. Edited by M. Black and H. H. Rowley. London: Thomas Nelson and Sons, 1967. Pp. 168–207.

Kidner, D. *Genesis.* Tyndale Old Testament Commentaries. 4th reprint. London: Tyndale Press, 1973.

Maly, E. H. "Genesis," *The Jerome Biblical Commentary,* vol. 1. Englewood Cliffs, New Jersey: Prentice-Hall, 1968. Pp. 7–46.

Marks, J. H. "The Book of Genesis," *The Interpreter's One-Volume Commentary on the Bible.* Edited by C. H. Laymon. London: William Collins Sons & Co., 1972. Pp. 1–32.

Montet, P. *Egypt and the Bible.* Philadelphia: Fortress Press, 1968.

Morgenstern, J. *The Book of Genesis.* 2nd ed. New York: Schocken Books, 1965.

Parrot, A. *Abraham and His Times.* Philadelphia: Fortress Press, 1962.

von Rad, G. *Genesis.* The Old Testament Library. Philadelphia: Westminster Press, 1966.

Richardson, A. *Genesis 1-11.* Torch Bible Commentary. 7th impression. London: SCM Press, 1971.

Simpson, C. A. and W. R. Bowie. "The Book of Genesis," *The Interpreter's Bible,* vol. 1. Nashville: Abingdon-Cokesbury Press, 1952. Pp. 439–829.

Skinner, J. *Genesis.* The International Critical Commentary. New York: Charles Scribner's Sons, 1910.

Speiser, E. A. *Genesis.* The Anchor Bible, vol. 1. Garden City, New York: Doubleday & Company, 1964.

Wright, G. E. and F. V. Filson. *The Westminster Historical Atlas to the Bible.* Philadelphia: Westminster Press, 1956.

In addition, the serious student should consult the articles on "Abel," "Abraham," "Adam," "Assyria and Babylonia," "Egypt," "Eve," "Genesis," "Hagar," "Hittites," "Hurrians," "Isaac," "Ishmael," "Jacob," "Joseph," "Pentateuch," etc., in leading Bible dictionaries, such as:

The Interpreter's Dictionary of the Bible
The International Standard Bible Encyclopedia
Dictionary of the Bible, by J. L. McKenzie, S. J.
Theological Dictionary of the Old Testament
Wycliffe Bible Encyclopedia

The following journals contain numerous articles on different aspects of Genesis studies (most of the foreign language journals listed frequently contain articles in English):

Annual of the Swedish Theological Institute
Biblische Zeitschrift
Bulletin of the John Rylands Library
Catholic Biblical Quarterly
Dansk Teologisk Tidsskrift
Expository Times
Harvard Theological Review
Hebrew Union College Annual
Interpretation
Israel Exploration Journal
Jewish Quarterly Review
Journal for the Study of the Old Testament
Journal of the American Oriental Society
Journal of Bible and Religion
Journal of Biblical Literature
Journal of Cuneiform Studies
Journal of Jewish Studies
Journal of Near Eastern Studies
Journal of Northwest Semitic Languages
Journal of the Palestine Oriental Society
Journal of Semitic Studies
Journal of Theological Studies
Nederlands Theologisch Tijdschrift
Oudtestamentische Studiën
Palästina-Jahrbuch

Palestine Exploration Quarterly
Review and Expositor
Revue Biblique
Revue de Qumran
Rivista degli Studi Orientali
Scottish Journal of Theology
Scripture
Studia Theologica
Svensk Exegetisk Årsbok
Theological Studies
Theologische Literaturzeitung
Theologische Rundschau
Theologische Zeitschrift
Trierer Theologische Zeitschrift
Uppsala Universitets Arsskrift
Verbum Domini
Vetus Testamentum
Zeitschrift für die Alttestamentliche Wissenschaft
Zeitschrift des Deutschen Palästina-Vereins
Zeitschrift für Theologie und Kirche

II

The Creation

(Chapters 1–2)

A PANORAMIC DESCRIPTION
OF CREATION (1:1–2:3)

A careful analysis of Genesis 1:1–2:3 shows that the author of this material followed a set pattern in presenting the story of creation. It starts with an introduction (1:1-2), which states what God made "in the beginning" (apparently before the first day), and ends with a conclusion (2:1-3), which describes what God did after he had finished his creative work. He divides the body of the account (1:3-31) into six days so that each of the first three days corresponds to its parallel in the second three days. On the first three days God created "habitats," and on the second three days "creatures" to dwell in them. *Chart I* demonstrates the literary coherence of this section.

CHART I

**The Literary Structure of the Account of Creation
in Genesis 1:1–2:3**

Introduction—1:1-2

Habitats	Creatures
Day 1—Light—1:3-5	Day 4—Light bearers—1:14-19
Day 2—Sky and separation of the waters—1:6-8	Day 5—Birds and fish—1:20-23
Day 3—Dry land and vegetation—1:9-13	Day 6 —Land animals and man—1:24-31

Conclusion—2:1-3

The author repeats expressions in every (or almost every) paragraph. Each begins with the words "And God said, Let there be" (or something similar, vss. 3, 6, 9, 14, 20, 24). After describing God's creative work, the writer says, "and it was so" (vss. 7, 9, 15, 24, 30). Over and over again, he emphasizes "and God saw that it was good" (vss. 4, 10, 18, 21, 25, 31). Several other phrases and words are repeated throughout the chapter. (Attention is called to these in the comments on individual verses.)

Introduction (1:1-2)

[1] The precise meaning of the Hebrew text of Genesis 1:1-3 is hard to determine. (a) Some scholars interpret the first Hebrew word in verse 1 (*bere'shith*) as an independent statement, **In the beginning God**, and understand this verse as a sweeping introductory statement summarizing the entire following account of creation. (b) Others interpret it as an independent statement and take it to include the creation of chaos in verse 2. (Many translations are ambiguous on this point.) A major weakness in these views is that *bere'shith* is in the construct in Hebrew and ordinarily should be translated as a subordinate temporal clause. *Bare'shith* is the absolute form, which would ordinarily be translated as an independent clause. (c) Accordingly, the best biblical linguists translate this term "In the beginning of God's creating [or When God began to create] the heavens and the earth, the earth was without form and void." (d) On the other hand, if it is to be connected with verse 3, verse 2 must be interpreted as a parenthesis, and one would read: "In the beginning of God's creating the heavens and the earth (the earth being without form and void, etc.), God said, Let there be light, etc." This last interpretation seems to be best in keeping with the syntax of the Massoretic text (MT).

The Hebrew verb translated **created** (*bara'*) occurs forty-eight times in the OT (including five times in Gen. 1—once each in vss. 1 and 21 and three times in vs. 27; and twice in Gen. 2—vss. 3 and 4) and always describes an act of God. A study of the use of this word in various OT contexts (for a complete list of passages see *The Englishman's Hebrew and Chaldee Concordance of the Old Testament* [5th ed.], p. 270) suggests that it means "to bring something new into existence," whether out of material already in existence (as in Isa. 43:15-16; 65:18; Jer. 31:22; Ezek. 21:30) or without any indication of already existing material (as in Ps. 89:12; Isa. 45:12). Isaiah 34:11 and Jeremiah 4:23-26 state that God created chaos, and Isaiah 45:7 says that he created darkness. The author of Genesis 1 surely believed that ultimately God created the heavens and the earth out of nothing, although the verb *bara'* and the syntax of Genesis 1:1-3 do not allow one to affirm dogmatically that this is the thought he intended to assert in verse 1. Hebrews 11:3 declares that "the world was created by the word of God, so that what is seen was made out of things which do not appear."

In Genesis 1, the verb *bara'* ("create") is used in conjunction with **the heavens and the earth** (vs. 1; see Ps. 148:5; Isa. 40:26, 28; 42:5; 45:18), "the great sea monsters and every living creature that moves, with which the waters swarm, . . . and every winged bird" (vs. 21) and "man . . . , male and female" (vs. 27; see Gen. 5:1-2; 6:7; Deut. 4:32; Ps. 89:47; Isa. 45:12; Mal. 2:10). However, Genesis 2:3-4 apparently uses this verb in summary fashion to encompass everything that God did in Chapter 1. It should be noted that Genesis 1:27 states God **created** man and that 2:7 says God "formed" man of "dust from the ground," which indicates that God can create something out of already existing material (in this case, out of dust).

[2] Verse 2 describes what might be called the "negative aspects of creation," which God counterbalances (but does not eliminate) in the ongoing creative process (vss. 3-31). (a) The earth is **without form and void**, which seems to mean that while it was covered with water its geographical and topographical features did not stand out and there was no life upon it (see Isa. 45:18; Jer. 4:23-26). (b) Everything was shrouded in **darkness**. (c) An inseparable mass of **waters** engulfed the earth.

It is impossible to know precisely what the author of
Genesis intended by the Hebrew phrase *ruach 'elohim*
(RSV **the Spirit of God**). *Ruach*, which occurs over 370
times in the Old Testament, is capable of several nuances
of meaning and is rendered in a variety of ways in all
English versions of the Bible. For example, the KJV translates it "cool" (Gen. 3:8); "breath" (Gen. 6:17; 7:15;
2 Sam. 22:16; Job 4:9); "mind" (Gen. 26:35); "blast"
(Exod. 15:8; 2 Kings 19:7); "anger" (Judg. 8:3);
"quarter(s)"(1 Chron. 9:24); "air" (Job 41:16); "tempest"
(Ps. 11:6); "wind" (Gen. 8:1; Exod. 14:21; 15:10;
Num. 11:31; 2 Sam. 22:11; 1 Kings 18:45; 19:11 [3 times];
2 Kings 3:17); etc.

'Elohim can mean the one true "God" or "foreign gods"
(e.g., Num. 25:2 [twice]; 33:4; Deut. 7:4; 32:17, 37; etc.),
and its meaning must be determined by each context. But
this Hebrew word can also be used as a "noun of quality,"
that is, it can function as an adjective and thus mean "divine," "awesome," "mighty," etc. Again, the KJV frequently translates *'elohim* in this way. For example,
"*mighty* prince" in Genesis 23:6 is literally "prince of
God"; "*great* wrestlings" in Genesis 30:8 is literally "wrestlings of God"; "*mighty* thunderings" in Exodus 9:28 is
literally "voices of God"; "*very great* trembling" in 1 Samuel 14:15 is literally "trembling of God"; "*exceeding great*
city" in Jonah 3:3 is literally "city of God"; etc.

Accordingly, there are several possible *literal* translations of *ruach 'elohim* in Genesis 1:2: "Spirit (spirit) of
God," "mighty Spirit (spirit)," "breath of God," "mighty
breath," "anger of God," "mighty anger," "wind of God,"
"mighty wind," etc. Thus, no group of translators of any
English version of the Bible can avoid *interpreting* what
the original writer had in mind when he used this phrase,
no matter how they finally decide to translate it.

(1) Many scholars interpret this phrase to mean *the Spirit
of God* (so the KJV, ASV, and RSV). Several of them
affirm that the Hebrew verb translated **was moving over** in
the RSV, *merachepheth*, really means "was brooding
upon," and so the Spirit functions as a setting bird who

hatches the world- (or cosmic-) egg and produces heaven
and earth, a concept derived from the *B*abylonian epic of
creation. (2) Some think that **Spirit of God** refers to the
Holy Spirit as a separate personality in the godhead, and
thus find the concept of the Trinity in Genesis 1. (3) It is
also possible that "spirit of God" is an anthropomorphic
expression. Just as the "spirit of Jacob" (Gen. 45:27)
means Jacob, and the "spirit" of Ahab (1 Kings 21:5)
means Ahab, so the "spirit of God" may mean God (see
Gen. 6:3). (4) Because of similarities between the context
of Genesis 1:2 and other passages in the Old Testament,
still others think the author meant *a mighty wind* when he
used this expression (so the NEB and the American Translation). Here the *ruach 'elohim* sweeps over the **waters**,
and in time the waters abate and dry land appears
(Gen. 1:9). Genesis 8:1 states that after the waters had
prevailed on the earth 150 days, God caused a *ruach* (KJV
"wind") to pass over the earth, the water subsided, and
dry land appeared. According to Exodus 14:21, God sent a
strong east *ruach* (KJV "wind"), which drove back the sea
and divided the waters, so that the Israelites could pass
over on dry land. The language of Exodus 14:21 is strikingly similar to that found in the creation story of Genesis 1: "and the Lord drove the sea back by a strong east
wind all night [cf. Gen. 1:2], and made the sea dry land [cf.
Gen. 1:9], and the waters were divided [cf. Gen. 1:6-7]."
On the basis of these considerations and other evidence,
some scholars believe that *ruach 'elohim* means "wind of
God" or "mighty (awesome) wind" in Genesis 1:2. (See
H. M. Orlinsky, "Plain Meaning of Ruach in Gen. 1:2,"
The Jewish Quarterly Review 49 [1957], pp. 174–82; and
G. H. Davies, "The Holy Spirit in the Old Testament," *Re-
view and Expositor* 63 [1966], p. 130.) It is impossible to
know which of these meanings the biblical author intended.

The Creation of Light (1:3-5)

[**3-4**] In describing God's creative work, the author of
Genesis 1 speaks of what *God said* (vss. 3, 6, 9, 11, 14, 20,

24, 26) and what *God did* (vss. 1, 7, 16, 17, 21, 25, 26, 27) interchangeably. When God "speaks," a creative energy is released that brings about the thing he utters. When the writer says that what God made was **good** (vss. 4, 10, 18, 21, 25, 31), he does not mean that it is "morally good," but that it is capable of doing what God designed it to do. One aspect of creation consists of untangling and arranging already existing elements. Thus, the author states that God **separated** the light from the darkness (vss. 4, 18), the day from the night (vs. 14), and the waters which were under the firmament from the waters which were above the firmament (vss. 6, 7), and that he "gathered together" the waters under the heavens into one place so that the dry land appeared (vss. 9, 10).

[5] Throughout Genesis 1, emphasis is placed on God's *naming* various things that he had made. He **called** the light Day, the darkness Night (vs. 5), the firmament Heaven (vs. 8), the dry land Earth, the gathering together of the waters Seas (vs. 10), and human beings (male and female) Man (Heb. *'adham*, i.e., Adam, 5:2). In OT thought, he who gives a name thereby declares his rightful dominion over that which is named and states the intended function of that which is named. In view of this, it is worthy of note that man *names* the cattle, the birds, and the beasts (2:19, 20), for God gave him dominion over them (1:28); that man *calls* his mate *Woman* (2:23) and *Eve* (3:20), for God gave him *rule* over her (3:16) and created her to *help* him (2:18, 20); and that a parent *names* his child (4:25), for God gave him authority over the child.

At the end of each paragraph in his presentation of creation, the author of Genesis 1 says, "And there was evening and there was morning, a . . . day" (vss. 5, 8, 13, 19, 23, 31). All sorts of theories have been spun on the basis of different interpretations of the word "day." In view of the structure and scope of Genesis 1, it is possible to interpret the statement "And there was evening and there was morning, a . . . day" as a *literary device* used by the author to conclude each of his six paragraphs, his purpose being to affirm the great religious truth that everything in the world was made by God. (See Excursus, "The Age of the Earth and Man," p. 92, below.)

The Creation of the Firmament (1:6-8)

The Hebrew word for "firmament" (*raqia*') means literally "beaten out, stamped (referring to metal)," and thus describes the sky as a solid, inverted dome which holds back the waters above it. Elsewhere, the Old Testament describes the sky as God's "upper chambers" (Amos 9:6) that resemble a "molten mirror" (Job 37:18) and rest upon "pillars" (Job 26:11). It seems most likely that these authors are using terms that pertain to the building of a large, impressive building to describe the earth and the sky. The author states that God made (*'asah*) the firmament (Gen. 1:7), the sun, moon, and stars (vs. 16), the beasts, cattle, and everything that creeps upon the ground (vs. 25), and man (i.e., male and female, vs. 26; cf. 2:18). One is hardly justified in trying to make a distinction between this verb and *create* (*bara*'), since both *make* (1:31; 2:2 [twice], 3, 4) and *create* (2:3, 4) are used to encompass everything described in Genesis 1 and to depict the creation of man (*make*—1:26; 2:18; 5:1; *create*—1:27; 5:1, 2 [twice]). "Heaven(s)" (Heb. *shamayim*; 1:1, 8, 9, 14, 15, 17, 20, 26, 28; 2:1, 4 [twice]) clearly means the sky, and not "the eternal dwelling place of the righteous."

The Creation of Dry Land and Vegetation (1:9-13)

These verses describe two creative works of God: (1) the subsiding of the waters under the heavens and the concurrent appearance of the dry land and (2) the springing forth of all types of vegetation from the dry land or earth. This corresponds to the two acts of creation on the sixth day: (1) the creation of land animals and (2) the creation of man, both of which require dry land and vegetation for their existence. This intimate connection between the accounts of God's creative activity on the third and sixth days is further emphasized by the statements that God gave the "earth" power to "bring forth" (Heb. *yatsa*') vegetation (vs. 12) and living creatures (vs. 24) and that he gave both plant life and animal life the power to reproduce "according to their own kinds" (vss. 11-12, 24-25). This is not to be taken to mean that God gave plants and animals the power to reproduce and then withdrew from them from then on, because other biblical texts affirm that God continues to sustain this reproductive power in his creation. For example, he *"causes* the grass *to grow* for the cattle" (Ps. 104:14); he *"gives"* his creatures food in due season (Ps. 104:27); he *"sends forth* his Spirit," and thus brings new life into existence on earth (Ps. 104:30).

Creation of the Sun, Moon, and Stars (1:14-19)

The heavenly bodies (and especially the sun) were regarded as deities and were worshiped in ancient Egypt, Babylon, and Syria. Even some of the Israelites adopted this worship (2 Kings 21:3, 5; Jer. 8:2; Ezek. 8:16), in spite of the fact that it was specifically condemned in the law (Deut. 4:19; 17:3). The author of Genesis 1 declares that the heavenly luminaries were created by God for three purposes. Each of these is stated twice in what appears to be an *a b c c b a* pattern. *Chart II* represents an attempt to analyze the literary structure of this pattern.

CHART II

The Three Purposes of the Luminaries in Genesis 1:14-19

Genesis 1:14-15	*Genesis 1:17-18*
A. To separate the day from the night—vs. 14	A. To separate the light from the darkness—vs. 18
B. To be for signs, seasons, days, and years—vs. 14	B. To rule over the day and over the night—vs. 18
C. To give light upon the earth—vs. 15	C. To give light upon the earth—vs. 17

Other Near Eastern religions taught that man should worship the sun, moon, and stars, but the author of Genesis 1 affirms that God created the sun, moon, and stars to serve man (see Ps. 104:19-23). God alone is to be worshiped, and not his creations, which were made by him and thus are his (see Pss. 74:16; 136:7-9).

There may be some sort of intentional parallel between the luminaries "ruling over" (Heb. *mashal*) the day and night (vss. 16, 18), and man "having dominion over" (Heb. *radhah*) the earth and all its creatures (vss. 26, 28), although the Hebrew verbs are different. The exact sense in which the heavenly bodies are thought to *rule over* the earth is not clear, but the apparent parallelism of this expression with the statement that the sun, moon, and stars are for signs, seasons, days, and years (vs. 14; see *Chart II*) should be kept in mind in attempting to determine this. The most natural view would seem to be that the various aspects of life on earth are limited by, subject to, and changed by the movements of the heavenly bodies.

Creation of Fish and Birds (1:20-23)

The author of the book of Genesis uses the Hebrew expression *nephesh chayyah*, literally "living soul" (RSV, "living creature" or "being") in speaking of marine life (1:20, 21), cattle, creeping things, beasts that live on dry land (1:24, 30; 2:19), birds (1:30; 2:19), and man (2:7). Thus, one must avoid reading the modern meaning of the word "soul" back into biblical texts. In Genesis 2:7 and most biblical passages, "soul" refers to *the whole man* as a living being, just as it refers to *the whole fish* as a living being in Genesis 1:20, 21, etc., and not to the spiritual aspect of man.

The overall thrust of Genesis 1 suggests that the "great sea monsters" (Heb. *tannin*, vs. 21) are real water creatures and not mythological monsters. The reference could be to sharks, whales, hippopotamuses, crocodiles, or other large animals that live in or near water. God "blesses" marine life with reproductive powers in saying, "Be fruitful and multiply, and fill the waters" (vs. 22), as he later "blesses" man with reproductive powers when he says, "Be fruitful and multiply and fill the earth" (vs. 28).

Creation of Land Animals and Man (1:24-31)

[24-25] The author divides land animals into three categories: (1) **cattle**, that is, domesticated animals—roughly, *herbivora*; (2) **creeping things**, evidently including reptiles, insects, and very small quadrupeds; (3) **beasts**, that is, wild animals—roughly, *carnivora*.

[26-27] These verses are filled with difficulties that scholars explain in various ways. The limited space allowed for the present commentary permits only a brief presentation of some of the more prominent views.

The first person plural (**us, our**) has been interpreted in various ways. (a) Some think the writer has in mind the three Persons of the Godhead—the Father, the Son, and the Holy Spirit. However, this concept cannot definitely be shown to exist in the OT (although, of course, the OT does not deny it). (b) Others suggest that since the Hebrew word used for God here (*'elohim*) is plural, the writer adjusted his verbs to fit this form. But elsewhere in Genesis 1 he uses this plural noun with singular verbs. (c) Still others believe that the author is depicting God as a mighty king issuing "creative decrees." Since it was customary for any ancient Near Eastern king to issue decrees in the first person plural (frequently called "the plural of majesty" or "the royal *we*"), the writer simply adopts this stereotyped literary form.

However, one of the two following explanations seems most likely. (d) The OT often depicts God as a king seated on his throne with his angels or heavenly council gathered about him (see 1 Kings 22:19-22; Ps. 82:1; Job 1:6; 2:1). Isaiah 6 describes him as "sitting upon a throne" (vs. 1) with angelic beings called "seraphim" gathered about him (vss. 2, 3, 6), and as saying, "Whom shall *I* send, and who will go for *us*?" (vs. 8). Apparently, the first person plural ("us") here refers to the Lord and his heavenly council. This may be what the author of Genesis 1:26 has in mind (see also Gen. 3:22; 11:7). (e) The first person plural may be a literary device designed to emphasize the importance or solemnity of the event being described. God is speaking to himself about the creation of his most important creature, man, so he uses a formal term. Then verse 27 describes the execution of what is announced in verse 26 and uses the singular to do so. (For this explanation, see E. A. Speiser, *Genesis,* AB, pp. 4, 7.)

The idea that God created man in his own **image** or **likeness** has also been interpreted in a variety of ways. (1) On the basis of a study of the Hebrew word translated **image** (*tselem*) and the statement in Genesis 5:3 that Seth was "in Adam's own likeness, after his image," many scholars contend that the author of Genesis 1:26-27 means that man's physical features are a copy of God's physical features. (2) A similar, although somewhat different view, is that man's upright posture (which distinguishes him for the rest of the animal kingdom) reflects God's posture. (3) In view of the emphasis on man's having dominion over the rest of created life (vss. 26, 28), some scholars have suggested that the divine image in man pertains to his dominion over other creatures. However, a closer look at the context indicates that man's dominion is the *result* of his being made in the image of God, and not the concept intended by the statement that he was made in God's image. (4) Several of the church "fathers" (as Gregory of Nyssa and Chrysostom) and the Roman Catholic Church in particular have contended that the divine image is something that God gave man when he originally created him but which he lost at the fall. But this seems untenable because even after the flood man is still said to have been created in the image of God with no hint that that image had been lost (Gen. 9:6). (5) Many scholars, even those who believe that the image of God in man may include man's bodily form, suggest that this means that God gave man spiritual qualities like his own (including the ability to think on a very high level, the power to communicate meaningfully, the ability to look beyond oneself to higher goals, and the propensity to examine one's own motives and actions).

It seems most likely that one of the two following views is what the author of Genesis intended. (6) He states that God created man in his own image in order to set man apart from the rest of God's creatures by emphasizing his dignity, which must be recognized and respected by one's fellows. (7) The sequence of thought in Genesis 1:26-28 is parallel to that found in Psalm 8:5-8. But in Psalm 8, the idea seems to be that man, although he has dominion over other creatures, is less than God, but only "*little less* than God" (Ps. 8:5, RSV), for he has been crowned with *glory* and *honor.* Accordingly, man's being made in God's *image* may mean that he is not God, but only a *likeness* of God, and at the same time is the most noble of God's creatures and thus stands above (has dominion over) all the rest. (For an excellent discussion of this problem, see N. W. Porteous, "Image of God," IDB, vol. 2, pp. 682–85.)

Man (Heb. '*adham*) in verses 26-27 is a generic term including **male and female**, as is clearly stated in verse 27. Sex is a vital part of man's nature—a gift of God. God commands man to "be fruitful and multiply" (vs. 28) *before the fall.* Thus, marriage, the sexual relationship, conception, and childbirth are all a part of man's life from the very beginning and not punishments that God imposed on the human race because of the sin of Adam and Eve. These functions are included in the statement, "And God saw everything that he had made, and behold, it was very good" (vs. 31). To picture the sexual drive as something sordid, sinful, or ugly in and of itself is to oppose the biblical teaching on this subject.

[29-30] The **food** available to man and beast on earth is a *gift* of God. Apparently the author of Genesis 1 emphasizes this so that his readers may be grateful and thankful for the means God provides to sustain them.

Conclusion (2:1-3)

Genesis 2:1-3 emphasizes the great variety in God's creative activity by repeatedly referring to "all his work which he had done" (vss. 2 [twice], 3; cf. "all the host of them" in vs. 1). Two words are used to describe God's activity on the seventh day: (1) he "finished" his work (vss. 1, 2); (2) he "rested from" his work (vss. 2, 3). It seems clear that these two words are intended to convey the same thought. But scholars are divided over the meaning.

(a) Some think "finish" and "rest" suggest that God "abstained from work" on the seventh day and resumed it on the next day. This would be parallel to man's working six days, resting on the seventh day, and returning to his work on the following day. Such an interpretation would help explain Exodus 20:8-11, where man is commanded to rest on the seventh day because God did. However, this interpretation is not the most natural one in the context of Genesis 1:1–2:3.

(b) On the basis of the Samaritan Pentateuch, LXX, and Syriac Peshitta others argue that the original reading of verse 2 was: "on the *sixth* day God finished his work . . . and he rested on the *seventh* day." In this case, "finish" and "rest" would mean that God *"ended his work"* of creating new things with the creation of man. However, since it is easy to see why a later translator would change "seventh" to "sixth," but difficult to understand why a later scribe would change "sixth" to "seventh," the MT ("seventh") in verse 2 probably preserves the original reading.

(c) Still others believe that the author means that God continued to create on the seventh day, but he terminated this activity some time during the day and rested. But what did God create on the seventh day? Some say he created "rest." This does not fit the context, however, which declares that it was "from all God's work that he had done" that he "rested."

(d) Therefore, it seems best to retain the MT and to translate verse 2a as a pluperfect: "And on the seventh day God had finished his work which he had done, and he rested . . . ." In fact, verse 1 has already stated that "the heavens and the earth were finished" (apparently at the end of six days, consummated with the creation of man), and it is hardly likely that the writer immediately contradicts himself and declares the God did not "finish" his work until some time on the seventh day. Of course, this does not mean that God quit working in his world and left it to "run down" or "wind down" like a clock. Throughout the book of Genesis and the rest of the Bible, God is the subject of verbs of action; he continues to work in the world which he made. When Jesus healed the man that had been sick for thirty-eight years on the sabbath day, the Pharisees opposed him for working on the sabbath. But Jesus replied, "My Father *is working still*, and I am working" (John 5:17). This statement is incorrect unless God continues to work in his world. Thus, Genesis 2:1-3 must mean that man was the highest and last creature that God made, and after this he brought his work of creating new things to an end. Exodus 31:17 seems to support this view: "*in six days* the Lord made heaven and earth, and on the seventh day he *rested* and was *refreshed*." Evidently, this statement assumes that God's creative acts were completed in six days and that God was refreshed by his rest on the seventh day so that he was ready to continue his work on the following day. To be sure, this is highly anthropomorphic language (i.e., language in which human actions are attributed to God) and is not to be taken literally, as if God needed rest like man (see Ps. 121:3-4; Isa. 40:28; and LWC-OT, vol. 1, ch. 1).

[1] At the end of the sixth day, all the **host** of the heavens and the earth was finished. Sometimes in the OT "host of heaven" means angels (1 Kings 22:19; 2 Chron. 18:18; Ps. 103:21; etc.), and sometimes the sun, moon, and stars (Deut. 4:19; 17:3; 2 Kings 17:16; 21:3; etc.). Obviously it means the latter in Genesis 2:1. Host of **the earth** is found here only in the entire OT. Evidently it means everything that is on the earth. Ezra's prayer in Nehemiah 9:6 provides a close parallel to the meaning here: "Thou hast made heaven, the heaven of heavens, with *all their host*, the earth and *all that is on it*, the seas and *all that is in them*; and thou preservest all of them; and the *host of heaven* worships thee."

[3] Not only does the biblical writer relate that God "rested" on the seventh day, but he declares that God **blessed** and **hallowed** the seventh day as a "sabbath" for man. The Hebrew word translated "rested" in verses 2 and 3 is *shabhath*, which is cognate with the Hebrew noun *shabbath*, meaning "sabbath." Here, man is summoned to

imitate God. God achieves or accomplishes his work; he rests and expresses satisfaction over what he has produced; then he undertakes a new task. Man is to model his life after this divine example. It is worthy of note that this verse affirms that the sabbath rest is intended for all mankind and not for the Jews only and that the sabbath day was observed prior to the time that God gave Israel the sabbath law through Moses (cf. Exod. 16:22-30; 20:8-11), and thus originated outside Israel.

EXCURSUS

The Age of the Earth and Man

Biblical truth does not conflict with scientific truth. If both the natural world and the Bible are the works of God, whenever they seem to contradict one another, man has misunderstood either the Bible or the natural world. Problems in this area arise when a scientific theory is assumed to be a demonstrated fact, or when a particular interpretation of a biblical text (frequently in Gen. 1) is assumed to be the precise meaning that the biblical writer intended. A few observations on Genesis 1 pertaining to this problem seem appropriate.

(1) As *Chart I* above shows, the author of Genesis 1 followed a specific scheme or order in writing the story of creation. However, he does not claim to be presenting God's creative acts in *chronological* order. Therefore, no geological explanation of the chronological sequence of the appearance of various phenomena or types of life on earth necessarily contradicts the *order* of Genesis 1.

(2) The author of Genesis does not date "the beginning" nor does he tell how much time transpired between "the beginning" (1:1-2) and the "first day" (1:3-5). In 1650–1654, Archbishop James Ussher of the Church of England published a study of OT chronology in which he concluded that God created the heavens and the earth in 4004 B.C. Because of his prominence in the Church of

England at that time, he was able to get his conclusions published in the margin of some editions of the KJV. This has led some readers of the Bible to conclude erroneously that these marginal dates were part of the original text. The truth is that they are one man's opinions, which have been disproved in the intervening centuries. Since the Bible does not state how long the earth was without form and void, any geological estimate of the age of the earth is compatible with what is explicitly stated in Genesis 1.

All theories that have been proposed to harmonize Genesis 1 and science (and they can be no more than theories) have their strengths and weaknesses. Perhaps there is some truth in each one. But it should be emphasized that "the first chapter of Genesis is clearly not intended to comprise a scientific document" (R. K. Harrison, *Introduction to the Old Testament*, p. 554; see also p. 553), but a religious affirmation. The truth it proclaims is that God created all that is, that he has adequately provided for the needs of all his creatures, that he has given man dominion over all other creatures on earth, and that the sum total of all he has made is very good. Apparently the author is not concerned about how long this took, the chronological sequence in which it was done, or the procedure God employed in doing it.

The length of time man has been on earth is a different problem from the age of the earth. Scientists generally agree that man is a latecomer among earth's creatures. However, there is good evidence that he was on earth long before 4004 B.C. Between 1937–1939, excavators unearthed fossil remains of human beings in caves at Mount Carmel and in Galilee dating between 150,000 and 120,000 years ago. Archeologists discovered the body of a baby in the Shanidar Cave in Mesopotamia dating about seventy-five thousand years ago. There is widespread evidence of human activity on earth from about 8000 B.C. In Palestine and Egypt, scientists have uncovered human skeletons, flint tools and artifacts, stone mortars, beads, pins, pendants, etc., made from animal bones, all dating from about 8000 B.C. Before 5000 B.C. Jericho had been inhabited several times by different ancient cultures, and pottery and flint industries flourished in this region. (See G. E. Wright and F. V. Filson, *The Westminster Historical Atlas to the Bible,* p. 15; Y. Aharoni and M. Avi-Yonah, *The Macmillan Bible Atlas* [London: Collier-McMillan, 1968], p. 20; Harrison, *Introduction*, pp. 152–63.)

By insisting that Genesis 1 covers a period of six twenty-four days and that the genealogical lists in Genesis 5 and 11:10-26 are exact, unbroken chronological timetables, some find a contradiction between the biblical and scientific computations of the time man has been on earth. However, such views are based on only one interpretation of these passages. For one thing, there is good reason to believe that the genealogical lists in Genesis 5 and 11:10-26 are not unbroken. A careful study of genealogical lists elsewhere in the Bible demonstrates that biblical writers often omitted several persons in such lists. First Chronicles 26:24 says that Shebuel the son of Gershom, the son of Moses, was chief officer in charge of the treasuries in the time of David! Obviously the writer skips several persons, and uses the word "son" in the sense of "descendant" or "grandson" or "great-grandson" or the like in this text. Ezra 8:2 states that Hattush of the sons of David accompanied Ezra when he went to Jerusalem from Babylon (458 B.C.)! A comparison with 1 Chronicles 3 (where Hattush is mentioned in vs. 22) shows that Ezra skips over several people here and uses "sons" in the sense of "descendants." (See J. M. Myers, *Ezra–Nehemiah,* AB, p. 70.) In the NT, the book of Matthew begins with the words "The book of the genealogy of Jesus Christ, the son of David, the son of Abraham" (Matt. 1:1)! Again the biblical writer omits several persons in his genealogical list and uses "son" in the sense of "descendant."

In keeping with this recurring practice, there is good reason to believe that the author of Genesis 5 and 11:10-26 skips many people between Adam and Abraham. Therefore, it is impossible to compute the length of time that man has been on earth by simply adding the numbers given in these two chapters.

EXCURSUS

The Babylonian Creation Epic and the Genesis Account

Competent linguists and biblical scholars have called attention to possible similarities between the Babylonian creation epic (Enuma elish) and the account of creation in Genesis 1. Some of these may be listed here. (1) The word translated "the deep" in Genesis 1:2 (*tehom*) is the Hebrew equivalent to the Babylonian *Tiamat*, meaning "the underworld ocean" and "the Chaos-dragon." (2) The "mighty (awesome) wind" of Genesis 1:2 (see the NEB and the note on "the Spirit of God" in Gen. 1:2) calls to mind the incident in the Babylonian epic in which Marduk (a Babylonian god) gathers up the winds to conquer Tiamat. (3) The Babylonian epic speaks of Marduk "fixing the destinies" of each element in creation, and Genesis 1 declares that God created a "habitat" for each of his "creatures." (4) Where there are points of contact between Enuma elish and Genesis 1, the order of events is the same.

CHART III

Order of Points of Contact Between Enuma Elish and Genesis 1

Enuma elish	*Genesis 1*
1. The gods and matter are coexistent and coeternal.	1. Yahweh creates matter; he exists independently of it.
2. There is primeval chaos; Tiamat is surrounded by darkness.	2. The earth is a waste; Tehom (the deep) is covered with darkness.
3. Light emanates from the gods.	3. Yahweh creates light.
4. The gods create the firmament.	4. Yahweh creates the firmament.
5. The gods create dry land.	5. Yahweh creates dry land.
6. The gods create the lightbearers.	6. Yahweh creates the lightbearers.
7. The gods create man.	7. Yahweh creates man.
8. The gods rest and celebrate.	8. Yahweh rests and sanctifies the seventh day.

(Adapted from A. Heidel, *The Babylonian Genesis*, p. 129)

These and other (alleged, but less convincing) similarities between these two accounts have led many scholars to conclude that the author of Genesis 1 borrowed his material directly from a Mesopotamian source or from a Canaanite source that in turn was based on an earlier Mesopotamian source. At least three observations should be made about this position.

First, that biblical writers used earlier sources and borrowed from oral and written traditions originating in other nations and cultures is in complete harmony with the biblical teaching of inspiration. For one thing, the biblical authors themselves *claim* to use sources (Luke 1:1-4; 2 Sam. 1:18; 1 Kings 11:41; 14:19, 29; etc.). Paul does not hesitate to quote words from pagan poets (Acts 17:28; 1 Cor. 15:33; Titus 1:12). Furthermore, if the inspired speakers and writers were serious about communicating the divine message to the people of their day, they had to use words, phrases, and concepts already familiar to those people. If they had invented or created new thought patterns to convey God's word, they would have *concealed* it rather than *revealed* it, because it would have been impossible for anyone to have understood them.

Second, it has not been proved conclusively that the author of Genesis 1 borrowed (directly or ultimately) from Babylonian sources. After an extensive analysis of this whole problem, Heidel concludes: "I believe that *the whole question must still be left open*" (*Babylonian Genesis,* p. 139). Admittedly, it seems quite certain that the Babylonian material could not have been borrowed from Genesis, because there is good evidence that the Babylonian epic goes back at least to the First Babylonian Dynasty (1894–1595 B.C.) if not earlier (Heidel, *Babylonian Genesis*, pp. 13–14), which by the most conservative estimate antedates the biblical record of creation. At the same time, it is possible that both Enuma elish and Genesis 1 are based on a common source earlier than both.

Third, whereas scholars of the late nineteenth and early twentieth centuries placed great emphasis on the affinities between Enuma elish and Genesis 1, more recent studies (based on and profiting from earlier works) rightly stress the unique nature of the Genesis record. "Since the religion of the Hebrews diverged sharply from the Mesopotamian norms, we should expect a corresponding departure in regard to beliefs about creation. This expectation is fully borne out" (Speiser, *Genesis*, p. 11). The biblical speakers and writers used words, expressions, and literary structures that already existed in the world around them to communicate the word of God, but they applied what they used in ways radically different from the nations around them. For example, Paul addressed the Athenians on the "unknown God" (Acts 17:23), but he did not mean the same thing by that expression as they did. "Identical phraseology does not necessarily imply identical theology" (Heidel, *Babylonian Genesis*, p. 138).

There are marked contrasts between Enuma elish and Genesis 1. (a) In Enuma elish there are many gods who fight one another, and as a result of a series of struggles the various elements in the universe come into existence. But in Genesis 1 there is only one God, who effortlessly creates the world and all that is in it by his own word and deed. (b) In Enuma elish and other Babylonian accounts of the creation of man, man is created to serve the gods by offering sacrifices which they eat to keep them alive and by building sanctuaries for the gods and caring for them. However, in Genesis 1 man is created in the image of God; he is dependent on God (God is not dependent on his service), and the work that he does is for his own sustenance, not to keep God alive. (c) Enuma elish is clearly mythological in nature, while Genesis 1 is a mixture of historical facts and religious truth based on these facts. On the other hand:

> The OT contains . . . no myth which traces the creation to a primordial battle between divine powers . . . . Mythological allusions have been torn out of their ancient context of polytheism and nature religion, and have acquired a completely new meaning within the historical syntax of Israel's faith.
>
> B. W. Anderson, "Creation," IDB, vol. 1, p. 726

It is possible that Genesis 1 was written to or for an Israelite audience that had been attracted to or influenced by Babylonian or Canaanite (derived from Babylonian) mythological beliefs and that the author's purpose was to present a polemic against these beliefs. An effective means of doing this would have been to use Babylonian terminology in order to inject it with new meaning or to attribute to Yahweh what the Babylonians attributed to their gods.

A More Detailed Description
of the Creation of Man (2:4-25)

In order to interpret Genesis 2:4-25 correctly in its present position in the book of Genesis, it is imperative that one keep in mind that the author said what he did in this section in light of what had already been said in 1:1–2:3, and that he would assume that his readers already would have read the earlier section. Thus, even if he used earlier sources (written or oral) under divine guidance to present the story of creation, it does not seem logical that he viewed them as two distinct and contradictory accounts of the same story (see the Excursus at the end of this chapter). In other words, he is *not beginning all over again* in 2:4-25. Rather, he follows a frequently used, universally accepted literary procedure. First, he presents a panoramic description of creation (1:1–2:3), and then he elaborates in detail on that part of the description that is most important for the religious message he is attempting to convey (viz., the creation of man [2:4-25]). In this process, to be sure, he alludes to other phases of creation already depicted in 1:1–2:3, because man was not created in a vacuum. But he does this with a view of showing the reader how man fits into the overall scheme of divine creation. To be more specific, when the author states that "God made the earth and the heavens" (2:4), he does *not intend to give new information* to his readers as if they had not been told this earlier; or when he alludes to a time "when no plant of the field was yet in the earth" (2:5), he is not speaking as if his readers had not already read 1:11-12; or when he describes in detail the creation of man (2:7) and woman (2:18-22), he is quite aware that his readers already know that God created "male and female" in his own image (1:27).

Genesis 2:4-25 falls naturally into three paragraphs, each of which builds on that which precedes, and which steadily grow in momentum until they reach a powerful climax: (1) God forms man from the ground (vss. 4-7); (2) God prepares a garden for man's happiness and satisfaction (vss. 8-17); (3) God creates woman for man to work with him (vss. 18-25).

God Forms Man (2:4-7)

A comparison of various English translations of the Bible reflects the difficulties scholars face in rendering the Hebrew verbs in verses 5-6. (a) Some understand verses 5(or 5b)-6 as a parenthesis, translate the verbs as pluperfects, and take verse 7 as the logical continuation of verse 4. This would suggest there was no vegetation on the earth when man was created and would contradict the sequence in Genesis 1 (vss. 11-12 precede vss. 26-27) and the idea that God gave man vegetation for food in 1:29, which naturally presupposes that vegetation had already begun to grow on the earth before man's creation. Indeed, some argue that the thought is that plants and herbs could not grow on the earth until God gave moisture to water the dry, parched soil and man to cultivate the soil.

(b) It seems better to render the verbs here in the past tense and to translate the Hebrew conjunction *we* at the beginning of verses 5, 6, and 7 by "and," which is its most common meaning. If this is correct, then the writer is elaborating on God's creative work on the third and sixth days described in chapter 1. After the waters receded and the dry land appeared, for an unspecified period of time there was no vegetation on the earth because no rain had yet fallen. In time, God watered the earth with a mist, and vegetation sprang up on the earth. (It is true that the author does not say this explicitly in 2:6, but surely it must have been obvious to those who first read 2:4-25 as a sequel to 1:1–2:3.) Now that everything had been prepared to enable man to survive on earth, God created him (2:7). The most casual observation shows that the growth of vegetation does not depend on human cultivation.

[4] The phrase **These are the generations** [or "descendants"] **of . . .** occurs ten times in the book of Genesis (2:4; 5:1; 6:9; 10:1; 11:10, 27; 25:12, 19; 36:1 ["these are the generations of Esau" is repeated in vs. 9]; 37:2) and apparently was intended by the author to divide the book into smaller units for more meaningful reading on the part of its original audience. (1) Some scholars believe that his expression in 2:4a is the conclusion of 1:1–2:3. (2) Others think that originally it appeared as the first line of 1:1 and the introduction to the first part of the book. (3) It seems most likely, however, that the writer of the book of Genesis intended for it to be understood as the beginning of the section 2:4–4:26. (If so, this book contains an introduction [1:1–2:3], and ten sections, each beginning with the phrase "These are the generations of . . . .") The following considerations support this view. First, elsewhere in the book of Genesis where this phrase appears, it always *introduces a new section* rather than concluding the previous one. Second, the Hebrew word translated "generations" or "descendants" (*toledhoth*) does not have reference to the thing or person named after it (the progenitor), but to that which is produced by it or him (the progeny). Thus, the phrase "These are the descendants of Terah" in 11:27 does not mean that what follows is the "story" or "history" of Terah, but rather that what follows has to do with the "descendants" (RSV) of Terah. Admittedly, Genesis 2:4a is unique because it speaks of **the generations of the heavens and the earth**, whereas all the other passages using this expression speak of some person. But still, it is easy to attach a similar meaning to this verse. The expression "must describe that which is generated by the heavens and the earth, not the process by which they themselves are generated" (J. Skinner, *Genesis*, ICC, p. 41). Third, verse 3 forms an excellent conclusion to 1:1–2:3, and it is difficult to discover any useful purpose that 2:4a would serve the reader following such an excellent conclusion.

The word "day" (Heb. *yom*) in 2:4b covers everything described in 1:1–2:3 and therefore cannot mean a period of twelve or twenty-four hours. It means "an indefinite period of time," as is the case also in Genesis 2:17; 3:5; Exodus 6:28; 32:34; Jeremiah 11:4; etc. Thus, it is impossible to show from the meaning of the word "day" in the Bible that it must mean a twenty-four hour period in Genesis 1.

[5] The precise meaning of the Hebrew word *śiach*, translated **plant** in the RSV, is hard to determine. The Syriac and Arabic versions understood it to denote "a desert shrub" of some sort, and this is the meaning of the Hebrew in Genesis 21:15 and Job 30:4, 7. But it may have a more comprehensive meaning in Genesis 2:5, as "plant" or "vegetation" (in general). Some scholars take "plant" to mean a wild plant, and "herb" to mean a cultivated plant. Others think "plant" has reference to perennials and "herb" to annuals. There is not enough evidence to be certain on this point.

The author of Genesis 2:4-25 repeatedly affirms that God performed mighty acts in creation by using verbs of action with God as the subject. God *made* the earth and the heavens (vs. 4), *formed* man from the dust (vs. 7), *planted* a garden (vs. 8), *put* the man in the garden (vss. 8, 15), *made to grow* every tree (vs. 9), *made* a helper for man (vss. 18, 22), *formed* every beast and *brought* them to man (vs. 19), *caused a deep sleep to fall* on the man, *took* one of his ribs (vs. 21), *made* woman and *brought* her to the man (vs. 22). In harmony with this, by implication he declares that God *caused it to rain* on the earth (2:5).

The initial reason God created man was **to till the ground** (2:5, 15; 4:2, 12). Work is not a curse that God placed on man when he ate the forbidden fruit. Genesis 3:23 is to be interpreted in the light of 3:17-19. The curse is the difficulty with which the work was to be performed, as is demonstrated by the hindrances placed in man's way (thorns and thistles) and the effort he has to extend to sustain himself (the sweat of his face).

[6] The Hebrew word translated **mist** in the RSV (*'edh*)

appears only in this verse and in Job 36:27 in the entire OT.
Its meaning is debated. (a) Some scholars think it refers to
an underground source of water because the text says it
went up from the earth. Then, they call attention to the
inconsistency between "rain" (which apparently is anticipated in vs. 5) and **mist** (vs. 6). (b) It seems more likely,
however, that the writer is using common biblical terminology for rain here. Frequently, the biblical writers speak of
moisture rising from the earth, gathering to form clouds,
then descending on the parched ground as rain (1 Kings
18:44-45; Ps. 135:7; Jer. 10:13; 51:16; and as a symbol for
invading armies, Jer. 4:13; 47:2; Ezek. 38:9). It is significant that all these passages use the same Hebrew verb
translated "went up" (*'alah*) that appears with **mist** in
Genesis 2:6. Accordingly, verse 6 describes the coming of
the rain anticipated in verse 5. The implication is that when
God finally caused it to rain, the plants and herbs sprang
up and the earth was covered with vegetation, so that
everything is ready for the creation of man.

[7] Here the inspired writer uses the word **formed**
(Heb. *yatsar*) to describe the creation of man. This word
frequently occurs in speaking of a potter's work with clay
(see Isa. 29:16; 45:9; 64:8; Jer. 18:2-4, 6, 11). Thus, the
author of Genesis 2:7 compares God's work in creating
man from the ground with a potter's creating a vessel from
clay. He borrows a well-known human activity to symbolize an obscure divine activity, and thus his readers understand the message. He uses what is known to explain what
is unknown and in this way *reveals* truth rather than *concealing* it. But the verb "to form" is not restricted to the
creation of man in the OT (in addition to Gen. 2:7, see
Ps. 33:15; Zech. 12:1). It is also used of summer and winter (Ps. 74:17), the dry land (Ps. 95:5), or earth (Isa. 45:18;
Jer. 33:2), Leviathan (the whale? Ps. 104:26), the eye
(Ps. 94:9), the mountains (Amos 4:13), the beasts (Gen.
2:19), and all things (Jer. 10:16; 51:19).

There is a wordplay in the Hebrew text of Genesis 2–3
that indicates an intimate relationship between man
(*'adham*) and the ground (*'adhamah*). A rather good En-

glish equivalent to this wordplay may be found in the KJV and ASV translation of 1 Corinthians 15:47: "The first man is of the *earth, earthy,*" a statement of Paul undoubtedly based on Genesis 2:7. God formed man of dust from the *ground* (2:7; 3:23), made him to till the *ground* (2:5; 3:23; cf. 2:15), cursed the *ground* because he sinned (3:17), and decreed that he should return to the *ground* whence he came (3:19). The context seems to indicate that **dust** (Heb. *'aphar*) is synonymous with **ground** here (see 2:7; 3:19). At the same time, it should be noted that *out of the ground* God made to grow every tree (2:9), and God formed every beast (2:19). The emphasis throughout Genesis 2–3 seems to be on the frailty and transitoriness of all God's creation, whether vegetable, animal, or man.

But this leads to another wordplay. The same God who formed man (*'adham*) out of the ground (*'adhamah*, 2:7) also took woman (*'ishshah*) out of man (*'ish*, 2:22-23). Just as man is intimately connected with the ground, woman is intimately related to man. Whereas Genesis 1:1–2:3 uses "man" (*'adham*) in the sense of mankind, 2:4-25 uses it of the first man as distinguished from woman.

The last two lines of verse 7 affirm that man's life is God-given. God enables man to breathe, and thus to be alive, as he does all other creatures (see Gen. 7:22). Some have tried to justify a threefold division of man into flesh (or body), soul, and spirit from Genesis 2:7. They equate **dust** with flesh or body, **breath** with spirit, and insist that the last phrase of the verse must be translated as "a living soul." However, this understanding reads much more into the biblical text than it really says. (1) The Hebrew words for "flesh" or "body" and "spirit" do not occur in this passage. (2) The Hebrew expression *nephesh chayyah*, which some insist on translating "a living soul," is used of fish and marine life in Genesis 1:20, 21; land animals in 1:24; beasts, birds, and reptiles in 1:30; and beasts and birds in 2:19. If "soul" means the eternal part of man or the sum total of man's "body" and "spirit" in Genesis 2:7, it must mean the eternal part of a fish or the sum total of a fish's "body" and "spirit" in Genesis 1:20, 21; etc. (3) The flow of the context in Genesis 2:7 indicates that the word translated **being** in the RSV (*nephesh*) means the whole person. The author's emphasis is on the gift of life. A potter might mold a man out of the ground, but God alone can give him life. "Modern science has done nothing to diminish the mystery of life or to suggest for it any other source than God" (A. Richardson, *Genesis 1–11*, TBC, p. 61).

God Prepares a Garden for Man (2:8-17)

Many scholars think the author of Genesis 2 affirms that man was created before vegetation, because this is the order in which they are mentioned in verses 7 (man) and 8-9 (vegetation). However, verses 8-9 do not have in mind the first springing up of plants on the earth but the special divine preparation of a garden as man's first home on earth. Verses 5-6 imply that plants and herbs sprang up before God placed man on earth. It is difficult to understand why the writer would mention that the reason no plant or herb had sprung up was that God had not caused it to rain on the earth (vs. 5) unless he meant to convey the thought that when moisture watered the earth, plants and herbs sprang up (vs. 6). Furthermore, it is not logical to believe that man could have been sustained without vegetation for food, and any reader (ancient or modern) would be puzzled (if not startled) by such an idea.

Thus, apparently the writer's primary purpose is to emphasize that God took great care in preparing man's first home on earth. (1) It was a "garden" (Heb. *gan*, probably park or orchard; vss. 8, 9, 10, 15, 16). (2) It was located "in the east" (vs. 8), that is, east of Palestine. (3) It had trees that were beautiful to the human eye, enjoyable to human taste, and nutritious to the human body (vs. 9). (4) The garden was watered by four rivers, so that there could be no doubt that its beauty and nutritiousness would continue on and on (vss. 10-14). (5) God gave man complete freedom to eat of every tree of the garden except the tree of the knowledge of good and evil (vss. 16-17).

It is most likely that the writer here is describing man's first dwelling place on earth, and not a mythological utopia. This must have been located somewhere in or near Mesopotamia, because the Tigris and Euphrates rivers are specifically named in verse 14. But beyond this general location, it is impossible to pinpoint the garden of Eden geographically. There is wide divergence of opinion among critics as to the identity of the "Pishon" river (the Indus or the Ganges rivers of India, the Pallakopas canal that feeds into the Euphrates in Mesopotamia, some river in Arabia, etc., vs. 11), the "land of Havilah" (the northeast district of Arabia, part of the great Syrian desert located south and west of the Euphrates, etc., vs. 11), the "Gihon" river (a river in Armenia or India, the Shatt-en-Nil canal that flows into the Euphrates on the east, the Nile in Egypt, etc., vs. 13), and the "land of Cush" (Ethiopia, a district in northern and central Babylonia, etc., vs. 13).

[9] God planted two special trees in the garden of Eden. One was the **tree of life.** Genesis 3:22 (cf. also vs. 24) states that if the first man ate of the fruit of this tree, he would live forever. Thus, the tree of life is a tree whose fruit gives life to anyone who eats it (objective genitive, see LWC-OT, vol. 1, ch. 1). The expression "tree of life" is used figuratively of wisdom (Prov. 3:18), the fruit of the righteous (Prov. 11:30), fulfilled desire (Prov. 13:12), and a gentle tongue (Prov. 15:4), to convey the same general idea. In the NT John uses certain pictures derived from the description of the garden of Eden in Genesis 2 to depict heaven, one of which is the "tree of life" (Rev. 22:2).

The other special tree which God planted in the garden was **the tree of the knowledge of good and evil** (Gen. 2:9, 17; 3:3-12, 17). By analogy with the interpretation of the tree of life suggested above, the tree of the knowledge of good and evil would be a tree whose fruit enables the eater to know good and evil. But to what does "the knowledge of good and evil" refer? There is great difference of opinion on this point.

(1) When the man and his wife ate the forbidden fruit, "they *knew* that they were naked" (3:7). Thus, some schol-

ars argue that the "knowledge of good and evil" in 2:9, 17 means the consciousness of sex. However, the divine command to "be fruitful and multiply, and fill the earth and subdue it" (1:28) is given before the fall and would be hard to explain if man and woman had no consciousness of sex at that time. It does not make sense for God to forbid man to eat the fruit of a tree that would make him conscious of sex (2:17) and then create woman and bring her to the man that she might become his wife (2:21-22), before he ever became aware of sex by eating the forbidden fruit.

(2) The statement "they *knew* that they were naked" in 3:7 would seem to be a deliberate contrast to 2:25: "the man and his wife were both naked, and *were not ashamed.*" Then, "they *knew* that they were naked" means "they *were ashamed* that they were naked." In this case, the knowledge of good and evil might mean "the feeling of shame at being naked."

(3) Others take this phrase to mean the ability to discern between right and wrong ethically or morally. It has been suggested that it is not the *fruit* of this tree that is central to the story, but the *command* of God that man not eat it, which God gave for the purpose of making man aware of the difference between good and evil. However, that God commanded man not to eat of the fruit of this tree presupposes that he already knew how to discern between right and wrong as a result of the divine act of creation prior to the fall. Such a command presupposes that man already knows it is good to obey God and evil to disobey him.

(4) The serpent equates the knowledge of good and evil with being "like God" (3:5). In this case, "good and evil" would be a comprehensive term meaning "everything." Indeed, the statement "my lord the king is like the angel of God *to discern good and evil*" in 2 Samuel 14:17 is equivalent to "my lord has wisdom like the wisdom of the angel of God *to know all things that are on the earth*" in 2 Samuel 14:20 (see also "good and bad" in Gen. 24:50 and 31:24). This would be further confirmed by God's own statement, "Behold, the man has become like one of us,

knowing good and evil," in Genesis 3:22. "Knowledge" here may mean something different from intellectual knowledge—for example, experience. And yet this view must be rejected on practical grounds, because surely the biblical writer does not mean that man knows or experiences everything (just like God does) as a result of the first man's having eaten of the forbidden fruit.

(5) Still others believe that the writer here is depicting a kind of comprehensive knowledge that comes to every person in the process of maturing from childhood to adulthood, including such things as sound reasoning, good judgment, moral discernment, etc. However, the author of Genesis is not describing the natural process of growth but a certain capacity that man attained, which is basically foreign to his original nature, as a result of eating the forbidden fruit. He does not mean that maturity is bad.

(6) According to the literal reading of 2 Samuel 19:35 (Hebrew 36), the aged Barzillai asks, "Can I know (discern) between good and evil?" (see the KJV, ASV, and NEB), a question expecting a negative answer. Since Barzillai was an excellent judge of right and wrong, this must mean that at the age of eighty he no longer had full possession of his mental and physical powers. To "discern between good and evil" may have the same meaning in 1 Kings 3:9. This has led some scholars to argue that "the knowledge of good and evil" in Genesis 2:9, 17 means full possession of one's physical and mental powers. However, the context of Genesis 1–2 would suggest that the man and his wife already enjoyed this before the fall.

(7) In view of the thrust of Genesis 1–11, perhaps the biblical author has in mind the proud self-confidence of individuals and of the human race collectively to solve all their problems and make all their dreams come true without God or contrary to him. Thus, Adam and Eve made aprons out of fig leaves to cover themselves when they knew they were naked (3:7); Cain killed Abel because he was jealous that God had accepted Abel's sacrifice but rejected his (4:8); the sons of God married the daughters of men, who bore them children that became mighty men or

men of renown on the earth (6:4); and men built a city and a tower in a plain in the land of Shinar to make a name for themselves (11:4). The knowledge of good and evil in itself was not wrong, for God himself had this knowledge (3:22). But such knowledge was dangerous to *man*, because he was not capable of possessing it without being naughty and thinking that he was on an equality with God (that he was "like God," 3:5, 22). The same picture appears in Ezekiel 28:11-19, where the overthrow of the king of Tyre is compared with God's casting Adam and Eve out of the garden of Eden because they ate the forbidden fruit. If this interpretation is correct, "the tree of the knowledge of good and evil" is an expression that means something like "the tree whose fruit gives the one who eats it astonishing ability." God can exercise this ability soberly, calmly, and naturally for the good of his world (especially man). But man uses it for his own selfish ends, and seeks to demonstrate his equality with God in so doing. Thus, each time man decides to take what God has given him into his own hands and to use it as he pleases, God intervenes and thwarts his efforts, as when he sends a flood to destroy the "mighty men" living in the days of Noah (6:13-17), or confuses the language of those building the city and tower in Shinar and scatters them abroad (11:7-9). This interpretation would seem to be supported by the similarity between the words God spoke after Adam and Eve ate the forbidden fruit and the words he spoke after work was begun on the city and tower in Shinar. In the former instance, he said: "Behold, the man has become like one of us, knowing good and evil; and now, lest he put forth his hand and take also of the tree of life, and eat, and live for ever" (3:22). And in the latter, he said: "Behold, they are one people, and they have all one language; and this is only the beginning of what they will do; and nothing that they propose to do will now be impossible for them" (11:6).

[15] It was common in the ancient Near East for kings to have gardens or orchards or parks around their palaces, which were constantly tended and cultivated by the king's gardeners. The author of the book of Genesis may be

drawing his imagery from this practice to describe the relationship between God and man. If so, his point is that God is the king of the earth, and the first man is the servant he placed in the garden of Eden to tend and cultivate it.

[17] It is difficult to interpret the divine warning to the first man: **in the day that you eat of it you shall die**, because he did not die *on the day* (at the moment) he ate the forbidden fruit. Several solutions have been offered. (1) Some early Jewish rabbis argued that since one day with the Lord is as a thousand years, the text means that Adam and his wife would die before they reached the age of one thousand, and they did. This explanation is very fanciful. (2) Others seek to relieve the difficulty by interpreting "death" as "spiritual death." However, the context suggests that the reference is to "physical death," that is, the withdrawal of the "life" that God gave when he breathed into his nostrils the breath of life (2:7). God's warning (2:17) and the understanding of the man and his wife (3:3) have in mind physical death. (3) Still others think the expression "you shall die" means "you shall be doomed to death." It is argued: "The point of the whole narrative is apparently man's ultimate punishment rather than instantaneous death" (Speiser, *Genesis*, p. 17).

(4) The view which seems to offer the fewest difficulties is this: First, this statement presupposes that man as he was originally created would not have died if he had not eaten the forbidden fruit. "Sin came into the world through one man and *death through sin*" (Rom. 5:12). Second, God did not create man to live for ever on the earth. "God *alone* has immortality" (1 Tim. 6:16). In order for man to live for ever, he would have to eat of the tree of life (or else it does not make sense for God to have created the tree of life, cf. Gen. 3:22), and therefore he was not immortal by nature in the character he had when he was originally created by God. Initially, God may have planned to "take" man from the earth to be with him (cf. Gen. 5:24), "so that he should not see death" (Heb. 11:5). Third, the most natural interpretation of God's warning, "in the day that you eat of it you shall die" (Gen. 2:17), is that man would die

the moment he ate of the forbidden fruit. However, this did not happen—not because God does not or cannot do what he says (as the serpent's assurance to Eve would imply, 3:4), but because he has a compassionate heart and had mercy on man when he disobeyed him. Of course, this did not invalidate God's threat, because the first man died eventually; but it put off the execution of that threat to a later time. This interpretation seems truer to the context and natural meaning of 2:17 than the view that "you shall die" means "the death process shall begin in your body."

God Builds Woman for Man (2:18-25)

Several scholars insist that the author of Genesis 2:4-25 is attempting to present *a chronological account* of creation: man was created first, then vegetation, then animals, and finally woman. On the basis of this interpretation, they reach conclusions concerning the thrust of verses 18-25 which hardly come from the biblical text itself (e.g., the author of this material depicted the creation of animals as an *unsuccessful experiment* by God in search for a mate for man, or that he portrayed the creation of woman as an *afterthought*). Apparently, Genesis 2:4-25 is a *theological* account. Man appears at the first of the narrative because the writer's purpose is to show that God provided for *all* of man's needs. He gave him food to sustain his body, an ideal home in which to live (vss. 4-17), dominion over other forms of animal life (vss. 19-20), and woman to help him and to share his dreams and disappointments (vss. 18, 21-25). In each case, the author graphically calls the reader's attention to man's needs and then proclaims that God fulfilled them. Thus, in verses 18-25, first he emphasizes that other animals God formed "out of the ground" (vs. 19) like man (vs. 7) were not suitable for him, and so God *built* (Heb. *banah*, RSV "made") a woman from man's rib to satisfy his deepest needs (vs. 22).

[18] Man is a creature made by God. Therefore, God knows his nature even better than he knows it himself. He did not make man to live alone. Of course, the reader of the present form of the book of Genesis already knows this

from 1:27; but now the writer wants to emphasize it in order that his audience might come to appreciate the importance, and actual indispensability, of a wife in man's life. When God says, **It is not good** [Heb. *ṭobh*] **that the man should be alone**, naturally the reader would place the creation of woman chronologically back into chapter 1, because the writer first related the creation of woman (1:27-29; note that the imperatives in vs. 28 and the pronoun "you" in vs. 29 are plural in Hebrew and thus refer to man and woman together, not separately), and then said, "God saw everything that he had made, and behold, it was very good" (Heb. *ṭobh*, vs. 31). In other words, it could not be said that "everything" God had made was "very good" until woman was created. *This* is the point of 2:18-25, and not that God created woman as an afterthought.

Some find a contradiction between Genesis 2:18 and Paul's statement in 1 Corinthians 7:1: "It is well [*good*] for a man not to touch [have sexual relations with] a woman." However, it should be noted carefully that Paul does not say "it is not good for a man to have sexual relations with his wife." Instead, he is speaking of unmarried Christians who are being criticized for being single—as if it were invariably necessary to be married to serve Christ acceptably. And it is in response to this that he declares it is good (quite acceptable) for a man not to have sexual relationships with a woman (i.e., not to get married) if he has sufficient self-control to avoid lust and fornication, adultery, or some other sexual abuse as a single person. But even here, the general principle "it is not good that man should be alone" is assumed; and a well-rounded, contented bachelor is the exception, not the rule.

[19] Like man, animals were **formed** (Heb. *yatsar*) from the **ground** (Heb. *'adhamah*) and are **living creatures** (beings; Heb. *nephesh chayyah*). And yet, there is a qualitative difference between men and animals, in that God created man "in his own image" (1:26-27). Thus, God brings the animals to man (not man to the animals), and he gives them names (they do not name him). This is possible because God has already given man dominion over his

other creatures (1:26, 28). When the writer states that **God formed every beast of the field**, etc., he is not describing the creation of animals for the first time, as though his readers had not been told this earlier (in 1:20, 22, 24-25) but is putting the creation of woman in a proper relationship to the creation of animals.

[20] God determined to create a **helper** for man before he ever brought the animals to him that he might name them (vs. 18). But he does not make woman until man can appreciate her value in the fullest sense. So first, he parades the animals before man that he might be convinced thoroughly that none of these could measure up to his aspirations or satisfy his needs. Clearly, the author's purpose is to extol the virtues of woman, and not to depict her creation as a "necessary evil" or "afterthought." Chapter 1 leaves the creation of mankind (man and woman) until last to emphasize the importance of mankind in relationship to the rest of God's creatures. Similarly, chapter 2 leaves the creation of woman until last to stress the woman's inestimable value to man in contrast to all other creatures. That this is his point is verified by his portrayal of women in later chapters of the book of Genesis.

[21] Judging from other passages in the OT that use the same Hebrew word for **deep sleep** (*tardemah*; Gen. 15:12; 1 Sam. 26:12; Isa. 29:10; Job 4:13; 33:15; Prov. 19:15) and from the context of the present passage, "deep sleep" means a trance, a swoon, a coma, ecstasy (see the LXX *ekstasin*), or hypnotic sleep.

[22] Man (vs. 7) and animals (vs. 19) were formed from the ground, but woman was "built" (Heb. *banah*, RSV **made**) from man's **rib**. By using these carefully chosen terms, the writer emphasizes the special care that God took to make woman the ideal companion and fellow worker of man. Woman is such an important and indispensable creature that a part of the body which God originally formed for man was selected by the Lord so that she could be made from it

Earlier, the verbs "create" (Heb. *bara'*, 1:27) and "make" (Heb. *'asah*, 1:26; 2:18) were used to describe the creation of woman, but in 2:22 the word is "build" (Heb. *banah*). It seems obvious that the author chooses this word to convey the idea that God took special care in making just the right kind of helper for man.

The biblical text suggests that man did not observe the creation of the animals or of woman. God created both and then **brought** (Heb. *hebhi'*, 2:19, 22) them **to the man**. God already knew the kind of mate man required, but it was best for man to discover this for himself in order to fully appreciate God's gift of woman.

[23] The Hebrew text of verse 23 exhibits man's excitement and inexpressible joy over finding a companion that suited him perfectly. It seems that he had been searching diligently for a long time for a suitable mate, and when he found her, he burst out, **This at last** [literally, "this time"] **is bone of my bones**, etc. And three times in this verse, he uses the word "this" in the feminine (Heb. *zo'th*). **"This is bone of my bones . . . ; *this* shall be called Woman, . . . *this* was taken out of Man."** Here, woman is not viewed first as a childbearer for man but is appreciated for her own worth as man's companion and fellow worker.

Bone of my bones and flesh of my flesh is a popular Hebrew expression for the closest kind of kinship or relationship (see Gen. 29:14; Judg. 9:2; 2 Sam. 5:1; 19:12; 1 Chron. 11:1).

As in English, so also in Hebrew, there is a pun or wordplay on **Man** (Heb. *'ish*) and **Woman** (*'ishshah*) here. Up to this time, the writer had been using the word *'adham* for man, but now he shifts to *'ish* in order to create the wordplay. As is common in OT puns, these words are not related to one another etymologically but simply sound alike. Since woman **was taken out of Man**, she is dependent on him. And since man *names* his companion, he has authority over her (just as his naming of the beasts and birds demonstrate his authority over them, vss. 19-20). Of course, this is not a hateful or exacting or overbearing kind of authority, but an authority that woman naturally respects from the man who provides for her and gives her protection and security. It is no more offensive to a Christian woman than Christ's authority is to the church (see 1 Cor. 11:3; Eph. 5:23). "False and sentimental notions of the equality of the sexes do not exalt but dishonor womanhood, which has its own distinctive excellence—an excellence that is different from man's" (Richardson, *Genesis*, p. 69).

[24] Verses 24-25 contain a religious message for the original readers of Genesis, namely, that the relationship between a man and his wife is stronger than that between a man (or woman) and his (or her) parents, and that there is no shame in nudity between a man and his wife. Some scholars think this verse means that at marriage a man is to leave his own family and live with his wife's kindred, as did Jacob (Gen. 29) and Moses (Exod. 2:15–3:1; the technical term for this is "beena marriage"). But it is more likely that the writer means to emphasize that when a man marries, it is important for him to sever the ties of dependence on his parents and set up a new, separate home for himself and his wife.

Because of one meaning of the Hebrew and Arabic words translated "flesh," some scholars have suggested that **they become one flesh** means "they become one clan." However, the context here indicates that it means that when a man and woman marry, they have sexual relations and produce children (see especially 1 Cor. 6:16; Eph. 5:31). This corresponds well with the end of chapter 1, where God creates man and woman and then tells them to "be fruitful and multiply" (1:26-28). Thus, it is clear that the sexual drive and the birth of children are functions God gave man before he sinned and therefore are good in and of themselves.

God created *one* woman for the man. He could have created any number he wished. A man is to **cleave to his wife**, that is, marriage is to be a permanent relationship. God hates divorce (Mal. 2:16; Matt. 19:3-9; Mark 10:2-9). He also hates fornication and adultery, for he ordained that a man and a woman marry before engaging in sexual intercourse.

EXCURSUS

The Coherence of Genesis 1 and 2

It has become a common practice in scholarly circles to assign Genesis 1:1–2:3 (or 2:4a) to one original source (P for the Priestly work) and 2:4 (or 2:4b)-25 to another (J for the Y[J]ahwistic work). This is based on three main arguments: (1) The account in 1:1–2:3 follows a rigid pattern of presentation, is very formal and schematic, and aims at scientific classifications for the various creatures, whereas 2:4-25 reflects a childlike simplicity. (2) The order of these two sections is different. (3) 1:1–2:3 uses *'elohim* (RSV "God") as the name for God, while 2:4-25 uses *yahweh 'elohim* (RSV "the Lord God"). But even beyond this, scholars are unable to find a coherence in the two separate paragraphs and thus proceed to subdivide them into smaller units. For example, many critics contend that 2:10-14 is a later insertion by someone who wanted to change the original mythical story into a historical account.

In dealing with narrative material, certainly there is great value in getting behind the present final form of a book to earlier stages of preservation of the material (as when 2 Sam. 1:18 refers to the Book of Jashar), and when possible back to the original event itself. But a preoccupation with this sort of scholarly endeavor often ends in a neglect of the material as it stands in the final form of the biblical text, which at some point was presented to a specific audience for a particular purpose. It would seem logical that the commentator's first task is to attempt to interpret the text as it now stands and move from this to earlier stages of the material. The present commentary attempts to follow the text of the Bible as it stands and to discover the meaning the text had for the audience that first read the book as a whole. Whatever the case before, there came a time when some audience read Genesis 1:1–2:3 before 2:4-25 and interpreted the latter in light of the former. In such a framework, "it is misleading to call 2:4-25 a second creation account" (D. Kidner, *Genesis,* TOTC, p. 58).

III

The Story of Human History
(3:1–11:26)

Out of the countless stories that might have been told about primeval man, the author of Genesis has selected some which teach a great religious truth that he wishes to emphasize to his readers: in spite of God's innumerable blessings, man has rebelled against him; because God loves man, he punishes him to keep him from destroying himself, and out of this punishment brings him new hope. He couches his theology in four stories: the fall of Adam and Eve (ch. 3), Cain's murder of Abel (ch. 4), Noah and the flood (chs. 6–9), and the tower of Babel (11:1-9). These stories are connected by genealogical lists, each covering a long period of time: from Adam to Noah (ch. 5), the genealogies of Noah's three sons (ch. 10), and from Noah to Abraham (11:10-26).

That the writer covers long eras with few words shows his deliberate selectivity (see John 20:30-31; 21:25) and implies that he (and possibly his readers) knew many details about other people and places that he mentions only briefly in passing. It is a mistake for the reader of Genesis to spend his time conjecturing about matters that the author avoided or failed to explain. The important thing is to try to understand what he intended to say to his first audience and then to apply this to the situation of modern man.

SIN AND PUNISHMENT,
GRACE AND RENEWAL (I):
THE FALL OF ADAM AND EVE (CH. 3)

The story of the fall of Adam and Eve (Gen. 3) follows a well worked-out pattern: (a) Man sins (vss. 1-6). (b) He strives to evade responsibility for his sin (vss. 7-13). (c) God pronounces punitive curses on him (vss. 14-19). (d) God puts man in a situation in which he can begin again (vss. 20-24). The writer's purpose is clearly religious.

Man Sins (3:1-6)

Apparently the biblical author's purpose in verses 1-6 is to show his readers the true nature of sin. Sin is much more than disobeying a specific commandment of God externally. Surely, God had forbidden man to eat of the tree of the knowledge of good and evil (2:17), and when the man and his wife ate of this fruit (3:6), he pronounced curses upon them (3:14-19). But the author forces the reader to look behind this external act to see *why* man would be so impudent as to disobey his own creator. He emphasizes that basically sin is a selfish desire coupled with a lack of confidence in God's goodness which lies at the very center of man's existence as a created being (even before the fall). In other words, essentially sin is a heart problem. The external act is merely a symptom of the problem, not the real disease.

The biblical writer paints the picture of sin in six successive steps. First, the woman is deeply disturbed by God's command not to eat the forbidden fruit. Somewhere deep within her is a burning desire to eat the fruit of *this* tree, and she cannot help but wonder if perhaps God is depriving her of something that would improve her life in some way. When the serpent asks her, "Did God say, 'You [plural] shall not eat of any tree of the garden'?" (vs. 1), he simply brings to the surface what had been irritating her subconsciously for a long time. The purpose of his question is to emphasize that God is depriving man of something that would be good for him. Thus, he exaggerates

God's hindering him from partaking of *everything* he has made. The woman's hidden desire for the forbidden fruit is revealed in her overreaction to the serpent's question: "We may eat of the fruit of the trees of the garden but God said, 'You shall not eat of the fruit of the tree which is in the midst of the garden, neither shall you touch it, lest you die'" (vss. 2-3). God's command in 2:17 contains no prohibition against *touching* the fruit. Of course, it could be argued that the original command included a prohibition against touching it, that we learn of this detail for the first time in 3:3, and that the biblical author chose to omit it from the account in chapter 2. However, if one puts himself in the position of the original readers and seeks to discover the impression the author is trying to convey, it is more natural to take the woman's reply to the serpent as an overreaction to his insinuations, reflecting her subconscious desire to eat the forbidden fruit.

Second, the serpent enforces the woman's desire to eat the fruit by telling her the advantages of eating from this particular tree. He insinuates that God had told man only the bad results of eating this fruit and had deliberately failed to mention the good ones. The context suggests that the advantages the serpent emphasizes are correct externally. (a) When he says, "You [plural] will not die" (vs. 4), apparently he means, "You will not die (physically) immediately," and they did not. As a matter of fact, after man eats the forbidden fruit, God drives him out of the garden "lest he put forth his hand and take also of the tree of life, and eat, and live for ever" (vs. 22). (b) He promises that the eyes of the man and the woman will be opened (vs. 5), and when they ate, "the eyes of both were opened" (vs. 7). (c) He promises that they will be "like God, knowing good and evil" (vs. 5), and after they ate God said, "Behold the man has become like one of us, knowing good and evil" (vs. 22). Thus, the issue here is whether these advantages outweigh the advantages man would have enjoyed had he not eaten the forbidden fruit. The Bible repeatedly admits that sin brings "fleeting pleasures" (see Heb. 11:25), but it also insists that the joys which God offers are much more wholesome and satisfying for man. In other words, there is more to life than mechanical cause and effect. God and man are not machines that react to each other automatically in preprogrammed ways. It is impossible to predict what man will do or what God will do under a given set of circumstances. True, when man ate the fruit he did not die (physically) immediately as God said, yet the reason for this is not that God was weak and unable to make man die (as the serpent's statement implied), but that he is compassionate and merciful to man even when he disobeys him (see comments on 2:17). Indeed, when man ate the fruit his eyes were opened, yet not to see secrets God had hidden from man that would prove to be advantageous to his life (as the serpent's words suggested), but to his own nakedness, which made him so miserable that he felt compelled to cover himself. To be sure, when man ate the fruit he received astonishing ability (he became like God, knowing good and evil), yet he is unable to use this ability for the good of the world (as God does), but only for selfish ends (see comments on 2:9).

Third, the woman's mind dwells on the desirable aspects of the forbidden fruit. She "saw" (here obviously referring to a function of the mind, not of the eye) that the fruit was good food (not poison), attractive or appealing, and could "make one wise" (vs. 6). The appeals to the lust of the flesh, the lust of the eyes, and the pride of life characterize the temptations of Jesus (Matt. 4:1-11; Luke 4:1-13) and of all men (1 John 2:16). These have the greatest attraction for man, who is already prone to be motivated by self-centered interests.

Fourth, the woman "took" some of the "fruit" of the tree (vs. 6). Perhaps she wanted to test the impression she got by looking at the fruit. It looked very good, but if she touched it she could find out if it also felt good. If she could touch it without being harmed, perhaps she could eat it without being harmed. She may have felt that she would not disobey the Lord's command to eat the fruit (2:17) by touching it, in spite of her statement to the serpent that God had commanded man not to touch it (3:3). Yet, he who plays with temptation soon discovers that sin is more powerful than he (Prov. 4:14-17; 6:27-29; 2 Tim. 2:22).

Fifth, the woman "ate" of the fruit (vs. 6). As yet, there was no sign of danger in doing so, and she was convinced that this would be beneficial to her.

Finally, she "gave some to her husband and he ate" (vs. 6). Since the woman did not die (physically) immediately when she ate of the fruit, her husband undoubtedly concluded that it would bring no harm to him either. The sinner feels more comfortable if others join him in his deeds; so the woman prevailed upon her husband to eat the forbidden fruit with her.

[1] Scholars interpret the identity and role of **the serpent** (Heb. *nachash*) in the story of man's sin (vss. 1, 2, 4, 13, 14) in various ways. (a) Some think the serpent is not a literal snake, but a personification of temptation within man. (b) Others insist that the original writer and readers of Genesis 3 would have understood the serpent symbolically, because the serpent was used symbolically in religious cults throughout the ancient Near East. Ancient Egyptian art depicts the naked Canaanite goddess of fertility holding a snake in her hand (see J. B. Pritchard, *The Ancient Near East in Pictures* [Princeton: Princeton University Press, 1954] pp. 470–74). Archeologists have unearthed several serpent figures made of metal in various parts of the ancient world, including a snake draped around a goddess in Egypt, snakes draped around cult objects in Beth-shan (Pritchard, *Pictures*, pp. 585, 590), and a god represented in the form of a serpent (ibid., p. 692). After the Israelites defeated the Canaanite king of Arad (Num. 21:1-3), they murmured against the Lord and he sent fiery serpents among the people. When Moses prayed for them, God told him to make a bronze serpent and set it on a pole so that the Israelites might look on it when the serpents bit them, and live (Num. 21:4-9). This may have involved an Israelite adaptation of Canaanite practices, or a mocking polemic against their trust in magical symbols such as the snake. In either case, the point that the Lord, and not a bronze serpent, is the source of healing.

However, many of the Jews themselves failed to grasp this truth and were attracted to the Canaanite snake cult. This is indicated by Hezekiah's reform (705 B.C.), which included the destruction of Nehushtan (from the root *nachash*, the Hebrew for "serpent" in Gen. 3), "the bronze serpent that Moses had made" (2 Kings 18:4). The themes of the naked couple (Gen. 2:25; 3:7), childbearing (3:16), and productive vegetation (3:17-19) are at home in Canaanite fertility cults.

Therefore, it may be that the author of Genesis intentionally used language taken from Canaanite religion in telling the story of man's sin (just as Paul borrowed language from Greek poets as a means of conveying God's message to his hearers, Acts 17:28; 1 Cor. 15:33; Titus 1:12), or that he used the story of the serpent's seduction of man and woman to symbolize Israel's seduction by Canaanite fertility gods of his day. After all, Paul used this story in warning Christians not to be led astray from singlehearted devotion to Christ (2 Cor. 11:2-3). The curse that the Lord pronounces upon the serpent (Gen. 3:14-15) calls to mind Job 26:13 and Isaiah 27:1, which speak of God's victory over various kinds of serpents. Apparently these serpents are symbolic representations of the ocean and foreign nations.

(c) On the strength of one possible interpretation of the last two lines of 3:15, some early church fathers and modern scholars interpret the serpent in Genesis 3 as the devil himself and contend that verse 15 contains the first biblical reference to the gospel of redemption (protevangelium). Revelation 12:9 and 20:2 call the devil "that ancient serpent," and Paul may have Genesis 3:15 in mind in Romans 16:20.

(d) The language and context of Genesis 3 seem to indicate that the serpent has a dual identity. First, it is a **wild creature** that God had made (vs. 1). God curses it "above all cattle" and "wild animals" and decrees that it shall go upon its belly and eat dust (vs. 14). Apparently the biblical author was thinking of a literal snake, not (just) a symbol.

When God created man, he decreed that he "have domin-ion over the fish of the sea and over the birds of the air and over every living thing that moves upon the earth" (1:28). This decree still stands after man sins, but now man en-counters hostility in the animal kingdom and must engage in an ongoing struggle with other creatures of God, espe-cially the snake (3:15). But second, the serpent of Gene-sis 3 is more than merely a wild creature. It has capacities that rise above the typical capabilities of animal life: it is subtle (vss. 1, 13), can speak in human language (vss. 1, 4-5), and is able to reason and to present convincing argu-ments to man that rival even the commandments of God himself in man's mind (vss. 4-5). This seems to suggest that the author of Genesis uses the serpent as a symbol of the power of temptation in human life, or that he thinks of the devil speaking to man through a serpent (which may be compared with the Lord speaking to Balaam through an ass, Num. 22:28). The "enmity" between the serpent and the woman (3:15) may be both the hostility between snakes and human beings, and man's constant struggle with the Tempter, the Devil. Just as 1 Peter 5:8 compares the devil with "a roaring lion," Genesis 3 compares him with a subtle serpent.

[5] Since God made man "after his likeness" (Heb. *kidhmuthenu*; 1:26), one might wonder why the serpent thought it would be tempting to promise him that if he ate of the forbidden fruit he would become **like God** (*ke'lohim*; 3:5, 22). Obviously two different concepts of being like God are intended. The point in 1:26 seems to be that al-though man has dominion over the rest of God's creatures on earth, he is not God, but only *like* God (see comments on 1:26). To "know good and evil" apparently means to have astonishing ability to deal with problems and make one's dreams come true. This is not bad in and of itself, because God possesses such ability (3:22). But it is bad *for man*, because he cannot use this ability unselfishly; with it he becomes haughty and thinks he is on an equality with God (see comments on 2:9). The serpent appeals to man's desire to become God's equal.

The Hebrew word here translated "God" (*'elohim*) is plural in form. Ordinarily, grammarians argue that if this word is used with a singular verb or is modified by a singular adjective or participle, it should be translated as a singular; but if it is used with a plural verb or is modified by a plural adjective or participle, it should be translated as a plural. In 3:5, the participle translated "knowing" is plural (*yodhe'e*), and this had caused the translators of the KJV and NEB to read "as [like] gods." This interpretation may find support in verse 22, where the Lord says, "Behold, the man has become like one of *us*." If this is the correct line of thought, the serpent did not assure the man and woman that if they ate the forbidden fruit they would be like *God*, but that they would be like *gods*, which in this context would mean "heavenly beings" or "angels." On the other hand, this grammatical rule is not invariable, and thus the translators of the ASV and RSV concluded that the singular "God" was the most likely meaning. There does not seem to be anything in the language or the context that would allow a dogmatic solution to this difficult problem. Either interpretation is significant.

Man Strives to Evade Responsibility (3:7-13)

As soon as man sins, he begins feeling guilty. This makes him uncomfortable with his own condition (vs. 7), in the presence of God (vss. 8-10) and around others (vss. 12-13). He feels he must do something about the sin he has committed and the guilt he has incurred. He must cover his sin and pretend that he is not to blame for his ungodly desires and rebellious actions. He feels that it is important to defend his righteousness and guard his innocence. He believes he is capable of dealing with his sin and guilt by his own ingenuity and creativity.

The first thing man does to try to hide his guilt is to cover his physical nakedness (vs. 7). It is characteristic of man to think he can deal with the deep problems of his heart by controlling his physical behavior. Such a philosophy runs rampant in circles which emphasize the correct observance of external religious acts rather than an inner change of motives and attitudes. The man and his wife felt compelled to cover themselves because when they ate the forbidden fruit, "the eyes of both were opened, and they knew that they were naked" (vs. 7). The serpent was correct in stating that if they ate the fruit their eyes would be opened (vs. 5), but his insinuation was that this would enrich man's life, whereas the truth was that it made him miserable.

The Hebrew word translated "know" (*yadha'*) has a wide variety of meanings in the OT, and therefore one must determine its precise meaning by each context in which it occurs. Some scholars equate "knowing good and evil" (vs. 5) with "knowing that they were naked" (vs. 7). However, it seems more natural to identify "knowing good and evil" in verse 5 with the same phrase in verse 22. Knowing "that they were naked" in 3:7 is the antithesis of not being ashamed that they were naked in 2:25. In 2:25 it is assumed that before the man and his wife ate the forbidden fruit they *knew* (intellectually) that they were naked, but this caused them no shame. So 3:7 means that as a result of eating this fruit they *knew* (i.e., became ashamed) that they were naked.

On their own initiative, they decided to make themselves aprons out of fig leaves. However, this was not adequate, and thus God made for them garments of skins to clothe them (vs. 21). It is not immediately clear why garments of skins are acceptable for man's clothing and aprons of fig leaves are not. But it does appear that the point the biblical writer is making here is that when man tries to deal with the consequences of his own sins he is destined to fail, but when he turns his problems over to God he will be adequately supplied.

Man's second means of covering his guilt is to hide from God (physically) "among the trees of the garden" (vss. 8, 10). Man sins, and suddenly he is aware that God is near; this makes him afraid (vs. 10), and instinctively he seeks protection behind some physical object. But the God who made the universe has no problem seeing through trees, or even through man's external pretenses:

Sheol and Abaddon lie open before the Lord,
how much more the hearts of men.

Proverbs 15:11

Man's third method of concealing his guilt is to shift the blame to someone or something else (vss. 12-13). Even while the man was confessing, "I ate [of the forbidden fruit]," he was trying to lay the responsibility for his sin on the woman (because she gave him some of the fruit—he did not take it from the tree with his own hands) and on God (because he gave the woman to him). And even while the woman was admitting, "I ate [of that same fruit]," she was claiming that the serpent had tricked (beguiled) her into doing something she would not have done otherwise.

The manner in which God deals with the man and his wife is very instructive. Had it not been for God's unwavering love for man, even in his rankest rebellion, God would have put them to death immediately as he originally threatened (2:17; see comments there). Instead, he sets in motion a chain of events intended to lift them out of the pit they had dug for themselves (see Ps. 7:15). First, he makes man aware of his presence (vs. 8). The biblical writer uses anthropomorphic language to convey this thought (see LWC-OT, vol. 1, ch. 1). He pictures God as a wealthy landowner strolling casually through his woods in the late afternoon. To conclude from this that God actually walks on two legs like a human being is to fail to appreciate the nature and purpose of figurative language in the Bible. Second, he asks the man and his wife a series of questions designed to help them see themselves as they really are. In verse 9 he calls to the man, "Where are you [singular]?" Of course, God could have *driven* or *flushed* man out of hiding, but compassion led him to *draw* him out. When the man responded, God said, "Who told you that you were naked? Have you eaten of the tree of which I commanded you not to eat?" (vs. 11). And after the man tries to blame his wife and God himself for his sin, God turns to the woman and asks, "What is this that you have done?" (vs. 13). Obviously none of these questions indicate that

God was ignorant of what the man and his wife had done and thus was seeking information. On the contrary, it was because he knew what they had done that he was asking these questions. And his purpose was to make them feel the full weight of responsibility for their motives and actions. Only then could he help them. God's fatherly love and concern for man is apparent in this approach. Third, God punishes man for his rebellion to make him realize the seriousness of sin (vss. 14-19). Fourth, he provides for the new needs that man has in the situation he has brought upon himself through sin (vss. 20-24).

[8] The KJV and ASV read, "And they heard the voice of the Lord God walking," but a "voice" does not "walk." To be sure, the first meaning of the Hebrew word *qol* is "voice," but the precise meaning must be determined by the context. The RSV and NEB have **sound**, which conveys a clearer impression of the original idea to the modern American mind. The word *qol* is connected with "marching" in 2 Samuel 5:24 and "feet" in 1 Kings 14:6 and 2 Kings 6:32. "The voice of feet [marching]" would mean "footsteps." And the idea in Genesis 3:8 is that the man and his wife heard the Lord's footsteps as he walked in the garden.

The Hebrew phrase translated **in the cool of the day** in the RSV, KJV, and ASV is *leruach hayyom,* which means literally "at the spirit (or wind) [time] of the day." *Ruach* is the same word translated "Spirit" in the KJV of Genesis 1:2. The Hebrew preposition *le* is used of *time* in the OT but not of temperature. Therefore, this phrase actually means "at the breezy time of the day," which is late in the evening when fresh breezes bring relief from the daytime heat (cf. NEB "at the time of the evening breeze").

God Pronounces Punitive Curses (3:14-19)

Like 2:23, 3:14-19 is in poetic form in the Hebrew (except for the introductory statements in vss. 14, 16, and 17). Perhaps these curses were given in poetry for easy memorization because they were frequently sung, or because it was customary to announce curses in poetic verse. Their concern is with all mankind, and not with Israelites alone, as is indeed the case throughout Genesis 1–11 (as well as with many other passages in the OT). According to the OT, God's rule and care are universal, not nationalistic. One should not forget this in attempting to understand the OT teaching on God's election of Israel. Israel's election does not reflect God's partiality toward Israel but his means of reaching all mankind, who had sinned and been cursed. In the early chapters of Genesis, it was because of man's rebellion that it became necessary for God to choose Seth or Noah or Abram to prevent the human race from being completely destroyed and to bring fallen mankind back to him. Thus, God's curses on man serve as the background for his attempts to redeem man described in the following chapters.

Genesis 3:14-19 contains a number of textual and technical problems, some of which must be disregarded in this commentary. These verses relate God's curses on the serpent (vss. 14-15), the woman (vs. 16), and the man (vss. 17-19). Structurally, the pattern here may be *a b a*, because the curses against the serpent and the man begin with an *explanation* for the curse: "Because you have [done so-and-so]" (vss. 14, 17), but the curse against the woman is not accompanied by an explicit explanation. At any rate, the theological emphasis throughout is that God does not punish man arbitrarily, but because of his sin. There is something about the seed of sin that brings forth the fruit of punishment (Gal. 6:7-8; James 1:14-15).

The curse on the serpent (vss. 14-15) must be interpreted in light of one's understanding of its (or his) identity. The context of Genesis 3 indicates that (a) the serpent is a wild animal, but also that (b) he has abilities above and beyond that which is typical of wild animals (see comments on 3:1). It is extremely difficult to determine what lines in God's curse are directed against the animal (the snake) and what lines are directed against the devil who used it to tempt the man and his wife. Possibly God announces two specific curses on the animal, and one on the devil. His first curse against the snake is that it will be punished more than other animals in that it will be forced to go on its belly, and thus be more susceptible to the annoyance of rising and blowing dust (vs. 14; this curse would hardly be suitable for the devil). Since man originally sinned in response to a beast's temptation, God apparently curses not only the serpent but all beasts (a view rejected by W. H. Bennett [*Genesis*, CB, p. 108] but advocated by J. H. Marks ["The Book of Genesis," IOVC, p. 6] and Alan Richardson [*Genesis 1–11*, TBC, p. 74]). This agrees with Paul's words in Romans 8:19-23 and with the obvious hostility that exists between man and beast. The translation "Banned shall you be from all cattle," which has been proposed by E. A. Speiser (*Genesis*, AB, pp. 22, 24), is not convincing.

The divine decree that the serpent go on its belly may be understood in one of two ways. (1) This does not necessarily imply that snakes had legs prior to man's temptation. Many species of snakes have the ability to erect relatively long portions of their bodies for certain periods of time. Originally serpents may have done this normally, but because of the curse they are forced to crawl on their bellies as a rule. (2) There were "creeping things" on the earth before the fall (Gen. 1:26, 30), which very likely included serpents. Thus, the divine curse may not be the crawling movement of the serpent but a new significance given to this as a result of the fall. As a parallel, it seems likely that there were rainbows prior to the flood, but after the flood God gave the rainbow a new significance for man (Gen. 9:13). Modern man may find it difficult to understand God's rationale for punishing a morally irresponsible animal that the devil used to accomplish his purposes. Perhaps there is no reasonable explanation for this that would satisfy the human mind. However, this is perfectly in harmony with other OT texts demanding the death of animals when they killed or desecrated human beings (Gen. 9:5; Exod. 21:28-39; Lev 20:15-16).

God's second curse against the serpent is that he will "put enmity between" the serpent and his "seed" and "the woman . . . and her seed"; serpents will harm people, but people will dominate and exterminate them (vs. 15). This would suggest that before the fall there was a harmonious relationship between man and other creatures. God had given man dominion over the rest of the animal kingdom (Gen. 1:28), and apparently they accepted this dominion with tranquility. God brought all the animals to man, and he gave them names (2:19-20). Certain prophetic texts seem to assume this harmony when they announce the coming of an age when harmony between man and beast will be restored (Isa. 11:6-9; 65:17-25; Hos. 2:18). Because of the serpent's role in the temptation, God puts enmity between it and the woman which had not been there before. The Hebrew word translated "seed" (*zera'*) is collective here (as is usually, though not always, the case throughout the Bible) and means "descendants," as the context shows. The devil does not have "descendants" (and the word here can hardly mean "followers," for if it did the "seed" of the woman would have to be "followers" of the woman), but the serpent does. "The woman" is obviously Eve (not the Virgin Mary), and her "descendants" are the human race. As long as time will last, there will be a continuing hostility between snakes and people; but people will prevail, and snakes will be the worse for the battle. Some scholars insist that there is no hopeful or optimistic outlook for the human race in Genesis 3–11, and certainly not in God's "curses" in 3:14-19; they assert that such passages of hope occur for the first time with the call of Abraham in 12:3-11. However, several texts in these chapters, including 3:15, indicate that this is not the case.

That the serpent was subtle (vss. 1, 13), could speak (vss. 1, 4-5), and was able to argue with man convincingly (vss. 4-5), shows that the author of Genesis has in mind more than merely a wild animal. Either the serpent symbolizes the power of temptation in man's life, or the text describes the devil speaking through the serpent to tempt man (see comments on vs. 1). If the curse on the serpent fits the situation described in the context, it must contain a curse on the devil. Nothing in verse 14 fits the devil, so this curse must appear in verse 15. Apparently the biblical author uses the physical hostility between snakes and people as a symbol for the spiritual hostility between mankind and the devil. The devil dealt a telling blow against man by persuading the man and his wife to sin against God, and he will continue to tempt man to sin. But ultimately man will prevail, and the devil will be conquered. This is as far as the text goes.

A brief sketch of the history of the interpretation of Genesis 3:15 may be helpful. Targum Jonathan and Targum Jerusalem applied it to the Jews and their victory over the devil in the days of the Messiah. The early church fathers generally understood the serpent to be the instrument of the devil, but Irenaeus was in the minority in interpreting the seed of the woman as Jesus Christ. Following Jerome's reading in the Vulgate, medieval Roman Catholic scholars insisted that the "woman" in this verse is the Virgin Mary. Luther rejected this explicit interpretation but thought that the verse as a whole announced the virgin birth of Christ. Several modern exegetes deny any reference whatsoever to the devil and Christ in this verse. The context of Genesis 3 seems to support the general view of Calvin and Protestant theologians, namely, that verse 15 announces there will be continual enmity between mankind and the devil throughout human history and promises that ultimately mankind will prevail. (A more detailed presentation of the various interpretations of this verse is given by J. Skinner, *Genesis,* ICC, pp. 80–82.)

There is no reference (explicit or implicit) to the Virgin Mary or to Jesus Christ in this text. Yet it is clear from the unfolding of God's purpose in scripture that the only way man's victory over the devil is possible is through Jesus Christ (see Rom. 16:17-20; Rev. 12:7-12; 20:1-6).

God's curse on the "woman" (vs. 16) is twofold. First, she will suffer pain in childbirth. God intended for man and woman to have children from the very first (see Gen. 1:28; 2:24); having children is not a curse. But apparently before the fall the woman could have given birth to children painlessly; as a result of the fall, giving birth to a child will be painful to her.

Second, the marital relationship will not be as naturally

harmonious as God originally intended. The precise nuance of thought in the last two lines of verse 16 is very hard to determine. Genesis 2:18-24 states that God created the woman to help the man (vss. 18, 20) and that the man named the woman (vs. 23), indicating that from the first God intended for the man to "rule over" the woman. This speaks against the view that whereas the man and the woman stood on an equality before God prior to the fall, after the fall God placed the woman under the man's rule. However, scholars have suggested several other interpretations.

(1) On the basis of the LXX and Syriac Peshitta, some emend *teshuqathekh,* "your desire," to *teshubhathekh,* "your return." The woman had failed in her responsibility to help the man by giving him the forgidden fruit (vs. 6) and encouraging him to eat it (vs. 17). Now she must return to the role originally intended for her, and her husband will make sure she discharges that role. However, it is best not to emend the MT unless absolutely necessary.

(2) The reading "your desire shall be *for* your husband" (RSV; cf. NEB), which is quite legitimate, may suggest that the woman's sexual or emotional passion for the man will be so strong that she will have difficulty mastering it irrespective of the adverse consequences that it might bring upon her. While this is linguistically possible, it is not a suitable punishment for the sin she committed.

(3) The KJV and ASV have the happiest translation: "thy desire shall be *to* thy husband," that is, "thy wishes shall be (subject) to (those of) thy husband." The previous context described what happened when the woman was left to follow freely her own desire. Her inability to cope with the situation made it necessary for God to impose a control upon her, which would be superior to her innermost wishes (viz., the decision of her husband). In matters of great importance and ultimate concern, it is his decision that must prevail, no matter how strong the woman's desire for a different route of action may be. This does not mean that God decreed a harsh, authoritarian rule of the husband over the wife, for then the divine curse would inject still

another evil into the marital union. Thus, it is difficult to accept the view of some scholars that here the biblical author was trying to explain the woman's place as the husband's possession or slave, which was a widespread belief in the ancient Near East. Instead, the husband is to *rule* lovingly, but firmly, always in the best interest of his wife. This is the same picture of the marriage relationship as that painted in Ephesians 5:22-33.

God also pronounces two curses on the man (vss. 17-19). First, he must work especially hard for his food (vss. 17-19a). God curses "the ground" because of man's sin. Thus, the only abundant crop the ground produces easily and rapidly is thorns and thistles, which choke out good grain, the sustenance on which man depends. This suggests that before the fall the ground yielded good food for man quickly and easily and that man did not have to work extraordinarily hard to secure it. Work is not a curse God placed on man as a result of the fall, because God commanded the man to till and keep the garden before he sinned (2:15). The curse consists of the difficulty of the work and the hindrances man has to overcome to procure his food. Second, man must die physically (vs. 19b). C. A. Simpson argues that the curse God placed on the man was not physical death itself but a terrible fear of death ("The Book of Genesis," IB, vol. 1, pp. 512–13). Now it is true that the Bible nowhere suggests that God created man to live on earth for ever. That he created the tree of life before the fall (see 2:9) suggests that at that time man was not capable of living on earth for ever (see 3:22). At the same time, physical death is undoubtedly the consequence God said would come from eating the forbidden fruit (see 2:17; 3:3, 4). Originally, therefore, God may have intended to transform man into a different form (see Gen. 5:24; Heb. 11:5; 1 Cor. 15:51-54), not to put him to death. It was man's sin, then, that brought death into the world (Rom. 5:12; 1 Cor. 15:21-22).

[15] The verb **bruise** seems suitable to describe the result of man's action on the serpent but not the result of the serpent's action on man. Some scholars try to solve this

problem by arguing that the Hebrew verb *shuph* comes from the root, *sh-'-p,* meaning "to trample upon, to crush," but this does not improve the situation. In light of what one would expect the text to mean, commentators have suggested that *shuph* (or a similar Hebrew word) be translated "lie in wait for," "lay snares for," "snap at," "strike at" (NEB), etc., but as yet no certain solution is evident.

[16] For **your pain in childbearing** (RSV), the MT has two nouns joined by "and," which may be translated literally, "thy sorrow and thy conception" (KJV), "thy pain and thy conception" (ASV); similarly the LXX reads, "your labour and your groaning" (so the NEB). However, this is clearly an instance of hendiadys, in which two words are joined by "and" to express one thought. Thus, the reading of the RSV is best here. (See Speiser, *Genesis,* p. 24, and most exegetes.)

[17] From the unpointed Hebrew text, it is impossible to tell whether *l'dm* here and verse 21 means **to Adam** or "to the man." The Massoretic (pointed) Text has "to Adam," if it can be shown that it is invariably true that without the article the Hebrew word 'adham means "Adam" (which is the interpretation of the KJV, ASV, and RSV). However, there is no apparent reason why the proper name "Adam" is appropriate before Genesis 5:1, and thus most commentators read "the man" in 3:17, 21 (so the NEB).

Some scholars want to emend the Hebrew expression translated **because of you** (*ba'abhurekha*) to *be'o-bhadhekha,* "when you till it" (following the LXX, Symmachus, and the Vulgate), which would agree with a similar expression in a similar context in 4:12. However, the same Hebrew word found in the MT here appears in 8:21, which clearly refers back to 3:17. Furthermore, the Hebrew text of 3:17 as it now stands contains a wordplay on *'arurah,* "cursed," and *ba'abhurekha,* "because of you," which would be somewhat destroyed by adopting this emendation. It seems best, therefore, to retain the reading of the MT.

[19] Surely the biblical author does not mean that man

shall sweat as a result of the effort he puts forth in *eating* bread. Rather, the effort man expends is in *producing* the bread that he eats. Here the biblical writer is using metonymy (cf. LWC-OT, vol. 1, ch. 1), substituting "eat" for the closely associated verb "earn." Thus, "you shall gain your bread by the sweat of your brow" (NEB) best conveys the real thought of the original Hebrew expression.

God Enables Man to Begin Again (3:20-24)

God could have put man to death (physically) immediately when he rebelled against him; in fact, he warned man that if he ate of the forbidden fruit he would do just that (cf. 2:17). Instead, he cursed sinful man so that he could never forget the seriousness of alienation from God (3:14-19). The purpose of this divine punishment was not to destroy man but to bring him back to God.

In verse 20, man, apparently optimistic about the future, describes his wife as the mother of all living; in verse 21, God makes clothes for the man and his wife; but in verses 22-24, God drives man out of the garden of Eden. Many scholars see great disharmony in these verses because (a) verses 20-21 are optimistic, while verses 22-24 are pessimistic; and (b) it is difficult to see how the man could think of his wife as the mother of all living when as yet there is no indication that they had any children. The most common explanation for this is that verse 20 is a marginal gloss on 4:1 which a later scribe wrongly inserted between 3:19 and 3:21, that originally verse 23 was the immediate continuation of verse 19, and that verses 21-22 and 24 are (at least in part) from a different source. However, the commentator is faced with the responsibility of making sense out of the text as it now stands, for it does not seem likely that the author of the book of Genesis would have written an obviously contradictory narrative, no matter how many sources he may have used in the preparation of his work.

Two considerations may go a long way in alleviating the supposed difficulties in this paragraph. First, there is nothing in verses 22-24 that warrants the conclusion that the

biblical writer saw God's driving man out of the garden of
Eden as a punitive (pessimistic) action. It may well have
been the most compassionate thing God could have done
under the circumstances. Numerous scholars contend that
in verse 22 God (like pagan deities) is panic-stricken by the
possibility that man might eat of the tree of life and thereby
become a formidable threat to him, and so he feverishly
drives him out of the garden (see Skinner, *Genesis*,
pp. 87–88, 97, where he says that "3:22 borders hard on
the pagan notion of the 'envy' of the godhead"; and Simpson, "Genesis," p. 501). However, this idea is so foreign to
the rest of the Bible, including the surrounding context,
that it is hard to believe this is what the author of Genesis
really had in mind. Indeed, God acts here not out of fear
for his own supremacy, but out of concern for man's welfare. Man had eaten of the tree of the knowledge of good
and evil, and in so doing had acquired abilities that he was
not able to use unselfishly, and thus that ultimately hurt
him (see comments on 2:9). Now, if God allows him to eat
of the tree of life, he will receive immortality, which God
can use meaningfully and beneficently, but which will be
harmful to man because (not being God) he cannot use it
wisely, especially now that he has sinned. To prevent man
from injuring himself even more with gifts too complex for
his nature, God lovingly seals off any possibility of his
eating of the tree of life by driving him out of the garden
and making it impossible for him ever to return.

Second, the statement that Eve was the mother of all
living (vs. 20) is unsuitable in its present position *only* if it
can be established that the biblical writer intends to be
giving a chronological sequence of events here. However,
there is no compelling reason to believe this. Just as the
author of the book of Judges summarizes the entire period
of the Judges for his readers (Judg. 2:11-23) *before* he
relates events pertaining to specific judges (Judg.
3:7–16:31), the author of Genesis prepares his readers for
the births of Cain (4:1), Abel (4:2), and Seth (4:25) by declaring Eve to be the mother of all living (3:20). If he can
refer to a man's leaving his father and mother before he

tells of the existence of fathers or mothers (2:24), there is no reason why he cannot speak of Eve as the mother of all living before he tells of her having children. And if the reference to Eve as the mother of all living is out of place in 3:20, the allusion to the woman's seed in 3:15 is also out of place.

Consequently, Genesis 3:20-24 states in summary fashion the things God did for man after his rebellion to enable him to make the most out of his life, in spite of the curses he had called down upon himself by disobeying God (3:14-19). First, although the man and his wife were destined to die (vs. 19), God enabled them to have children as he originally planned (see 1:28), so that human life would continue on earth even after their deaths (3:20). Second, God apparently slew some animals and made the man and his wife garments of skins (3:21), which were much more adequate for their needs than the aprons of fig leaves that they had made for themselves (3:7). Third, God drove them out of the garden to prevent them from eating of the tree of life (3:22-24), which undoubtedly would have made life on earth even more unpleasant for mankind than it is as a result of their having eaten of the tree of knowledge of good and evil.

[20] There is a wordplay in the Hebrew text here. **The man called his wife's name Eve** [Heb. *chawwah*], **because she was the mother of all living** [Heb. *chay*]. Obviously the expression "all living" is limited to human life (as in Job 30:23; see Ps. 143:2).

[22] The plural **us** probably means God and his heavenly council, the angelic hosts gathered around his divine throne (see the comments on 1:25 and 3:5).

The progression of temptation and sin from **knowing good and evil** to *putting* **forth his hand** to *taking* to *eating* to *living* in this verse is strikingly similar to the progression from *being deeply disturbed by God's command* to *doubting God's motives* to *seeing* to *taking* to *eating* to *having the eyes opened* in 3:1-7 (see comments on 3:1-6).

[24] The original reading of verse 24 is debated. Some scholars follow the LXX, which says: "And he drove out

the man, and caused him to dwell to the east of the garden of Eden; and he stationed the cherubim and a flaming sword, which turned every way to guard the way to the tree of life." The KJV, ASV, RSV, and NEB all agree in following the MT. In either case, the text says that when God drove man out of the garden of Eden, he went eastward. This agrees with 11:2, which tells of men migrating "from the east" to a plain in Shinar (in Mesopotamia).

Apparently **cherubim** are angelic beings or man-made representations of angelic beings (see Exod. 36:35; 37:7-9; 1 Kings 6:23-27), whose purpose was to **guard** the divine throne or a holy place. The context of Genesis 3 (see "us" in vs. 22) and the parallel concepts in Ezekiel 28:11-19 suggest that angelic beings are intended here.

There is nothing to suggest that one of the cherubim is wielding the **flaming sword**. This sword probably represents an additional obstacle to man's getting to the tree of life. Many scholars conjecture that it is here a symbol for lightning.

EXCURSUS

The Biblical Fall and Babylonian Parallels

Modern scholarship has called attention to three possible Babylonian parallels to the biblical account of the fall of man in Genesis 3, in search of an ancient Near Eastern source for this narrative. One is a cylinder seal in the British Museum depicting a male and a female under a tree, seated, facing one another, fully clothed, with arms and hands stretched out toward the tree, and an upright wriggling snake behind the female. However, there is no writing with this picture, and one is left to conjecture what it means. More recent experts believe that these two figures are a god and goddess sitting under a date palm, and that the serpent is an emblem of the goddess. There is no evidence that what is portrayed on this seal has any connection with Genesis 3. (See A. Heidel, *The Babylonian Genesis*, pp. 124–25.)

A second alleged Babylonian parallel to the account in Genesis 3 is the Gilgamesh Epic, especially Tablet XI, which dates from about 2,000 B.C. or before. The hero Gilgamesh, who is part god and part man, is shocked by the death of his friend Enkidu and determines to search for immortality, in spite of the fact that the gods jealously reserved this for themselves. Having heard that the gods had given Utnapishtim immortality after the great flood, Gilgamesh sets out to find Utnapishtim.

After an arduous journey, he meets Utnapishtim, who suggests that if he can overcome sleep by staying awake six days and seven nights, he might be able to overcome death. But Gilgamesh is so exhausted from his journey that he falls asleep almost immediately. After he awakes, he sets out to return to his home, but as he departs Utnapishtim tells him that if he will secure a thorny plant at the bottom of the sea and eat it when he becomes an old man, his life will be rejuvenated. Gilgamesh secures the plant, but later, while he is bathing in a pool and carrying the plant in his hand, a serpent snatches the plant from him and eats it, thus receiving the power to shed its old skin and to renew its life. In this way Gilgamesh loses his last hope of immortality. (For a more detailed account of this epic, see A. Heidel, *The Gilgamesh Epic and Old Testament Parallels*, pp. 5–13, 15–101, especially pp. 80–93.)

Now one must have a strong predisposition to find parallels between this epic and Genesis 3 to see any obvious parallels at all. It is by no means certain that 3:22 depicts God as selfish with immortality and panic-stricken at the thought that man might become a formidable rival by eating of the tree of life (see comments on 3:22). In fact, God is in complete control of the situation at all times. The major theme of the Gilgamesh Epic is man's search for immortality. Gilgamesh has two opportunities to receive it and loses it once because of his inability to stay awake and a second time because the serpent eats the plant that can give it to him. By way of contrast, the major theme of Genesis 3 is man's sin. Man eats of the fruit that God has forbidden because he becomes convinced that this will bring him advantages superior to those God had already given him. The serpent encourages man to disobey God.

A third and most frequently cited Babylonian parallel to Genesis 3 is the Adapa legend (see Bennett, *Genesis*, p. 103; Skinner, *Genesis*, p. 92; and S. H. Hooke, "Genesis," PCB, p. 180), dating from the fourteenth century B.C. or before. Adapa, who is part god and part man, is the servant of the god Ea. One day while he is fishing, the south wind overturns his boat and casts him into the water. Adapa curses the south wind, and the sky god Anu summons him before his throne to answer for his deed. Ea warns Adapa that Anu will offer him the food and water of death and instructs him not to eat or drink them. When Adapa comes before Anu, Tammuz and Gizzida, the gate-keepers of heaven, intercede for him, and Anu decides to bless Adapa by giving him food and water that will make him immortal. However, Adapa refuses them, thinking that they are the food and water of death. Thus, he loses his opportunity to live for ever, goes back to earth, and dies like other men.

Once again, it is the differences between the Adapa legend and Genesis 3 that stand out, not the similarities. In Genesis 3 man is forbidden to eat of the tree of life because of his sin, while Adapa refuses the food and drink of immortality because his god told him that it was the food and drink of death. Genesis 3 is concerned with temptation and the origin of sin in the world, which are not even mentioned in the Adapa legend. In Genesis 3 God pronounces death on mankind because of human sin, whereas Adapa must die because he did not take advantage of his opportunity to become immortal. "It is a misnomer to call the Adapa legend the Babylonian version of the *fall* of man. The Adapa legend and the biblical story are fundamentally as far apart as the antipodes" (Heidel, *Babylonian Genesis*, p. 124).

Now in order to communicate the divine message, the biblical writers clearly used words, expressions, and stories already familiar to the people of their day. But this does not mean that they attached the same meanings to these means of communication as did their neighbors. And frequently the biblical authors used extraneous material for polemical purposes. This would be effective, for example, in claiming for Yahweh the works or attributes that pagan peoples claimed for the multiplicity of gods. The more one studies comparative religious texts in the ancient Near East, the more he becomes aware of the uniqueness of the OT. Even those who apparently are most anxious to establish parallels between Babylonian materials and the account of the fall of man in Genesis 3 are compelled to admit:

> It should be obvious that none of these [Babylonian] traditions parallels the biblical story of the Fall closely enough to be considered a direct antecedent. As a matter of fact, the differences are almost as striking as the similarities.
>
> S. J. De Vries, "The Fall," IDB, vol. 2, p. 235

For more extensive comments, see the Excursus, "The Babylonian Creation Epic and the Genesis Account," page 95, above.

Excursus

The Responsibility for Sin

Both Christians and non-Christians have written endless volumes on the question of how sin came into the world. This brief excursus cannot deal with the many and complex problems involved. However, any treatment of Genesis 3 is compelled to offer a few suggestions on this point. Some contemporary scholars seek to evade the whole problem in Genesis 3 by arguing that this account does not deal with the origin of sin but is the story of every man told in the form of a parable, or the like. But in the subsequent chapters, which describe the growth of sin in the world, the biblical writer assumes that sin originated with the eating of forbidden fruit. Following the lead of the great church father Augustine (A.D. 354–430), large sections of Christendom (including Roman Catholicism, Lutheranism,

Calvinism, etc.) conclude that not only death, the consequence of Adam's sin, but sin itself, is transferred to all men as his descendants. Historically, the crucial text used in defense of this position has been Romans 5:12-21; then Genesis 3 and other passages constitute supportive evidence. Simply stated, Augustine argued that before the fall Adam was able not to sin if he so chose. But when he chose to sin, God punished him by changing his basic nature, so that now he was not able not to sin. Since children inherit their parent's nature, all Adam's decendants are not able not to sin. (For an extended discussion of the views of Augustine, Thomas Aquinas, Luther, Calvin, and others on this issue, see R. Seeberg, *Text-Book of the History of Doctrines,* vols. 1-2 [Grand Rapids, Mich.: Baker Book House, 1958].)

In attempting to speak to this problem, one should keep in mind that the Bible makes certain crucial affirmations that have a direct bearing on this issue. (1) God is wholly good (Ps. 100:5), and everything he created is good (1 Tim. 4:4). How then can one explain sin in the world? (2) Each man is responsible for the guilt of his own sins (Jer. 31:20-30; Ezek. 18; Rom. 14:12; 2 Cor. 5:10). If so, whatever it is that the human race inherits from Adam, it cannot be guilt for his sin. (3) Sin is too powerful for man to overcome by himself (Rom. 6:17, 20, 23; Eph. 2:1-3), or else some people could save themselves, and thus Christ would not be necessary. How is this to be explained if the human race has not inherited the sinful nature from Adam?

Plato and, later, the Gnostics sought to solve this problem by arguing that matter and God have always coexisted in the universe. Matter is evil and thus the origin of evil on earth. However, the Bible affirms (and modern science agrees) that there was a time when matter did not exist. Before anything else was, God was; and he is the Creator of all that is (Gen. 1:1; Ps. 90:2; John 1:1-3; Col. 1:17).

Others insist that ultimately God must have been the originator of sin, because nothing exists apart from him. Again, the scriptures specifically deny this (James 1:13). Even the author of Genesis 3 seems to be opposing this notion by relating that the man tried to blame God for his sin by chiding him for giving him the woman (Gen. 3:12).

Still others (like Eve—Gen. 3:13) blame the devil for their sins. But if he is really responsible and is able to overpower man with sin apart from man's own willful submission to temptation, it would not be right for God to hold man accountable for that over which he has no control.

A long-standing Jewish explanation for sin in the world is the evil inclination (*yetser hara'*) in man (Gen. 6:5; 8:21). However, this inclination is not the cause of the first man's sin but the result of it.

The Bible teaches that man's willful choice of sin in preference to doing God's will is the original cause and continuing cause of sin in the world. Not only was Adam free to choose (Gen. 2:16-17; 3:6, 17), but also God urged Cain to "master" sin that was couching at his door (Gen. 4:7), which does not make sense if Cain had no free choice in the matter. God created man so that he could make free choices, while he himself wills for man to choose the good and reject the evil (James 1:14). So God is not responsible for man's sin. Before Adam sinned, he lived in an environment free from sin and its influences, an environment which never again can be duplicated in human history. Because of the new sinful environment created by Adam's fall, all men are born into sinful surroundings (Pss. 51:5; 58:3) and thus from their earliest moments have a predisposition or tendency to sin, which appears to be Paul's point in Romans 5:12-21 (see the exegesis of W. Sanday and A. C. Headlam, *The Epistle to the Romans*, ICC, pp. 130–53). And sin is so powerful that all men yield, not because of a sinful nature inherited from Adam, but because they freely choose to do so.

SIN AND PUNISHMENT, GRACE AND RENEWAL (II): CAIN AND ABEL (CH. 4)

Certain modern scholars have obscured the religious emphasis obviously intended in Genesis 4 by proposing theories that this chapter actually reflects tribal conflicts between the Kenites (represented by Cain) and the Israelites (represented by Abel), or a religious polemic against the settled agricultural Canaanites by the seminomadic, sheepherding Israelites, or an Israelite rendition of a Babylonian sacrificial ritual. The story of Cain and Abel follows essentially the same pattern as that of Adam and Eve in Genesis 3: (a) Cain sins (vss. 1-8); (b) he strives to evade the responsibility for his sin (vss. 9-10); (c) God pronounces punitive curses on him (vss. 11-16); (d) God puts mankind in a new situation in which he can begin again (vss. 17-26). The biblical writer is striving to make his readers aware that man is essentially the same in each generation and that God patiently seeks to bring him back from the rebellious course of life he has chosen.

Cain Sins (4:1-8)

Again the biblical author emphasizes that sin is much more than the overt act of murder; it is a problem that originates in the heart. Here he describes sin in four successive stages.

First, Cain brings an inadequate offering to the Lord (vss. 4-5). There are several views as to why God rejected Cain's sacrifice and accepted Abel's. (1) The translators of the LXX (ca. 280 B.C.) apparently thought that God had told Cain and Abel how he wanted their sacrifices prepared, but Cain did not prepare his offering the way God directed, for they read in verse 7: "Is it not so—if thou offerest rightly, but dost not cut in pieces rightly, thou has sinned? Be still!" However, (a) this does not make sense in speaking of a vegetable offering; (b) it is not certain whether this reading is a translation of an earlier Hebrew text differing from the MT; and (c) other details in the context seem to favor a different view.

(2) Some modern commentators argue that the reason Yahweh rejected Cain's sacrifice is that only animal (bloody) sacrifices were acceptable to him (see Skinner, *Genesis*, pp. 105–106). However, long after this God commanded the Israelites to offer sacrifices of the fruit of the

ground (see Lev. 2; Deut. 26:1-11) as well as animal sacrifices.

(3) The biblical texts dealing with Cain and Abel would seem to indicate that there were three main reasons why God rejected Cain's sacrifice and accepted Abel's: (a) Abel gave the Lord the best that he had, but Cain gave a mediocre portion of the fruit of the ground. "Cain brought . . . an offering of the . . . ground [nothing special; vs. 3]," but "Abel brought of the firstlings [something special] of his flock and of their fat portions [again something special; vs. 4]." Cain appears to have kept back the best for himself, whereas Abel gave the best he had to the Lord.

(b) Abel first yielded *himself* to God, and then he brought his sacrifice as a genuine outward expression of his commitment; but Cain was content to give God his sacrifice. This seems to be the point in verses 4-5. The Lord had regard not first or simply for Abel's offering, but for Abel; contrariwise, the Lord had no regard first for Cain, and then for his sacrifice. God's first concern is with a man's life and motives and then with his outward deeds. In 1 John 3:12, John warns Christians "not [to] be like Cain who was of the evil one and murdered his brother. And why did he murder him? Because his own deeds were evil and his brother's righteous." Because Cain had yielded his life to the evil one and did evil deeds, he murdered his brother. It was possibly for the same reason that God rejected his sacrifice (see Prov. 21:27).

(c) Hebrews 11:4 says, "By faith Abel offered to God a more acceptable sacrifice than Cain." While Cain trusted in his own goodness at bringing a sacrifice to the Lord, Abel trusted in God and not in himself, his sacrifice, or anything that he did. "It was Abel's attitude of faith in God's righteousness, and not (like Cain's) in his own, that made his oblation acceptable" (Richardson, *Genesis*, p. 82). Cain's anger at God for rejecting his sacrifice (vs. 5) would suggest that he was more concerned about receiving proper recognition for what he had done than about pleasing God.

Second, Cain becomes "very angry" at God because he

GENESIS 4:1-8 / *145*

had rejected his sacrifice and at his brother Abel because he is jealous that God had accepted Abel's sacrifice. He is also quite dejected; "his countenance fell" (vss. 5-6). Like Jesus (Matt. 5:21-22) and NT teachers in general (see 1 John 3:15), the author of Genesis emphasizes that man's real problem is anger of the heart, which may express itself, among other ways, in murder.

Third, Cain refuses to exert the internal effort necessary to resist temptation. God warns him that "sin is couching at the door" like a wild animal lying in wait to pounce on its prey (see 1 Pet. 5:8-9) and urges him to "master it" (vs. 7). But Cain's pride has been hurt, and he is so self-centered that he is determined to retaliate by hurting his brother. At the end of verse 7, the KJV reads, "unto thee shall be *his* desire, and thou shalt rule over *him.*" If one adopts this translation, "his" and "him" must refer to Abel. Then God would be telling Cain that there is no need for him to be jealous of Abel, because if he would "do well," Abel his younger brother would respect him just as a wife respects her husband (see 3:16, where the same Hebrew word for "desire" [*teshuqah*] occurs). However, the flow of the context makes much better sense if one reads "its" and "it" with the ASV, RSV, and NEB and thinks of "sin" as their antecedent.

Finally, Cain plans to murder Abel, lures him into the field (apparently on false pretenses), and deliberately murders him (vs. 8; see Matt. 23:35; Luke 11:51; Heb. 12:24). The MT at the beginning of verse 8 reads, "And Cain said to Abel his brother." One expects this to be followed by what Cain said, but this is missing. Some scholars seek to solve the problem by emending *wayyo'mer* ("and he said") to *wayyishmor* ("and he eyed," "and he lay in wait for"), a change of only one Hebrew consonant. Others translate the Hebrew text in uncommon ways. For example, the translators of the KJV read, "And Cain *talked with* Abel his brother," while the translators of the ASV read, "And Cain *told* Abel his brother." However, many early versions, including the Samaritan Pentateuch, LXX, Syriac Peshitta, Aramaic Targum, and Vulgate, have the expected statement of Cain, "Let us go out to the field" (RSV). It is easy to see how a scribe's eye skipped from the word "field" in this phrase to the same word in the next phrase, thus causing him to omit Cain's statement. So, the reading adopted by the RSV and NEB seems to be best here. If so, the text describes how Cain deliberately planned how he was going to murder Abel, how he lured him into open country where no one would see him do it, and then murdered him. It is a clear case of willful, premeditated murder. Adam and Eve had sinned against God by eating the forbidden fruit. Now their son Cain becomes angry with his brother and murders him. Sin against God breeds and is inseparably connected with sin against man. The contagion and powerful influence of sin spreads.

[1] This verse represents a typical way of telling about the birth of a child in the OT: (a) the man knew his wife; (b) the wife conceived; (c) she bore or gave birth to a son (or daughter); (d) she (or her husband) named the child (see 4:17, 25; 16:4, 15; 21:2-3; 1 Sam. 1:20; 1 Chron. 7:23; Isa. 7:14; 8:3; Hos. 1:3-4).

The verb **knew** (Heb. *yadha'*) is a euphemism (see LWC-OT, vol. 1, ch. 1) meaning "had sexual intercourse with." "To know" in the Bible involves much more than obtaining facts. It means to have a daily, personal, intimate relationship with some other person, whether it be God or man.

There is a wordplay in Hebrew on **Cain** (Heb. *qayin*) and **I have gotten** (Heb. *qanithi* from the root *q-n-h*). Eve called her first son Cain to symbolize that (in spite of her sin and punishment) she had gotten a man-child **with the help of the Lord**. This is the first of many biblical texts that teach that conception and birth are a cooperative enterprise involving man and woman and God. If God "closes" a woman's womb, a couple cannot have children (Gen. 20:18; 1 Sam. 1:5-6). And it is only if he "opens" the womb that they can have children (Gen. 29:31; 30:22). God "makes," "fashions," "forms," and "knits together" a person in his mother's womb (Job. 31:15; Ps. 139:13; Jer. 1:5). Consequently, children are God's "gifts" to man and woman (Gen. 33:5; 48:9; Ps. 127:3). Modern man finds it very difficult to accept the biblical claim that God is actively at work in conception and birth. Their frequent repetition leads him to conclude that these are "natural laws" that God established when he created man, or that biblical writers simply reflect rather unscientific and unenlightened views on this subject. Of course, one cannot prove or disprove scientifically whether God supplies the life-giving power necessary to bring a new person into existence. But the Bible consistently maintains that he does. There is absolutely no reason to limit this divine activity to Bible times or to a few select individuals. It is clear that the biblical writers taught that the origin and preservation of every person is directly dependent on life and energy given by God. Naturally, he who takes this seriously has the highest regard for all his fellowmen, whether rich or poor, large or small, black or white, educated or uneducated.

[2] Since the statement "and she conceived" is not repeated here, some scholars think Cain and Abel were twins. However, this is inconclusive because the same phrase is omitted in verse 25. The biblical writer wants to impress his readers with the fact that sin is so powerful that it causes a man to hate and kill his own **brother**, as is clear from the fact that he refers to Abel as Cain's brother seven times in verses 2-10.

The Bible does not explain the origin of the name **Abel**. The Hebrew word *hebhel* means "breath" or "vapor," and some have conjectured that this name was given because Abel was killed while he was still relatively young or to emphasize the brevity of life now that death had entered the picture. But none of this is certain.

[3] Just as the biblical author skips over many years between verses 2a and 2b, so **in the course of time** indicates that he skips another interval of many years between verses 2 and 3. He omits many events because they do not fit his purpose or the spiritual needs of his audience.

Modern man would like to know many details about the origin of sacrifice. It is clear that it originated long before Moses gave the law at Sinai and Israel became God's people and that it was widely practiced in the ancient Near East. However, the Bible does not say how or where it originated.

The author of Genesis does not specify how God let Cain and Abel know whether their offerings were acceptable or not. In harmony with Leviticus 9:24 and 1 Kings 18:38, Theodotion (second century A.D.) and Ibn Ezra and Rashi (twelfth century A.D.) proposed that fire came down from heaven and consumed Abel's offering. Others conjecture that the manner in which the smoke ascended from the two sacrifices indicated whether they were accepted or rejected. Still others believe that Cain and Abel gradually came to know whether their offerings were accepted by subsequent events that occurred in their lives. The Bible is not clear on this point.

Cain Strives to Evade Responsibility (4:9-10)

Like Adam and Eve (see comments on 3:7-13), Cain tries to evade the responsibility for killing Abel by telling God an outright lie, namely, that he does not know where Abel is (vs. 9). Cain's motive is apparently completely self-centered. He does not want to be punished any more than is absolutely necessary. Thus, he complains of the severity of his punishment (vs. 13) and seeks protection from anyone who would kill him to avenge the murder of Abel (vss. 14-15). His concerns call to mind the "thief who is shamed when caught" (Jer. 2:26). Instead of being filled with remorse over having killed his brother, Cain desires to avoid as much punishment for his crime as possible. Evidently the biblical writer is stressing the growing power of sin's grip over the human race.

Again, as in the case of Adam and Eve (see comments on 3:7-13), God's way of dealing with Cain reveals great truths concerning man's rebellion and God's nature. God had every right (legally) to destroy Cain. But due to his great love for and optimistic attitude toward man (even in the face of deliberate rebellion), he patiently works to help him become what he originally made him to be. First, the Lord refuses to accept a sacrifice that comes from a heart seeking divine praise and recognition (vs. 5; see the comments on vss. 1-8). If he had accepted this sort of gift, God would have been encouraging man to become even more proud than he had already become. Second, God asks Cain a series of questions designed to make him see that he was fully responsible for his motives and actions. When Cain becomes angry because his sacrifice is rejected, God chides, "Why are you angry, and why has your countenance fallen?" (vs. 6). Clearly Cain had offered his sacrifice in order to secure divine approval and praise, and he became angry because he did not get what he was seeking. God continues, "If you do well, will you not be accepted?" (vs. 7). The way one acquires God's approval is not by offering sacrifices or by doing impressive deeds for his own exaltation but by doing good. In this context, apparently this means to worship God out of sincere gratitude for all his blessings and to think and act lovingly toward one's brother. After Cain kills Abel, God asks, "Where is Abel your brother?" (vs. 9). He stubbornly refuses to let Cain forget or avoid the responsibility for his sin. Finally, when Cain insolently lies about his knowledge of Abel's death, God queries, "What have you done?" (vs. 10)—essentially the same question he had asked Eve (3:13). Clearly, God is not seeking information when he questions Cain. As a father attempts to stop and change the devious and destructive course of his rebellious son, the Lord seeks to compel Cain to look at himself as he really is, for only then can he hope to bring him to his senses and alter the pattern of his life. Third, God punishes Cain to make him see the seriousness of his sin (vss. 11-16). Fourth, he enables man to use the earth's resources and his own God-given talents to establish an environment in which man can return to God (vss. 17-26).

[10] Obviously, **blood** does not have a **voice** that cries out. The Lord is using personification (see LWC-OT, vol. 1, ch. 1) in speaking of blood here, in order to emphasize that no matter how cleverly man covers up his sin, God has ways of bringing his sin out into the open (see Num. 32:23; Gal. 6:7-8). According to the ancient law of

blood vengeance, the nearest relative of a murder victim was to vindicate the deceased by killing his murderer (Num. 35:19-21). This relative was called a "redeemer" (Heb. *go'el*) or "avenger of blood." But when circumstances were such that this blood avenger could not or would not function, God assumed his role (see 2 Kings 9:26; Job 16:18; 19:25-26; Isa. 26:21; Ezek. 24:7-8), for he is personally concerned to defend the helpless and unsuspecting from evil men (see Exod. 22:21-24).

God Pronounces Punitive Curses on Cain (4:11-16)

As with Adam and Eve (see comments on 3:14-19), God decrees that Cain be "cursed from the ground" (vs. 11). The context indicates that this has a twofold meaning. (1) The ground, which had yielded abundant crops for Cain when he had tilled it (vss. 2-3), will cease to give him its produce, and thus he will no longer be able to practice agriculture (vs. 12). (2) The ground or earth will not make Cain feel he is a welcome inhabitant, so that wherever he goes he will be "a fugitive and a wanderer" (vss. 12, 14; see Jude 11).

But God tempers his punishment of Cain with mercy and compassion. When Cain realizes that as a fugitive his life will be in constant jeopardy (vs. 14), God promises him that if anyone kills him, "vengeance shall be taken on him sevenfold" (vs. 15), that is, seven of the murderer's kinsmen will be slain. Thus, the *mark* that God puts on Cain is not a punitive stigma or brand indicating that he is a murderer, but a warning to anyone that might contemplate killing him and thus a divine protection. It must have been a conspicuous symbol of some sort, the meaning of which would be immediately apparent to any would-be assailant. This could have been something attached to Cain's body or clothing or a mark like a tattoo made in the flesh. Elsewhere we are told of signs or marks put on the hand or the forehead (Exod. 13:9, 16; Deut. 6:8; 11:18; Ezek. 9:4, 6), and this could be the kind of thing intended here.

[11] The **ground** does not really have a **mouth**, nor does it **receive** [drink] **blood**. As in verse 10, the Lord uses per-

sonification (see LWC-OT, vol. 1, ch. 1) to emphasize that he will not allow Cain to escape punishment for his sin.

[14] In the interest of the theory that the original author of Genesis 4 is describing activities and characteristics of the Kenite tribe, several exegetes argue that **the ground** in verse 14 is the land of Canaan, that to **be hidden** from the face of the Lord and to go "away from the presence of the Lord" (vs. 16) mean to leave the land over which Yahweh gives protection (see 1 Sam. 26:19) and thus to lose his protection, and that "east of Eden" (vs. 16) is a late gloss.

However, such interpretations of these particulars are fraught with serious difficulties. (1) No matter how many sources (oral or written) the author of Genesis used, surely he presented them to his readers in a consistent, understandable manner in keeping with his purposes. Since "the ground" (Heb. *'adhamah*) up to this point in the book of Genesis has been the dry land on which man and animals live, since there is nothing in the text to suggest any other meaning here (note the admission of Skinner, *Genesis*, p. 110), and since it surely has this meaning in verses 10-12, there is every reason to believe that the biblical writer intended dry land in general, and no geographical area in particular.

(2) The book of Genesis begins with the affirmation that Yahweh created the earth. As it unfolds, the biblical writer assumes and declares that Yahweh can and does work anywhere and everywhere on this earth that he had made. Therefore, to believe that he would limit the Lord's sphere of activity to Canaan or any other geographical region is incredible. The remaining chapters in the book of Genesis picture God working in places far distant from one another geographically, as Ur of the Chaldees, Haran, Canaan, and Egypt. Furthermore, God's promise to protect Cain (especially in vs. 15) is conceivable only if God continues to be with Cain and watch over him. Thus, it is necessary to interpret the expressions "to be hidden from the face of the Lord" and "to go away from the presence of the Lord," not in a literal or geographical sense, but in a technical or figurative sense.

To be sure, there is a clear parallel between Adam and Eve and Cain at this point. God "drove" Adam and Eve out of the garden of Eden (3:24), and he "drove" Cain away from the ground (4:14; in both texts the Hebrew verb translated "drove" is *garash*). Obviously this means that they changed the geographical locations of their homes. But this does not mean in either instance that they were literally or physically separated from the Lord (see Ps. 139:7). Rather, as the whole tenor of both contexts show (for the expressions involved, compare 3:8 with 4:14, 16), "to be hidden from the face of the Lord" and "to go away from the presence of the Lord" mean to cease to enjoy the kind of relationship with and blessings from the Lord that existed prior to their sinning (see the similar statements in Lev. 22:3; Pss. 27:9; 51:11; Isa. 59:2). Cain no longer has that deep, personal, cooperative relationship with God that satisfied his heart and enabled him to harvest bumper crops when he tilled the land.

Cain's statement, **whoever finds me will slay me** (vs. 14), God's response, "If any one slays Cain" (vs. 15), and the biblical writer's explanation that the Lord put a mark on Cain "lest any[-one] who came upon him should kill him" (vs. 15) imply that the earth had become fairly well populated. That Cain built a city (vs. 17) supports this, as does the fact that civilization was becoming rather advanced by this time. The biblical author failed to record many details about the length of time covered in these stories, the nature and size of the numerical growth of mankind on earth, the major areas of population, the character of human life in general, and the intellectual advancement of ancient man, all of which are of major interest to modern man. Scholars have advanced various theories on these matters, but the Bible itself offers no information on such issues.

[15] The translation **Not so!** or "No" of the RSV and NEB follows the reading *lo' khen*, which apparently lies behind the LXX, Symmachus, Theodotion, Syriac Peshitta, and Vulgate. The MT has *lakhen*, "therefore," a reading adopted in the KJV and ASV. The difference in the

Hebrew is very slight. Either translation is understandable.

[16] **The land of Nod** has never been identified geographically. In the Hebrew, there is a wordplay on *nadh* ("wanderer") in verses 12 and 14 and *nodh* ("Nod," "Wandering") in verse 16. It could be that the biblical writer did not have any particular geographical location in mind, but only wished to symbolize that Yahweh made Cain a wanderer.

When God drove Adam and Eve out of the garden of Eden, they established a new home "east of the garden of Eden" (3:24). Now that God drives Cain from his home, he sets up a new home **east of Eden.** It is from this area that mankind later migrates westward and in other directions (11:2).

God Enables Mankind to Begin Again (4:17-26)

Genesis 4:17-24, 25-26, and 5:3-32 should be studied together. Each section begins with one of Adam's sons (Cain in 4:17-24 and Seth in 4:25-26 and 5:3-32) and traces his genealogy to a certain point. That 4:25-26 and 5:3-8 are parallel and cover the same period is obvious, and it is likely that the biblical author is using two earlier sources here. Obviously the biblical author is not presenting this material in chronological order. Instead, he brings his readers up to a certain point, leaves the sequence never to be resumed, or to be resumed later, and goes back to an earlier period to begin another line of thought. This approach is quite typical of history writing. Because of the similarities in some of the names, several scholars argue that 4:17-24 and 5:3-32 are actually the same genealogy and contend that the differences in order and in the spelling are due to the fact that the two lists come from different sources. But it is evident that the author of Genesis intends to be tracing two genealogies: that of Cain and that of Seth. The names are similar because people are fond of repeating names of important ancestors and because in any society the same names are given to several different people. (This is a well-known fact in biblical history.)

It is true that the biblical writer does not give an *explicit* evaluation of either genealogy. However, several things would seem to suggest that he is deliberately emphasizing a contrast between the descendants of Cain and the descendants of Seth. (1) The major concerns of the descendants of Cain are materialistic. They spend their time and efforts in building cities (vs. 17), tending cattle (vs. 20), manufacturing and playing musical instruments (vs. 21), and making tools and weapons of metal (vs. 22). By way of contrast, the descendants of Seth are primarily concerned with spiritual matters. Eve called her third son Seth to express her appreciation for God having given her "another child instead of Abel" (vs. 25). After Seth's son, Enosh, was born, "men began to call upon the name of the Lord" (vs. 26). The biblical author interrupts his otherwise stereotyped genealogy to point out that "Enoch walked with God" (5:22, 24) and that Lamech called his son "Noah," saying, "Out of the ground which the Lord has cursed this one shall bring us relief from our work and from the toil of our hands" (5:29). (2) In bold contrast to God's initial plan for marriage (2:22-24), Cain's descendant Lamech takes two wives, thus initiating the practices of bigamy and polygamy, which God tolerated for some time but never authorized. (3) Lamech's song of boasting to his wives (vss. 23-24) indicates that sin is getting an even firmer grip on the human race. After some inner struggle, Cain had yielded to jealousy and anger and had killed his brother; but Lamech relishes the thought of killing someone. Cain had sought protection from anyone that might avenge the blood of Abel by trying to kill him; but Lamech repeatedly avenges the slightest injury to himself by killing men and boys who are relatives of the one who attacks him.

Now the biblical author's point is not that cultural advancement and refinement are evil. As a matter of fact, human talents and the earth's resources (both God-given) collaborate in an excellent way for the improvement of life on earth. However, "the advance of civilization does not of itself make men more reverent towards God or more humane towards one another" (Richardson, *Genesis*, p. 86).

The more man accomplishes with the skills and products God has given him, the more he tends to feel self-sufficient and able to manage his life without God. "Culture, with all the benefits it brings to mankind, does not close the spiritual rift which has opened between men and God" (Marks, "Book of Genesis," p. 6).

> The Bible nowhere teaches that the godly should have all the gifts . . . . The family of Lamech could handle its environment but not itself . . . . Cain's family is a microcosm: its pattern of technical prowess and moral failure is that of humanity.
>
> D. Kidner, *Genesis*, TOTC, p. 78

[17] Various scholars express three perplexities over this verse. (1) It places the building of cities before wandering nomadic life (vs. 20). (2) Although Cain has been consigned to the role of a wanderer (vss. 12, 14), verse 16 says he *dwelt* in the land of Nod, and verse 17 says he **built a city**. (3) Cain names the city he built, not after his own name, but after the name of his son Enoch. These critics contend that these problems arose from the fact that the author of Genesis has used two conflicting sources without reconciling their discrepancies. However, a "city" is not necessarily a large, impressive metropolis, but may be a small, unimposing village of relatively few inhabitants. Chapter 4 apparently covers many years, and the fact that Cain was a wanderer and fugitive would not militate against his spending some time in a settled community. And while it was customary for the builder of a city to name it after himself, there is no good reason why he could not name it in honor of his son.

[19] **Lamech** is the first man mentioned in the Bible who had **two wives** (see also vs. 23). There are several cases of bigamy and polygamy in the OT, but this does not justify assertions or implications that the biblical writers looked on such as an "advance in civilization" or that it is "commended by the example of the patriarchs" (Bennett, *Genesis*, p. 121). For example, just because the author of Genesis relates Cain's murder of Abel does not mean he com-

mends that act. And just because the author of 2 Samuel records David's adultery with Bathsheba and his murder of Uriah (2 Sam. 11) does not indicate that he approves those deeds. Likewise, that the author of Genesis relates Lamech's bigamy does not show that he approves bigamy or polygamy. As a matter of fact, this stands in bold contrast to his description of the first marriage, according to which God created *one woman* for the man (2:22-24), whereas theoretically he could have created any number that he thought it best for him to have.

[20] As frequently in the Bible, the word **father** here and in verse 21 is not used literally, but metaphorically (see LWC-OT, vol. 1, ch. 1), and means "founder," "originator," or "precursor."

[22] "Cain," the last element in **Tubal-cain**, can be interpreted in one of three ways: (1) as part of a proper name, "Tubal-cain"; (2) as "smith," in which case this text should be read "Tubal, the smith"; (3) as a reference to the first or major ancestor in a genealogical line, so that one could translate "Tubal, (the family of) Cain."

[23] Like 2:23 and 3:14-19, 4:23-24 is in poetry. Scholars generally agree that this is a very ancient poem used by the author of Genesis. If so, this would indicate that blood vengeance was an exceedingly old pre-Israelite practice, like sacrifice (see comments on vs. 3).

[24] Some of the early church fathers believed that in this song Lamech was expressing remorse over having slain one young man. However, the context shows that Lamech is daring anyone to try to slay him and boasts that he will promptly and completely avenge any such attempt. Lamech points out that his ancestor Cain had killed his own brother in cold blood but declares that he had killed and would kill only in self-defense. If God had ordained that Cain, who was guilty of premeditated murder, would be avenged by the death of seven relatives of anyone who murdered him, Lamech concludes that he was justified in killing seventy-seven relatives of anyone who attempted to murder him. This attitude is vindictive and self-centered. Jesus reverses the entire quality of such an attitude when

he tells Peter that if his brother sins against him, he should forgive him seventy-seven times, that is, indefinitely (Matt. 18:23-25).

[25] As in the account of the naming of Cain (vs. 1), there is a wordplay in Hebrew on *sheth* ("Seth") and *shath* ("appointed"). And here again Eve expresses her gratitude to God for giving her a son (see comments on vs. 1). By naming him **Seth**, she voices her appreciation to the Lord for enabling her to have **another child instead of Abel**, apparently indicating her wish that he have the same spiritual qualities as Abel. Her hopes were not disappointed.

[26] Instead of **men began to call upon the name of the Lord**, the LXX and Vulgate read "he [i.e., Enosh] began [was the first] to call on the name of the Lord." According to either text, the name of the Lord was called upon for the first time in the days of Enosh. Many scholars argue that this means that the first time the name "Yahweh" was invoked was in the days of Enosh. Then they find a contradiction between this (ascribed to J) and Exodus 3:13-15; 6:2-3, which declare that the worship of "Yahweh" in Israel originated with Moses, and conclude that Genesis 4:25-26 must be from the J source, Exodus 3:13-15 from E, and 6:2-3 from P. In an attempt to harmonize these passages, Speiser (*Genesis*, pp. 37–38) explains them as two stages in the history of ancient religion. He believes that among the patriarchs there was "a small body of searchers" that originated the worship of "Yahweh." Later all Israel adopted this worship under the influence of Moses. However, there are two other ways to explain this statement. (1) God may have made himself known by the name "Yahweh" for the first time in the days of Enosh without fully revealing the characteristics that this name was intended to suggest until the days of Moses. (2) The author of Genesis may be saying that whereas the tendency of men in ancient time was to trust their own power and achievements, Enosh initiated the practice of giving God thanks for his blessings and accomplishments. There are several passages in the OT where the phrase "call upon the name of the Lord" appears in parallelism with

"praise or give thanks to the Lord" (see Isa. 12:4;1 Chron. 16:8; Pss. 105:1; 116:17). In this case, the emphasis would not be on the divine name "Yahweh" (as is often assumed), but on "calling the name of" Yahweh, and "Yahweh" would be used because this was the name familiar to the author of Genesis and his readers at the time of the writing of this book.

A GENEALOGICAL LIST
FROM ADAM TO NOAH (CH. 5)

Genesis 5 consists of a genealogical list containing the names of ten persons. The author of Genesis seems to have two purposes in mind in placing this list in its present position. First, he wishes to cover the long period from Adam to Noah (from the creation of man to the flood) in a relatively short space. It is quite conceivable that he knew about many interesting things that happened or were said to have happened during this time, but they did not lend themselves to the religious message he intended to convey to his audience (see John 20:30-31). Several things would seem to suggest that in order to cover this period he used an ancient genealogical list that had been handed down to him. (1) The statement "This is the book of the generations of Adam" (vs. 1) indicates that at one time chapter 5 existed as a separate written work. (2) Verses 1-2 repeat information already given in 1:26-27. (3) The genealogy from Adam to Enosh in 5:3-6 is virtually a repetition of the information given in 4:25-26. (4) For the most part, chapter 5 follows a rigid literary pattern: (a) the author gives the age of the patriarch at the birth of his firstborn; (b) he tells how long the patriarch lived after this; and (c) he states the age of the patriarch at his death.

Since Oppert's work in 1877, scholars have called attention to certain similarities between the genealogical list in Genesis 5 and the Babylonian king list of Berossus. (1) Both lists contain ten names. (2) The name of the third person in each list means "man" (Akkadian *Amelu*; Heb. *Enosh*). (3) The seventh person in each list

(Akk. *Enmeduranna*; Heb. *Enoch*) enjoys a special intimate relationship with his God. (4) Both lists end with the
great flood, and the tenth person in each list
(Akk. *Ziusudra*; Heb. *Noah*) is the hero of the flood story.
At the same time, there are striking differences between
these two lists. (1) None of the names in either list correspond to any name in the other list. (2) The time from the
beginning to the flood is 432,000 years in the Babylonian
list, while it is only 1,656 years in Genesis 5. There is no
evidence to support the theory that the author of Genesis
borrowed from the Babylonian list.

In the Excursus, "The Age of the Earth and Man" (see
p. 92, above), evidence was cited from 1 Chronicles 26:24,
Ezra 8:2, and Matthew 1:1 to indicate that genealogical
lists in the Bible often omit several persons. A clear example of this appears in Matthew 1:8, which states that Joram
(i.e., Jehoram) begat (was the father of) Uzziah (KJV,
Ozias). A study of the pertinent texts in the OT shows that
Jehoram was the father of Ahaziah (2 Kings 8:25), Ahaziah
was the father of Joash (11:2), Joash was the father of
Amaziah (14:1), and Amaziah was the father of Uzziah
(15:1). In other words, Matthew 1:8 says Jehoram begat
(was the father of) Uzziah, in spite of the fact that Jehoram
was Uzziah's great-great-grandfather. Similar gaps may well
have occurred in the genealogical list in Genesis 5. Therefore, no dogmatic position on the age of the earth or of
man can be derived from the material given in this chapter.
"Because of the possibility of the omission of necessary
links and uncertainty about the length of the generation,
genealogies offer comparatively little certain chronological
assistance" (R. A. Bowman, "Genealogy," IDB, vol. 2,
p. 365).

[1-2] It is worthy of note that verses 1-6 do not record
events chronologically later than the events recorded in
chapters 1-4. Rather, verses 1-2 cover virtually the same
ideas as those expressed in 1:26-27, and verses 3-6 repeat
some of the information given in 4:25-26. It is a common
practice in writing history to take the reader up to a certain
point and then to drop back in time to pick up a thread that

was left dangling in order to move the story in a different direction. The result of such a procedure is that the book which is thus produced (in this case, the book of Genesis) does not follow (or even intend to follow) an exact chronological sequence. To insist that it do so is to deny clear statements in the text itself, such as those before us.

The Hebrew word *'adham* is used in two senses in verses 1-3. In verses 1a and 3, it has reference to the first man and so should be translated as a proper name, **Adam**. However, in verses 1b and 2 it means "mankind" and thus should be translated **man**. This is remarkably illustrated in verse 2, where the biblical author states, **Male and female he created them . . . and named them** [Heb. *shemam*, plural] **Man**. "It takes the two sexes together to express what God means by 'human' " (Kidner, *Genesis*, p. 80). Paul says in 1 Corinthians 11:11: "in the Lord woman is not independent of man nor man of woman."

[3] That Adam became the father of a son **after his image** argues against the view that the image of God in man was lost as a result of the fall.

[22] The statement **Enoch walked with God** (vss. 22, 24) is very general, and therefore it is very difficult to determine its exact meaning. The only other place in the Bible where this exact expression appears is Genesis 6:9, where it is connected with being "righteous" and "blameless." Other passages (such as Pss. 14:2-3; 130:3; Prov. 20:9; Rom. 3:23) suggest that this does not mean Enoch was sinless. The same Hebrew phrase translated "walk with" (the hithpael of *halakh* + *'eth*) occurs in 1 Samuel 25:15, where the servants of Nabal tell Abigail concerning the men of David, "we did not miss anything when we were in the fields, as long as we *went* [*walked*] *with* them." A very similar phrase (the qal of *halakh* + *'eth*) is found in Malachi 2:6, where God says of Levi, "he *walked with* me in peace and uprightness" (see also Mic. 6:8, which uses the qal of *halakh* + *'im* in the expression translated "to *walk* humbly *with* your God"). In light of these texts, Genesis 5:22, 24 would seem to mean that Enoch enjoyed an intimate, personal relationship with God. The LXX

reads, "Enoch *pleased* God."

[24] When the biblical writer says that Enoch **was not, for God took him,** apparently he means that Enoch did not die. Hebrews 11:5 declares, "By faith Enoch was taken up *so that he should not see death.*" God did not create man originally to live on the earth for ever, for it was necessary for him to eat of the tree of life to do this (see Gen. 3:22 with the comments there). Likewise, God did not originally intend for man to die, because death was the curse God placed on man as a result of his sin (see Gen. 3:17-19 and the comments on 3:14-19). Apparently, then, God originally planned to "take" man from the earth to himself in glory when his life on earth was finished. The Hebrew verb translated "took" (*laqach*) in Genesis 5:24 is also used in 2 Kings 2:3, 5, 10 of Elijah's translation into heaven by a whirlwind, but also in Psalms 49:15 and 73:24 of God receiving the righteous to himself (evidently after they have died physically). In these texts, it appears that the word "take" functions as a technical term for man's translation by God to a higher existence.

[29] The expression **out of the ground which the Lord has cursed** clearly presupposes and alludes to 3:17, thus showing how closely these early chapters in Genesis are knit together.

The way that Noah is to **bring us relief from our work and from the toil of our hands** is not by being saved from the flood in the ark, but by becoming "the first tiller of the soil" and discovering how to cultivate the grape vine (see Gen. 9:20; and compare Judg. 9:13; Ps. 104:14-15).

Lamech called the name of his son **Noah** (Hebrew *noach*) because he would bring man **relief** (KJV "comfort"; Heb. *nacham*) from his work.

SIN AND PUNISHMENT, GRACE AND RENEWAL (III): NOAH AND THE FLOOD (CHS. 6–9)

In spite of God's punishment of Cain (4:11-16) and the material and intellectual successes of his descendants

(4:17-24), human corruption increases, and for the third time in the early chapters of Genesis, the same pattern is presented: (a) all mankind (with the exception of Noah and his family) becomes corrupt (6:1-12); (b) God punishes mankind by sending a flood to destroy the whole human race except for Noah and his family (6:13–7:24); (c) God puts man in a new situation by sparing Noah and his family in the ark, by blessing them, and by establishing a covenant with them (8:1–9:19); (d) however, Noah gets drunk, his son Ham sees his nakedness, and Noah curses Ham's son Canaan (9:20-29).

All Mankind Sins (6:1-12)

It seems best to interpret this very difficult paragraph as parallel to the accounts of the sins of Adam and Eve (3:1-6) and of Cain (4:1-8). Thus, "the sons of God and the daughters of men" (vs. 2) are human beings (not the assembly of the gods or angels), as confirmed by the divine response ("My spirit shall not abide in *man* for ever," vs. 3), the birth of mighty men or men of renown (vs. 4), and Jesus' reference to this event (Matt. 24:38-39; Luke 17:26-27; see notes on vs. 2).

Mankind's sin is that the sons of God "saw" (Hebrew *ra'ah*; cf. the first step in the sins of Eve, 3:6; Achan, Josh. 7:21; and David, 2 Sam. 11:2) that the daughters of men were fair, they "chose" (Heb. *bachar*) from them indiscriminately (following their own passions and desires, unconcerned about God's will) whomever they wished, and they "took" (Heb. *laqach*; cf. the sins of Eve, 3:6; Achan, Josh. 7:21; Saul, 1 Sam. 15:21; and David, 2 Sam. 11:4) them as wives. Surely the idea is not that marriage as such is wrong, because the author of Genesis has already portrayed marriage as divine in origin and as the highest human relationship (cf. 1:26-27; 2:18-24). Rather, the purpose, nature, or result of these marriages must have been wrong. The pattern of Genesis 1–11 suggests that these marriages constitute an attempt on man's part to rise in power or intellect so that he might live independently of (if not in rivalry with) God (cf. Eve's desire to be like God,

3:6; Cain's anger at God's rejection of his sacrifice, 4:5-6; and the desire of the people at Babel to make a name for themselves, 11:4, 6). This would seem to be corroborated by the fact that their children were "mighty men, men of renown" (6:4).

But the writer emphasizes that behind these acts of "flesh" (vs. 3) was man's fundamentally corrupt *heart*: "every imagination of the thoughts of his heart was only evil continually" (vs. 5; cf. 8:21). Sin is a heart problem, which leads to "violence" (vss. 11, 13), corruption (vss. 11, 12), and divine destruction (note the verbs "blot out," 6:7; 7:4, 23 [twice]; and "destroy," 6:13, 17; 8:21; 9:15), and in time permeates "all flesh" (i. e., all mankind, cf. 6:3, 12, 13)—that is, all flesh but Noah and his family, who still walk "with God" (vs. 9), and who look to him to supply their needs and depend on him in all circumstances.

[2] At least four identifications of **the sons of God** and **the daughters of men** have been suggested. (1) The majority of scholars argue that **the sons of God** are angels, because of the use of this phrase in Job 1:6; 2:1; Psalms 29:1; 89:6 (Hebrew 7); Daniel 3:25 (see also Enoch 6:2; the Qumran Genesis Apocryphon, col. II); and the supposed allusions to this passage in 2 Peter 2:4-5 and Jude 6. They further suppose that **the daughters of men** are human females. However, this view demands that Genesis 6:1-4 be regarded as unhistorical and mythological, which does not agree with God's determination to destroy man from the earth, or with the births of human children, or with the function of these verses in the overall pattern evident in Genesis 1–11. In light of the rest of the book of Genesis (and of the entire Bible, for that matter), it is incredible to think that any biblical author would promote the idea that angels actually had intercourse with women and that children were born to them. Nor is it clear that 2 Peter 2:4-5 and Jude 6 have Genesis 6:1-4 in mind. Second Peter 2:6-8 refers to the destruction of Sodom and Gomorrah, which is recorded in Genesis 19:24-29—eleven chapters after the chapter which relates the destruction of the world by the flood and the divine deliverance of Noah, mentioned in

2 Peter 2:5. Similarly, the event alluded to in 2 Peter 2:4 may be separated from that mentioned in verse 5 by several chapters in Genesis, because verse 4 apparently has in mind the fall of Satan and his angels, which is the natural presupposition lying behind the story of the temptation in Genesis 3:1-6.

(2) Ancient Jewish authorities, including Targums Onkelos and Pseudo-Jonathan, Symmachus, the Midrash Bereshith Rabba, Rashi, and Ibn Ezra, interpreted **the sons of God** as persons who came from aristocratic families (in the OT, "son of God" is frequently a title for a king—cf. 2 Sam. 7:14; 1 Chron. 22:10; 28:6; Pss. 2:7; 89:26-27 [Hebrew 27-28]; etc.), and **the daughters of men** as individuals coming from poor families. But distinctions between royalty and commoners do not occur in Genesis 1–11, and the OT does not specify that kings or people of high rank must avoid marriage with commoners. Certainly such would not have been regarded as so corrupting that it would evoke God's anger to the extent that he would destroy all mankind by a flood! Verses 5 and 11 indicate that these marriages corrupted mankind morally or religiously. The term **daughters** is just as comprehensive in verse 2 as it is in verse 1 and thus cannot denote only a part of the marriageable female population in verse 2.

(3) **The sons of God** could be the men that called upon the name of the Lord (see 4:26), and who **walked with God** (5:22, 24; 6:9; the OT and NT frequently refer to God's people as "sons of God"—cf. Prov. 3:12; Isa. 1:2, 4; Heb. 12:5-9), and **the daughters of men** might be "worldly-minded or materialistically-minded women," such as those condemned in Isaiah 3:16–4:1; 32:9-13; and Amos 4:1-3. As a matter of fact, the "violence" (man's inhumanity to man) mentioned in Genesis 6:11 and 13 calls to mind the evils perpetuated by the women described in these passages. A driving concern for materialistic success finds striking parallels in the stories of Adam and Eve (3:6), Cain (4:3, 5; see notes on these verses) and his descendants (4:17-24), and the people at Babel (11:1-9).

(4) Since 6:1-4 immediately follows the genealogical lists

of the descendants of Cain (4:17-24) and Seth (4:25–5:32), it would be natural to think of **the sons of God** as the descendants of Seth and **the daughters of men** as the descendants of Cain.

The last two views have three considerations in their favor: (a) they do not destroy the historical character of the narrative, which is so typical of the Genesis stories; (b) they provide a reason why God felt that he must destroy mankind; (c) they explain everything as belonging to human affairs, rather than injecting an angelic element into the text. If indeed angels were intended by the author, then one is hard put to explain why God did not become grieved with them and destroy them rather than mankind, why the children born to these marriages were not half-angel and half-human or some angels and some humans, and why such a thought as angels having intercourse with women, which is so foreign to the religious and moral principles of the rest of the book of Genesis and of the Bible, was perpetrated in this text.

[3] This verse is filled with difficulties, for which numerous solutions have been offered. Only a few observations can be made here, and the reader is urged to examine good commentaries and journal articles to acquire a deeper understanding of the problems involved.

The precise meaning of God's **spirit** is debated. Some think the Holy Spirit is intended (this may explain why the ASV capitalizes Spirit). Others believe it is an idiomatic expression for God himself. Just as man's spirit may be used for man himself (cf. 41:8; Dan. 2:3), so God's spirit may refer to God himself. The present context would seem to suggest that it means the God-given breath which sustains human life on earth (note this connotation of *ruach*, "spirit," in Num. 16:22; 27:16; Job 10:12; 27:3; Ps. 104:29, 30; Isa. 57:16; see BDB, p. 925). But one's interpretation of this term is inseparably connected with his understanding of the rest of this verse.

Again, the verb *yadhon* is problematic. The translation "strive with" (KJV, ASV) is hard to justify. Symmachus, Targum Pseudo-Jonathan, and Luther read "judge," appar-

ently deriving this form from the root *din*. Then the connotation would be that God was continually trying to turn
man back to him from sin by judging or striving with him
through punishment (cf. Isa. 63:10), but to no avail
(Amos 4:6-11 conveys a similar thought). Consequently,
God must resort to a much severer punishment (viz., the
flood). The LXX, Syriac, Vulgate, and Targum Onkelos
read **abide in** (RSV) or "remain in" (NEB), perhaps suggesting that the original Hebrew text read *yadhur* or *yalun*,
either of which requires only a slight emendation of the
consonantal text. This seems to be the correct reading (see
below).

Further, one must decide whether **man** (Heb. *'adham*)
refers to individual human beings in a more or less timeless
sense or to the human race as a whole living in the days of
Noah. The context would appear to support the latter.

The word **flesh** obviously stands in contrast to **spirit**, but
man was already flesh, physically speaking, before the fall
and before the sons of God married the daughters of men
(cf. 2:7; 3:19—although the word **flesh** does not occur in
these verses). Thus, **flesh** must refer here to man's worldly
inclinations and ambitions, his unspiritual aspirations (see
BDB, p. 142).

Finally, what does God mean when he says, **but his**
[i. e., man's] **days shall be a hundred and twenty years?** A
number of scholars argue that this indicates God had determined to reduce the average life span from several hundred
years (ch. 5) to 120, just as later he reduces it to seventy or
eighty (cf. Ps. 90:10). However, after this the descendants
of Shem live to be much older than 120 (cf. 11:10-32), as do
Abraham (25:7) and Isaac (35:28), and this interpretation
does not fit well into the context of Genesis 6. Consequently, it is preferable to agree with Targums Onkelos and
Pseudo-Jonathan, Jerome, Rashi, Ibn Ezra, and Calvin in
understanding God to mean that he would allow man another 120 years to repent before destroying him by a flood
(see Speiser, *Genesis*, p. 46). Peter apparently alludes to
this when he says that "God's patience waited in the days
of Noah" (1 Pet. 3:20).

In the context of Genesis 6, therefore, God appears to mean this in verse 3: I will not keep mankind alive with my life-giving breath indefinitely, because he is worldly-minded; instead, I will destroy him in 120 years if he has not repented by that time.

[4] The reading "giants" (KJV) is based on the LXX. Numbers 13:33 indicates that the **Nephilim** (RSV, ASV, and NEB) were large in stature, and that the sons of Anak (cf. Josh. 14:15; 15:13-14; Judg. 1:20) descended from them. The context of Genesis 6 suggests that the Nephilim were the children born to **the sons of God** and **the daughters of men**, who became **the mighty men, the men of renown.** The phrase **came in to** (Heb. *bo' 'el*) is a euphemism for "had sexual relations with" (cf. LWC-OT, vol. 1, ch. 1).

[5] When God finished creating the world and all things therein, he "*saw* everything that he had made, and behold, it was very good" (1:31). But now, as man increasingly ignores God and follows his own fleshly pleasures, God **saw that the wickedness of man was great** (cf. vss. 11-12). These anthropomorphic statements declare that God sees everything man does (cf. Prov. 15:3). Man's deeds are the natural, external expressions of what is already going on in his **heart** (cf. 8:21; Deut. 31:21; 1 Chron. 28:9; 29:18; Jer. 17:5-10), and God knows everything that man intends (cf. Ps. 139:1-6, 23-24). There seems to be an intentional contrast between what the sons of God "saw" (vs. 2) and what God **saw** (vs. 5), perhaps to emphasize that God punishes man at the very point where he thinks he is succeeding in his sinful ways (cf. Num. 32:23).

[6] The translation "it repented the Lord" (Jehovah, KJV, ASV; cf. also vs. 7) has given rise to no little discussion. Certainly the biblical writers nowhere suggest that God must repent of sin, and they firmly declare that when God says something, he does not lie or go back on his word (cf. Num. 23:19; 1 Sam. 15:29; Mal. 3:6). Thus, the Hebrew verb *nicham* here must mean that God **was sorry** [RSV, NEB] **that he had made man** (cf. this same basic meaning of "repent" in Exod. 32:14; 1 Sam. 15:11;

Jer. 18:7-8; 26:3, 13; Joel 2:13; Jon. 3:10; 4:2), which finds support in the companion word **grieved** in the parallel line. God is not impersonal. He is deeply involved in human affairs and in men's lives, and he is deeply moved by man's actions. When man sins, God is sorry—he is grieved. Whereas *man's* heart was only evil continually (vs. 5), *God's* **heart** was grieved at man's wickedness (vs. 6).

[9] The author of Genesis uses the expression **These are the generations of** to divide his work into smaller sections (see note on 2:4). He describes Noah as **righteous** (cf. 7:1), "perfect" (KJV, ASV) or **blameless** (RSV, NEB), and as a man who **walked with God** (cf. 5:22, 24). Surely he does not mean that Noah was sinless (cf. 9:21), because elsewhere biblical writers (some, if not all, of whom undoubtedly knew the story of Noah) declare that no one is without sin (cf. Pss. 14:1-3; 130:3; Prov. 20:9; Rom 3:23). Noah is pleasing to God because he is different from the people of his day. While they are violent (vss. 11, 13) in their treatment of their fellowmen, he is **righteous** (i.e., he treats them justly; note this meaning of the word in Amos 5:7, 24); whereas they are "corrupt" (vss. 11, 12), he is perfect or **blameless**; and while they satisfy their own desires, he wishes to satisfy God.

God Sends the Flood (6:13-7:24)

As in the cases of Adam and Eve (3:14-19) and Cain (4:11-16), God punishes man for his sin. He announces to Noah that he has determined to send a flood over all the earth to destroy every living creature. He instructs him to build an ark in a rectangular shape approximately 450 feet long, 75 feet wide, and 45 feet high; to bring every type of land animal into the ark, one pair of unclean animals and seven pairs of clean animals; and to store up every kind of food that these animals and his household can eat. Noah does all that God commands him (6:13–7:10).

When the time arrives for the flood to begin, God tells Noah to bring his family and all the animals into the ark. Noah does so, and God shuts them in. God sends the flood and destroys every creature outside the ark (7:11-24).

[14] The Hebrew word here translated **ark** (*tebhah*) is an Egyptian loanword meaning "chest" or "sarcophagus." **Gopher** (KJV, ASV, RSV) is simply the English transliteration of a Hebrew word, the meaning of which is uncertain. Some scholars connect it with the Greek word *kupárissos*, "cypress" (so the NEB), a wood which the Phoenicians used in building ships and the Egyptians in building sarcophagi. Others think it may be "pine." There is a Hebrew wordplay here on *gopher* and *kopher*, **pitch** (bitumen).

[15] The length of a **cubit** varied in the ancient Near Eastern world from time to time and from place to place. It is generally thought that it was the distance from the fingertip to the elbow, or about eighteen inches, which would mean that the ark was 450 feet long, 75 feet wide, and 45 feet high.

[16] The meaning of this verse is admittedly obscure. Depending on ancient versions, cognate words in other Semitic languages, and subjective interpretation of the evidence, the Hebrew word *tsohar* has been understood as "light" (KJV), "window" (ASV), and **roof** (RSV, NEB). The two most likely views seem to be: (1) an opening to allow light into the ark was made all the way around the ark (interrupted only by the beams supporting the roof), and extending from the roof one cubit below; (2) this opening began a cubit below the roof and extended downward an unspecified distance.

[17] The context indicates that, whereas **all flesh** means "all mankind" in verses 12 and 13 (cf. the word "flesh" in vs. 3), it means "all animal life" in 6:19; 7:15, 16; 8:17 (cf. 9:4); and both "human and animal life" in 6:17; 7:21; 9:11, 15 (twice), 16, 17.

[18] God enters into an intimate, personal relationship with Noah. The biblical word for such a relationship is **covenant** (Heb. *berith*); the nature of this covenant is described in 9:1-17.

[21] Up until the flood, God had "given" man only plants to eat (1:29); after the flood, he "gives" him "every moving thing that lives" (9:3). Just as Noah "gathers"

(KJV, ASV) or **stores up** (RSV, NEB; Heb. *'asaph*) food in preparation for the flood, so later Joseph "gathers" (Heb. *qabhats*) grain (wheat) into the store-cities of Egypt in preparation for the seven-year famine (cf. 41:35, 48).

[22] Throughout the account of the flood, emphasis is placed on the fact that Noah **did all that God commanded him** (6:22; 7:5, 9, 16; 8:18).

> By faith Noah, being warned by God concerning events as yet unseen, took heed and constructed an ark for the saving of his household; by this he condemned the world and became an heir of the righteousness which comes by faith.
>
> Hebrews 11:7

[7:1] Several times in the biblical story of the flood, the anthropomorphic terms "see" and "eyes" are used of God. God saw that man's wickedness was great (6:5) and thus that the earth was corrupt (6:12), but he also saw that Noah was righteous (7:1; cf. 6:9), and so Noah found favor in his eyes (6:8). God did not discover that Noah was **righteous** when he obeyed him by building the ark, but he knew he was righteous and thus commanded him to build it. Obedience is the natural fruit of righteousness, that is, a right human relationship with God (which means that man trusts in God and not in himself; cf. Heb. 11:7); righteousness is not the result of obedience. A comparison of 6:9 and 7:1 would seem to suggest that it is incorrect to distinguish between walking "with" God and walking **before** him (on the latter, cf. 17:1).

[2] The distinction between **clean** and unclean animals here indicates that laws making such distinctions existed in the ancient world long before Moses made decrees concerning them at Sinai (cf. Lev. 11; Deut. 14:3-20), just as was the case with the sabbath (Gen. 2:1-3) and circumcision (17:1-14). A law or a truth does not have to have its origin with a certain individual or religion to be a vital part of that religion or to be distinctive in that religion. For example, Jesus did not originate the ideas of loving God with all one's heart (cf. Deut. 6:5), of loving one's neighbor as oneself (cf. Lev. 19:18), or of loving one's enemies

(cf. Exod. 23:4-5; Prov. 25:21-22), and yet these concepts are central to his message (cf. Matt. 22:34-40 and 5:43-48, respectively).

It is impossible to determine certainly whether the Hebrew phrase *shibh'ah shibh'ah* (see also vs. 3) means "by sevens" (KJV), that is, seven animals of all clean species, or "seven and seven" (ASV) or **seven pairs** (RSV, NEB), that is, fourteen animals of all clean species. Some scholars have taken the former view, and have conjectured that the seventh animal was a male which was to be sacrificed after the waters of the flood subsided. But there can be no certainty on this point.

[3] If one follows the MT as it stands, no distinction is made between clean and unclean birds, as is attested later by the specific reference to the raven (cf. 8:7), which is unclean (cf. Lev. 11:15; Deut. 14:14). However, after the word **female**, the LXX has this sentence which is missing in the MT: "and of all the birds that are not clean a pair, male and female." It is possible that a copyist's eye skipped from the word **female** in the first line to the same word in the second (a phenomenon called homoioteleuton), thus omitting the sentence found in the LXX from the present Hebrew text. As is usually the case, the singular noun *zera'* (RSV **kind**; KJV and ASV "seed") is a collective meaning "descendants" or "offspring."

[4] The context would suggest that God gave Noah **seven days** to bring all the animals into the ark (see especially vs. 10).

[6] The MT says literally, "Noah was a son [Heb. *ben*] of" **six hundred years**, which is a Hebrew idiom meaning that Noah was six hundred years old. Here is one of many instances in which the literal translation is not superior.

[11] Beginning here, the key events connected with the flood are dated precisely according to the year of Noah's life. These are briefly outlined in *Chart IV* (see p. 172).

The careful manner in which these details are related favors the historicity of this account, although it is impossible to assign a date to the flood described here.

Instead of **seventeenth**, the LXX reads "twenty-seventh."

172

CHART IV

Chronology of the Flood

(Dates in parentheses are not specifically stated in the text.)

Event	Year of Noah's Life	Reference
The rain begins.	600th yr.; 2nd mo.,17th day	7:11
After forty days and nights, the rain stops.	600th yr.; (3rd mo., 26th day)	7:4, 12, 17
On the 150th day the flood peaks.	600th yr.; (7th mo., 16th day)	7:18-20, 24; 8:3
The day after the waters begin to subside, the ark runs aground on submerged land.	600th year.; 7th mo., 17th day	8:4
The tops of the mountains become visible.	600th yr.; 10th mo., 1st day	8:5
Forty days after the mountain tops become visible Noah sends out a raven and a dove.	600th yr.; (11th mo.,10th day)	8:6-7
Seven days later, Noah sends out a dove for the second time.	600th yr.; (11th mo., 17th day)	8:10-11
Seven days later, Noah sends out a dove for the third time.	600th yr.; (11th mo., 24th day)	8:12
Noah removes the covering of the ark and sees dry land.	601st yr.; 1st mo., 1st day	8:13 (cf.8:3)
Noah and his family leave the ark.	601st yr.; 2nd mo., 27th day	8:14-19

Unfortunately, it is impossible to know whether the years in these chapters are reckoned according to the ancient Hebrew calendar beginning in October or according to the Babylonian calendar beginning in April.

The flood resulted from massive amounts of water gushing upward from **the great deep** (underground rivers and streams) and pouring down from heavy clouds, which are called figuratively **the windows of the heavens** (cf. 8:2; 2 Kings 7:2, 19; Isa. 24:18; Mal. 3:10). It was as if the waters above and the waters below, which God had separated by the firmament when he was creating the world (cf. 1:7), returned to their former combination during the period of chaos, and thus God had reversed his initial creative acts (an interesting description of the reversal of creation also appears in Jer. 4:23-26).

[13] In contrast to the ungodly marriages described in 6:1-4, Noah and his sons practice monogamy and regard the intimate relationship between husband and wife in that high and noble way indicated by God in the very institution of marriage itself (cf. 1:26-27; 2:18-24 and the notes there).

[16] At the same moment when God was about to unleash his punishment on impenitent and persistent sinners, he manifested his tender love to the faithful and obedient Noah, for when he and his family had gone safely into the ark, **the Lord shut him in.**

[18] The Hebrew verb translated **prevailed** (vss. 18, 19, and 20) is *gabhar*, which means literally "to be strong." One gets the impression that the author is describing a mighty battle between **the waters** and the **earth** or dry land, and the waters are victorious.

[19] The statement **all the high mountains under the whole heaven were covered** (with water) can be interpreted in a universal sense or in a local sense, and the same is true of the terms "all flesh" (for the passages, see note on 6:17), **earth**, and the like. The reader will normally encounter one of three views in scholarly works. (1) Most liberal scholars argue that the author was thinking of a global flood, but that such a flood never occurred (cf. Skinner, *Genesis*, pp. 165, 175). (2) Some conservative critics think that the

flood was universal and seek to demonstrate this by linguistic and geological evidence (so J. C. Whitcomb, "Flood," *Wycliffe Bible Encyclopedia*, vol. 1, pp. 613–17). (3) Other conservative scholars think that the flood occurred in the Mesopotamian region inhabited by ancient biblical man and thus was not a universal flood; they also appeal to linguistic and geological evidence (so R. K. Harrison, *Introduction to the Old Testament*, p. 558, and Kidner, *Genesis*, pp. 93–95).

There is simply not sufficient concrete information to allow a dogmatic judgment on this matter. A few observations may give a slight indication of the complexity of the problem. The Hebrew word translated **earth** (*'erets*) means the globe in some passages in Genesis (e.g., 1:1-2; 2:4), and a certain land or region in others (e.g., 41:57 [twice]); obviously, it could mean either in Genesis 6–8. The Hebrew word rendered all, whole, or **every** (*kol*) may have a universal connotation (as 1:21, 26), but it may also have a localized significance as viewed by the speaker or writer with reference to his particular audience (as 41:57 [twice]; cf. Acts 2:5; Col. 1:23, where the word "every" cannot be all-inclusive in the absolute sense). Geologists have discovered ample evidence of flooding all over the globe but no conclusive evidence of one universal flood. Rather, available remains can as easily point to local floods that occurred at different historical periods.

[20] Since the waters rose **fifteen cubits** (about twenty-two and one-half feet) above the mountains of Ararat (cf. 8:4), the ark floated just above them, as it would have sunk down into the water about half its height (30 cubits or 45 feet; cf. 6:15). Thus, the very next day after the waters began to subside, the ark struck the land and grounded (see *Chart IV,* above).

God Gives Man a New Start (8:1–9:19)

After all men and animals on earth perish in the flood, God remembers Noah and those with him in the ark and causes the rain to cease. The ark then comes to rest on the mountains of Ararat in Armenia north of Mesopotamia

(8:1-5). After waiting forty days, Noah sends out a raven and then three doves (or a dove three times) to see if the land is dry enough for the inhabitants of the ark to disembark. When the dove does not come back and God tells him to go forth, Noah and all in the ark abandon it (8:6-19). Noah offers a sacrifice to God, and God resolves never to destroy life on earth by a flood again (8:20-22).

God encourages Noah and his sons to be fruitful and multiply on the earth. He allows them to eat meat and vegetation but warns them not to eat blood with meat or to kill their fellowmen (9:1-7). God makes a covenant with Noah, promising never to destroy life on earth again by a flood; the sign of this covenant is the rainbow (9:8-19).

[1] The statement **God remembered** [Heb. *zakhar*] **Noah** is anthropomorphic and in no way implies that God forgets or might forget his people or his commitments. In a text like this, "remember" conveys the idea of concern which motivates to immediate and positive action (cf. 19:29; 30:22; Exod. 2:24; 1 Sam. 1:19; Jer. 31:20).

The Hebrew word translated **wind** is *ruach*, the same word that is rendered "Spirit" in 1:2. The purpose of the **wind** here is to dry up the waters, as is the case also in Exodus 14:21 in the account of the drying up of the waters of the Reed Sea. Since this also seems to be the function of the *ruach* in Genesis 1:2, it may be best to read "wind" there (see note on that verse). The author of Genesis apparently thinks of the flood as bringing upon the earth a chaotic condition similar to that which existed before the establishment of the firmament and the appearance of the dry land.

[4] Instead of **seventeenth**, the LXX has "twenty-seventh" (cf. 7:11). The expression **came to rest** translates a form of the verb *nuach*, which in Hebrew forms a word-play with *noach*, "Noah" (vs. 1), on the one hand, and with *ruach*, "wind" (vs. 1), on the other.

The phrase **mountains of Ararat** is not specific enough to locate the precise mountain on which the ark landed. **Ararat** is the name of a rather large country north of Mesopotamia, called Urartu in Assyrian. The Peshitta and

Targum Onkelos suggest that the mountain on which the ark landed was in Kurdistan southwest of Lake Van, but the traditional view is that it was the highest mountain in the range to the northeast of Lake Van, that is, Mount Massis, the modern Mount Agridagh, some seventeen thousand feet above sea level.

[7] Apparently it was not necessary for the **raven** to return to the ark, because it could perch and feed on the carrion floating in the water.

[8] As the MT stands, one would assume that Noah sent out the **dove** on the same day he dispatched the raven. However, the statement in verse 10, "he waited another seven days", has led some scholars to conjecture that the original Hebrew text of verse 8 began with the words "Noah waited for seven days" (NEB), or something similar. (Note that *Chart IV* follows the MT.)

[11] **Olive** trees do not grow at high altitudes. So, when the dove brought back **a freshly plucked olive leaf** in its beak, Noah knew that the waters had subsided sufficiently for the inhabitants of the ark to think seriously about disembarking.

[13-14] The words **dried** and **dry** in verses 13 and 14 translate two different Hebrew words. In verse 13 (twice), the word is *charebh*, which seems to suggest that the waters had receded from the land, but the ground was still extremely muddy and too soft to support living creatures. In verse 14, the word is *yabhesh*, which apparently indicates that the ground was now sufficiently firm to maintain such creatures.

[17] When God first created the sea creatures (1:22) and man (1:28), he told them to **be fruitful and multiply**. Now that all life on earth has been destroyed, God gives the same command to birds, beasts (8:17), and man (9:1, 7). The same terminology is used at other strategic points in the book of Genesis, namely, when the Lord reveals himself to Jacob at Bethel on his return from Paddan-aram in Mesopotamia to Hebron in southern Canaan (35:11), and when the household of Jacob settles in the land of Goshen in Egypt (47:27).

[20] Although animal sacrifices are mentioned earlier (viz., in 4:4), this is the first time an **altar** is mentioned. **Burnt offerings** were the most self-denying gifts that man had to offer God in ancient times, because the '*olah* was a whole burnt offering, that is, the entire animal was burned on the altar, and the worshiper received nothing to eat for himself, as in other sacrifices. The context indicates that Noah offered these sacrifices for two purposes: (1) to express deep gratitude to God for sparing those in the ark and (2) to make expiation or propitiation for himself and the rest of mankind for their sins in the hope that God would not destroy the human race again by a flood.

[21] The OT emphasizes that God does not get hungry, yearn for food, and eat the animals that man offers on earthly altars (cf. Ps. 50:9-13). In this, he is strikingly different from the ancient Mesopotamian gods of the Gilgamesh Epic, who were so hungry after going without food during the seven days that the flood was supposed to have lasted that they gathered around Utnapishtim's sacrifice like flies (for further details, see the Excursus, "The Genesis Flood and Babylonian Parallels," p. 184, below). Accordingly, the statement **the Lord smelled the pleasing odor** is simply an anthropomorphic (and perhaps idiomatic) metaphor meaning that the Lord accepted or approved of Noah's sacrifice (the same root is used in this sense in Exod. 29:18, 25, 41; Lev. 1:9, 13, 17; 2:2, 9, 12; 3:5, 16; 4:31; 6:15, 21 [Hebrew 8, 14]; 8:21, 28; etc.; Num. 15:3, 7, 9, 13, 14; 18:17; 28:1, 6, 8, 13, 24, 27; 29:6, 8, 13, 36; etc.; 1 Sam. 26:19; Ezek. 20:41; and of sacrifices made to idols in Ezek. 6:13; 16:19; 20:28). Paul uses virtually the equivalent imagery in Greek (Eph. 5:2; Phil. 4:18).

A biblical writer could know what **the Lord said in his heart**, that is, "thought," only by divine revelation or by observing the results of God's thinking manifested in his acts.

God had **cursed the ground** by causing it to bring forth thorns and thistles when Adam and Eve sinned (3:17-18), by reducing its yield when Cain sinned (4:11-12), and by sending a flood because of mankind's corruption (8:21).

Now, he promises not to send this sort of curse on the ground again, in spite of man's rebellion (cf. Isa. 54:9). Unfortunately, the flood, while punishing man for his sinfulness, did not change his nature; his situation is still the same (cf. 6:5): **the imagination of man's heart is evil from his youth,** that is, from the time he is old enough to be able to discern between right and wrong.

[22] God promises to maintain the rhythm of nature without ceasing until the world comes to an end (cf. Col. 1:17), which assumes, of course, that he is active in what unbelievers call "natural law." Simpson notes:

> In those days it was perhaps easier for men to see the hand of God in the catastrophic and the sudden than it was in the ordered quiet of the succession of the seasons. Nor can it be claimed that man's realization of God's activity is generally more adequate even in this age. For the tendency is still to take for granted the ordered, stable elements of life, and to say "Thy will be done" only in the face of the catastrophic.
>
> "Genesis," p. 549

By purposefully and actively "making his sun rise" and "sending rain" on the evil and unjust as well as the good and just, God shows his people a living example of the way that he wants them to respond to their enemies (Matt. 5:43-48, especially vs. 45).

[9:1] After the flood, and in spite of man's continued sinfulness (cf. 8:21), God gives man great blessings for the purpose of making his life on earth as pleasant and as productive as possible under the new set of circumstances. First, he reiterates his initial decree that man **be fruitful and multiply** (cf. 1:28; 9:7).

[2] Second, God reaffirms man's dominion over the rest of his creatures. Many scholars suggest that this verse indicates a distinction between man's relationship to animal life before and after the flood. Before the flood, this association was peaceful and harmonious, and afterwards it became hostile. Some have proposed that Isaiah 11:6-9 anticipates a return to the ideal antediluvian situation. However,

such a view is by no means certain. If **fear** and **dread** are understood in a positive sense, the thought is that animals generally respect man for his obvious superiority in intellect and ability. If they are interpreted in a negative sense, the meaning still seems to be fundamentally the same as that presupposed in 1:26, 28, where God authorized man to "have dominion over" the rest of created life. Man's rule over all other life on earth is a divine gift and naturally calls for sincere gratitude.

[3] Third, God allows man to eat meat, whereas before the flood he could eat only plant life (cf. 1:29). Food is a continuing gift of God (cf. Matt. 6:11) and thus evokes man's constant appreciation and thanksgiving (cf. Rom. 14:6; 1 Tim. 4:3).

[4] However, mankind (not merely Israel) is forbidden to eat the blood of an animal with its meat, possibly partly explaining why the early church avoided this practice (cf. Acts 15:19-20, 28-29; 21:25). There are at least three reasons why man is forbidden to eat blood: (1) The blood is regarded as the seat of life itself (Lev. 17:11, 14; Deut. 12:23). (2) Even though God allows man to kill animals for his sustenance, they are God's property, and man is to recognize this by abstaining from that which signifies the life which God gives his creatures (viz., the blood). (3) God's portion in all animal sacrifices is at least the blood (cf. Lev. 3:12-17; 7:22-27; Deut. 12:26-27; 15:19-23; 1 Sam. 14:31-35; Ezek. 33:25).

[5-6] These two verses should probably be taken together. On the one hand, if a beast kills a human being, he is to be put to death (cf. Exod. 21:28-29). On the other hand, if a man kills his fellowman, the dead **man's brother** is to avenge his blood by killing the murderer. **By man shall his blood be shed** is a divine command that the human race punish murderers by capital punishment. Logically, since God gives life, he alone is authorized to take life. However, when God *commands* man to execute murderers, he delegates this task to him, and it becomes his God-given responsibility. (This principle is assumed in Rom. 13:4; 1 Pet. 2:14.) To be sure, man can use this prerogative un-

justly and be subject to God's wrath (cf. 1 Kings 21:8-13; Luke 23:18-25), but he can also refuse to exercise it when it is justified and be the object of divine disapproval. The reason man is forbidden to commit murder is that **God made man in his own image** (cf. 1:26-27; 5:1), and murder is the most flagrant denunciation of man's dignity. "It is only God's image in man that implies sacredness, and . . . where belief in God is lacking respect for human personality does not long survive" (Richardson, *Genesis*, p. 110). Some theologians argue that when Adam and Eve ate the forbidden fruit, they lost the image of God which Yahweh gave them in the beginning. However, verse 6 refutes this because it bases the prohibition of murder on the assumption that after the fall man still possesses God's image.

[9-10] God's **covenant** here amounts to a divine promise to all mankind and to all animal life "for all future generations" (vs. 12; cf. "never" in vss. 11 [twice] and 15) that he will never destroy life on earth again by a flood.

Although the Hebrew word *zera'*, translated "seed" in the KJV and ASV, is singular in form, it obviously has a collective meaning (here **descendants,** referring to all mankind), as it normally does throughout the Bible.

[13] God is portrayed as a mighty archer who shoots his arrows (lightnings; cf. Pss. 7:13 [Hebrew 14]; 18:14 [Hebrew 15]; Hab. 3:11) from his bow (cf. Ps. 7:12 [Hebrew 13]; Hab. 3:9). Now, however, he promises to lay aside his bow in the sky, thus symbolizing his intention never to destroy the earth by a flood (on the rainbow, cf. also Ezek. 1:28).

[15-16] In highly anthropomorphic language (see LWC-OT, vol. 1, ch. 1), God states that the purpose of the rainbow is to cause him to **remember** his **covenant** with man and **every living creature.** God's promise never to destroy the earth again by a flood is an **everlasting covenant** with all human and animal life. Richardson comments:

> Without the constant covenanted care and protection of God, whether men recognize the fact or not, human life could not continue for a single day . . . . No man is be-

yond the care and loving kindness of God, despite his depravity.

Genesis, p. 107

Noah Gets Drunk, Curses Canaan (9:20-29)

After the flood, Noah becomes a vinedresser, plants a vineyard, and one day gets drunk on the wine. His youngest son Ham sees his drunken father lying naked in his tent and tells his two brothers. They take a garment, walk backward into the tent to avoid seeing their father's nakedness, and cover their father. When Noah becomes sober, he realizes what Ham has done to him, and so he pronounces a curse on his son Canaan and consequently also on his descendants, the Canaanites. Noah lives to the age of 950.

[20] A literal translation of the Hebrew of this verse would be, "and Noah, a man of the ground, began and planted a vineyard." This can hardly mean that **Noah was the first tiller of the soil** (RSV), as Adam had done this before him (2:15; 3:17-19). The idea could be that Noah "began the planting of vineyards," that is, he was the originator of vinedressing (just as Jabal initiated tent dwelling and cattle raising, Gen. 4:20; or just as Jubal originated the playing of lyres and pipes, 4:21), or that after the flood Noah began working as a husbandman or vinedresser for the first time in his life (so the KJV and ASV).

[21] Some scholars seek to relieve Noah of any blame for becoming drunk by arguing that mankind had had no experience with wine prior to this time, and thus Noah could not have known that it would make him inebriated. However, since the author's interest is in the sinful activity of Ham rather than in explicitly expressing a value judgment concerning Noah's action, this conclusion builds too heavily upon what is not said in the text and cannot appeal to a specific biblical statement for support. Elsewhere the Bible condemns drunkenness (cf. Prov. 20:1; 23:29-35; Gal. 5:19-21). Frequently a drunken person will undress without realizing what he is doing (cf. Lam. 4:21).

[22] The Lord told ancient Israel that only a man's wife

was to see her husband's nakedness, that is, sexual organs
(Lev. 18:6-7). The present verse in Genesis indicates that
this same idea was held by ancient man long before Moses.
Thus, Ham's offense is that he did not honor his father's
dignity by allowing him personal privacy at a time when his
genitals were exposed. Habakkuk 2:15 condemns those
who make people drunk in order that they might gaze on
their shame. Perhaps Ham got some sort of perverted sen-
sual pleasure out of observing his naked father. This event
naturally calls to mind the story of how Lot's daughters
made him drunk in order that they might have intercourse
with him to preserve his posterity (Gen. 19:30-38). The
text does not make it clear what Ham **told** his brothers or
the attitude with which he told it. Was he inviting them to
share his perverted pleasure? Was he ridiculing his father's
behavior? Was he so bewildered by this episode that he
was seeking their advice? Since Noah curses Ham's son,
and Shem and Japheth know it is wrong to look on their
father's nakedness, it seems likely that Ham knew right
from wrong in this circumstance but deliberately did what
was wrong because of selfish desires.

[24] The statement that **Noah knew what** [Ham] **had done**
(Heb. *'asah*) to him suggests that more was involved in
this incident than Ham's simply viewing his father's nakedness. The Bible does not make clear what this was, either
because the original readers of Genesis already knew, or
the biblical author felt a minimum of words was sufficient
to indicate its nature because of general practices of the
day, or because the activity was too base and delicate to be
described explicitly.

[25] The theme of Noah's curse is that Ham's son **Canaan**
shall be a **slave** (vss. 25, 26, 27) because his father saw
Noah's nakedness. By way of contrast, Shem and Japheth
will be richly blessed because they refused to look on their
father's nakedness and covered him while he was in his
drunken stupor.

Some scholars find two originally independent sources
woven together in verses 22-27 because Ham was the one
who saw Noah's nakedness, but Noah **cursed Canaan**. This

is not necessary, however, because in the patriarchal blessings and curses, the action of the father often determines the fate of his descendants. For example, Jacob curses the descendants of Simeon and Levi because they killed the men of Shechem (49:5-7; see notes on these verses and the account of the activity of Simeon and Levi at Shechem in Gen. 34:25-30). So, in the present context, Ham's transgression consigns the descendants of his son Canaan (the Canaanites) to a role of subjection and servitude to the descendants of Shem and Japheth.

It should be noted in passing that some (particularly in North America) have used this verse as a proof text for their prejudice against blacks. They wrongly assume that the curse is placed on Ham, whereas the Bible says quite clearly that it was placed on Canaan. Since some of the descendants of Ham settled in Egypt (cf. the synonymous parallelism of "Egypt" and "Ham" in Pss. 105:23; 106:21-22), and since early settlers brought black slaves to America from Africa (of which Egypt is a part), it has been erroneously contended that God intends for the white man to be superior and for the black man to be his slave. This is "a noteworthy example of the danger of a strained literalism in the interpretation of the Scripture" (Bennett, *Genesis*, p. 157).

[26] The reading "Blessed be the Lord God of Shem" (KJV) or "Blessed be Jehovah, the God of Shem" (ASV) does not make sense in this context, where a man (Canaan) is cursed in the preceding verse, and a man (Japheth) is blessed in the following verse. On an analogy with 24:31 and 26:29 (where the same construction occurs), it is possible to read here **Blessed by** [of] **the Lord my God** [reading *'elohay* instead of *'elohe,* which requires no change whatsoever in the Hebrew consonantal text] **be Shem** (so the RSV). Or it may be that a copyist accidentally reversed the letters *he* (h) and *lamedh* (l) (a phenomenon called metathesis, which is quite common in handwriting, typing, and printing) in the word *'elohe,* "God of," and that the original text was *barekh yhwh 'ohole shem,* "Bless, O

Lord, the tents of Shem" (so the NEB). (The phrase "tents of Shem" actually occurs in vs. 27 of the MT.)

[27] The first line in this verse contains a wordplay in Hebrew on *yapht,* **enlarge,** and *yepheth,* **Japheth.**

It is impossible to determine the meaning of this verse with certainty. While the descendants of Shem are undoubtedly the Israelites (see 11:10-27), the descendants of **Japheth** have been variously interpreted as allies of the Habiru who invaded the land of Canaan in the fourteenth century B.C., the Hittites, the Phoenicians, the Philistines, and even Gentile converts to Christianity! That the coastland peoples were descendants of Japheth (10:5) would seem to favor the Phoenicians or the Philistines, but the Philistines are listed as descendants of Ham in 10:14.

But to complicate matters even more, the expression **dwell in the tents of** (Heb. *shakhan be'ohole*) is sometimes used in the OT in a hostile sense of invading armies driving their enemies out of their tents and dwelling in them (cf. 1 Chron. 5:10; Ps. 78:55) and sometimes in a friendly sense of peaceful coexistence or alliance (cf. Pss. 84:10 [Hebrew 11]; 120:5). Since the whole context indicates that Noah is asking God to curse Ham's son Canaan and to bless Shem and Japheth, it seems best to interpret this phrase in a friendly sense here. However, there is not enough information to attach the fulfillment of Noah's wish to any specific historical setting.

EXCURSUS

The Genesis Flood and Babylonian Parallels

Stories of a mighty flood belong to some of the earliest extant literature of the ancient Near East. Among the more significant of these are a Sumerian fragment and an Old Babylonian fragment from Nippur, the Atrahasis epic, the Gilgamesh Epic (all certainly extant as early as the first half of the second millennium B.C. and probably much earlier), and the account of Berossus (third century B.C.). Tablet XI of the Gilgamesh Epic contains a full account of the typical Mesopotamian version of the flood, which may be summarized here.* Gilgamesh, king of Uruk, becomes very fearful of death and so decides to go to Utnapishtim in a far distant land to learn how he had obtained immortality. Utnapishtim tells him in great detail his experience in the flood, which led to his immortality. The god Enlil had determined to destroy a certain city by a flood, but another god, Ea, warned Utnapishtim, telling him how he could survive the flood by building a ship of specified dimensions. When the flood came, Utnapishtim took his family, sailors, well-educated craftsmen, and every kind of animal into the ark. Then Ea shut them in. The storm raged six days and destroyed all living creatures on earth, and on the seventh day the ship grounded on a high mountain. After seven days, Utnapishtim sent out a dove, then later a swallow (both of which soon returned), and finally a raven (which never returned). Then Utnapishtim brought all the people and animals out of the ship and offered a sacrifice. The gods swarmed around the sacrifice like flies, because they had not eaten since man had last offered sacrifices; their survival depended on eating the sacrifices which men offered to them. The other gods pacified Enlil, and in time he bestowed on Utnapishtim and his wife eternal life.

A study of this account shows that there are similarities between the story of the flood in Genesis 5–8 and Babylonian parallels. (1) In both, the deity singles out one man to deliver from a universal flood. (2) Each is told to build a ship according to certain specifications. (3) The different accounts give a rather detailed description of the coming of the flood, the destruction of all life on earth, and the salvation of those in the ship. (4) In both cases, the ship is grounded on a tall mountain. (5) The heroes in both stories

---

*English translations of the Gilgamesh and Atrahasis epics with related materials may be found in Heidel, *Gilgamesh Epic*, pp. 16–136; E. A. Speiser, "The Epic of Gilgamesh" and "Atrahasis," with additions by A. K. Grayson, in *Ancient Near Eastern Texts Relating to the Old Testament*, ed. J. B. Pritchard, 3rd ed.(Princeton, N.J.: Princeton University Press, 1969), pp. 72–99, 104–6, 503–7, 512–14.

release birds in order to determine whether it is safe to leave the ark—each account mentions a dove and a raven. (6) Both accounts describe the disembarking from the ark and the sacrifice of thanksgiving offered by the hero.

At best, however, these similarities may indicate that the biblical writer adopted some of the literary style and structure and some terminology already familiar to himself and his readers from earlier ancient Near Eastern accounts of a mighty flood, because the differences between the biblical story and other extant flood stories of the ancient world are much more extensive than the similarities. (a) In the OT only one God is involved, but in the Babylonian accounts the flood is sent by an assembly of gods—but they are not in agreement about whether it is best to send the flood or about which persons are to be killed and which to be spared. (b) In the OT God sends the flood to punish man for his sin, whereas in the Gilgamesh Epic the gods do it just because they decide to do it. (In the Atraḥasis epic Enlil does it to repay men for depriving him of his sleep by being noisy.)

(c) The name of the OT hero is Noah, but the names of Babylonian heroes vary from Ziusudra to Utnapishtim to Atraḥasis to Zisuthros; the name of the mountain range on which Noah's ark landed is Ararat, while the name of the mountain on which Utnapishtim's ship grounded is Mount Nisir. (d) The OT indicates that God revealed to Noah directly that he was going to destroy the earth by a flood, whereas the Babylonian records state that the gods involved in the respective accounts indicated to the hero in a dream that they were going to send a flood. In the Gilgamesh Epic, the god Ea gives Utnapishtim only hints or slight indications of what is going to happen and leaves it up to him to draw the correct conclusions. (e) Genesis 6:3, 1 Peter 3:20, and 2 Peter 2:5 indicate that God instructed Noah to warn mankind of the impending doom in the hope of bringing them to repentance and that he gave them ample time to repent (see note on Gen. 6:3); but in the Babylonian stories, the gods try very hard to keep their destructive intentions from man, and Ea reveals their plan to

Utnapishtim only indirectly because he is Ea's favorite.
(f) Noah's ark has three stories with an unspecified number of rooms, whereas Utnapishtim's ship has seven stories with sixty-three rooms. (g) Noah's ark is 450 feet long, 75 feet wide, and 45 feet high, giving it a displacement of about 43,000 tons; Utnapishtim's craft is a perfect cube of 180 feet each way, giving it a displacement of some 228,500 tons. (h) The only human inhabitants of Noah's ark are Noah and his wife, their three sons and their wives; Utnapishtim is accompanied by his wife, several sailors, and learned craftsmen. (i) Noah sends out four birds, or two birds four times: a raven (8:5-7) and three doves (or the same dove three times; 8:8-12); but Utnapishtim sends out three: a dove, a swallow, and a raven. (j) Whereas Noah does not leave the ark until God commands him to do so, Utnapishtim leaves the ship at his own discretion. (k) When Noah offers his sacrifice, God smells its pleasing odor and determines that he will never destroy the earth again by water; but when Utnapishtim offers his sacrifice, the gods hungrily swarm about it because they have not eaten since the last sacrifice had been made before the flood began. (l) In the OT, after the flood, God tells Noah and his family to be fruitful and multiply and to have dominion over all animal life; in the Gilgamesh Epic, Enlil transforms Utnapishtim and his wife into gods, thus making them immortal.

These considerations (and others of a more technical nature which cannot be discussed here) indicate that

> the arguments which have been advanced in support of the contention that the biblical account rests on Babylonian material are quite indecisive .... We ... do not know how the biblical and Babylonian narratives of the deluge are related historically. The available evidence proves nothing beyond the point that there is a genetic relationship between Genesis and the Babylonian versions. The skeleton is the same in both cases, but the flesh and blood, and above all, the animating spirit are different.
>
> Heidel, *Gilgamesh Epic*, pp. 267–68

THE NATIONS THAT
DESCENDED FROM NOAH (CH. 10)

God had told Noah and his sons to "be fruitful and multiply, and fill the earth" (9:1). Genesis 10 sketches very broadly and briefly how this occurred, and thus obviously covers hundreds of years. The structure of this chapter is very symmetrical. It begins (vs. 1) and ends (vs. 32) with a summary statement affirming that the passage deals with the descendants of the sons of Noah. Then it lists the peoples that emerged from Japheth (vss. 2-5), Ham (vss. 6-20), and Shem (vss. 21-31). Each of these shorter units itself ends with a summary statement pertaining to the lands, languages, families, and nations connected with the three main groups (vss. 5, 20, 31).

The reason that Shem's descendants are mentioned last is not because he is Noah's youngest son (for Ham was the youngest, 9:24), but because it is through him that Abram comes (cf. 11:10-27). The author of Genesis is more concerned with theology than with chronology, as is evident in numerous points throughout the book.

The contents of this chapter indicate that the phrase "the sons of" in verses 2, 6, and 22 means "the descendants of." In the three lists, some of the names are those of peoples and tribes (e.g., Madai in vs. 2 refers to the Medes), some of countries (e.g., Mizraim in vss. 6, 13 is Egypt); some are plural (e.g., all the words ending in *-im* in vss. 13-14, since *-im* is the ending of the masculine plural in Hebrew); and some are gentilic, that is, they refer to certain peoples (with the normal gentilic ending *-i* in Hebrew, e.g., all the words ending in English "-ites" in vss. 16-18). In very general terms, the descendants of Japheth occupied the region to the north and west of Palestine, those of Ham to the south, and those of Shem to the east. But there is some overlapping, as Havilah (vss. 7, 29), Sheba (vss. 7, 28), and Ludim (vs. 13) or Lud (vs. 22), all of which are listed under both Ham and Shem. Perhaps this may best be explained by assuming that descendants of one son inhabited a certain region in an earlier period and were later displaced by descendants of the other, or that descendants of both lived side by side in the same region. At any rate, the arrangement here is not based on skin color, race, or language, but on geographical settlement. It is hazardous and unnecessary to think of these peoples as contemporaries. Rather, the different groups lived and flourished at different times. The same list occurs in 1 Chronicles 1:4-23 with some variations.

When Paul preached to the Athenians, he affirmed God's impartial love for all men by declaring that "he made from one every nation of men to live on all the face of the earth, having determined allotted periods and the boundaries of their habitation" (Acts 17:26). Basically, this is the religious thrust of Genesis 10. "Theologically it affirms the unity of the human race and sees the peopling of the earth as the result of the divine blessing (cf. 9:1); it is a new creation, but now of the nations of the earth" (E. H. Maly, "Genesis," JBC, vol. 1, p. 17). Again:

> God's purpose embraces all the nations, for all are in truth one big family, sprung from a common ancestor . . . . Nothing could indicate more clearly than does this chapter the firmness and antiquity of the Hebrew conviction that Jehovah is the God of all the earth, the Lord of the nations and the hope of the Gentiles.
>
> Richardson, *Genesis*, pp. 116–17

As Jeremiah puts it very clearly and succinctly: "Who would not fear thee, O King of the nations?" (Jer. 10:7). God's care of and concern for all men of all nations permeates OT thought and is emphasized forcefully in Genesis 10, where a Jewish writer under divine inspiration takes the time and trouble to enumerate with proper appreciation the peoples of the earth prior to and contemporary with his age, and classifies them all as the descendants of the faithful Noah.

[1] For the fourth time, the author of Genesis begins a section in his book with the expression **These are the generations of** (cf. 2:4; 5:1; 6:9; KJV, ASV, RSV), here apparently meaning "These are the descendants of" (so NEB).

The Descendants of Japheth (10: 2-5)

The author enumerates seven groups which descended from Japheth. The first (Gomer) he further divides into three groups, and the fourth (Javan) he further divides into four, finally commenting that the coastland peoples spread from these.

[2] **Gomer** (cf. Ezek. 38:6) represents the Gimirray of Assyrian inscriptions and the Cimmerians of classical Greek writers, a people living in southern Russia who swept into western Asia in the late eighth or early seventh century B.C. **Magog** (cf. Ezek. 38:2; 39:6) has not been identified with certainty. **Madai** stands for the Medes (cf. 2 Kings 17:6; 18:11; Isa. 13:17; 21:2; Jer. 25:25; 51:11, 28; Esth. 1:3, 14, 18, 19; 10:2; Dan. 8:20; 9:1; 11:1). **Javan** is a common OT term for the Ionians (Greeks who settled in Asia Minor; Isa. 66:19; Ezek. 27:13; Joel 3:6 [Hebrew 4:6]; Zech. 9:13; Dan. 8:21; 10:20; 11:2). **Tubal** and **Meshech** (cf. Isa. 66:19; 27:13; 32:26; 38:2, 3; 39:1; Ps. 120:5) are peoples who lived southeast of the Black Sea in eastern Anatolia. **Tiras,** which is mentioned only here in the OT, is generally understood to represent the Etruscans of Italy.

[3] **Ashkenaz** (cf. Jer. 51:27) apparently refers to the Scythians, a marauding people who swept into the Palestinian region in the latter half of the seventh century B.C. The meanings of **Riphath** ("Diphath" in 1 Chron. 1:6) and **Togarmah** are unknown, although **Togarmah** (cf. Ezek. 27:14; 38:6) may indicate inhabitants of a place called Tegarama in Akkadian, located near Carchemish.

[4] **Elishah** (cf. Ezek. 27:7) is apparently the Alashiya of the Tell el-Amarna Tablets, and so the island of Cyprus. **Tarshish** (cf. Ps. 72:10; Isa. 23:1, 6, 10; 66:19; Jer. 10:9; Ezek. 27:12; Jon. 1:3; 4:2) is probably the same as the Greek Tartessos in southern Spain, which was a Phoenician mining and trading center in ancient times. **Kittim** (cf. Num. 24:24; Isa. 23:1, 12; Jer. 2:10; Ezek. 27:6; Dan. 11:30) is identical with the Greek Kition, which is the modern city of Larnaka on the island of Cyprus. It seems

likely that the original spelling of the last name in this verse was "Rodanim" (so the NEB) rather than **Dodanim** (KJV, ASV, RSV, following the MT), because the letters *daleth* (d) and *resh* (r) are very similar in the Hebrew square script. (The Samaritan Pentateuch, the LXX, and the parallel passage in 1 Chronicles 1:7 all read Rodanim.)

[5] The allusion to the various **languages** spoken by the peoples listed in verses 2-4 indicates that the writer is describing movements that occurred *after* the incident pertaining to the city and tower of Babel in 11:1-9, although it is recorded *before* that event. This further indicates that the historical books of the OT do not necessarily present events in chronological order.

The Descendants of Ham (10:6-20)

The author lists four groups that descended from Ham, the third of which (Put) is not traced further. However, the first (Cush) gives rise to five groups, and one of them (Raamah), in turn, to two; the second (Egypt) produces seven groups; and the fourth (Canaan), eleven.

[6] **Cush** (cf. Isa. 18:1; Jer. 13:23; Ezek. 29:10; Zeph. 3:10) here possibly refers to the Kassite rulers of Babylon (as vss. 8-12 would seem to suggest) rather than to Ethiopia. "Mizraim" (KJV, ASV, NEB) is the common word for **Egypt** (RSV) in the OT. **Put** (cf. Jer. 46:9; Ezek. 27:10; 30:5; 38:5; Nah. 3:9) is either Punt (the entire African coast of the Red Sea) or Libya. **Canaan** has reference to the pre-Israelite inhabitants of Palestine.

[7] **Seba** (cf. Ps. 72:10; Isa. 43:3; 45:14), **Havilah, Sabtah, Raamah** (cf. Ezek. 27:22), and **Sabteca** are unknown, but their associations in the present context indicate that they are to be located in or near North Africa and Arabia. **Sheba** (cf. 1 Kings 10:1, 4, 10, 13; Job 6:19; Ps. 72:10, 15; Isa. 60:6; Jer. 6:20; Ezek. 27:22; 38:13; Joel 3:8 [Hebrew 4:8]) stands for the Sabeans, who settled south of Babylon in Arabia on the western side of the Persian Gulf, and **Dedan** (cf. Isa. 21:13; Jer. 25:23; 49:8; Ezek. 25:13; 27:15 [MT], 20; 38:13) represents the Dedanites, who lived in the same general region.

[8] Nimrod (cf. Mic. 5:6 [Hebrew 5]) has been variously identified with the Babylonian god Marduk, Gilgamesh, and one of the early Babylonian kings. However, the Bible does not give enough information to help one reach a definite conclusion.

[9] Assyrian and Babylonian monuments often depict some king as killing a lion or some other wild beast. Thus it was characteristic of ancient Mesopotamian kings to boast of their ability in the chase. That Nimrod was a mighty hunter **before the Lord** would seem to suggest that his success in the chase was due to abilities that Yahweh had given him and to Yahweh's help. Even in such mundane matters as hunting, the Bible declares that a man's success depends on the Lord.

[10] Nimrod's principal cities were **Babel** (i.e., Babylon, which is located on the west bank of the Euphrates about fifty miles south of Bagdad), **Erech** (i.e., Uruk or Warka, about 100 miles southeast of Babylon), and **Accad** (whose identification is uncertain, but is frequently equated with Agade, perhaps a few miles north of Babylon).

The translation of the next term is debated. Some follow the MT *kalneh* and read "Calneh" (so the KJV and ASV), which a few identify with the city of Nippur. Others, however, change the vowel points to give *kullanah* (the consonants remaining the same), **all of them** (so the RSV and NEB, as in 42:36). **Shinar** (cf. 11:2; 14:1, 9; Josh. 7:21; Isa. 11:11; Zech. 5:11; Dan. 1:2) is the biblical word for Sumer, that is, the land of Babylon.

[11] The first phrase of this verse does not mean "Out of that land went forth Asshur" (KJV), but **From that land he** [i.e., Nimrod] **went into Assyria** (RSV, ASV, NEB). Archeological discoveries bear out the fact that Assyria owed a great debt to Sumer (Babylonia) for her development. The ruins of **Nineveh**, the most important city of Assyria, lie on the east side of the Tigris River across from Mosul. If **Rehoboth-Ir** is a place name, its location is unknown. However, some scholars think it should be translated "broad places of a city," indicating that Nineveh was a city with broad streets.

[12] This verse shows that **Resen** is located between Nineveh and Calah, but its exact location is unknown. **Calah** is the modern Nimrud, located twenty miles south of Nineveh at the confluence of the Tigris and Upper Zab. **The great city** intended in the last line is enigmatic. Some scholars think it is Nineveh, others that it is Calah, and still others that it is Resen, Nineveh, and Calah viewed as a unit. There is not enough evidence to reach a decision on this point.

[13] The **Ludim** (cf. Isa. 66:19; Jer. 46:9; Ezek. 27:10; 30:5), **Anamin,** and **Naphtuhim** are unknown, while the **Lehabim** may be the Libyans, and thus identical with the Lubim (2 Chron. 12:3; 16:8; Dan. 11:43; Nah. 3:9).

[14] The **Pathrusim** (cf. Isa. 11:11; Jer. 44:1, 15; Ezek. 29:14; 30:14) are the inhabitants of Pathros, that is, southern or Upper Egypt. The **Casluhim** are unknown. The **Caphtorim** are the inhabitants of Caphtor, but scholarly opinion on the location of Caphtor varies widely, including a region in Egypt, the lands of the eastern Mediterranean, the territories of southwest Asia Minor, Phoenicia, Cyprus, Cilicia, and Crete. Since Jeremiah 47:4 and Amos 9:7 (cf. Deut. 2:23) state that the **Philistines** came from Caphtor, many exegetes think it best to place **and Caphtorim** immediately before the author's explanatory statement to his audience, **whence came the Philistines** (cf. the NEB), rather than in its present position in the MT (which is followed in the RSV, KJV, and ASV).

[15] **Sidon** represents the Sidonians of Phoenicia (cf. Judg. 3:3; 18:7; 1 Kings 5:6 [Hebrew 20]; 16:31). **Heth** is variously interpreted as the Hittites and the Hurrians.

[16] The **Jebusites** were pre-Israelite Hurrian inhabitants of Jerusalem (cf. Josh. 15:8, 63; 18:28; Judg. 19:10; 2 Sam. 5:6, 8). The **Amorites** were a major group of pre-Israelite inhabitants of Canaan (cf. Num. 13:29; 21:13, 31; Deut. 1:7; Josh. 24:8; Judg. 1:34), who had come into Canaan from northern Mesopotamia. The **Girgashites** (cf. Gen. 15:21; Deut. 7:1; Josh. 3:10; 24:11; Neh. 9:8) have not certainly been identified.

[17] The **Hivites** lived in central Palestine at Gibeon

(Josh. 9:7), Shechem (Gen. 34:2), and the surrounding region. The **Arkites** were inhabitants of the city of Arka, the modern Tell ʿArka, located about twelve miles northeast of Tripolis near the Mediterranean coast in Syria. The **Sinites** lived at the city of Sianu, but the location of this city is not certainly known.

[18] The **Arvadites** were inhabitants of the city of Arvad (cf. Ezek. 27:8, 11), located on an island just off the northern coast of Phoenicia, thirty-five miles north of Tripolis. The **Zemarites** lived at Zemar in northern Phoenicia, and the **Hamathites** were inhabitants of Hamath (cf. Num. 34:8; 2 Kings 14:25; Amos 6:2, 14), a powerful city and territory in Syria. From these areas, **the Canaanites spread** into the geographical region defined in verse 19.

[19] The author describes the territory of the Canaanites by delineating imaginary lines from **Sidon** in the northwest down along the Mediterranean coastline to **Gaza** in the southwest near **Gerar,** then across eastward to the cities of the Valley of Siddim or Salt Sea, that is, **Sodom, Gomorrah, Admah,** and **Zeboiim** (cf. Gen. 14:2-3, 8, 10, 17, 21; 19:1, 24, 28-29; Deut. 29:23 [Hebrew 22]; Isa. 1:9-10; 3:9; 13:19; Hos. 11:8; Amos 4:11), then apparently northward to **Lasha,** which cannot be certainly identified but may be the same as Leshem (cf. Josh. 19:47) or Laish (cf. Judg. 18:27-29), which the Danites captured toward the end of the period of the Judges and renamed Dan.

The Descendants of Shem (10: 21-31)

In line with his religious emphasis, the author lists four groups and one individual who descended from Shem, the fifth of whom (Aram) he further divides into four groups. He traces the individual (Arpachshad) through four generations (cf. 11:10-17) with a special interest in the descendants of Eber through Peleg and Joktan. Although **Shem** was the oldest son of Noah (cf. 5:32; 6:10; 9:18; 10:1), the author leaves his descendants till last because his religious concern lies first with the descendants of Shem, through whom Abram is to come (11:10-27). Thus, he explains to his readers that Shem was **the elder brother of Japheth** (vs. 21, RSV, ASV, NEB; the translation "the brother of Japheth the elder" [KJV] is certainly incorrect). Of Shem's descendants, the author's main interest here is in **Eber,** from whom come the "Hebrews." So he mentions **Eber** at the beginning of the section on Shem (vs. 21), in spite of the fact that he is the great-grandson of Shem (see vss. 22-24).

[22] **Elam** (cf. Gen. 14:1, 9; Isa. 11:11; 21:2; 22:6; Jer. 25:25; 49:34-39; Ezek. 32:24; Dan. 8:2) has reference to the Elamites who lived in the large territory east of Assyria and Babylon; **Asshur,** to the Assyrians; **Lud,** to the Lydians of Asia Minor or to some unknown people in the general Mesopotamian region; and Aram, to the Arameans, who settled over a wide territory, the most notable area being Syria.

[23] First Chronicles 1:17 omits the words **the sons of Aram,** listing the four following names of this verse as sons of Shem. This further indicates that "sons" can mean "grandsons" or "descendants" in the Bible. (This must be determined in each case from the context.) Unfortunately, **Uz, Hul, Gether,** and **Mash** (or "Meshech," 1 Chron. 1:17) have not been identified.

[25] This verse contains a Hebrew wordplay on *pelegh,* **Peleg,** and *niphleghah,* **was divided.** This line may mean that it was during the days of Peleg that the scattering of man over all the face of the earth as a divine punishment occurred (cf. 11:8-9). However, this interpretation is not absolutely certain.

[26] The identities of **Almodad** and **Jerah** are unknown. **Sheleph** is a Yemenite tribe or district, and **Hazarmaveth** is the modern Ḥaḍramaut in southern Arabia east of Yemen.

[27] The identities of **Hadoram, Uzal** (cf. Ezek. 27:19), and **Diklah** are not certainly known.

[28] **Obal** (or "Ebal," 1 Chron. 1:22) and **Abimael** have not yet been identified. **Sheba** (cf. vs. 7) apparently refers to the Sabeans, who lived south of Babylon in northern Arabia.

[29] Although **Ophir** occurs frequently in the OT (cf. 1 Kings 9:28; 10:11 [twice]; 22:48 [Hebrew 49];

1 Chron. 29:4; Job. 22:24; 28:16; Ps. 45:9 [Hebrew 10]; Isa. 13:12), the place where the Ophirites lived is much debated. The different contexts involved here would seem to indicate that it was located on the east coast of Arabia. **Havilah** and **Jobab** have not been identified.

[30] Undoubtedly the region defined by the borders described in this verse was well known to the author of Genesis and his readers, but modern scholarship has not been able to identify **Mesha** or **Sephar** with any certainty.

SIN AND PUNISHMENT, GRACE AND RENEWAL (IV): THE TOWER OF BABEL (11:1-26)

The flood deterred man's sinful deterioration only temporarily. Now, for the fourth time in the early chapters of Genesis, the same pattern appears: (a) the people living in the land of Shinar (Babylon) seek to become famous by building a magnificent city and tower (vss. 1-4); (b) God punishes them by scattering them abroad and causing them to speak in different languages (vss. 5-9); (c) God creates a new possibility for a bright future for sinful man by raising up Abram through Shem (vss. 10-26). Richardson comments:

> The story of the Gift of Tongues at Pentecost is nothing other than the Babel story in reverse. When men in their pride boast of their own achievements, there results nothing but division, confusion and incomprehensibility; but when the wonderful works of God are proclaimed, then every man may hear the apostolic Gospel in his own tongue.
>
> *Genesis*, p. 126

Men Seek Their Own Praise (11:1-4)

After the flood, men are able to live in harmony for a while. In time, however, they migrate from the east and settle in the plain in the land of Shinar. Here their ambitions consume them, as is indicated by the ascending suggestions they make to each other in hortatory statements beginning with "Let us": Let us make bricks and burn them thoroughly (vs. 3); Let us build ourselves a city (vs. 4); Let us make a name for ourselves (vs. 4).

[2] The expression *miqqedhem* has been variously rendered as "east[ward]" (ASV), "in the east" (NEB), and "from the east" (KJV, RSV). As the preceding verb *nasa'*, **migrate** (RSV), "journey" (KJV, ASV, NEB), means literally "to pluck up (tent pegs)" (cf. Isa. 33:20), that is, "to break up camp, to start on a journey" (cf. Gen. 33:12; 35:5, 16, 21; 37:17), it is most natural that it be followed by a reference to the point of departure rather than by a reference to the destination; so, the best translation seems to be **from the east** (*miqqedhem* has this same meaning in Isa. 2:6; 9:12 [Hebrew 11]). **Shinar** is another name for Babylonia (cf. the note on 10:10).

[3] Building stones are very scarce in the Tigris-Euphrates Valley, but **bitumen** is plentiful. Accordingly, it is customary here to build great edifices out of burned clay bricks and to cement them together with bitumen. In Hebrew there is a wordplay on *lebhenah*, **brick,** and *'ebhen*, **stone;** and also on *chemar*, **bitumen,** and *chomer*, **mortar.**

[4] The **tower with its top in the heavens** is a good description of a Babylonian ziggurat, which is a large tower shaped like a pyramid, usually 70 to 160 feet high, often made in seven terraces, centered in the temple area, with a shrine on top. Scholars have variously identified the tower in Genesis 11:4 with Etemenanki, the ziggurat of Esagila, the temple of Marduk in Babylon; Euriminanki, the ziggurat of Ezida; the temple of Nebo at Borsippa; and the ziggurat of the moon-god Sin at Ur; but such conjectures are inconclusive.

Certainly it is not sinful in and of itself to build a city and a tower. The real sin is the self-centered attitude of the heart which often motivates such activity: **Let us make a name for ourselves.** Many worldly-minded individuals have been driven to long and hard work and to impressive achievements by the desire to be famous. (Second Sam. 8:13, Jer. 32:20, and Neh. 9:10 show that this expression means to "become famous.") However,

> with only this one purpose and this one ambition we can
> never succeed. We can never become great just by work-
> ing to be great, for this is a selfish end, and no one can
> become great by being selfish. No one ever deserved to be
> called great merely because of what he did for himself.
>
> J. Morgenstern, *The Book of Genesis,* p. 89

Men's desire to make a name for themselves stands in bold antithesis to God's promise to make Abram's name great (12:2).

God Punishes the Proud (11:5-9)

Seeing that men are gaining more power and accomplishing more feats than their human frailties can endure and than is in their best interest, God intervenes, scatters men abroad, and makes them speak in different languages so that it will be difficult for them to understand one another. The name of the place where men tried to build the city and tower in the plain of Shinar is called Babel (Heb. *babhel*), because there the Lord "confused" (Heb. *balal*) the language of all the earth. Again the writer employs a Hebrew wordplay and has no intention of giving a scientific, etymological explanation for the origin of the name Babel.

[5] The statement that the Lord **came down** to the city and tower (cf. also vs. 7) is anthropomorphic and thus is not to be taken to mean that God is limited by space (which would contradict the biblical emphasis on his omnipresence, cf. Ps. 139:7-12; Jer. 23:24), or that he is unaware of man's activities (which would contradict the biblical affirmation that he knows everything, cf. Ps. 139:1-6; Prov. 15:3; Heb. 4:13). Rather, apparently this language is carefully selected to emphasize how small and insignificant was this undertaking, which loomed so gigantic in the eyes of men (cf. Isa. 40:15, 17, 22-24).

[6] Here, God is not acting out of the fear of man's power or wisdom, nor does he fear man as a formidable rival. But, like a loving father, he is concerned for their

welfare and is determined not to allow them to follow their extravagant ambitions so far that they will destroy themselves. (The thought is the same as that found in 3:22-23.)

[7] Men's resolutions ("come, let us," vss. 3, 4) are nullified and terminated by God's resolutions ("Come, let us," vs. 7). "He who sits in the heavens laughs" (Ps. 2:4) at man's foolproof schemes.

> Many are the plans in the mind of a man,
>> but it is the purpose of the Lord that will be established.
>>> Proverbs 19:21

[8] Without divine support and help, no human endeavor can really be successful.

> Unless the Lord builds the house,
>> those who build it labor in vain.
> Unless the Lord watches over the city,
>> the watchman stays awake in vain.
>>> Psalm 127:1

> Commit your work to the Lord,
>> and your plans will be established.
>>> Proverbs 16:3

Abram and New Hope (11:10-26)

Genesis 11:10-26 briefly sketches the genealogy from Noah's son Shem to Abram (cf. 1 Chron. 1:24-27). Even a cursory reading of this paragraph reveals the rigid, stereotyped, repetitious manner in which each succeeding individual is described. It is likely that the writer has omitted a number of people in the family tree, as is frequently the case in genealogical lists in the Bible. (See the lists in 1 Chron. 1–9 and Matt. 1:1-17; the genealogical information in ch. 10, which covers roughly the same time span; the Excursus, "The Age of the Earth and Man," p. 92, above, and the introductory paragraphs to Gen. 5, p. 158, above.) The MT, Samaritan Pentateuch, and LXX differ greatly on the ages of the individuals listed here at the birth of their firstborn, and on the number of years they lived after this. These will be noted at the appropriate places in the notes that follow. (Consult the charts in Bennett, *Genesis*, p. 171; and Skinner, *Genesis*, p. 233.) It is probably no accident that, just as the genealogical list in chapter 5 contained ten persons and ended with the three sons of Noah (Shem, Ham, and Japheth–5:32), so the present list contains ten persons and ends with the three sons of Terah (Abram, Nahor, and Haran–11:26).

[10] For the fifth time in the book of Genesis, the author begins a section with the words **These are the descendants of** (cf. 2:4; 5:1; 6:9; 10:1). That Shem became the father of Arpachshad **two years after the flood** when he was **a hundred years old** does not necessarily contradict 5:32 and 7:6, which make him 100 years old when the flood came. On the one hand, 5:32 may mean that Noah became the father of Shem, Ham, and Japheth **after** he was 500 years of age (so the RSV), for if one takes the MT of that verse literally ("and Noah was five hundred years old, and Noah begat Shem, Ham, and Japheth" [so the KJV, ASV, and NEB]), it would mean that the three sons of Noah were triplets, which is certainly not the case. On the other hand, the **hundred years** of 11:10 could be a round number.

[12-13] The Samaritan Pentateuch says **Arpachshad** was 135 years old when **Shelah** was born and that he lived 303 years after Shelah's birth; the LXX says he begat Cainan when he was 130 and that he lived 330 years after Cainan's birth. Then it states that Cainan was 130 when Shelah was born to him and that he lived 330 years after Shelah's birth.

[14-15] The Samaritan Pentateuch and the LXX say that **Shelah** was 130 when **Eber** was born; after this, the former states that he lived an additional 303 years, while the latter says it was 330 years.

[16-17] The Samaritan Pentateuch and the LXX agree that **Eber** was 134 when **Peleg** was born; but the former says that he lived 270 years after this, while the latter says it was 370 years.

[18-19] The Samaritan Pentateuch and the LXX state that **Peleg** was 130 when **Reu** was born; the LXX agrees with the MT that he lived 209 years after this, whereas the

Samaritan Pentateuch says it was 109 years.

[20-21] The Samaritan Pentateuch and the LXX concur that **Reu** was 132 when **Serug** was born; the LXX agrees with the MT that he lived 207 years after this, while the Samaritan Pentateuch reads 107 years.

[22-23] The Samaritan Pentateuch and the LXX both state that **Serug** was 130 when **Nahor** was born; the LXX agrees with the MT that he lived 200 years after this, whereas the Samaritan Pentateuch says it was 100.

[24-25] The Samaritan Pentateuch and the LXX agree that **Nahor** was seventy-nine when **Terah** was born; the former says he lived sixty-nine years after this, and the latter states that it was 129 years.

[26] The MT, Samaritan Pentateuch, and the LXX agree that **Terah** was seventy when **Abram** was born (assuming that Abram was the oldest son of Terah and that **Nahor** and **Haran** were born later); however, while the LXX agrees with the MT that Terah lived 135 years after this, the Samaritan Pentateuch states that it was seventy-five years (vs. 32). In Hebrew, **Haran** (*haran*) the man (vss. 26, 27 [twice], 28, 29, 31) is spelled differently from **Haran** (*charan*) the city (vss. 31, 32), and the two are not to be confused, although there may be an intentional wordplay on these words in the MT.

IV

The Life of Abraham
(11:27–25:18)

The phrase "these are the descendants of" (vs. 27) marks the beginning of a new section in the book of Genesis (cf. 2:4; 5:1; 6:9; 10:1; 11:10). Whereas the former chapters are concerned with four great events in the early history of mankind, illustrating man's continual persistence in sin and God's determination to redeem him through didactic punishment and renewed opportunity, the rest of the book of Genesis describes the early stages in a series of events that finally bear fruit in the emergence of a chosen people (Israel), whose divine purpose on earth was intended to be the missionization and conversion of all the nations of the world to the one true and living God (cf. 12:3; 18:18; 22:18; 28:14; Exod. 19:5-6; Isa. 19:23-26; 41:8-10; 42:18-20; 43:8-10; Jer. 1:5, 10; Pss. 100; 105:1-2; 117; the books of Ruth and Jonah; etc.).

One biblical word that is used frequently to describe Abraham is "father." Emphasis is placed on his role as "father" of his own household (18:19), of Israel (Luke 16:24; John 8:39, 56), and of all nations (spiritually) (Gen. 17:4-5; Rom. 4:9-12). Yet Abraham was human and thus had many faults. Sometimes he manifested great faith in God, but sometimes he was overcome by fear and demonstrated a lack of faith. The section dealing with Abraham presents an interesting and challenging mixture of the patriarch's faith and unbelief.

FROM UR TO HARAN:
ABRAM'S FAITH WAVERS (11:27-32)

Some of the details of Abram's life at Ur and Haran must be supplied from passages outside the book of Genesis. Joshua 24:2 states that when Terah, Abraham, and Nahor lived "beyond the Euphrates" (evidently meaning in Ur of the Chaldees), they served other gods. Thus, one hindrance to Abram's faith in the one true and living God was that he had been raised to believe in and worship many gods. A second situation that in time was to pose a problem was that his brother Haran died (Gen. 11:28), and he took Haran's son Lot into his household to care for him (cf. 12:4; 13:2-13). A third obstacle that was destined to become a great anxiety in Abram's life was that he married his paternal half-sister Sarai (cf. 20:12) only to discover later that she was unable to conceive and bear children (11:30). A fourth negative force was his dominating father Terah, who was actually the authoritative head of Abram's family long after Abram married—in fact, until Terah died (11:32–12:3; Acts 7:4). A fifth hindrance was the feeling of security that comes from staying in familiar places among familiar people. God charged Abram in Ur of the Chaldees to depart from his land and kindred and to go into a land that he would show him (the land of Canaan; Acts 7:2-3), but Abram did not leave his kindred. He allowed Terah to continue to direct his life. "Terah took Abram" and the rest of his household to Haran, and "they settled there" (Gen. 11:31). The culture, environment, customs, and beliefs at Haran were strikingly similar to those at Ur.

It is only when Terah died that God called Abram a second time (this time at Haran) to go into the land of Canaan (11:32–12:3; Acts 7:4), and it was only then that Abram launched out by faith and did what God commanded him (Gen. 12:4). Hebrews 11:8 extols Abram's faith manifested at Haran; it does not have in mind the journey guided and controlled by Terah from Ur to Haran. Evidently Abram experienced great struggles with his faith as he abandoned his former manner of life and committed himself more and more into the care and keeping of God. In this process sometimes he failed to believe, as in the present instance when he capitulates to his father's desire and settles in Haran far short of the destination which God intended for him in the land of Canaan.

[27] This verse obviously covers a great number of years in a few words. The writer does not say how many years transpired between the births of Terah's three sons, nor how old Haran was when Lot was born.

[28] **Ur of the Chaldeans** (cf. vs. 31; 15:7; Neh. 9:7) is the southern Babylonian city of Uru, whose remains were found several decades ago in the mounds of al-Muqayyer, 125 miles from Babylon and twenty-five miles southeast of Uruk. It was a major religious center for the worship of the moon-god Sin.

[29] Abram marries his paternal half-sister **Sarai** (see 20:12), and Nahor marries his niece **Milcah** (see 22:20, 23; 24:15, 24, 47), the daughter of his brother Haran. According to the Nuzi Tablets (fifteenth century B.C.), the uncle could adopt his niece and marry her after his brother's death. If the marriage of Nahor and Milcah took place *after* the death of Haran, it may be that this custom was followed here. However, there can be no certainty on the point, because verses 28 and 29 may not be sequential.

[30] In time, Sarai's barrenness becomes a great challenge to Abram's faith, especially when God promises him that he will make of him a great nation (12:2) and that Sarai herself will give birth to a son (17:15-16).

[31] Although the book of Genesis never so states, it is clear from this verse that God had commanded Abram to go to **the land of Canaan** (as Acts 7:2-3 explicitly states), because it says that when Terah and his household left Ur, their intention was to go to Canaan. **Haran** is located on the great trade route between Nineveh to the east and Carchemish to the west. It was a notable ancient Hurrian city in the days of Abram, and (like Ur) a prominent center for the worship of the moon-god Sin. Both Ur and Haran had magnificent temples dedicated to the worship of this god. It may very well be that Terah and his household

settled there because they continued to be attracted to the worship of this god and felt at home in Haran, where the culture, life-style, and customs were very similar to those of Ur. This last chapter in the first large section of the book of Genesis (chs. 1–11) vividly depicts two instances of the futility of man's following his own desires and will: (1) The men of Shinar failed to complete the city and tower which they had begun because God confused their language (vss. 7-9); and (2) Terah's household failed to reach Canaan because they were satisfied with Haran (vs. 31).

[32] Acts 7:4 states that Abram and his household left Haran after Terah died, thus agreeing with Genesis 11:32–12:4. Genesis 11:26 is sometimes taken to mean that Terah was seventy when Abram was born. But Abram left Haran when he was seventy-five (12:4), making Terah 145; however, Genesis 11:32 says Terah died at the age of 205.

A *certain* solution to this numerical dilemma is impossible because of a lack of information. Still, two options lie open to the investigator. On the one hand, 11:26 does not necessarily mean that Terah was seventy when *Abram* was born. Abram may have been mentioned first here because of his importance in the following chapters, not because he was the oldest son of Terah. Since Haran died before Terah's household left Ur (11:28), it may be that he was the oldest. It is not inconceivable that Abram was born when Terah was 130. Noah was 500 when his oldest son was born (5:32), and Shem was 100 (11:10). Also, like Abram (16:3, 25:1), Terah undoubtedly had several wives and concubines (both Abram and Sarai were his children, but by different wives, 20:12), and thus even though he was old at 130, one of his wives or concubines may have been considerably younger. On the other hand, the Samaritan Pentateuch of 11:32 says that Terah died at the age of 145, and some scholars think this was the original text.

ABRAM AND YAHWEH (12:1-9)

Unlike the previous paragraph (11:27-32), this little section depicts a series of incidents in which Abram manifested his faith in Yahweh. It is true that apparently the death of Abram's father, Terah, was necessary before Abram was able to sever the ties with his family and begin to trust in Yahweh meaningfully (see Acts 7:4), yet this is typical of mankind. Furthermore, Abram had much in his background to overcome, for he had been raised in pagan polytheism (cf. Josh. 24:2), and his faith must have been very great for him to do the things which Yahweh required of him, as recorded in 12:1-9.

Yahweh's Call (12:1-3)

Yahweh *asks* far less of Abram than he *offers* him. Specifically, he calls on Abram to do only two things and promises him six divine blessings (three with each request—see *Chart V*).

CHART V

Yahweh's Requests of and Promises to Abram

Requests	*Promises*
1. *Leave your country, kindred, and father's house and go to the land I will show you.*	1a. *I will make you a great nation.*
	1b. *I will bless you.*
	1c. *I will make your name great.*
2. *Be a blessing.*	2a. *I will bless those who bless you.*
	2b. *I will curse those who curse you.*
	2c. *In [By] you all the families of the earth will be blessed.*

[1] Yahweh called Abram the first time in Ur of the Chaldees (Gen. 24:7; Neh. 9:7; Acts 7:2-4). But Terah, evidently as patriarch of the family, had taken charge of the situation. He took his family out of Ur, but when they came to Haran they "settled there" (Gen. 11:31), apparently for many years and thus did not fully carry out the divine charge. Now Haran had become Abram's **country**, so that later when Abram sends his servant to Haran in

search for a wife for Isaac, he charges him not to take a
wife for Isaac from the daughters of the Canaanites, but to
go to his country, and to his kindred, and to his father's
house (Gen. 24:4, 27, 38, 40, 41, 48). Thus, Yahweh again
tells Abram that he must leave his country.

God makes three requests of Abram that only faith could
motivate one to obey. First, he challenges him to sever his
ties with his country, his kindred, and his father's house.
This calls to mind Jesus' call to discipleship: "If any one
comes to me and does not hate his own father and mother
and wife and children and brothers and sisters, yes, and
even his own life, he cannot be my disciple" (Luke 14:26;
see Matt. 10:37). Second, God charges him to go to a land
that he would choose without giving any description of that
land or telling its name. Abram "went out, not knowing
where he was to go" (Heb. 11:8). Third, God admonishes
him to be a blessing to the nations about him and to the
peoples with whom he comes in contact. How difficult this
would be for a man who was accustomed to taking second
place under the patriarchal oversight of his father!

[2] God's promise that he would make of Abram **a great
nation** must have seemed most incredible to a man who
could not even have a child because his wife was barren
(11:30). It is ironic that God promises to **make** [Abram's]
name great, for this is the very thing a previous generation
had attempted to do by their own power and wisdom by
building the tower of Babel (Gen. 11:4).

The expression translated **so that you will be a blessing** in
the RSV has been interpreted in at least three ways:
(1) The Samaritan Pentateuch reads *wehayah,* "and [so
that] it [i.e., Abram's name, mentioned in the previous line]
will be a blessing." Skinner (*Genesis*, ICC, p. 244) and
others (e.g., E. A. Speiser, *Genesis*, AB, p. 86) adopt this
interpretation. This is the interpretation adopted in the
NEB: "I will . . . make your name so great that it shall be
used in blessings." (2) The RSV and many scholars take
the Hebrew expression here as a promise. If so, it can be
interpreted in different ways. If **blessing** means "prosperity," then God means that Abram will become the very

epitome of prosperity, a living example of prosperity. Or, if **blessing** means "happiness," Yahweh may be promising Abram that his good fortune will become proverbial among men, so that they will say: "So-and-so is as happy (blessed) as Abram" or "may So-and-so be as happy (blessed) as Abram" (see the similar wish that the inhabitants of Bethlehem uttered for Ruth—Ruth 4:11). (3) However, *wehyeh* is the imperative second person masculine singular (GHG, p. 168, par. 63q) and thus indicates a divine command: "Be thou a blessing" (so the ASV; the KJV "and thou shalt be a blessing" is ambiguous and can be taken as a promise or a command).

[3] The expression which the RSV translates **by you all the families of the earth shall bless themselves** is the subject of continuing scholarly debate. Two basic interpretations have emerged. On the one hand, numerous scholars understand the verb in a reflexive sense—"bless themselves" (so the RSV and NEB). Then the promise would be that "the nations of the world will point to Abraham as their ideal, either in blessing themselves or one another" (Speiser, *Genesis*, p. 86). This is based on two linguistic arguments and one critical argument. (1) While it is true that the niphal form of the verb occurs here and in 18:18 and 28:14, and that the niphal is ordinarily translated passively ("be blessed"), the hithpael form appears in the same expression in 22:18; 26:4, and the hithpael is reflexive ("bless themselves"). (2) The fundamental form of the root *b-r-k*, "to bless," is the piel, but the passive of the piel is the pual, not the niphal, suggesting that the niphal was understood in a reflexive sense. (3) Due to the influence of Wellhausen, other literary-historical scholars, and certain history-of-religion analysts, it is widely believed that Israel's interest in and concern for the nations was highly improbable before she was carried into Babylonian exile. But the same critics assign Genesis 12:1-3 to an early source (usually J—tenth century B.C.). Thus, they conclude that these verses could not manifest a universal concern and therefore translate it in a nonuniversal sense.

On the other hand, many scholars interpret this verb in a

passive sense—"be blessed" (so the KJV and the ASV). This view is also supported by two linguistic arguments and one theological argument. (1) The LXX translates this expression passively, and the NT follows this reading (Acts 3:25; Gal. 3:8). (2) The LXX renders the hithpael of Genesis 22:18 and 26:4 passively. Just as the niphal sometimes has a reflexive sense, so the hithpael sometimes has a passive sense (see GHG, p. 150, pars. 54g-h). (3) A major theological scheme in Genesis 1-11 is: (a) Man sins. (b) Yahweh punishes man for his sin. (c) Yahweh gives mankind a new lease on life by raising up one individual who was ultimately intended to bless the rest of mankind (such as Cain, Seth, and Noah). Genesis 11:1ff reflects just this scheme: (a) Man sins by building a city and tower for his own glory (11:1-4). (b) Yahweh punishes man by confounding his language and scattering him to distant places on earth (11:5-9). (c) Out of this mass of humanity, Yahweh raises up Abram to bless the rest of mankind (12:1-3). (See G. von Rad, *Genesis,* OTL, p. 156; D. Kidner, *Genesis,* p. 114; E. H. Maly, "Genesis," JBC, vol. 1, p. 18.)

The latter seems to be the preferable view. The thought is that Yahweh chose Abram and his descendants, the Israelites (see Gen. 22:18; 26:4; 28:14), to carry his saving message to all nations by teaching and example. That generally speaking the Israelites did not do this does not prove that Yahweh did not want them to do so, just as the failure of the church to carry the gospel to all nations does not show that Christ does not intend for her to do so (see Matt. 28:18-20; Acts 1:8).

Abram's Response (12:4-9)

It is noteworthy that Abram responded to Yahweh's call by doing what he had said, and not by talking about what he had said. The author of the book of Hebrews emphasizes that Abram's faith motivated him to obey God, and that this obedience required him to abandon the settled life he had come to enjoy in Haran in order to become a sojourner in a foreign land (Heb. 11:8-10).

Genesis 12:4-9 covers a great deal of time and territory

in a few brief sentences. Obviously many events transpired between Abram's departure from Haran and his arrival in the Negeb (southern Palestine), but most of these are omitted because they would not have made a significant contribution to the author's theology. The distance from Haran to the Negeb is over 450 miles. From the lay of the land, from what is known of ancient caravan routes and religious shrines, and from the biblical text, it seems clear that Abram and his companions went from Haran (Gen. 11:31) west to Carchemish or Til Barsip on the Euphrates, southwest to Aleppo, due south to Qatna (the Mari texts show that there was widespread travel and communication between Aleppo and Qatna), Damascus (where Abram acquired Eliezer, Gen. 15:2), Shechem (Gen. 12:6), the region between Bethel and Ai (Gen. 12:8), and the Negeb (Gen. 12:9). (For a detailed discussion with maps and documentation, see A. Parrot, *Abraham and His Times*, pp. 57–84.) The migration of Abram's household was one of many similar migrations of West Semites out of the Hurrian territory around Haran to the southwest. The same God who had appeared to Abram in Ur (Acts 7:2-3) and Haran (Gen. 11:31–12:3) appears to him in Shechem in central Canaan (Gen. 12:7), and Abram builds an altar to him at Shechem (Gen. 12:7) and between Bethel and Ai (Gen. 12:8). Apparently the author points this out in order to emphasize that Yahweh's activities are not restricted to a certain geographical region on earth, but as creator of heaven and earth he is active throughout his universe (see Gen. 1–2; Ps. 148:13).

The biblical text does not specify how many persons were in Abram's household (Gen. 12:5). However, Genesis 13:7-8 makes it clear that both Abram and Lot had many herdsmen (most of whom undoubtedly had families), and Genesis 14:14 states that Abram had 318 trained fighting men who had been "born in his house." Hence, it would be conservative to estimate that there were at least two thousand people in his house. (See W. H. Bennett, *Genesis*, CB, p. 175.)

[5] The Hebrew word translated **persons** in the RSV and

dependants in the NEB is *nephesh*, which literally means "soul" (so the KJV and the ASV). But many modern English readers define "soul" as the eternal part of man, which is certainly not the meaning in our text or in verse 13. "Persons," "individuals," "dependants," and the like are better renderings. This is another instance in which the literal translation is not the best translation.

[6] Shechem is the modern Nablus, located between Mount Ebal and Mount Gerizim in central Canaan. The **place at** [or of] **Shechem** means the Canaanite sanctuary at Shechem (as in the NEB). The Hebrew word *maqom*, "place," frequently has this meaning in the OT (cf. Gen. 22:4; 28:11; Exod. 3:5; Jer. 7:12). It was customary for the Israelites to take over a sanctuary that had been dedicated to a pagan god and to establish the worship of Yahweh in its stead.

Instead of **oak of Moreh** (RSV, ASV), the Aramaic Targum Onkelos (apparently the source for the reading of the KJV) reads "plain of Moreh." However, the MT and all the ancient versions have "terebinth of Moreh" (so the NEB), which is undoubtedly the correct reading. Since "Moreh" means "oracle," this was probably a terebinth tree where the Canaanites received oracles, located at the Shechem sanctuary (cf. Gen. 35:4; Deut. 11:30; Josh. 24:26; Judg. 9:37).

The last statement in verse 6, **At that time the Canaanites were in the land,** was obviously written long after the events being related here as an explanation to a later generation, for those participating in this event would have known this. As an author's later explanation, it has a function similar to John 2:21-22, namely, to explain something to the later audience in order to emphasize a religious truth. Apparently the point the author wants to stress here is that in spite of the fact that Canaanites were already in the land of Canaan when Abram's family arrived (vs. 6), Yahweh promised Abram that he would give this land to him and to his descendants (vs. 7). Many scholars understand this phrase to suggest that when the author wrote it the Canaanites, who had lived in this land, no longer lived there and thus conclude that it was written long after the conquest after the Canaanites had been driven out. However, it seems more likely that his meaning is that when Abram's family came into the region around Shechem, the Canaanites had already begun to settle there.

[7] In spite of the fact that the Canaanites had already begun to settle in Palestine, Yahweh promised Abram that he would **give this land** to his **descendants.** Thus, Israel's ultimate possession of Canaan was not a powerful human military achievement which gave the Israelites a license to boast of their own strength or wealth or righteousness, but a gift of God for which they should be ever grateful. That God is the subject of the active verb **give** presupposes that he is alive and working powerfully to carry out his will in behalf of his chosen people and mankind. The Hebrew word translated **descendants** (RSV, NEB) is *zera'*, which is a singular form meaning literally "seed" (KJV, ASV). However, like the English words "sheep" and "fish," the word "seed" in Hebrew is collective and should be translated or understood as a plural. In the present passage, it is clear that the "seed of Abram" are the Israelites. This is consistently the meaning of this expression throughout the OT.

Abram apparently built altars at Shechem (vs. 7) and between Bethel and Ai (vs. 8) in response to Yahweh's promise that he would give this land to Abram's descendants. He built these altars to Yahweh at already established Canaanite sanctuaries to symbolize Yahweh's claim on this land to give it to the Israelites.

[8] To **call on the name of** Yahweh in this context evidently suggests that Abram worshiped Yahweh rather than the gods he and his father's family had worshiped in Mesopotamia (Josh. 24:2) or the gods being worshiped by the Canaanites at these sanctuaries (cf. Gen. 4:26). This manifested Abram's trust in Yahweh and his gratitude for having been led safely thus far.

ABRAM AND THE PHARAOH (12:10–13:1)

A great deal of time probably transpired between the

events recorded in verses 1-9 and those related in verses 10ff. A famine in the Negeb forces Abram and his household to go to Egypt (vs. 10), apparently in search of food, just as Jacob and his household later go from Canaan to Egypt (Gen. 41:53ff.). This creates a new test for Abram's faith. Apparently he had heard that the Egyptian Pharaoh had killed prominent men with beautiful wives in order to take their wives into his harem. So he is confronted with the alternatives of trusting in Yahweh to protect him or of pretending that Sarai was not his wife. The faith Abram had manifested from Haran to the Negeb (vss. 4-9) would make one anticipate continued manifestations of his trust in Yahweh, but instead he becomes afraid and exhibits a lack of faith. He asks Sarai to say that she is not his wife. She consents, and the Pharaoh takes her into his harem (vs. 15) to be his wife (vs. 19). Yahweh had wanted to bless all nations through Abram (vs. 3), but when Abram sins he afflicts the Pharaoh's house with great plagues (vs. 17). The Pharaoh rebukes Abram sharply for lying about Sarai's relationship to him and sends him out of the land (vss. 18-20). He returns to the Negeb, from which he had originally entered Egypt (13:1).

In spite of Abram's unbelief, Yahweh cares for him in various ways: (1) When the famine arose in the Negeb, it is noteworthy that Egypt was nearby with an ample supply of food and with a Pharaoh and a people who were willing to accept foreigners and share their food with them. (2) God had promised Abram that he would make of him a great nation (vs. 2). Yet now, not only was his wife Sarai barren (11:30), but she had become the wife of another man (12:19). It is striking that the Pharaoh did not kill Abram when he discovered Sarai was his wife but, being a man of high moral principles, returned her to him safely and gave him safe conduct out of the land (vss. 18-20). (3) Verse 17 does not say that plagues came on Pharaoh and his house, but that Yahweh "afflicted" Pharaoh and his house with great plagues. God is actively working to carry out his purposes (he is the subject of a verb of action).

[10] The author uses the verb **went down** (Hebrew

yaradh) because Egypt is at a lower topographical elevation than Canaan.

[11] Verses 11 and 14 state that the Pharaoh took Sarai as his wife because she was very **beautiful**. It may be that he also took her to enhance his ego or his political strength because she was a relative of a wealthy and powerful nomadic sheik, but the OT text does not say this.

Genesis 17:17 indicates that Abram was ten years older than Sarai. So, if he was seventy-five when they left Haran (Gen. 12:4), she must have been sixty-five. The incident recorded in Genesis 12:10ff. must have taken place a few years after this. At sixty-five to seventy, how could it be that Sarai was "very beautiful"? Many scholars solve this problem by contending that the reference to Abram's age in Genesis 12:4 is from one source (P), while the story in Genesis 12:10ff. is from another (J). However, this does not explain why the collector of these sources or the author of the book of Genesis let this enigma stand in the text of the final form of the book. Abram was 175 when he died (Gen. 25:7) and Sarai was 127 (Gen. 23:1). Apparently men and women aged more slowly in the early part of the second millennium B.C. than in more recent times. If so, Sarai would have lived only approximately half of her life at sixty-five to seventy and thus would have had the appearance of a woman in her late thirties or early forties in modern times.

[13] Sarai was Abram's half-**sister**, as they had the same father (Terah) but different mothers (Gen. 20:12). Archeological evidence indicates that she was probably also his **sister** legally. The Nuzi Tablets from Mesopotamia (fifteenth-fourteenth centuries B.C.) show that in Hurrian society (Haran was a major Hurrian city), sometimes when a man married a woman, he adopted her as his sister in a legal transaction. In such arrangements, the man had greater authority than in a common marriage contract, and the woman enjoyed greater protection and a higher social status. (For further details, see E. A. Speiser, "The Wife-Sister Motif in the Patriarchal Narratives," *Biblical and Other Studies*, 1 [1922], pp. 15–28.)

Abram's fear is due to self-centeredness, as his statements to Sarai in verse 13 show. It is significant that he pleaded with her not to reveal to the Pharaoh that she was his wife and did not command her to do this. Like Adam and Eve (Gen. 3:1-7), both the man and the woman yield to the pressures of the fleeting moment and lie about their relationship.

[16] Instead of **he dealt well with Abram**, the KJV has "he entreated Abram well." But the text certainly does not mean that the Pharaoh pleaded with Abram or petitioned him with urgency. In an earlier stage of the English language, the word "entreat" meant "treat, deal with." Apparently the thought here is that the Pharaoh gave Abram sheep, oxen, etc. (see 20:14).

Many scholars think that the reference to **camels** in the list of possessions that Abram acquired in Egypt is an anachronism. This is because domestic camels are not mentioned or depicted in ancient Near Eastern literature and art until several centuries after Abram. The earliest extant reference to domestic camels is in an Assyrian record from the days of Tiglath-pileser I (ca. 1100 B.C.). At the same time, excavations at Mari in Mesopotamia have unearthed bones of camels in houses from the eighteenth century B.C. Absence of extrabiblical data does not necessarily prove that a biblical detail such as this is nonfactual. (For a more detailed discussion with documentation, see J. A. Thompson, "Camel," IDB, vol. 1, pp. 490–92.)

[17] The contrast between Abram's growing prosperity (vs. 16) and the **plagues** on the Egyptians in their own land (vs. 17) is strikingly similar to the contrast between the growth and prosperity of the Israelites in Egypt (Exod. 1:7, 20) and the ten plagues that God brought on the Egyptians (Exod. 7–12). The Bible does not specify the kind of plagues with which Yahweh afflicted the Pharaoh and his house. A comparison with the similar incident in chapter 20 would seem to suggest that they were a kind of disease which made it impossible for the women to conceive and bear children (Gen. 20:17-18). Furthermore, the text does not explain how the Pharaoh learned that these plagues

were an indication that Yahweh was displeased because he had taken Sarai as his wife.

[18] The question **What is this you have done to me?** is rhetorical. The Pharaoh knew what Abram had done before he asked, as his next question shows, but he asked nevertheless because he wanted Abram to see the deep implications of what he had done. It is interesting that this pagan ruler would try to help Abram, the elect of God, understand himself, his relationship to God, and his attitudes toward his fellowman better. God had asked virtually the same question of Eve (Gen. 3:13) and Cain (Gen. 4:10).

[19] Verses 18-19 suggest that the Pharaoh's moral and ethical ideals were much higher than Abram had heard or imagined. If one is chosen by God to bless mankind, he must believe that mankind is worth blessing. The assumption that pagans are guilty until proven innocent is a fundamental deterrent to establishing a divinely appointed relationship with them.

The KJV tries to avoid the idea that the Pharaoh actually married Sarai by translating: "Why saidst thou, She is my sister? So I might have taken her to me to wife." But this avoids the clear meaning of the MT, and the RSV, ASV, and NEB are correct in translating **so that I took her for my wife**. The Pharaoh is obviously morally correct in chastising Abram. Thus, Abram has nothing to say in response. A dead silence temporarily surrounds everyone present.

[20] One should not construe verse 20 to mean that the Pharaoh drove Abram out of Egypt in anger because he had lied to him. Rather, he gave Abram and his household safe escort out of the land to make sure that nothing else was done to harm them in any way, lest Yahweh afflict Egypt with new plagues.

EXCURSUS

The Three Accounts of a Patriarch's Lie about his Wife

The book of Genesis contains three accounts of a patriarch who lies about his wife: one concerning Abram in Egypt (Gen. 12:10–13:1), one pertaining to Abraham in Gerar (Gen. 20), and one about Isaac in Gerar (Gen. 26:7-11). There are obvious differences in these records, but there are also striking similarities. These similarities have led many scholars to conclude that these accounts go back to one event or tradition which was handed down in three separate sources lying behind the Pentateuch: two J sources in 12:10–13:1 and 26:7-11 and the E source in chapter 20.

But there is another way to explain this phenomenon. On the one hand, it must be admitted that "there is no impossibility in supposing that these were . . . duplicated incidents" (H. H. Rowley, *The Growth of the Old Testament* [London: Hutchinson's University Library, 1953], p. 18). In other words, if Abram lied about his wife once, he could have done so twice, and if Abram did it, his son may have imitated his father under similar circumstances. On the other hand, the similarities between these two stories may be due to the fact that the same traditionist or author used the same or similar words or phrases in relating or handing down these accounts. Presentations of events in the books of Judges and Kings provide analogies to this. (For more detailed discussion of this problem with suggestive insights regarding conservative and liberal attitudes toward it, see E. H. Maly, "Genesis 12, 10-20; 20, 1-18; 26, 7-11 and the Pentateuchal Question," CBQ 18 [1956], pp. 255–62.)

ABRAM AND LOT (13:2–14: 24)

Reasons for the Strife between Abram and Lot (13:2-7)

From the Negeb, Abram and his household return to the place between Bethel and Ai where he had built an altar to Yahweh (cf. 12:8). Here the households of Abram and Lot separate. This is because Abram (13:2) and Lot (vs. 5) are increasing in livestock, and the region is not able to provide sufficient pasture for their herds (vs. 6) or enough water for so many animals. Thus, when Lot decides what land he will choose, he selects an area that is green and "well watered everywhere" (vs. 10).

[2] Abram's wealth was a gift of God (see Gen. 24:35). He probably received **silver** and **gold** from the Pharaoh in Egypt (cf. Gen. 12:16), just as he did later from Abimelech in Gerar under similar circumstances (Gen. 20:16).

[6] There is a striking similarity between the circumstances that led to the separation of Abram and Lot and to the separation of Esau and Jacob (36:6-7). In both instances, **the land could not support both of them**. It was customary for nomads like Abram and Lot to seek for harvested fields on which to graze their flocks and herds in the summer. In doing so, they yielded to the wishes of the permanent inhabitants of the territory, which were governed by the law of the change of pasture.

[7] It was common for **strife** to arise between herdsmen over wells from which water was drawn for their livestock. Similar incidents arose between Isaac's herdsmen and the men of Gerar (Gen. 26:12-33) and between the daughters of Reuel and some shepherds in Midian (Exod. 2:16-19). With **the Canaanites and the Perizzites** nearby, it would have been very dangerous for the households of Abram and Lot to engage in an open, violent struggle. Later, Jacob feared being attacked by the Canaanites and Perizzites when Simeon and Levi killed the men of Shechem because Shechem the prince raped their sister Dinah (Gen. 34:30). In the course of the conquest of Canaan, the tribe of Judah had to defeat the Canaanites and the Perizzites at Bezek (Judg. 1:4-5). On the basis of the Hebrew root *p-r-z*, some scholars argue that "Perizzites" should be translated "hamlet-dwellers," to be distinguished from the "Canaanites" who lived in fortified cities. However, it is more likely that the Perizzites are ancient Hurrian inhabitants of Palestine prior to the Israelite conquest of the land.

Abram's Magnanimous Proposal (13:8-9)

In reality, the strife between Lot's herdsmen and Abram's

herdsmen provided a new test for Abram's faith. He had not believed when the crisis arose in Egypt (12:10-20); how would he fare in this new situation? Yahweh had told Abram that he would give the land of Canaan to his descendants (12:7); might he not lose this promised possession to Lot and his descendants (the Moabites and the Ammonites) if he did not claim it for his own now? And he had every right to do so because he was the older of the two and had cared for Lot when his father Haran died (11:27, 31; 12:4-5; 13:5). And if he made his claim, he could know what land his descendants would possess. But instead, he decided to act on the basis of faith. He gave Lot his choice of land and trusted in God that things would work out for the best according to his divine purposes.

> Opportunities to do great things come only occasionally, even to great people. But the little things which must be done, and done right, come constantly to both great and small. If a man should do a few big things well, but should fail in all the little things, we could hardly consider him truly great. Perhaps the true test of greatness is the way a man does the little things. If he finds them hard, or if they take too long, or if he hesitates too much, or does them in slip-shod manner, we may be sure that he will never be able to do great things. But if he does the little things right and promptly, without doubt and hesitation, if he shows himself the master in little things, then he may believe that he will be equal to the big things when they come....The great man must be always ready to do the right thing in the right way.
>
> J. Morgenstern, *The Book of Genesis*, p. 106

Lot's Choice (13:10-13)

Whereas Abram acted by faith, Lot acted by sight (cf. the contrast that Paul makes in 2 Cor. 4:18; 5:7). He chose the territory in the southern part of the Jordan valley just north of the Dead Sea because it looked good to him in the fleeting moment. It was like "the garden of the Lord," the garden of Eden (cf. Gen. 2:10-24), like "the land of Egypt" where Abram and his household went to get food when a great famine swept through Canaan (12:10), for it was "well watered everywhere" (13:10).

The author of Genesis describes Lot's life as a progressive entanglement in the web of sin. First, Lot "saw" the Jordan valley (13:10) and "chose" it as his home (13:11). Second, he "moved his tent as far as Sodom" (13:12), not intending to live within its borders or to partake of the sins of its inhabitants but still placing himself in dangerous proximity to them (13:13). Third, he "dwelt in Sodom" (14:12), perhaps enticed by the conveniences he could enjoy in a settled life and confident that he could resist worldly temptations. Fourth, he acknowledged the men of Sodom as his "brothers" (19:7) and offered them his two daughters to do to them as they pleased sexually (19:8). Finally, when the two angels urged him to flee from the city to escape destruction, "he lingered" (19:16). (Similar pictures of the progressive nature of sin appear in the stories of Adam and Eve in Genesis 3:1-6 and of Cain and Abel in Genesis 4:1-8.) The great beauty of the land and the great sinfulness of its inhabitants stand in sharp contrast to one another.

[10] There has been a great deal of discussion among scholars as to whether the Jordan valley (RSV) or "the plain of Jordan" (KJV, ASV, NEB) includes the Dead Sea or terminates north of it. It is now generally believed that the ancient cities of Sodom, Gomorrah, and Zoar lie beneath the waters of the Dead Sea on the eastern side of its southern portion. At one time this region was not covered with water but came to be later by certain changes in the earth's surface. This would explain how the four Mesopotamian kings could fight against the five kings of this region "in the Valley of Siddim (that is, the Salt Sea)" (Gen. 14:3). If this is the case, the Jordan valley in 13:10 encompasses the Dead Sea. (For a more detailed discussion, see J. P. Harland, "Sodom," IDB, vol. 4, pp. 395-97.) Although certain Syriac manuscripts read "Zoan" (the Egyptian city of Tanis or Avaris) instead of Zoar, it is best to read Zoar, which is often connected with Sodom and Gomorrah in the OT (cf. Gen. 14:2, 8; 19:22-24, 30).

The phrase **this was before the Lord destroyed Sodom and Gomorrah** is a chronological explanation by the author of Genesis intended for his audience. It implies that in the days of his audience the situation in this region was different and anticipates the story of the destruction of Sodom and Gomorrah in 19:24-28, although his readers would not know of this event until they got to this passage in the book, unless they had already learned of it by word of mouth or from some other written source.

[13] Like the last line of verse 10, this verse is the author's explanation to his later audience. Its purpose is to show that Lot's choice was foolish because he put a great deal of importance on temporal earthly attractions but failed to properly evaluate the dangers of a wicked environment. The Greeks had a proverb which said: "Bad company ruins good morals." This was incorporated into Menander's play *Thais,* and Paul cited it in one of his letters to the Corinthian Christians (1 Cor. 15:33). The author here gives the reason for Yahweh's destruction of Sodom, which is described in chapter 19. As that passage shows, Sodom's wickedness consisted of the worst kinds of sexual immorality, including fornication, adultery, and homosexuality. In man's eyes, these might appear to be sins against one's fellowman, but the present verse describes them as sins **against the Lord.** Since God made man in his own image (Gen. 1:26-27), when one does something to harm man he sins against his maker, whether this harm be in the form of murder (Gen. 9:6), oppression (Prov. 14:31), or sexual abuse.

Yahweh's Renewal of the Promise (13:14-18)

The author of Genesis makes a sharp contrast between the consequences of Lot's choice and the results of Abram's trust. This is quite clear from the statement, "Lot lifted up his eyes and saw" (vs. 10), and Yahweh's charge to Abram, "Lift up your eyes, and look" (vs. 14). Lot made a selfish choice of land and associates, and it led to the corruption of his descendants and the loss of good territory. Abram unselfishly accepted what was left, and

Yahweh promised to give his descendants that fruitful land (vss. 14-15, 17) and to multiply his descendants as the dust of the earth (vs. 16), which are renewals of the promises made in 12:7 and 12:2 respectively. Inspired by this new promise, Abram moves to the oaks (or terebinths) of Mamre at Hebron and lays claim to the land as Yahweh's gift by building an altar with which to worship him (vs. 18), just as he had done earlier at Shechem (12:7).

[15] The Hebrew word translated **descendants** in the RSV is *zera'*, "seed," which is singular. But this is a collective singular, referring to all the descendants of Abram, that is, the Israelites (cf. 12:7), as is quite clear from the occurrences of this same word in verse 16.

The expression **for ever** (Heb. *'adh 'olam*) does not mean (1) endless time, for this would assume that the physical universe will exist continually without end (which contradicts 2 Pet. 3:10; etc.); or (2) as long as the earth shall last, for Christianity erases the distinction between Jews and Gentiles (Gal. 3:28; Eph. 2:11-16), a distinction which physical control of the land of Canaan presupposes; but (3) a relatively long period of time in contradistinction to a relatively short period of time (cf. 1 Sam. 1:22). In light of the Christian view that all men can serve God in Christ wherever they live on earth, the claim or belief that any group of people should live "for ever" on any particular region on the globe loses all significance.

[17] After **I will give it to you**, the LXX adds "and to your descendants for ever." This may be because the eyes of the Greek translator(s) jumped back to verse 15 and copied this phrase after the statement "I will give [it] to you" (which occurs in vss. 15 and 17) or because the Greek translator(s) thought this phrase belonged here to complete the thought and because it occurred in verse 15. However, in Hebrew thought what is said about or promised to one person as the great ancestor of the group is understood to apply to the whole group, so that when God says to Abram, "*by you* all the families of the earth shall be blessed" (12:3), he means "*by you and your descendants* all the families of the earth shall be blessed" (22:18; 28:14).

[18] Like the "oak [terebinth] of Moreh" at Shechem (12:6), **the oaks** [terebinths] **of Mamre** at Hebron probably marked the site of a Canaanite sanctuary that was already in the land before Abram arrived. By building an altar to Yahweh there, Abram was laying claim to this region as Yahweh's rather than Baal's or some other god's.

Abram's Rescue of Lot from Invaders (14:1-24)

Not only did Lot's selfish choice (13:10-11) put him and his family in a sinful environment (13:13), but it also subjected him to the political situation which existed at that time in Sodom, Gomorrah, and their sister cities. These five cities in the Dead Sea region (14:2) were vassals to the Elamite king Chedorlaomer and his Mesopotamian allies for twelve years (14:4). But they decided to rebel in the thirteenth year, and thus in the fourteenth year Chedorlaomer and his allies came into Palestine to put down the rebellion and to subject this region to themselves once again (14:4-5). These foreign invaders first went south into Edom (14:6), then turned back north and fought the Amalekites and the Amorites (14:7) before they engaged in battle against Sodom and Gomorrah and their neighbors. Thus it seems quite clear that these Mesopotamian peoples had controlled a much larger area in Canaan than merely the five cities at the Dead Sea, and that the rebellion against them was much more widespread than simply among these cities. But as the biblical writer is concerned primarily with Abram and Lot, he preserves only that portion of the political and military situation that is relevant to their lives and to the religious point that he wishes to emphasize to his readers.

Some scholars have contended that Genesis 14 "is a legend pure and simple, without the slightest historical basis" (Morgenstern, *Genesis*, p. 113). However, by no means is this the common view, for there is weighty archeological and linguistic evidence indicating that the core of this chapter is very ancient and historical. (1) The author's explanations for his later audience in verses 2, 3, 7, 8, and 17 indicate that he is using a very ancient source containing place names that were no longer used or known in his day, thus necessitating a contemporary identification.

(2) The names of the four invading kings in verse 1 are clearly historical, although admittedly none of them have certainly been identified with specific ancient Mesopotamian rulers. Amraphel is not Hammurabi (who ruled Babylon 1728–1686 B.C.), as was once thought, but this name in Hebrew agrees with a number of Akkadian or Amorite name combinations. Arioch is equivalent to the Hurrian name Arriwuk, which was worn by a vassal of Zimri-lim of Mari (contemporary with Hammurabi), and which does not occur in any extant document later than about 1500 B.C. "Its appearance in the present context thus presupposes an ancient and authentic tradition. No late Hebrew writer would be likely to invent such a name and to assign it correctly to a neighbor of Babylonia" (Speiser, *Genesis*, p. 107). Chedorlaomer is the Hebrew spelling of Kudur-lagamar, a genuine Elamite proper name. Tidal is undoubtedly the same as the cuneiform Tudḥaliya, a name worn by at least five rulers of the Hittites and dating back to the period before the Hittites. A late Hebrew writer would hardly have invented this name.

(3) Archeologists have unearthed evidence that the Elamites ruled Palestine and surrounding areas near the beginning of the second millennium B.C. It is well known that vassal kings in this region often united their forces and rebelled against their overlords when seemingly advantageous circumstances arose, and that their overlords frequently brought their armies against them to put down revolts. (4) The names of the peoples and places invaded by the Mesopotamian armies, as well as the description of the route which they chose for their invasion (vss. 5-7), would hardly have been invented by a late author. It was not uncommon in ancient times for an army to bypass a city or cities, then later turn back and attack, as when Joshua and the Israelites went from Eglon to Hebron and then turned back to rout Debir (Josh. 10:36-39).

(5) Had a later writer invented this story, there is no logical reason why he would have placed the number of

Abram's trained men at 318 (vs. 14). If Gideon defeated the Midianites with 300 men (Judg. 7:7, 15-25), there is no reason why Abram could not have defeated the army of Chedorlaomer and his allies with 318 men, for the victory is Yahweh's. Furthermore, Abram had additional allies in Aner, Eshcol, and Mamre and their men (vss. 13, 24). He attacked the Mesopotamian army by night (vs. 15), when the element of surprise would have been in his favor and when his enemies could not tell how large Abram's army really was, and he may have attacked only that portion of the Mesopotamian army which was holding Lot and his relatives captive (vs. 16).

(6) Melchizedek's name for God is 'el 'elyon, "God Most High" (vss. 18-20), which is a Canaanite divine name and thus would be expected to be used by a Canaanite priest. It is significant that in his response to the king of Sodom, Abram calls God "Yahweh [RSV the Lord] God Most High" (vs. 22). This is to affirm that the "maker of heaven and earth," whom Melchizedek worships under the name El Elyon or "God Most High," is none other than Yahweh or the Lord. Abram here is doing much the same thing that Paul did in Athens when he identified the "Unknown God" whom the Athenians worshiped with the true God "who made the world and everything in it,...[the] Lord of heaven and earth" (Acts 17:23-24). This sort of response on Abram's part further supports the authentic historical ring of this chapter. In view of these considerations, it may be concluded that "the narrative itself has all the ingredients of historicity" (Speiser, *Genesis*, p. 109).

Mesopotamians capture Lot and his household (14:1-12). During at least part of the time that Lot lived in Sodom, this city and a large area around it in southern Palestine were under the control of the Elamite king Chedorlaomer and his allies for twelve years. Sodom and her allies decided to rebel in the thirteenth year of that subjugation, probably as part of a much larger united rebellion (vss. 4-7). The following year Chedorlaomer and his allies swept into Palestine to put down this rebellion and to punish the rebels (vss. 5-10). At first, they bypassed Sodom and her immediate allies and overran territories to the south (vss. 5-7). Then they turned back north, fought against and defeated Sodom and neighboring cities, and carried off survivors (including Lot and his household) and their provisions toward Mesopotamia as spoils of war (vss. 8-12).

[1] The KJV translates the Hebrew word *goyim* as a plural noun, "nations," and this word has that meaning in most OT texts. However, the context here calls for a proper name, "Goyim" (NEB) or **Goiim** (ASV, RSV), which many scholars identify with Guti or Gutium (Kurdistan), north of Babylonia.

[3] In relating historical events, it is not always best to follow a chronological sequence, which helps explain why verse 3 is in its present position in the text, although it describes the same event as that reported in verse 8. Once the author states that Sodom and her allies prepared their armies for battle (vs. 3), he must explain to his readers what caused them to do this (vss. 4-7), and then he can return to that scene (vs. 8) and continue his story (vss. 9-12). The battle between Sodom and her allies and the Mesopotamian invaders under Chedorlaomer was fought in **the Valley of Siddim,** which was later submerged under the waters of the Dead Sea in its southern extension. Today the water in this area is quite shallow. The OT often calls the Dead Sea **the Salt Sea** (Num. 34:3; Deut. 3:17; Josh. 3:16; 15:5) for obvious reasons.

[4] The situation described here and other similar OT texts suggest that Sodom and her allies **served** the Mesopotamian kings by pledging loyalty to them and by paying them annual tribute, and they **rebelled** against them by asserting their independence and by ceasing to pay them annual tribute (see 1 Kings 20:1-7; 2 Kings 18:7, 13-16; 24:1-2, 20).

[5-7] Probably following the usual route from Carchemish to Damascus, Chedorlaomer and his allies marched due south on the eastern side of the Jordan River. They overran **the Rephaim** at **Ashteroth-karnaim** (possibly Ashtaroth) in the land of Bashan east of the Sea of Galilee

(see Josh. 12:4; 13:12; cf. also Deut. 1:4; 2:11, 20; 3:11, 13; Josh. 9:10; 13:31), moved further south and subdued **the Zuzim** (perhaps the Zamzummim) at **Ham** in the territory later inhabited by the Ammonites (Deut. 2:20), continued south and smote **the Emim** at **Shaveh-kiriathaim** (possibly Kiriathaim) in the region later possessed by the Moabites and then Reubenites east of the central portion of the Dead Sea (vs. 5; see Num. 32:37; Josh. 13:19; Jer. 48:23; Ezek. 25:9), drove on south to **Mount Seir** and overran **the Horites** in the land which was later to be taken over by the Edomites (Gen. 36:20; Deut. 2:12, 22), and ultimately swept on as far south as **El-paran** (vs. 6), which many scholars regard as the ancient name for Elath and Eziongeber (see Deut. 2:8; 2 Kings 14:22; 16:6) in **the wilderness** of Paran. There may have been two reasons why the Mesopotamian invaders followed this course rather than first attacking Sodom and her surrounding cities immediately. (1) These nations that they subdued perhaps participated in a large-scale revolt against their Mesopotamian overlords. (2) They may have felt it imperative to overthrow these places first in order to keep their southern trade route open from the Red Sea to Egypt and southern Arabia.

From **El-paran** Chedorlaomer and his allies turned northwest to **Enmishpat**, which is the ancient name for **Kadesh-barnea** (see Gen. 16:14; 20:1; Num. 34:4; Deut. 1:2, 19; 2:14), located about fifty miles south of Beersheba and defeated **the Amalekites** living in this region. Then they turned northeast to **Hazazon-tamar,** the ancient name for En-gedi (2 Chron. 20:2), which is located on the western bank of the central portion of the Dead Sea, where they smote **the Amorites** that inhabited that territory (vs. 7). From here the Mesopotamian invaders attacked Sodom and her allies (vss. 8-9).

[10] Ancient Greek writers refer to **bitumen** floating on the surface of the water at the southern end of the Dead Sea, and large clumps of this material have been seen floating on the water in this area in modern times. It is impossible to tell whether the subject of the Hebrew

word translated **fell** (*yippelu*) here is the kings of Sodom
and Gomorrah (so the KJV, ASV, NEB) or some of their
soldiers (so the RSV). Verses 17, 21-22 describe a meeting
and conversation between Abram and the king of Sodom.
Thus, either the king of Sodom is not part of the subject of
the verb **fell** in verse 10, or the people of Sodom procured
another king shortly after the one mentioned in verse 10
died while fleeing from the enemy.

[12] The NEB interprets the **goods** (Heb. *rekhush*) of
Sodom, Gomorrah, and Lot in verses 11, 12, and 16 as
their "flock and herds," but the Hebrew word is apparently
more comprehensive than this in the present context
(cf. BDB, p. 940). It is noteworthy that the NEB translates
the same word by "property" in verse 21.

Lot was **the son of Abram's brother,** Haran (Gen. 11:27).
In verses 14 and 16, the KJV calls Lot Abram's "brother"
(Heb. *'ach*). But the word **brother** in Hebrew encompasses
relationships beyond that intended by the modern English
word "brother." Thus, the RSV and NEB correctly translate *'ach* by "kinsman"; or this word could conceivably be
rendered "nephew" in these verses. (For a fuller discussion, see H. Ringgren, "'ach," TDOT, vol. 1, pp. 188–93.)

Abram Rescues Lot (14:13-16). An escapee from the
Mesopotamian rout of Sodom and her allies, perhaps
knowing Abram's concern for Lot and his household,
comes to Abram and tells him Lot had been captured
(vss. 13-14). Abram gathers together his allies (vs. 13) and
his 318 trained men (vs. 14) and pursues the invaders. At
Dan (vs. 14), he attacks by night (vs. 15) the part of the
enemy army that was holding Lot's household, drives them
as far as Hobah, north of Damascus (vs. 15), and brings
Lot and his household back to Sodom (vs. 16).

[13] In other OT texts, **Hebrew** is a term that foreigners
use in speaking of Israelites (Gen. 39:14, 17; Exod. 1:16;
1 Sam. 4:6), or that Israelites use when they identify themselves to foreigners (Gen. 40:15; Exod. 1:19), or that biblical authors use when speaking of a relationship between
Israelites and foreigners (Gen. 43:32; Exod. 1:15). Repeated references to Ḥabiru or Ḥapiru in texts found at

Mari and Nuzi in Mesopotamia, at Tell el-Amarna in Egypt, at Alalakh in Syria, and at Boghazköy in Turkey indicate that this term is used sometimes of an ethnic group and sometimes of a social class encompassing many ethnic groups. As a social class, the Ḥabiru apparently are considered to be below the free citizens and above the slaves. Frequently they are mentioned as mercenaries in an army. It is not clear whether the Ḥabiru are to be identified with the OT Hebrews. Possibly the Hebrews were a part of a larger ancient Near Eastern ethnic or social group called the Ḥabiru. (For a more detailed discussion, see A. Haldar, "Habiru, Hapiru," IDB, vol. 2, p. 506.)

The KJV, ASV, RSV, and NEB all leave the impression that Mamre, Eshcol, and Aner were brothers. This could be the case. On the other hand, the same Hebrew word (*'ach*) is used to describe the relationship between Abram and Lot in verses 14 and 16, where it must mean "kinsman" or "nephew." Possibly it has the same meaning here. Verse 24 would seem to suggest that as **allies of Abram,** these three individuals and their fighting men went with Abram in pursuit of the Mesopotamian invaders and participated in Lot's rescue.

[14] The equivalent of the Hebrew word translated **his trained men** [or "servants"] in the RSV, KJV, and ASV (*chanikhayw*) appears in the Egyptian execration texts, where it means the "retainers" of a Palestinian chieftain, thus lending support to the accuracy of the NEB here. Slaves **born in** a man's house were considered part of his household (see Exod. 20:10, 17) and were regarded as more trustworthy than slaves that were bought.

The city name **Dan** would have been incomprehensible to readers living before the end of the period of the Judges, because prior to that time this town was called Leshem (Josh. 19:47) or Laish (Judg. 18:7, 14, 27, 29), and it was not until then that its name was changed to **Dan** (Judg. 18:29). Therefore, the date of the present final form of the book of Genesis cannot be earlier than that time, although the events that it relates and the oral or written sources from which it was composed are much earlier.

[15] Several things contributed to Abram's success in defeating the Mesopotamian invaders and in rescuing Lot and his household. (1) He **divided his forces** into several groups, possibly three, as this seems to have been customary (see Judg. 7:16; 1 Sam. 11:11; 13:17; Job 1:17; 1 Macc. 5:33). Undoubtedly, his men surrounded those that they planned to attack, as this was the normal procedure. (2) He attacked **by night,** which must have caused panic and confusion in the enemy camp, as this apparently took them completely by surprise. (3) He attacked that portion of the Mesopotamian army that held Lot and his household captive, and not the entire army under Chedorlaomer. (4) Yahweh was with him and gave him the victory (vss. 20, 23).

Hebrew geographical terminology is a bit strange to modern Western man. For the Israelite, the point of reference was the east, so this was "in front of" him. The west was "behind" him. So, the KJV and ASV translate *miśśem'ol* very literally "on the left hand of," while the RSV and NEB render it more correctly for modern man by the equivalent English idiom **north of. Hobah** has not yet been identified.

Abram meets the kings of Salem and Sodom (14:17-24). On his way back to his home by the oaks of Mamre at Hebron (see 13:18; 18:1), Abram passes through the "Valley of Shaveh" or the "King's Valley" (vs. 17) near Jerusalem, that is, "Salem" (vs. 18; see Ps. 76:2), where Absalom later was to set up a pillar or monument to himself (2 Sam. 18:18). Here the king of Salem (Melchizedek) and the king of Sodom (Bera?—see vs. 2) go out to meet him.

Melchizedek, in his dual role as king of Salem and priest of "God Most High" (Heb. *'el 'elyon*; vs. 18), which was a rather common combination in the ancient Near Eastern world, gives Abram bread and wine (vs. 18). He praises "God Most High" for giving Abram the victory over the Mesopotamian invaders (who, undoubtedly, had also been a threat to Jerusalem, possibly as one of the allies of Sodom and Gomorrah; vss. 19-20) and receives a tenth of all the spoil Abram had brought back (vs. 20).

By way of contrast, the king of Sodom proposes a business deal to Abram. He requests (demands?) the persons that Abram had brought back (possibly because they were the citizens of Sodom under his rule—this included Lot and his household) and suggests that Abram keep the goods (vs. 21). To a great extent, the goods would have been booty that the Mesopotamian invaders had carried off from Sodom and her allies, and so one can understand the concern of the king of Sodom and his intention of showing gratitude to Abram for defeating his enemies and rescuing his subjects. However, Abram rejects his proposal, lest the king of Sodom might claim that he had made Abram rich and lest Yahweh not get the glory for this victory (vss. 22-23). All Abram takes is what his soldiers had eaten, the share of the men that were with him, and the share of his allies, Aner, Eshcol, and Mamre (vs. 24). Morgenstern comments that Abram

> had done the right and fought for the weak, and had rescued Lot and the other captives, not thinking of reward, but only of duty. It was a rich reward which the king of Sodom offered, and many might think that Abraham was entitled to it, and might have taken it without compunction. But Abraham did not hesitate an instant. Of course he had no right to refuse the reward for the three allies who had accompanied him; they must speak for themselves. But for himself, he would take not so much as a shoestring. It was enough to know that he had done his duty, and had made people happy....One can serve God only by serving fellowmen loyally and usefully, entirely forgetful of self, and without thought of reward for the performance of duty.
>
> *Genesis,* pp. 109–10

[17] If verse 10 means that Bera, king of Sodom (vs. 2), fell into a bitumen pit and died while fleeing from the invading army (KJV, ASV, NEB), verse 17 would indicate that the people of Sodom had gotten a new king in the meantime. But if verse 10 means that Bera successfully escaped (RSV), it is he who met Abram as he returned

with the spoil from the north. The latter view seems more likely.

[18] **Melchizedek** was a pagan priest-king of the ancient Canaanite city of **Salem** (later Jerusalem) during the time of Abram. He worshiped the god El Elyon (God Most High), whom he believed to be the only God (monotheism), who made heaven and earth (vs. 19; see Ps. 124:8) and was able to defeat the enemies of the allies of Salem (vs. 20). Abram identified this God with Yahweh by expanding Melchizedek's phrase **God Most High** (vss. 19-20) to "the Lord [Yahweh] God Most High" (vs. 22; in much the same way, Paul identified the "Unknown God" of the Athenians with the one true God, who "made the world and everything in it" and was "Lord of heaven and earth" [Acts 17:23-24]). A later OT poet used Melchizedek as a model or prototype of an Israelite king who ruled in Jerusalem (Ps. 110:4), and the author of the NT book of Hebrews used him as a model or prototype of Christ (Heb. 5–7).

It is fanciful indeed to identify the **bread and wine** that Melchizedek brought to Abram with the Lord's Supper, even in a typological sense. The NT never mentions or implies such a connection. This verse probably means nothing more than that Melchizedek offered the weary Abram and his companions food as they returned from the battle with the Mesopotamian invaders. At best, it might mean that Melchizedek proposed and Abram accepted a covenant meal to indicate their common political opposition to the foreign invaders and their common religious commitment to the worship of only one God. Having come out of a polytheistic background himself (Josh. 24:2), Abram would have readily understood Melchizedek's courage in worshiping only one God in the midst of a polytheistic society in the city-states around him.

'El (**God**) is the name of a Ugaritic deity, and *'Elyon* (**Most High**) is the name of a Phoenician god. Outside Genesis 14, these two terms are combined into the name of a single deity in Psalm 78:35 and in the Aramaic inscription from Sujin. Each appears by itself or in other combinations frequently in the OT. (For more extensive discussions of

this matter, see B. W. Anderson, "God, Names of," IDB, vol. 2, p. 412; and F. M. Cross, Jr., "'el," TDOT, vol. 1, pp. 242–61.)

[19] The Hebrew word *qoneh* (RSV **maker**) comes from a root that has two meanings in the OT: (a) "to buy, purchase, acquire by purchase" (Gen. 47:20, 22; 50:13; Exod. 21:2; Isa. 1:3; etc.); and (b) "to create, make, produce" (Deut. 32:6; Ps. 139:13; Prov. 8:22). The latter is clearly the meaning in Gen. 14:19, 22, and thus **maker** (RSV) and "creator" (NEB) are much better renderings than "possessor" (KJV, ASV). (See BDB, pp. 888–89.)

[20] The text here and in Hebrews 7:4, 6 does not make it clear why Abram gave Melchizedek **a tenth of everything,** that is, apparently of the booty that he had brought back from his victory over that part of Chedorlaomer's army that held Lot and his household captive. It certainly suggests that Abram is acknowledging that, at least from a human point of view, Melchizedek is his superior—possibly because Melchizedek was king of Salem (Jerusalem) and had control over Hebron where Abram was living at the time. Also, it may be Abram's way of identifying his monotheistic commitment with that of Melchizedek and of proclaiming that if **God Most High** is identified with "the Lord" (Yahweh, vs. 22), it is right to pay tithes to him through his priest, thereby glorying the Lord for the victory that he had given his people north of Dan.

[22] The Hebrew phrase which the RSV translates **I have sworn** (*harimothi yadhi*) means literally "I have lifted up my hand" (so the KJV, ASV, and NEB). It was customary among the ancient Israelites, when taking an oath, to lift up the hand as a sign that they were sincere and could be trusted to carry out what they promised (see Exod. 6:8; Num. 14:30; Deut. 32:40; Ezek. 20:23 [all of which use this expression of divine oaths]; Dan. 12:7 [referring to an oath taken by the man clothed in linen speaking to Daniel]).

[23] Although Abram accepted wealth from Abimelech the king of Gerar (Gen. 20:14-16) and possibly also from the Egyptian Pharaoh (Gen. 12:16; 13:2), he refused to accept what the king of Sodom offered him. This is appar-

ently because the psychology of the situations was different. Presumably Abimelech and the Pharaoh acknowledged that man's possessions and other blessings come from a higher power, but the king of Sodom viewed man as the highest power in the universe. Furthermore, the king of Sodom would never have offered Abram any of the possessions in his city had he not rescued them from invaders that carried them off as booty, and even then he did so grudgingly and with ulterior motives. Aware of his attitudes and motives, Abram declined the offer so that God might be credited with giving him his wealth.

GOD'S PROMISE OF A SON TO ABRAM AND SARAI (15:1–18:15)

God Strives to Strengthen Abram's Faith (15:1-21)

Sarai's barrenness (11:30), the constant threat of danger from the Canaanites (or Amorites) and Perizzites (12:6; 13:7), the severing of ties with Lot (13:7-13), the Mesopotamian invasion of southern Palestine (14:5-12), and a lack of any secure indication that God was going to keep the promises he had made to Abram (12:1-3), were daily reminders to the patriarch of the uncertainty of the future. That this was very unsettling to him is clear from the two questions he poses to God in chapter 15: (1) "What wilt thou give me, for I continue childless?" (vs. 2); and (2) "How am I to know that I shall possess [Canaan]?" (vs. 8). God deals with these two concerns in the present chapter.

A son of his own (15:1-6). When God calls Abram in Haran, he promises: "I will make of you a great nation" (12:2). Such a promise presupposes that Abram would have a son. But Abram is already seventy-five (12:4), Sarai is sixty-five (ten years younger than Abram, 17:17), and the years are swiftly passing. Each day, to Abram it seems less and less likely that Yahweh's promise could ever come true. Thus, when God appears to him in a vision (vs. 1) at night (see vs. 5), Abram complains because the Lord had not given him a child as he had promised (vs. 2). Yahweh assures Abram that he will indeed have a son of his own (vs. 4) and that his descendants will be numberless (vs. 5). Abram believes the Lord that he can and will do what he said, and the Lord reckons it to him as righteousness (vs. 6), that is, he approves of and accepts this trusting, inner attitude of the sinful Abram and enters into a deep, personal relationship with him, as if Abram were actually righteous. Since no man can stand before God as morally and religiously righteous (Ps. 130:3; Prov. 20:9) or save himself by his own good works (Eph. 2:8-10; Titus 3:4-7), the only basis for a right relationship (righteousness) between God and man is faith. And this righteousness or right relationship is a divine gift to man, not a goal that he earns or achieves.

[1] The Bible does not explain why God told Abram, **Fear not.** It could be that the Lord's appearance in a vision was ordinarily terrifying to man (cf. vs. 12), or that Abram was afraid of enemies or potential enemies in the world about him such as Chedorlaomer and his allies (ch. 14), or that he was afraid that he would die without having a son (as the immediate context might suggest).

Yahweh's assurance, **I am your shield,** would seem to suggest that Abram is threatened by enemies, because other texts speak of God as a shield to emphasize that he protects his people from their enemies (Deut. 33:29; Pss. 3:3; 7:10; Prov. 2:7; 30:5). On the other hand, his assurance, **your reward shall be very great,** would seem to imply doubts on Abram's part that he would have a son of his own or that he and his descendants would inherit the land of Canaan, as God had promised.

[2] The Hebrew expression *ben mesheq,* which the ASV translates "possessor" and the RSV and NEB translate **heir,** is etymologically difficult. The KJV does not follow the MT, but Theodotion, the Vulgate, and the Targums Onkelos and Jonathan in reading "steward," which is actually a conjectural rendering. However, the context and ancient Near Eastern customs make it clear that **heir** is the correct reading. Abram's response in verse 3, "a slave born in my

house will be my heir" (Heb. *yoresh,* a common OT word for heir), corresponds to the last statement in verse 2, **the heir of my house is Eliezer of Damascus.** The Nuzi Tablets (fifteenth-fourteenth centuries B.C.) show that, among the Hurrians who lived in and around Haran (from which Abram came into Canaan), if a man did not have a son of his own he could adopt a slave to be his heir (the legal term for this kind of heir was *ewuru*). If he later had a son of his own, that slave would lose his inheritance to the son (the legal term for the natural heir was *aplu;* see Parrot, *Abraham,* p. 103). It is likely that *ben mesheq* is a Hebrew idiom meaning literally "son of acquisition," which would mean "he who is to acquire, heir of" (cf. BDB, p. 606). Abram chose to use this expression here to create a word-play with *dammeśeq,* **Damascus.**

[5] The Hebrew word translated **descendants** in the RSV and NEB is *zera‘*, which is singular. The KJV and ASV render it very literally by "seed." However, the comparison with the numberless **stars** shows clearly that God has a large multitude of people in mind. *Zera‘,* though singular, is a collective and must be translated or understood in a plural sense. The "seed" of Abram are the Israelites (see the same word in vss. 16 and 18).

Abram's descendants to possess Canaan (15:7-21). On another occasion (beginning during the daytime [vss. 12, 17] and not at night [vs. 5]), God appears to Abram and promises to give his descendants the land of Canaan (vss. 7, 18). When Abram asks the Lord how he can know that they will possess it, God gives him two assurances: (1) he makes a covenant with Abram through sacrifice (vss. 7-11, 17-21); (2) he briefly reveals to Abram that his descendants will go into captivity for 400 years and only after this will take possession of the promised land (vss. 12-16). Here is an example of the biblical claim that God predicts future events accurately.

[7] Yahweh identifies himself as the God who **brought** Abram from **Ur of the Chaldeans** (see 11:31; Acts 7:2-4) to give him the land of Canaan. Neither the departure of Terah's household from Ur nor the migration of Abram's

household to Canaan was accidental. Both were the result of God's intervention and guidance.

[10] The animals were **cut in two** and then each half was laid over against the other. Jeremiah 34:18-19 (describing an event that took place during Nebuchadrezzar's siege of Jerusalem, 589–587 B.C.) alludes to the practice of cutting a calf "in two" and the participants in the covenant "passing between its parts." Apparently those who walk between the two portions of the bisected animal invoke the same fate on themselves if they are unfaithful to their covenant partners. It is noteworthy that in the account in Genesis 15 only Yahweh's "flaming torch passed between these pieces" (vs. 17), evidently signifying that he was binding himself to give the promised land to Abram's descendants (vss. 18-21) without putting Abram under any obligation.

[12] The OT frequently refers to a **deep sleep** (Heb. *tardemah*) that comes from God (Gen. 2:21; 1 Sam. 26:12; Isa. 29:10; Job 4:13; 33:15). This seems to have been a kind of God-induced trance which was imposed on a man so that the Lord could do some sort of necessary work involving him.

[13] God promises to give Abram's descendants the land of Canaan, but this does not mean they will possess it immediately, as Abram might wish. Instead, they must first become **sojourners** and slaves **in a land that is not theirs.** The Bible emphasizes that God gives different parts of the earth that he has created to different peoples. They do not take it by force, but God gives it to them. And this is true even of his own chosen people. They cannot disgorge another people from a land that God has given to that people (see Deut. 2:4-5, 9, 19; 32:8). And **in a land that is not theirs,** like Egypt, they are **sojourners** and can become **slaves.** In Egypt, the Israelites may think that God will never give them the promised land, because they will be there **four hundred years** (see Acts 7:6), which is a round number for 430 years (Exod. 12:40).

[15] God's promise that Abram would **go to his fathers in peace** does not mean that he would be buried in Ur of the Chaldees or in Haran, but simply that he would live to

be an old man, as the next line suggests. Abram lived to the **good old age** of 175 (Gen. 25:7).

[16] Some scholars find a contradiction between the "four hundred years" of verse 13 and the **fourth generation** of this verse, thinking that four generations would be about 100 years. However, the Hebrew word translated **genera- tion** (*dor*) can have a variety of meanings (see Speiser, *Genesis*, p. 113). In the days of the patriarchs, when man lived considerably longer than in more recent times, it is not inconceivable that a generation was considered to be about 100 years.

God refuses to give the land of Canaan to his chosen people until the **Amorites** (another term for Canaanites) have sinned so much that they defile the land and prove themselves no longer worthy to live upon it. Apparently this is the meaning of the phrase **for the iniquity of the Amorites is not yet complete** (or "full," KJV and ASV), which the NEB happily translates: "for the Amorites will not be ripe for punishment till then." This rationale for God's driving the pre-Israelite inhabitants of Canaan out of their land and giving it to the Israelites also occurs in Leviticus 18:24-25, Deuteronomy 9:5, and 1 Kings 14:24. In complete harmony with this, God warns the Israelites that if they sin so as to defile the land, he will cast them out and give the land to other peoples (Josh. 23:11-13).

[17] The **smoking fire pot** and the **flaming torch** evidently symbolize the presence of God, as other OT texts connect his appearance with fire and smoke (see Exod. 19:18; 24:17; 2 Sam. 22:9; Ps. 18:8).

[18] In the act of passing between the pieces of the sacri- ficial animals, God **made a covenant with Abram** to give his descendants the land of Canaan. "The sense is that Yahweh obligates himself to keep his promise of land to Abraham in a way which Abraham can accept with renewed confi- dence" (J. H. Marks, "The Book of Genesis," IOVC, p. 15).

In spite of the fact that the Israelites were not to possess this land for several centuries, God says, **To your descen- dants I give** [so the RSV and NEB translate the Heb.

nathatti; KJV and ASV read "I have given"] **this land.** The context shows that this verb is a prophetic perfect, that is, it speaks of an event in the distant future as if it had already occurred, since it would certainly occur because God had promised that it would, and he has the power and integrity to do what he promises.

The extent of the land which Yahweh promises to Abram's descendants is **from the river of Egypt** (which apparently is not the Nile, but the "Brook of Egypt" of 1 Kings 8:65 and Isa. 27:12, i.e., the "Sea of the Arabah" of 2 Kings 14:25 or the "Brook of the Arabah" of Amos 6:14, which runs into the Mediterranean Sea about fifty miles southwest of Gaza) to **the river Euphrates** northeast of Damascus. One encounters these same idealistic boundaries frequently in the OT (see Deut. 1:7; Josh. 1:4; Ps. 72:8), but it was only in the time of David(?) and Solomon that the Israelites actually controlled the full extent of this territory (1 Kings 4:21, 24; 8:65). Man often fails to accept all that God is willing to give.

[19-21] The ten groups listed in these verses indicate the variety of peoples living in Canaan when Abram sojourned there and the lack of unity existing in this region.

Sarai's Plan to Fulfill the Promise (16:1-16)

One of Sarai's servants was an Egyptian slave girl named Hagar. Sarai may have procured her while Abram and his household were in Egypt during the famine in Canaan (12:10–13:1). Abram and Sarai had now lived in Canaan ten years (16:3) since they came out of Haran (see 12:4; 16:16; 17:17); thus Sarai was seventy-five years of age (cf. 12:4 with 17:17).

By this time, Sarai must have been quite certain that she could never have a child of her own. Furthermore, she had come out of a Mesopotamian culture in Ur and Haran which had laws specifying that if a man's wife could not have a child of her own, she could commit her slave girl to her husband; he could have sexual relations with her, and any child born to that relationship would be regarded as the wife's legal child. The Code of Hammurabi, paragraph 146, states that a certain kind of priestess could marry but could not bear children. However, she could give a slave girl to her husband so he could have offspring. In such an arrangement, if the slave girl tried to establish herself on equal status with her mistress, her mistress could reduce her to slavery once again but could not sell her. This would help explain why Sarai gave Hagar to Abram (vss. 2-3) and why she "dealt harshly with her" (vs. 6) when "she looked with contempt on her mistress" (vss. 4, 5), instead of expelling her. Furthermore, Nuzi Text number 67 states that if a man and his wife have no children, the wife must give her husband a concubine. Any children born to the concubine would legally be considered the wife's children. The Code of Hammurabi, paragraph 146, and Deuteronomy 21:14 both forbid the expulsion of a slave girl under circumstances like the ones described in Genesis 16, which may explain why Sarai did not really expel Hagar but did deal harshly with her.

Because she is barren, because the laws to which she had become accustomed demand it, and because she yearns to have a son as Yahweh had promised Abram, Sarai offers her Egyptian maid Hagar to Abram that she might have children by her (vs. 2). When Hagar becomes pregnant, she treats her mistress disrespectfully (vs. 4). As Hagar now is apparently directly responsible to Abram, Sarai urges him to deal with her because of her behavior (vs. 5). Abram puts Hagar back under Sarai's jurisdiction; Sarai deals harshly with her, and she flees toward her home in Egypt (vs. 6).

As she nears the outer border of Egypt in the wilderness of Shur (vs. 7), the angel of the Lord meets her at a well and tells her to return to Abram's household and to submit herself to Sarai (vss. 8-9). He promises her that she will have a son and that her descendants will be innumerable (vss. 10-12). Hagar returns to Abram's household and gives birth to Ishmael (vss. 15-16).

Once again, Abram's faith falters. Reason tells him that Sarai cannot bear children, yet he wants Yahweh's promise of a son to come true. When his wife suggests that he go in to her slave girl, as was customary in the Hurrian society whence Abram came at Haran, Abram readily agrees. How empty and hopeless he must have felt when Hagar fled back toward Egypt! And how relieved he must have been when she returned and gave birth to a son! But Ishmael was not the promised child that God had in mind. "This chapter marks another stage in eliminating every means but miracle towards the promised birth" (Kidner, *Genesis*, p. 126). Sarai and Abram here reflect "a fainthearted faith that cannot leave things with God and believes it necessary to help things along" (von Rad, *Genesis*, p. 191). Paul compares man's attempts to save himself by his own works with the human plans of Abram, Sarai, and Hagar to produce a child for Abram, and the Christian's trust in God with the trust that the Lord desired of Abram and Sarai in his promise of a son of their own (Gal. 4:21–5:1).

[2] According to the Bible, God "opens" (Gen. 29:31; 30:22) and "closes" or "shuts" (Gen. 20:18; 1 Sam. 1:5, 6) wombs, and children are God's "gifts" to parents (Gen. 33:4-5; 48:8-9; Ps. 127:3-5). Thus, when Sarai speaks of her barrenness, it is natural for her to say, **the Lord has prevented me from bearing children.** "The OT recognizes the hand of God in *all* the events of nature and history, and does not limit the Divine activity to 'special providences' " (Bennett, *Genesis*, p. 204).

The Hebrew phrase that the RSV translates **it may be that I shall obtain children by her** is *'ulay 'ibbaneh mimmennah*, which means literally "perhaps I shall be built up from her." Here again it is clear that the literal translation is not the best translation (since it does not make sense to the modern English reader) and that one must determine the meaning of this expression from the context and from similar phrases elsewhere in the OT. The law in Deuteronomy 25:5-10 states that if brothers live together and one brother dies, the dead man's brother must marry his widow (vs. 5), bear children by her (vs. 6), and thus perpetuate his brother's name in Israel (vss. 6-7, the Levirate law). But if the living brother refuses to marry his dead brother's widow, she shall go up to him in the presence of the elders,

take his sandal off, spit in his face, and say, "So shall it be
done to the man who does not build up [*yibhneh*] his
brother's house" (vss. 8-9). Here, to "build up" one's
brother's house (vs. 9) means the same thing as to "bear" a
son or children by his brother's wife (vs. 6). Logically,
then, to "be built up" by one's handmaid means for the
handmaid to bear children to one's husband. Almost the
same Hebrew phrase as that found in Genesis 16:2 appears
in Genesis 30:3, where the barren Rachel says to Jacob
(ASV), "Here is my maid Bilhah; go in to her, that she may
bear upon my knees, and *I also will be built up from her*"
(*'ibbaneh gham 'anokhi mimmennah*; RSV "and even I
may have children through her"). Again, the context indicates that Rachel wants her maid Bilhah to bear children
by Jacob that can be legally considered her own. In view of
this, the translation of the NEB in Genesis 16:2 has captured the meaning of the original Hebrew text very well for
modern English readers: "perhaps I shall found a family
through her."

[4] The precise meaning of the statement **she** [Hagar]
looked with contempt on her mistress is not quite clear. The
general circumstance would suggest that she felt her conception elevated her to a position above Sarai, who was
apparently unable to conceive, and thus she should no
longer be her servant. It may be that she even desired to
displace Sarai as Abram's wife (cf. Prov. 30:21-23).

[5] Sarai's statements here are based on legal concepts
derived form the Hurrian background out of which
Abram's family came. The Hebrew phrase *chamasi
'aleykha*, literally "my wrong [be, is] upon you" (KJV and
ASV), is ambiguous. It could mean "the wrong that I have
done be upon you," but there is every reason to believe
that Sarai did not mean this in this context. Therefore, the
correct interpretation must be **May the wrong done to me be
on you** (RSV), or "I have been wronged and you must
answer for it" (NEB). When Sarai gave Hagar to Abram as
a wife (vs. 3), Hagar ceased to be her responsibility and
became the legal responsibility of Abram. Thus, when
Hagar looked with contempt on Sarai (vs. 4), Sarai had no

means, legal or otherwise, to deal with the problem. All she could do was to tell Abram of Hagar's behavior and to leave it up to him as to whether he thought she was telling the truth. In order to convince him of her sincerity, she declared that she was not afraid for Yahweh himself to decide the case.

[6] Abram decides to relinquish his legal control over Hagar and to return her to her former legal position under Sarai (vss. 1, 3). Sarai cannot legally expel her, but nothing in the ancient laws indicates that she could not deal **harshly with her**. It is not clear whether this means Sarai beat Hagar (cf. Exod. 21:20), or made her work load unbearable, or punished her in some other way; but any of these would have been particularly hard on a pregnant woman. Sarai's treatment became so severe that Hagar **fled from her** toward her native land of Egypt (cf. vs. 7). The tensions, harsh feelings, and general unrest reflected in this story indicate some of the deep problems faced in a polygamous marital situation, which stands in sharp contrast to God's original divine intention that each man have only one wife (Gen. 2:18-24).

[7] In this context, the expression **the angel of the Lord** (vss. 7, 9, 10, 11) is simply a term that the writer uses to speak of **the Lord** himself, as verse 13 shows. **Shur** is a wilderness located on the northeastern frontier of Egypt (cf. Gen. 20:1; 25:18; Exod. 15:22; 1 Sam. 15:7; 27:8).

[8] The angel possesses superhuman knowledge. He knows Hagar without having been introduced to her. His questions **where have you come from and where are you going** are rhetorical. They are designed to help Hagar evaluate the consequences of her decision to flee from Abram's household.

[10] The angel persuades Hagar to return to Abram's household and to submit to Sarai's harsh treatment (vs. 9) by promising, **I will greatly multiply your descendants.** Since the Lord alone has the power to carry out such a promise, the angel of the Lord here must be the Lord himself. God made a similar promise to Abram (13:16; 15:5). Here again, the Hebrew word *zera'* is a singular

collective, "seed" (KJV and ASV), which actually means **descendants** (RSV and NEB), as the context makes quite clear.

[11] The angel tells Hagar to call her son **Ishmael** (Heb. *yishma'e'l*, meaning "May God hear" or "God will hear" or "God hears"), to commemorate the fact that **the Lord has given heed to** (hearkened unto, heard; Heb. *shama' 'el*) her **affliction** (i.e., Sarai's harsh treatment of her, vs. 6). This type of wordplay is common in the OT.

[12] Unfortunately, Ishmael (and like him, his descendants, the Ishmaelites) will be antagonistic to his kinsmen, and they in turn will be antagonistic to him. Some scholars translate the Hebrew phrase *'al pene* by "to the east of" or "in the presence of" (KJV). However, the same phrase in Deuteronomy 21:16, 25:18, and the present context indicates that the meaning is that Ishmael **shall dwell over against** [i.e., in defiance of, in disregard of] **all his kinsmen** (so ASV and RSV; cf. NEB).

[13] This verse is very difficult linguistically. As the Hebrew text stands, it reads literally: "And she called the name of Yahweh who was speaking to her, 'Thou are El Roi,' for she said, 'Have I also seen hither after the one seeing me?' " The KJV and ASV basically follow this reading, but it does not make sense. El Roi apparently means "God of vision," that is, a God that had appeared (in the event recorded in vss. 7-12), a God whom Hagar had seen. If so, it seems best to follow Wellhausen's suggestion that the last line be slightly amended to read *hagham ha'elohim ra'ithi wa'echi 'achare ro'i*, **Have I really seen God and remained alive after seeing him?** (so RSV, NEB, and most scholars). The idea that a man who saw God could not survive is quite prevalent in scripture (Gen. 32:30; Exod. 19:21; 33:20; Judg. 6:22-23; 13:22-23).

[14] The "lahai" (Heb. *lachay*) in **Beer-lahai-roi** lends support to the insertion of *wa'echi*, "and remained alive," in the previous verse. Again, by a slight emendation of the text, the name of the well seems to mean "The well of living seeing [sight, vision, appearance]," that is, the well where one lives (survives, continues to live) after seeing

God. The original participants would not need to be told where **Beer-lahai-roi** was located. Clearly, then, the statement **it lies between Kadesh and Bered** is the author's explanation for his later audience. The exact locations of **Bered** and **Beer-lahai-roi** are not yet known.

[15] Although the angel told Hagar, "You [feminine singular] shall call his name Ishmael" (vs. 11), the present verse says that **Abram** named Hagar's child. It was customary for the father to name the children (Gen. 5:3; 21:3), but this was by no means always the case (Gen. 30:6, 7).

Abram's Plan to Fulfil the Promise (17:1–18:15)

When God told Abram that he would make him a great nation (12:2), Abram concluded that God would do this legally through his slave Eliezer of Damascus (15:2), but God told him that his own son would be his heir (15:4). Sarai, assuming that she could never have a child of her own, gave her maid Hagar to Abram, and she bore Ishmael to him (16:2, 11, 15-16). But now God comes to Abraham and tells him that Sarah will have a son (17:16). Assuming this was impossible, Abraham assures God that he would be quite satisfied if his promise were fulfilled through Ishmael (17:17-18). But the Lord insists that Sarah will have a son, and through him God's promises will be fulfilled (17:19; 18:9-15).

Genesis 17:1–18:15 is vividly outlined by the biblical author. In chapter 17, the first three sections begin with what God said to Abraham (vss. 1 [cf. vs. 3], 9, 15), and by Hebrew expressions which can be translated "As for me" (vs. 4 [but this could also be the case in vs. 1]), "As for you" (i.e., Abraham, vs. 9), and "As for Sarai" (vs. 15). Each of these sections introduces a new element intended to symbolize a fresh beginning for the personalities involved: in the first section God reveals himself under the new name of "God Almighty" (El Shaddai; vs. 1) and changes Abram's name to "Abraham" (vs. 5); in the second, God commands Abraham to circumcise himself and all the males in his household (vs. 10); and in the third,

God changes Sarai's name to "Sarah" (vs. 15) and declares that she will have a son. The last section of chapter 17 begins with the statement "When he [God] had finished talking with him [Abraham]" (vs. 22), which makes a natural connection with the phrase "And God [or the Lord] said to Abraham" in verses 1, 9, 15. Then 18:1-15 tells of another divine appearance to Abraham, in which God repeats his promise that Sarah will have a son.

God reaffirms his promises to Abraham (17:1-18). God reasserts three covenant promises that he had already made to Abraham: (1) Abraham will be the father of a multitude of nations (vss. 2, 4-6; cf. 13:16; 15:5); (2) Yahweh will be the God of Abraham and his descendants (vss. 7-8; cf. 15:1, 7); (3) Yahweh will give the land of Canaan to Abraham and his descendants (vs. 8; cf. 12:7; 13:14-15, 17; 15:7, 16, 18-21). That this divine revelation is viewed as a turning point in Abraham's life is symbolized by God's revealing himself under the new name El Shaddai (vs. 1) and by his changing Abram's name to Abraham (vs. 5).

[1] Possibly because of the importance of the present occasion, Yahweh reveals himself to Abram by a new name, **God Almighty** (Heb. *'el shadday,* usually transliterated in English Bibles as El Shaddai; cf. also Gen. 28:3; 35:11; 43:14; 48:3; 49:25; Exod. 6:3). There is no agreement among scholars as to the meaning of *'el shadday.* An early rabbinic view was that it means "God who is self-sufficient." Others have suggested that it means "the Exalted One," "the Destroyer," "God all-knowing," or "God of the mountain." The translation **God Almighty** follows the interpretation of the LXX.

God's command to Abram, **walk before me,** means "live in the way that I approve" or "always be conscious of my constant presence as you live out your life" (cf. Gen. 24:40; 48:15; 1 Sam. 12:2; Isa. 38:3). The command **be blameless** (RSV), or "be perfect" (KJV, ASV, NEB), calls for a quality of life evoked by the consciousness of God's presence but is not an impossible requirement of sinlessness (cf. Gen. 6:9; Deut. 18:13; Pss.

18:23, 101:2; 119:1; 1 Tim. 3:2; Titus 1:6). "It signifies complete, unqualified surrender" (von Rad, *Genesis*, p. 193).

[3] Falling on one's face was an ancient way of showing respect to one's superior and of assuming the role of servant or subject (see vs. 17).

[4] God promises Abram that he will be **the father,** not of Israel alone, but **of a multitude of nations,** a promise that is repeated to Jacob in Genesis 28:3 and 35:11, and to Joseph in Genesis 48:4. These nations are the Ishmaelites, the Edomites, and the descendants of Abram through Keturah (cf. Gen. 25:2-6).

[5] God changes **Abram's** name to **Abraham.** Such a change in name is a symbol that a new era is beginning for a person. The phrase **for I have made you the father of a multitude of nations** is not intended to be an etymological explanation of the name **Abraham,** for "father of a multitude" is *'abh hamon* in Hebrew. Instead, there is a wordplay here on *'abhraham,* "Abraham," and *'abh hamon,* "father of a multitude."

[6] God promises both Abraham (vs. 6) and Sarah (vs. 16) that **kings** will be in their descendants.

[7] The word **covenant** denotes an intimate personal relationship between God and his people (Abraham and his descendants). God promises this will be an **everlasting covenant** (cf. vs. 13). And yet, in Christ God's special relationship to the descendants of Abraham has been superseded by his special relationship to Christians (Heb. 8:1-13). The word **everlasting,** then, does not mean endless time but rather a relatively long period of time.

[8] God promises Abraham that he will give his descendants all the land of Canaan for an **everlasting possession.** Again, the word **everlasting** can hardly mean endless time because this would necessitate the idea that the earth will continue for ever, which is denied in 2 Peter 3:10-13.

Circumcision, the sign of the covenant (17:9-14). The quality of God's love for man and his willingness to make and keep promises for man's good demand a human response in kind. God summons Abraham and all his household, including those born in his house, those purchased by him (vss. 12-13), and all subsequent generations, to be circumcised as a sign of the covenant between God and Abraham (vs. 11). At first glance, it may appear that God asked Abraham for very little in requiring circumcision. But actually, this was but a "sign" that indicated Abraham's total commitment to the Lord as his master—a commitment which God also expected in all Abraham's descendants.

[10] One should be aware of the use of the singular and the plural of the second person pronoun in the Hebrew of this verse (which the KJV and ASV indicate by using the archaic form "thou" for the singular and "you" or "ye" for the plural): **This is my covenant, which you** [plural] **shall keep, between me and you** [plural] **and your** [singular] **descendants after you** [singular]: **Every male among you** [plural] **shall be circumcised.** It is quite clear that God did not design circumcision for Abraham alone but for all those in his household and for his descendants.

Circumcision was widely practiced throughout the ancient Near Eastern world at a very early time. It was practiced by the Egyptians, the Arabs, the Moabites, the Edomites, the Ammonites, and the Canaanites, but not normally by the Philistines (2 Sam. 1:20), the Hivites (Gen. 34:15), or people in Mesopotamia. The use of a "flint knife" in the operation (cf. Exod. 4:25; Josh. 5:2-3; and the pictures of circumcision on the wall of the tomb in Sakkara, Egypt, dating from the Old Kingdom) takes this practice back into the Stone Age. There is good evidence that at an early period it was performed at puberty in preparation for marriage or to initiate a boy into full manhood. Among Abraham and his descendants, it was a sign of total commitment to the Lord. A number of passages seem to suggest that circumcision of the flesh was merely an external symbol that the person's heart was circumcised (cf. Deut. 10:16; 30:6; Jer. 4:4; 9:25-26; Rom. 2:28-29; for a fuller discussion, see J. P. Hyatt, "Circumcision," IDB, vol. 1, pp. 629-31).

[11] **You** is plural throughout this verse.

[12] **You** is also plural throughout this verse except for its last appearance in **your** [singular] **offspring,** and so Abraham's offspring. The circumcision of the male child **eight days old** (Gen. 21:4; Luke 1:59; 2:21; Phil. 3:5) is connected with the purification of his mother, who remains unclean for seven days after the birth (Lev. 12:1-3).

[14] The text here does not make clear how an uncircumcised male was to be **cut off from his people,** nor what is meant by the verb **cut off** (Heb. *karath*). This same verb appears in Exodus 31:14, where it is used as the equivalent of "putting to death." If this is a proper guide, Genesis 17:14 means that the Israelite community (the descendants of Abraham) is to put to death an uncircumcised male. However, the verb **cut off** also occurs in Leviticus 17:10; 20:3, 6, where God is the subject. If we follow this lead, Genesis 17:14 means that God himself will cut off the uncircumcised male from his people.

God insists that Sarah will have a son (17:15-21). That the confrontation between God and Abraham is a turning point in the lives of Abraham and his household is further emphasized by the changing of Sarai's name to "Sarah" (vs. 15), by the announcement that she herself will have a son (vss. 16, 19, 21), and by the declaration that she will become "a mother of nations" (vs. 16). Abraham, believing it impossible for a ninety-year-old woman to have a child, urges God to fulfil his promise through Hagar's son, Ishmael (vss. 17-18). God agrees to make Ishmael "a great nation" (vs. 20) but insists that his promise of a son will be fulfilled in the birth of Isaac to Sarah (vss. 19, 21).

[15] **Sarai** and **Sarah** are simply two spellings of the same name, meaning "princess."

[16] Biblically speaking, the power to beget, conceive, and give birth to a child is a "gift of God," whether a woman is of normal child-bearing age (like Jacob's wives, Gen. 33:4-5; or Joseph's wife, Gen. 48:8-9; or Hannah, 1 Sam. 1:5-16, 11, 19-20, 26-28) or older. It is tempting to interpret these gifts as "natural" because of their constant recurrence. But when a woman is too old to have children yet conceives and gives birth to a child anyway, the evi-

dence of God's power at work in his world again confronts man. It is significant that God says to Abraham, **I will *give* you a son by her**.

The phrase **a** [the] **mother of,** which occurs in the RSV and NEB, and in italics in the KJV and ASV, is not in the Hebrew text, which says literally, "she shall be for [become] nations." Speiser translates: "she shall give rise to nations" (*Genesis,* pp. 123, 125). The meaning is clear— nations will come from Sarah. It is more difficult to give a good English rendering; and again, the literal translation is not the best translation because it does not convey a clear and smooth thought to English readers.

[17] When God told Abraham that Sarah would have a son, he **laughed** (Heb. *yitschaq*; see the note on vs. 19). Unfortunately, it is impossible for modern man to comprehend precisely what kind of laugh this was. Whether it was a smile or a loud guffaw, the context shows that it expressed Abraham's certainty that it was impossible for Sarah to have a child, that is, his lack of faith in God's power.

To be technical, this conversation between God and Abraham took place when Abraham was ninety-nine years old (see vs. 24) and Sarah was eighty-nine. Abraham's reference to himself as **a hundred years old** and to **Sarah** as **ninety** is due to his projecting himself approximately a year into the future, when the child would be born if God's statement were correct.

[19] Ordinarily (though not always) the father named the child, so God says to Abraham, **You shall call his name Isaac**. The word **Isaac** in Hebrew is *yitschaq*, which is the same Hebrew word as that translated "[he] laughed" in vs. 17. Here again we are dealing with a wordplay. The line of reasoning seems to be this: Because Abraham "laughed" when God told him that Sarah would have a son, God told Abraham to call his name "Isaac" (laugh), perhaps to emphasize that nothing is too hard for God (see 18:14; for this same wordplay on "laugh" and "Isaac," see Gen. 18:12-13; 21:3, 6).

For the fourth time in this chapter, we encounter the

word **everlasting** (vss. 7, 8, 13, 19; see also "throughout their/your generations" in vss. 7, 9, 12). Twice it is applied to God's covenant with Abraham and his descendants (vss. 7, 8), once to God's covenant with Isaac and his descendants (vs. 19), and once to the possession of the land of Canaan by Abraham and his descendants (vs. 13). **Everlasting** can hardly denote "endless time" in these verses. Instead, it must mean "a long period of time."

The reader should also note again that throughout this chapter the Hebrew word *zera'*, which the KJV and ASV translate "seed" (vss. 7 [twice], 8, 9, 10, 19), is a collective noun and thus should be understood and/or translated as a plural (e.g., **descendants**, as in the RSV and NEB).

[20] Just as there is a wordplay in Hebrew on the words "laugh" and "Isaac" in verses 17 and 19, so there is a wordplay on the words "Ishmael" (Heb. *yishma'e'l*) and "hear" (Heb. *shama'*) in verse 20. ("Ishmael" is also connected with "hearing" in Gen. 16:11; 21:17.)

Just as twelve sons and eventually twelve nations were to come forth from Isaac's son Jacob (Gen. 29:31ff.), so God promises that **twelve princes** and ultimately twelve tribes would come forth from Ishmael (cf. Gen. 25:12-18).

[21] Even though God's **covenant** with Abraham involves "a multitude of nations" (vss. 4, 5, 6), including the Ishmaelites (who practiced circumcision, the sign of the covenant, beginning with Ishmael himself, cf. vss. 23, 25-26), there is a special sense in which God can say, **I will establish my covenant with Isaac.**

Abraham and his household are circumcised (17:22-26). When the conversation between God and Abraham terminated, Abraham was circumcised along with Ishmael and all his servants, both those born in his house and those bought by him.

The sequence of events in Genesis 17 may "suggest that only after Abraham's acceptance of God's covenant, signified in his own circumcision, is he eligible to receive the promised heir" (Marks, "Book of Genesis," p. 16).

Heavenly visitors promise a son (18:1-15). This paragraph is the end of a rather long section in Genesis (beginning with 15:1), which deals with a series of divine promises that Abraham would have a son through whom a populous nation would arise—a nation that would live in the land of Canaan. At the same time, it is closely connected with 18:16–19:38. The three heavenly messengers come to Abraham's tent to announce two significant events: the birth of a son to Abraham by Sarah (vss. 1-15) and the destruction of Sodom and Gomorrah (vss. 16-21).

While the aged Abraham is resting at the door of his tent in mid-afternoon (see 2 Sam. 4:5), suddenly "three men" appear off in the distance (vs. 2). He runs to meet them and begs them to share his shelter and food (vss. 3-8). After the meal, one of the visitors ("the Lord," vs. 10) announces that Sarah will have a son. Sarah, who is listening at the tent door, "laughed to herself" (Heb. *titschaq*, vs. 12) thus providing a reason later for calling the child *yitschaq*, "Isaac" (cf. Gen. 17:17-19; 21:2-6). The Lord chides her for her unbelief (reflected in her laughing) that anything might be "too hard for" him (vs. 14).

[1] The author of the book of Genesis discloses to his readers from the very outset that one of the three heavenly visitors ("men," vs. 2) that came to Abraham's tent is **the Lord** (see also vss. 10, 13, 14, 17, 19, 20, 22, 25, 26, 27, 30, 31, 32, 33). However, Abraham does not discover this until one of the visitors tells him that he will return and Sarah will have a son (vs. 10). Abraham's address to the spokesman of the three men in verse 3 ("my lord") is a courteous address approximating the modern English word "Sir." The other two visitors are "angels" (19:1), who later go on toward Sodom while the Lord and Abraham discuss the fate of the cities of the valley (KJV "plain"). Abraham is still living **by the oaks** [terebinths] **of Mamre** at Hebron at this time (13:18).

[2] The exclamation, **behold** [Heb. *hinneh*], **three men stood in front of him,** further shows the reader that these are heavenly visitors; they appear suddenly out of nowhere. However, Abraham, who may have been dozing, and whose eyesight may have been failing, does not register anything extraordinary in their sudden appearance. The

brightness of the scorching sun may have made him think that he was unable to see their approach across the burning sand.

Abraham is an exemplary model of unselfish, enthusiastic hospitality:

> Abraham had no idea who the strangers were; nor did he ask. It was enough that they were tired and spent. But unconsciously he was entertaining God Himself. . . . True hospitality consists, not merely in giving food and lodging to friends, but in opening heart and hand to all, not asking who they are, in sharing what we have, what God has given us, with all who need, in truly loving our neighbor as ourselves.

> Morgenstern, *Genesis,* pp. 117–18

Reflecting on this story, the author of Hebrews advises Christians: "Do not neglect to show hospitality to strangers, for thereby some have entertained angels unawares" (Heb. 13:2).

When Abraham first saw the strangers, he **ran to meet them** (at age ninety-nine!). Then he **bowed himself** before them. This does not mean he recognized the presence of God at this point and thus bowed in worship. Genesis 23:7, 12 speak of Abraham "bowing" before the Hittites, and 1 Samuel 24:8 tells how David "bowed" before Saul. This physical gesture is simply a courteous way of showing another person the highest honor.

[3] Addressing the man who seems to be the leader of his three visitors (**My lord**), Abraham further manifests the kindest form of courtesy when he begs, **Do not pass by your servant**, or "Do not pass by my humble self without a visit" (NEB). It would have been a great disappointment to Abraham if travelers felt that he did not genuinely want to share his blessings with them or thought that his home was unworthy of their presence.

[4] Abraham refers to what he offers his guests as only a small amount (**a little water** to wash their feet, vs. 4; "a morsel of bread" [NEB "a little food"], vs. 5), in order to emphasize that he is putting forth very little effort on their

behalf, and that they are not depriving him of goods that he needed, in an effort to make them feel at ease in his home.

Abraham invites his guests to wash their feet with water that he provides and to rest under **the tree** (oak or terebinth) at Mamre where he had pitched his tent (cf. Gen. 14:13). In the ancient Near East, the unpaved roads were very dusty, and travellers wore sandals. Consequently, when they came to some stopping place on their journey, it was refreshing and cleansing to have their feet washed. Washing weary travellers' feet or providing for their feet to be washed was a vital part of genuine hospitality (see Gen. 19:2; 24:32; 43:24; Judg. 19:21; 2 Sam. 11:8; Luke 7:44; 1 Tim. 5:10).

[5] The Hebrew phrase translated **that you may refresh yourselves** in the RSV and NEB is *wesa'adhu libbekhem,* which means literally "that you may sustain [KJV "comfort," ASV "strengthen"] your heart." The context shows that Abraham is describing the result of eating a meal (see the same or similar terminology in Judg. 19:5, 8; 1 Kings 13:7; Ps. 104:15). The "heart" here is not the blood pump but the whole person. A good translation would be "that you may receive strength."

[6] Apparently oblivious of his age and anxious to make his guests feel at home and to provide for their needs, Abraham **hastened** into his tent and asked Sarah to make **cakes** (i.e., small, round loaves of bread) out of **three measures of fine meal,** which was the best quality of flour known at that time. The Hebrew word translated **measures** is *se'im,* which is the plural of *se'ah* (see the note in the RSV). Scholars are not agreed as to the size of a seah, but if one follows the LXX it would be about one and one-half pecks. Accordingly, three seahs of fine flour would be about four and one-half pecks, or a little more than a bushel (see O. R. Sellers, "Weights and Measures," IDB, vol. 4, pp. 834–35).

[7] Abraham continues to hurry so that his visitors will not grow restless or have to wait any longer than necessary for their meal. He **ran to the herd** and selected one of his finest calves, and one of his servants **hastened to prepare**

it. Although it was costly, and although meat was a rare treat for nomadic travellers, Abraham did not hesitate to prepare meat for his guests.

[8] Abraham served his guests **curds** (a kind of soured milk much like yogurt) and **milk** with their meat and bread. As a mark of the highest courtesy, he **stood** while they ate—possibly to show them respect and to be ready to bring them anything else they might need. Here and in Genesis 19:3 heavenly beings (here including the Lord himself) are said to have eaten earthly food.

[9] After a meal, it was customary to engage in polite conversation. In the course of the conversation, the three guests startled Abraham by asking, **Where is Sarah your wife?** How could they have known the name of Abraham's wife? They had never been introduced to her prior to this occasion. This is the first indication to Abraham that his guests are no ordinary men but beings with divine or superhuman knowledge.

[10] Instead of **The Lord said**, the MT has simply "And he said" (so KJV and ASV). However, the statements that follows and the explicit mention of **the Lord** in the MT of verse 13 show that the Lord is the speaker.

The Hebrew phrase *ka'eth chayyah* means literally "according to the time of life" (so KJV) or "at the time when it revives," which is usually interpreted as an idiom meaning **in the spring**. The ASV reads "when the season cometh round" and the NEB "about this time next year." The context suggests that this strange expression means something like "at the end of the period of pregnancy" (see vs. 14 and 17:21; cf. Skinner, *Genesis*, p. 301; and Speiser, *Genesis*, p. 130).

Sarah was inside the tent behind the Lord as he spoke to Abraham and **was listening** to the conversation, thinking that she would not be detected for eavesdropping. When Abraham's guest disclosed that he knew Sarah had laughed and did not believe she would have a son (vs. 13), he gave Abraham further clues that he was no ordinary man but a divine or superhuman being. This must have had a great deal to do with Abraham's believing him when he promised to give him a son by Sarah and when he announced the destruction of Sodom and Gomorrah.

[11] Suddenly the author of Genesis breaks into the story to remind his readers that Abraham and Sarah were old and that Sarah was past the normal age of child-bearing when the Lord promised Abraham that he would have a son by her. He does this for at least two reasons: (1) to emphasize to his readers that the conception and birth of Isaac was miraculous, and (2) to explain why Sarah laughed (vs. 12).

[12] **Sarah laughed to herself,** that is, silently, in derision and unbelief, when she heard Abraham's visitor say that she would bear a son. The Lord's stern rebuke of Sarah (vs. 15) seems to suggest that Abraham had told her of God's promise that she would have a son (Gen. 17:16, 19), but she persisted in unbelief. This might explain why the Lord felt it necessary to come to Abraham a second time and announce the birth of a son by Sarah. The Hebrew word translated **laughed** is *titschaq,* which forms a word-play with *yitschaq,* "Isaac" (cf. Gen. 17:17, 19; 21:3, 6).

[14] The question **Is anything too hard for the Lord?** is actually the central issue throughout the story of the divine announcements that Abraham would have a son in his old age (Gen. 15:1–18:15). It is also one of the most vital questions facing contemporary man as he agonizes with the difficult problems of life.

[15] Sarah is startled when Abraham's guest exposes her unbelieving thoughts. She tries to avoid accepting the responsibility for her unbelief by denying that she had laughed. She sounds like Eve, when the Lord asked her, "What is this that you have done?" Eve blamed the serpent for deceiving her and persuading her to eat the forbidden fruit (Gen. 3:13). The human race has devised many ways to excuse itself for its sins. The sinner is afraid of being exposed. Exposure is embarrassing. Thus, when the Lord exposes Sarah, she denies it, **for she was afraid.** But the Lord forces man to face his deeds, so he refuses to allow Sarah to get by with her lie. He states firmly and confidently, **No, but you did laugh.**

THE DESTRUCTION OF
SODOM AND GOMORRAH (18:16–19:38)

The inspired author now returns to the vicissitudes of Abraham's nephew Lot, who had chosen to live in wicked Sodom (Gen. 13:11-13), and whom Abraham had rescued from Chedorlaomer and his Mesopotamian allies (Gen. 14:14-16). By now, Sodom and the cities of the valley had become so wicked that the Lord had decided to destroy them. But because of Abraham's faith in him and his love for Abraham, the Lord decides to tell the aged patriarch what he is planning to do (18:16-21). Abraham pleads with the Lord to spare the city if he can find only ten righteous people within it, and the Lord agrees (18:22-33). Unable to find ten righteous people within the city, the Lord determines to destroy it. The two angels who had accompanied him to Abraham's tent go ahead of him to Sodom to warn Lot and his family to flee. They do so, but only after much persuasion (19:1-23). Then the Lord destroys Sodom and the cities of the plain (19:24-29). Lot's two daughters, having concluded that they would never get married (their fiancés had been destroyed with Sodom, vs. 14) and have children, make their father drunk, have sexual relations with him, and give birth to Moab and Ammon, who are destined to become the fathers of the Moabites and the Ammonites, respectively (19:30-38).

God Announces the Destruction to Abraham (18:16-21)

The meal and the conversation now ended, Abraham courteously escorts his guests down the road toward their next destination (vs. 16). The Lord decides to tell Abraham that he is going to destroy Sodom because of its sins (vss. 17-21).

[16] That Yahweh and the two angels **looked toward Sodom** would have been some indication that they had a mission of some sort to that city. If they could see Sodom from the road, they must have walked about three miles east of the terebinths of Mamre at Hebron, where the hills of Hebron overlook the Dead Sea and the adjoining region.

[17] Just as verse 12 reveals the thoughts of Sarah, verses 17-19 reveal the thoughts of the Lord. The only way the divine author could have known what the Lord was thinking is for the Lord to have revealed it to him or for the Lord to have told Abraham, who related it to others.

[18] The Lord decides to tell Abraham of his intention to destroy Sodom, because he has promised to make him **a great and mighty nation** (see Gen. 12:2; 13:16; 15:5; 17:4-6), and that in him **all the nations of the earth shall** be blessed. The Hebrew verb translated "be blessed" is *nibhrekhu,* which is niphal and therefore passive (see the note on 12:3).

[19] The Hebrew word translated **chosen** (RSV footnote "known"; Heb. *yadha'*) has a wide variety of meanings in the OT, and its exact meaning must be determined by the context. Here, God means, "I have entered into a deep, intimate, daily, personal relationship with him" (see Amos 3:2; Hos. 13:5). This same word is used to describe the marital relationship (cf. Gen. 4:1, 25).

In response to God's having entered into this deep relationship with him, Abraham is responsible as a father to teach his children **to keep the way of the Lord by doing righteousness and justice.** It is rather amazing that throughout the history of Christendom, there have been those who have advocated that God's people can keep God's way without practicing righteousness and justice toward their fellowmen. The frequent emphasis on the indispensability of righteousness and justice throughout the Bible shows that this cannot be the case. Correctly performed external acts of religion—as important as they may be—can never substitute for loving attitudes and acts of goodwill toward one's fellowman (see Amos 5:21-24; Hos. 6:4-6; Isa. 1:10-17; Mic. 6:6-8; Ps. 50:7-23).

The divine fulfillment of many predictions (both announcements of destruction and promises of great blessings) in the Bible is dependent on man's response to God's love, which is manifested by his fidelity to God and his behavior toward his fellowmen. Jonah told the people of Nineveh that they would be overthrown in forty days

(Jon. 3:4), but this prediction was never fulfilled because the Ninevites repented (Jon. 3:6-10; cf. Matt. 12:41). God himself explains that *at any time* he promises to bless a righteous nation, if they digress into evil he will not do the good that he promised (Jer. 18:7-10). And in Genesis 18:19, God makes it clear that the fulfillment of the promises that he had made to Abraham depend on Abraham's faithfulness.

[20] The Hebrew expression rendered **the outcry against** [NEB "over"] **Sodom and Gomorrah** (cf. vs. 21 and 19:13) means literally "the cry of Sodom and Gomorrah" (so KJV and ASV). This difficult expression can be explained in at least three ways: (1) Yahweh may be personifying Sodom and Gomorrah and saying that they are crying out to him to punish the people living within them (the cry *of* Sodom). (2) He may mean that innocent people who are hurt by the sins of the inhabitants of Sodom and Gomorrah cry out to God for justice (the outcry *against* Sodom; cf. Exod. 22:21-24 [Hebrew 20-23]), as when the voice of Abel's blood cried to God from the ground (Gen. 4:10). (3) There seems to be a parallelism between the two lines in Genesis 18:20, indicating that "cry" or **outcry** has basically the same meaning as **sin**. If so, the idea is that God knows man's sins even when he tries very hard to hide them. When Moses allowed the tribes of Reuben, Gad, and the half-tribe of Manasseh to settle east of the Jordan, he told them that if they did not help their brethren take the land west of Jordan, they would be sinning against the Lord. And then he warned: "Be sure your sin will find you out" (Num. 32:23). If this is the interpretation that fits our passage, Yahweh means that the sins of the people of Sodom, which they are trying desperately to hide, are quite apparent to him (the cry=the sin *of* Sodom). This last view is probably the correct one.

[21] The idea that God must **go down to see** whether the sins of the people of Sodom are great enough to warrant severe punishment is an anthropomorphism (i.e., speaking of God in language that is ordinarily used of men) and consequently is not to be taken literally (cf. Gen. 11:5; Exod. 2:25). To deduce from this that God is not omni-

scient is to miss the point entirely and to contradict clear passages of scripture elsewhere (Ps. 139:1-18; John 21:17; Rom. 11:33-36).

Abraham Pleads for Sodom (18:22-33)

God had chosen Abraham to bless mankind (Gen. 12:3; 18:18), not to curse them. Thus, Abraham was greatly troubled when the Lord told him that he was contemplating the destruction of the cities of the valley. Furthermore, Lot and his family were living in Sodom, and Abraham's heart went out to them in spite of the fact that Lot had been selfish in choosing what appeared to be the best land when the strife arose between the herdsmen (Gen. 13:2-13). Abraham pleads fervently with God to spare Sodom if he can find ten righteous persons within the city, and God agrees.

> He who would do God's service and go as God's messenger unto his fellowmen must have a great heart, filled with love for those of his brethren who need him most. He must be slow to condemn and quick to excuse and forgive . . . Abraham knew full well the wickedness of the people of Sodom and Gomorrah. Nevertheless his loving heart overflowed with pity and compassion for them, and the thought of their destruction moved him to intercede on their behalf even with God Himself. . . . A few righteous men might yet convince the people of the evil of their ways, and cause them to repent and return to God . . . . True justice must always be tempered by mercy. For if God should judge all men absolutely according to their merits, who could stand before Him in judgment? What man doeth good ever, and sinneth not? Everyone does wrong at times for no man is perfect, but only God . . . . Surely not to punish is God's desire, but to forgive; not to chastise in anger, but to pardon and correct in love . . . . Even the wicked inhabitants of Sodom and Gomorrah were still [Abraham's] brothers, and his heart was still filled with love and compassion for them.
>
> Morgenstern, *Genesis*, pp. 124–26

[22] **The men** who leave Abraham and go on toward Sodom are the "two angels" who came to Abraham's

tent with the Lord (cf. 19:1). The third is **the Lord** himself, who stays behind to talk with the patriarch.

The phrase **but Abraham still stood before the Lord** is one of the eighteen ancient "corrections of the scribes" (Heb. *tiqqune sopherim*). The original text is said to have been "But the Lord still stood before Abraham," which was offensive to the scribes, because in their thought world one who stood before another was inferior to him and his servant. However, Genesis 19:27 would seem to favor the reading in the MT. In either case, the point of this line is that Yahweh was willing and anxious to listen to Abraham and to avoid the destruction of Sodom if at all possible.

[25] In verses 23-25, Abraham reasons that there is more injustice in destroying a few righteous people than in sparing a large number of wicked persons and assumes that a small number of righteous individuals can deliver their neighbors from terrible affliction and destruction because the Lord looks with favor on their commitment and devotion to him (cf. Jer. 15:1; Ezek. 14:12-20).

Here Abraham states one of the great truths of the Bible, which is that the world is governed by a God who is fair in all his dealings, even when it might seem to man that he is unjust (cf. Deut. 32:4; Rom. 2:6-11). And he is not a God of Canaan alone, where his chosen people live, but as the creator of all the earth (Gen. 1-2) he is also **the Judge of all the earth**. God's universal rule was as fully proclaimed in OT times as it is in NT times.

[27] While he is pleading with the Lord to spare Sodom, Abraham does not forget that he is speaking to the creator and judge of all the earth, and that he is one of his creatures, made in his image. Consequently, he speaks to God very humbly. In fact, four times in the course of their conversation he betrays his reluctance in being so bold as to think that he could speak to the Lord about the fate of Sodom and ask the Lord to spare the city for the sake of a few righteous people (vss. 27, 30, 31, 32). He is careful to assure Yahweh that he has no intention of being presumptuous in interceding for this wicked city. He acknowledges that he is **but dust and ashes**, that is, feeble and weak and

destined to die and return to the dust (cf. Gen. 2:7; 3:19; Ps. 103:14).

[32] Abraham decided to stop when he asked the Lord if he would spare Sodom if he found **ten** righteous persons living within the city. One wonders why he stopped. (1) Perhaps he felt that surely there were ten righteous persons in Sodom! (2) Or perhaps he was judging God by human standards—no righteous man would spare a city if he found fewer than ten righteous people living there, so the same must be the case with God! On the contrary, Paul makes it clear that Christ went beyond man's fondest dreams and noblest compassion by dying for sinners (Rom. 5:6-8). (3) Or possibly he assumed that God was precisely the way he had pictured, and he felt he would be asking far too much to ask him to spare Sodom if fewer than ten righteous persons lived there! However, God's forgiveness far transcends man's most profound picture of him, as Jesus' parable of the two debtors (Matt. 18:21-35) emphasizes. Perhaps Abraham should have continued and asked God to spare Sodom if fewer than ten righteous persons could be found in the city.

[33] When the conversation between Yahweh and Abraham comes to an end, Yahweh leaves him and apparently goes on to Sodom (cf. 19:24-25), and Abraham returns **to his place**, that is, to his tent by the oaks of Mamre at Hebron (cf. 13:18; 18:1).

Lot and His Family Flee Sodom (19:1-23)

The visit of the two angels at Sodom was the final expression of Yahweh's desire to spare the city (cf. 18:20-21). The angels did not come to destroy the city immediately but to spend the night (vs. 2) and to determine firsthand the true character of the citizens of Sodom. They were looking for ten righteous people. However, no one offered them any sort of hospitality—except Lot, who was not really a full-fledged citizen, but a "sojourner" (vs. 9). But worse than this, "the men of Sodom, all the people to the last man" (vs. 4), came to Lot's house during the night and demanded that he send the two men out to them that they might have homosexual relationships with them (vs. 5). The sins of Sodom were many: injustice (Isa. 1:10-17; 3:9), adultery, lying, condoning evil, encouraging wickedness (Jer. 23:14), pride, gluttony, prosperous ease, neglect of the poor (Ezek. 16:49), and homosexuality (Jude 7); and the people of Sodom had indulged in these sins for many years. Consequently, there could be no doubt that the only right course of action was to destroy the city. The people of Sodom were so steeped in sin that nothing could bring them to repentance, so "God gave them up" (Rom. 1:24, 26, 28).

Instead of influencing the people of Sodom for good, Lot was influenced by them for evil. He became "conformed to this world" (Rom. 12:2). To be sure, he was "greatly distressed by the licentiousness of the wicked" and "was vexed in his righteous soul day after day with their lawless deeds" (2 Pet. 2:7-8), and since he did not go as far as they did in sin, he could be described as "righteous" in a comparative sense. But there is ample evidence that the people of Sodom were making a strong impact on his life and character. Lot's hospitality toward the two angels, which undoubtedly he had learned from Abraham, was much less personal and genuine than Abraham's had been (vss. 1-3). That Lot "urged them strongly" to spend the night in his house rather than in the street (vs. 3) shows he knew that his neighbors were sexual perverts, yet he was content to live among them and to raise his family in that sort of environment. Lot even called the men of Sodom his "brothers" (vs. 7). Of course, he may have used this expression merely as a psychological means of strengthening his appeal to them not to abuse his guests, but still it is an indication of his desire to make them think that he wanted to be their friend and supporter. But they did not even appreciate this subtle courtesy, for they reminded him harshly and spitefully that he was but a sojourner in their city and not a full-fledged citizen (vs. 9). Lot was willing to offer his two virgin daughters to the wicked sexual perverts of Sodom to do with them as they pleased, just as long as they agreed to leave his two guests alone (vs. 8). Lot had allowed his daughters to date and to become engaged to young men who lived in Sodom, who were just as corrupt as everyone else in the city, and who obviously had no respect for Lot (vs. 14).

When the time came for Lot and his family to leave the doomed city, Lot lingered, and it was only because God was merciful (vs. 16) and Lot was Abraham's nephew (vs. 29) that the two angels "seized him and his wife and his two daughters by the hand" and forced them to go out (vs. 16). When the angels told Lot to flee to the hills, he argued with them and insisted that they allow him to go to Zoar (vss. 17-19). Later, he became afraid to stay in Zoar and fled to a certain cave in the hills (vs. 30). Here, his daughters made him drunk and had sexual relations with him so that he would have descendants (vs. 35). It may be safely conjectured that their moral values also had been blunted by the evil influences of Sodom.

The powerful influence of sin on Lot's heart and life is emphasized by his reluctance to go with the "two angels" (vs. 1) and to do what they say. in spite of clear evidence that they were sent from God and possessed supernatural powers. When the men of Sodom try to break into Lot's house, the angels strike them with blindness and render them incapable of forcing their way into it (vs. 11). They tell Lot plainly, "We are about to destroy this place" (vs. 13)—which would be possible only by supernatural power. They know in advance what is going to happen and tell Lot and his family where they can find safety (vs. 17).

[1] Speiser assumes that the two angels arrived at Sodom at the southern end of the Dead Sea in the evening of the same day that they ate with Abraham (*Genesis*, pp. 138, 142–43). The distance from Hebron to this region is about forty miles, normally a two-day trek on foot. If Speiser is correct, this is another indication (to the reader of the book of Genesis, but not to Lot, who would not have known of their previous whereabouts) of the supernatural powers of these angels. However, it is also possible that the angels came to Sodom two days after they had visited Abraham. Then, the concern of the biblical writer would have been to

indicate the time of day when the angels arrived and not to imply that they arrived there on the same day they left Abraham.

The gate of an ancient city was the center of various activities, such as hearing and judging legal cases (Gen. 34:20; Ruth 4:1, 11; 2 Sam. 15:2; Job 29:7; Amos 5:12, 15), transacting business (Gen. 23:10), proclaiming divine oracles (Amos 5:10; Prov. 1:21), discussing the day's activities (Ps. 69:13 [Hebrew 12]), and the like. It has been suggested that Lot was **sitting in the gate of Sodom** in the hope that he might show hospitality to any strangers that might come into town for the night, or as a member of the men of the city who heard legal cases, but the Bible does not explain why he was there.

The Tell el-Amarna tablets (fourteenth century B.C.) show that it was customary for courtiers and clients to address their superiors with their **face to the earth.** Lot seems to have adopted a servile role toward his guests.

[2] Lot dwelt in a **house,** which was apparently well-built (cf. vss. 6, 9, 11), in striking contrast to Abraham, who dwelt in a tent (18:1, 6, 9, 10). But in this case the more elaborate and comfortable abode was no indication of a closer relationship with God or of greater blessing from God.

When the angels say, **We will spend the night in the street,** it is not clear whether they were simply being polite or intended to spend the night investigating the city, or wanted to test the sincerity of Lot's offer, or wanted to help Lot realize how well he knew the wickedness of his environment.

[3] In contrast to the "cakes" that Abraham had made out of "fine meal" for his guests, Lot hurriedly makes them baked flat pieces of **unleavened bread.**

[5] The verb **know** (*yadha'*) here means "to have sexual relations with" (cf. Gen. 4:1, 25; 19:8; Judg. 19:25; 1 Sam. 1:19), and thus the NEB is correct in translating: "Bring them out so that we can have intercourse with them." Homosexuality is consistently condemned throughout the Scriptures (Lev. 18:22; 20:13; Rom. 1:26-27; 1 Cor. 6:9;

1 Tim. 1:10), and its promotion and/or practice can in no way be justified by God-fearing people.

[8] It is incredible that some scholars suggest the inspired author of Genesis is commending Lot for offering his two virgin daughters to the men of Sodom to abuse them sexually any way they wished in order to protect his guests. A biblical writer often reports the thoughts, words, and acts of different people without commending or condoning them. Was the author of 2 Samuel 11 commending David for adultery and murder? Was Luke commending Saul of Tarsus for persecuting the church (Acts 8:3; 9:1-2)? Was the author of Genesis commending the serpent for beguiling Eve (Gen. 3:1-5)?

[9] This verse is a bit difficult to understand because the audience addressed by the men of Sodom alternates. First they say *to Lot*, **Stand back** (the Hebrew verb *gesh* here is an imperative *singular*). Then they say *to one another,* **This fellow** [i.e., Lot] **came to sojourn** [he is not a full-fledged citizen, but only an alien or a foreigner], **and he would play the judge** (i.e., he dares to tell us how to run our affairs in our own hometown of Sodom, where we are the natives; the translation "and he will needs to be a judge" [KJV and ASV] is unclear, to say the least). Then they say *to Lot,* **Now we will deal worse with you** [singular] **than with them** (i.e., the two angels).

[11] The Hebrew word translated **blindness** here is not from the normal root for blindness ('-*w-r*) but is *sanwerim*, which is a loanword based on a cognate Akkadian root. It conveys the idea of a blinding flash, similar to that with which Yahweh smote the Syrians in response to Elisha's prayer at Dothan (2 Kings 6:18) or with which God smote Saul on the road from Jerusalem to Damascus (Acts 9:3; 22:6; 26:13). It is the kind of light that leaves its victims in a dazzled and confused state so that they cannot do what they intend.

[14] The Hebrew lying behind the phrase **who were to marry** can be interpreted equally well in either of two ways. The KJV and ASV render it "which [who] married," in which case the meaning would be that Lot had two married daughters whom he had to leave behind in Sodom when he fled because their husbands did not believe that the city would be destroyed (vs. 14) and two single daughters who fled with him and his wife (vs. 15). On the other hand, the translation of the RSV (cf. NEB) would mean that Lot had two daughters who were engaged to be married to two young men of Sodom; Lot tried unsuccessfully the same night that the angels came to his house to persuade them to flee from the city with his family but took his two daughters with him. The latter explanation seems preferable, because Lot's daughters are still living in their father's house and are virgins (vs. 8; cf. von Rad, *Genesis*, p. 214).

[15] The angels urge Lot to flee from Sodom, because the time set for the destruction of the city is sunrise (vss. 23-24). The context indicates that *'awon* means **punishment** here (so the RSV and NEB), and not "iniquity" (KJV and ASV). Some Hebrew words can have dual meanings like this, referring to cause or effect. The precise meaning must be determined by the context in each case.

[17] It is noteworthy that the urgent command to **flee** occurs five times in verses 17-22, thus indicating the hesitancy of Lot and his family to leave their home in Sodom. The Hebrew verb for **flee** is *malaṭ*, so there is a wordplay on the words *malaṭ* and *Loṭ* in the MT.

The **hills** (RSV, NEB) or "mountain" (KJV, ASV) to which Lot was told to flee are the hills on the Moabite plateau east of the Dead Sea. These hills stand between 2,500 and 3,000 feet above the Dead Sea.

[20] Again, there is a Hebrew wordplay on the word for **little** (*mits'ar*, vs. 20) and the name of the town "Zoar" (*tso'ar*, vss. 22, 23).

In verses 19 and 20, the KJV and ASV translate the Hebrew word *naphshi* literally by "my soul." However, the context shows that Lot is not talking about the internal and eternal part of his being (as a modern might be tempted to understand this), but about his whole being. Thus, it is better to read **my life** (with the RSV and NEB) or simply "me" (vs. 19) or "I" (vs. 20).

God Destroys Sodom and Gomorrah (19:24-29)

Yahweh rains fire and brimstone on Sodom and Gomorrah and the cities of the plain, destroying the people and the vegetation (vss. 24-25; see Luke 17:28-30). Lot's wife disobeys the divine command (vs. 17) by looking back toward Sodom and becomes a pillar of salt (vs. 26; see Luke 17:31). Not long after sunrise (vs. 23), "early in the morning" (vs. 27), Abraham comes to the place where he had pleaded with God to spare Sodom if he could find ten righteous persons within it (18:22-33) and looks down on the smoldering ruins of the cities (19:27-28); but at least Lot and his daughters have escaped the divine destruction (vs. 29).

The biblical text clearly affirms that Yahweh destroyed the cities of the plain (vss. 24-25, 29). However, it does not give a complete description of *how* he did this. The references to "brimstone and fire" (vs. 24), the dying of vegetation (vs. 25), and smoke going "up like the smoke of a furnace" (vs. 28) seem to suggest that lightning ignited a great field of petroleum, bitumen (or asphalt), and accompanying gases seeping up out of the ground, setting off massive explosions which demolished everything in the low-lying region. Archeologists generally agree that Sodom and Gomorrah and the cities of the plain were located under what is now the southern tip of the Dead Sea, where the water is still quite shallow, the maximum depth being about eighteen feet. Since the site of Bab edh-Dhra' in this region was visited regularly from 2300 to 1900 B.C. but not afterwards, it is likely that this destruction took place about 1900 B.C. Along the southern end of the western side of the Dead Sea is located the mountain called Jebel Usdum, which is largely a mass of crystalline salt. One calls to mind Lot's wife, who looked back and became a pillar of salt (vs. 26; for a fuller discussion of the location and destruction of the cities of the valley, see Harland, "Sodom," pp. 395–97).

[26] Kidner (*Genesis*, p. 135) has suggested that Lot's

wife was covered by molten materials that rained down on her from an explosion. If so, in time the materials under which she was buried may have been covered with salt deposits common in this region. Apparently, she did not think it was as urgent to flee from the city as the angels had indicated (vs. 17) and thus lagged behind; she turned around to have one last look at the city where she had lived so long and was trapped in the flying debris.

Lot's Daughters Bear Moab and Ammon (19:30-38)

Although God had promised Lot that he would not destroy Zoar (vs. 21), Lot is afraid to dwell there (vs. 30), evidently lest God destroy this little town as he had overthrown the other cities of the plain. So Lot flees to a certain cave in the hills with his two daughters. Convinced that they might never marry, Lot's daughters make him drunk, have sexual relations with him (vss. 31-36) and bear Moab and Ammon, who were destined to become the ancestors of the Moabites and the Ammonites (vss. 37-38).

Because Lot's daughters say, "There is not a man on earth to come in to us after the manner of all the earth" (vs. 31), several scholars have argued that the story of Lot is a parallel or alternative to the account of Noah and the flood. They contend that Lot and his daughters were the last survivors on earth, and in order to perpetuate the race, the daughters did the only thing they could do. However, the whole context shows that this is not the case. Abraham and his family are very much alive, as are thousands of other people, including the citizens of Zoar (vss. 20-23, 30). The picture the Bible paints is that Lot's daughters feared that since they lost their fiancés in the destruction of Sodom (vs. 14), they could never marry and bear children, so they resorted to having intercourse with their own father. That the author of Genesis condones or commends Lot's daughters' having sexual relationships with their own father is incredible (cf. Lev. 18:7), especially in view of his exalted view of marriage expressed elsewhere in the book (cf. 2:18-24).

[30] At one time, Lot had "flocks and herds and tents"

(13:5), "great possessions" (13:6), and many "herdsmen" (13:7-8), and lived in a well-built "house" (19:3, 4, 6, 8, 9, 10, 11); but now, because of his foolish choice to dwell among sinful people, his household is reduced to three persons, and he dwells **in a cave.**

[32] If it had been acceptable for Lot's daughters to have sexual relations with their father, there is no reason why they would have felt it necessary to make him drunk. The surreptitious air that hangs over their behavior shows they know their father would not have approved of such perverted sexual practices and they feel so guilty in executing them that they are willing to stop at nothing to keep them hidden. One is reminded of David's attempt to hide his adultery with Bathsheba by getting her husband drunk so that he would go home and have sexual relations with her (2 Sam. 11:13). At the same time, Lot is no less guilty or responsible just because he was so drunk that he did not know what his daughters were doing. That his daughters knew he was so weak as to be susceptible to much wine is a further reflection on his inferior character and influence.

[34] The sinner is a coward. He is miserable sinning alone. He has a passionate drive to bring others into his plans to join him in his deeds. When Eve ate the forbidden fruit, "she also gave some to her husband" (Gen. 3:6). Lot's firstborn daughter initiated the plot to get her father drunk and have sexual relations with him (vs. 31). She keenly felt the need for her sister to join her in this plan. After she had sexual relations with her father, she urged her sister to do likewise. Those who are young and impressionable need to learn the importance of choosing friends with high moral principles and of rejecting sinful plots (cf. Ps. 1:1; Prov. 4:14-17; 1 Cor. 15:33).

[37-38] The Moabites and the Ammonites are distant relatives of the Israelites, as they descended from Lot's children through his daughters, while the Israelites were the descendants of Abraham's grandson Jacob. Throughout OT history, the Moabites and Ammonites were political and religious enemies of Israel. To mention just one incident

involving each people, during the wilderness wanderings many Israelites were seduced by the women of Moab at Baal of Peor to practice prostitution and sacrifice to foreign gods (Num. 25:1-9); and Solomon built a high place for Molech, the god of the Ammonites and burned incense and sacrificed to this god (and others) to please his foreign wives (1 Kings 11:5, 7-8).

NEW TESTS OF ABRAHAM'S AND SARAH'S FAITH (20:1–21:21)

Abraham Lies Again about His Wife (20:1-18)

Having completed the account of the divine overthrow of Sodom and the cities of the plain (18:16–19:38), the author of Genesis now resumes the story of God's promise that Abraham would have a son by Sarah (15:1–18:15). He wishes to emphasize to his readers that it is not because of Abraham's righteousness or faith that God gave him a son, but out of God's own mercy and love.

For some reason, Abraham decides to leave the oaks of Mamre where he has lived so long (13:18–19:38; cf. 13:18; 14:13; 18:1). Perhaps the grazing land where he had been pasturing his flocks and herds had become depleted, or he had become discouraged by the sin and destruction of Sodom and the cities of the plain where Lot had been living, or he was being threatened by peoples living in the area (e.g., the Canaanites and the Perizzites, 12:6; 13:7) or other seminomadic tribes, or he simply got the urge to move to another region. Whatever his reason or reasons may have been, Abraham moved west-southwest toward Egypt and then north to the land "of Gerar" (vss. 1-2). Archeologists have discovered that Gerar was settled for a long time, beginning in the fourth millennium B.C. and continuing later than 1600 B.C. (For a fuller discussion of the location and discoveries at Gerar, see S. Cohen, "Gerar," IDB, vol. 2, pp. 381–82.)

As Abraham settles in new territory, he is afraid that Abimelech, the king of Gerar, will kill him in order to take

Sarah as his wife (cf. vs. 11 and the similar circumstance described in Gen. 12:11-12), and so he says that she is his "sister" (vs. 2). Abimelech takes Sarah into his harem (vs. 2), thus putting in jeopardy God's promise of a son to Abraham. God intervenes, smites Abimelech and his family with a disease that prevents them from bearing children (vss. 17-18), and tells Abimelech that he has taken another man's wife unknowingly (vs. 3). Abimelech pleads that he did not know Sarah was married (vss. 4-5), and God replies that he knew this and that this was the reason he kept Abimelech from sinning (vs. 6) by preventing him (possibly by smiting him with a disease, vss. 17-18) from having sexual relations with her (vs. 4). He commands Abimelech to return Sarah to Abraham (vs. 7). Abimelech chides Abraham for exposing him and his kingdom to the guilt and punishment of sin by lying about his relationship to Sarah (vss. 8-10).

Abraham tries to justify his actions with three arguments: (1) he was afraid that he would be killed if he did not tell this lie (vs. 11); (2) Sarah was indeed Abraham's half-sister through their common father, Terah (vs. 12); and (3) since God made Abraham a wanderer in the earth, his life was in constant danger. Thus he and Sarah had agreed that "at every place" she would say that Abraham was her brother (vs. 13)—if it worked elsewhere, it should work in Gerar! These call to mind similar excuses by Adam and Eve (3:12-13) and Cain (4:9) to justify their sinful actions. It is typical of man to make such excuses to try to cover his sins.

It is ironic that, whereas God had intended for all the families of the earth to be blessed by Abraham and his descendants, in this event Abimelech is the one who acts with integrity and thereby blesses Abraham. In order to show his high moral standards and honorable intentions, Abimelech gives Abraham "sheep and oxen, and male and female slaves," returns Sarah to him (vs. 14), and invites him to live wherever he wishes in the land of Gerar (vs. 15). Abraham then prays for Abimelech, and God heals him and his wife and his female slaves so that they can bear children (vss. 17-18).

Genesis 20 vividly demonstrates that ultimately God's promises do not depend on man's righteous performance but on God's mercy and love.

> On the brink of Isaac's birth-story [ch. 21] here is the very Promise put in jeopardy, traded away for personal safety. If it is ever to be fulfilled, it will owe very little to man. Morally as well as physically, it will clearly have to be achieved by the grace of God.
>
> Kidner, *Genesis*, p. 137

[1] Abraham goes from the oaks of Mamre toward **the Negeb**, through which he had passed on his way to Egypt at the time of the famine (12:9) and again on his way out of Egypt after his encounter with the Pharaoh (13:1, 3). Over an unspecified period of time, he pastures his herds in the region **between Kadesh and Shur**. Kadesh is located in the southern part of the Negeb, and the wilderness of Shur is located west of Kadesh toward Egypt. At this time, therefore, Abraham was in the vicinity of Beer-lahai-roi, where the angel had met Hagar and sent her back to Sarah (16:7, 14). During this period, Abraham makes a journey north to the land of **Gerar** (cf. Speiser's important note, *Genesis*, p. 148).

[2] **Abimelech** is a well-attested Canaanite word. It appears in the Tell el-Amarna tablets numbers 149–156 (early fourteenth century B.C.) as Abimilki, the name of the prince or ruler of Tyre. In our passage it is probably not a personal name but a royal title (like the Egyptian Pharaoh, the Roman Caesar, or the Russian Czar), since Genesis 26:1, 8, 16, 26 seem to refer to another king of Gerar called Abimelech, and the heading of Psalm 34 apparently refers to Achish the king of Gath as Abimelech (cf. 1 Sam. 21:10-15). Thinking that Sarah was Abraham's sister, Abimelech **took** her into his harem as his wife. Apparently he did not do this because of her beauty (as the Pharaoh of Egypt had done several years earlier, cf. 12:11, 14-15) but because he recognized the economic and military strength of Abraham (cf. 13:2; 14:14) and sought to

establish a friendly relationship with him by marrying his sister.

[4] The reason that Abimelech **had not approached** (i.e., had sexual relations with) Sarah is that God had smitten him and his family with a serious disease (vs. 17-18) and had thereby prevented him from being physically able to have sexual relations with her (vs. 6).

Abimelech, in his plea to God not to destroy him and his people for taking Sarah into his harem, does not claim that the people of Gerar are righteous (Heb. *tsaddiq*; KJV, ASV) in the abstract sense, but that he and his people are **innocent** (RSV, NEB) of any intention of doing wrong to Abraham by taking his wife into the king's harem. As a matter of fact, Abimelech had done this on the basis of a deliberate lie on Abraham's part. Ironically, Abimelech's plea for the deliverance of his own people calls to mind Abraham's plea for the deliverance of Sodom (18:22-33).

[5] Even the heathen king Abimelech knows that God is concerned not only with the works of the **hands**, but also with the **integrity of** the **heart** (the intentions or motives which lie behind man's external works).

[6] When a man has right intentions but is moving in the wrong direction, God has ways of protecting him from sin (cf. 1 Cor. 10:13). He used a dread disease to prevent Abimelech from having sexual relations with Sarah (vss. 17-18). Had Abimelech violated the marital bond between Abraham and Sarah by having sexual relations with her, he would have been sinning against God, for God is the source and sustainer of the sacredness of marriage (cf. 2:18-25).

[7] Although Abimelech had married Sarah in good faith, he was still a worldly-minded pagan. God's instruction to **restore** Sarah to Abraham and his threat that if he did not do so he would **die** from the disease seem to imply that Abimelech concluded that since Abraham had lied about his relationship to Sarah, he had a right to keep her. After all, what he had done could hardly be more sinful than what Abraham had done! However, God told him to return Sarah to her rightful husband and promised that when he

did so, Abraham would **pray** for Abimelech and his family
to recover from their disease, and they would recover
(cf. vs. 17).

Abraham is called a **prophet** (cf. Ps. 105:15) only because he interceded for Abimelech, because one function
of a prophet was to intercede for others (1 Sam.
7:5, 8, 9; 12:19, 23; Amos 7:2, 5; Jer. 7:16). He is a prophet
in a secondary sense. A NT illustration may clarify the
point. The Twelve (Matt. 10:2-4), Matthias (Acts 1:23, 26),
and Paul (Rom. 1:1) are called "apostles," but so are Jesus
(Heb. 3:1), Barnabas (Acts 14:14), and two unnamed
brethren (2 Cor. 8:18, 22) whom Paul sent to Corinth to
take up the collection made there for the poor saints in
Judea (2 Cor. 8:23). Surely these are not apostles all in the
same sense. Neither is Abraham a **prophet** in the same
sense as Samuel, Elijah, Isaiah, or Jeremiah.

[9-10] Abimelech's questions, **What have you done to us?**,
How have I sinned against you? (vs. 9), and **What were you
thinking of?** (vs. 10), are rhetorical. Here the king is not
seeking information but is forcing Abraham to look at his
own motives and actions. These questions call to mind
similar questions of God to Adam (3:9, 11), Eve (3:13), and
Cain (4:9, 10). Abraham, whom God had called to bless the
nations (12:3), brings a curse on Abimelech and the land of
Gerar. When Abimelech says to Abraham, **You have done
to me things that ought not to be done**, he means that there
are universal principles that govern a man's behavior toward his fellowman, principles which do not have to be
enunciated, because they lie at the very core of human
existence. One such principle is that when a man is kind
enough to let a stranger move about freely in his land, that
stranger should respond by showing concern for his well-
being (see Gen. 34:7; 2 Sam. 13:12). Instead, Abraham had
not considered the effect that his lie would have on
Abimelech and the people of Gerar but only the advantage
that he thought it would gain for him. Instead of **What were
you thinking of?** (vs. 10), the KJV and ASV read very literally, "What sawest thou?" (Heb. *ra'itha*), which means
something like "What did you (fore-)see?" (i.e., "What did

you expect to happen" that caused you to tell this lie?).

[11] Abraham argues that he assumed there was **no fear of God** in Gerar, and therefore the king would kill him to get his wife. Here the fear of God is inseparably connected with one's attitude and behavior toward his fellowman. Abraham doubted whether there was any respect for one's moral and social rights, or for human life, among the king and people of Gerar. For the believer, murder is sin because God made man in his own image (cf. 9:6). To respect (fear) God, one must naturally respect man who is made in his image. Abraham was dubious that the unbelieving people of Gerar had this sort of respect. The people of Sodom had no respect for a sojourner (Lot) in their midst (19:9); Abraham supposed that the people of Gerar would have no respect for a sojourner in their midst (20:1).

[12] Abraham told the truth as far as it went, but since he did not tell the whole truth about his relationship to Sarah (and this was crucial under the circumstances), it was a lie. Such a passage as this refutes biblical support for the principle of mental reservation. The Egyptians and ancient Semitic peoples allowed marriages between half-brothers and half-sisters, and apparently God allowed this in the time of Abraham. Genesis 11:27-29 apparently indicates that after Abraham's brother Haran died, his other brother Nahor adopted Haran's daughter Milcah and later married her (his own niece). This same text makes no mention of the relationship between Abraham and Sarah, evidently because both of them were Terah's own children (by different wives). At a later period, such marriages were forbidden (Lev. 18:9, 11; 20:17; Deut. 27:22).

[13] Here Abraham refers to the events recorded in Genesis 12:1-3, 11-13. It is difficult to see how this chapter and Genesis 12:1-20 can be two accounts of the same event from two different sources (as many source critics think), in view of the fact that the present account is based on a knowledge of and refers back to the account in 12:10-20. The similarity of order, vocabulary, and theme may be explained by the fact that the two events are similar and the same writer is relating them. Their differences

are due to the different details of the historical events themselves. (For a further discussion, see the Excursus, "The Three Accounts of a Patriarch's Lie about His Wife," p. 216, above.)

[14] Skinner thinks that Abimelech's gifts to Abraham are a "compensation for injury unwittingly inflicted" (*Genesis*, p. 319). It seems more likely, however, that they are Abimelech's way of demonstrating to Abraham that his intentions were honorable in taking Sarah into his harem.

[15] Whereas the Pharaoh had had his men escort Abraham and his family out of Egypt (12:20), Abimelech invites him to dwell in Gerar wherever he would like.

[16] This verse is extremely difficult to translate and interpret. It seems most likely that Abimelech is explaining to Sarah the customs or laws of Gerar pertaining to a man taking another man's wife without realizing that she was already married. The man who took her gives her husband **a thousand pieces of silver**. But since both Abraham (vss. 2, 5, 13) and Sarah (vs. 5, 13) had claimed that they were brother and sister, when Abimelech restores Sarah to her husband, he refers to Abraham ironically or sarcastically as **your brother**. Scholars are understandably divided over whether the **thousand pieces of silver** is the monetary value of the "sheep and oxen, and male and female slaves" mentioned in verse 14 or a gift in money in addition to these possessions.

According to legal customs in Gerar, this gift (**it**, not "he" [which would refer to Abraham], as in the KJV) functioned as "a covering of the eyes" (which is the literal translation of the Heb. *kesuth 'enayim*; KJV, ASV) to all that were with Sarah. In other words, it showed Sarah and her associates that Abimelech intended her and Abraham no harm or wrong but took Sarah into his harem without knowing she was Abraham's wife. It was a gift designed to show good faith on the part of Abimelech and to affirm that Sarah had not been defiled by her relationship with him. Accordingly, no one will have good reason to criticize or discredit Sarah because of this experience. In this way she was **righted** (ASV, RSV) or "completely vindicated"

(NEB), in the sight of others. The reading of the KJV, "thus she was reproved," is possible linguistically but does not fit the context.

[17-18] Verse 17 contains a sweeping statement that covers at least a nine-month period (of pregnancy) and possibly more.

The disease of Abimelech and his house caused sterility or barrenness. The Bible claims that God closes (1 Sam. 1:5, 6) and opens (Gen. 29:31; 30:22) wombs. Sometimes he closes wombs as a punishment for sin or to indicate that a sinful relationship exists. When man stops his sinning or dissolves his sinful relationship, God opens the wombs of the women in his house. The next chapter continues this line of thought by describing how God opened Sarah's womb that she might conceive and give birth to Isaac in her old age.

God Gives Abraham a Son (21:1-21)

Genesis 21 tells how God fulfilled his promise of a son through Sarah (vss. 1-21; cf. 15:4; 17:16, 19; 18:10) and how he continued to bless Abraham with indications that he would give the land of Canaan to him and to his descendants (vss. 22-34; cf. 12:7; 13:14-15, 17; 15:7, 16, 18-21).

That Isaac's conception and birth were possible only by divine intervention is emphasized by the verbs used with the Lord as subject ("visited," "did," vs. 1), by the repeated statement that Isaac was born in Abraham's "old age" (vss. 2, 5, 7; cf. 24:36), and by the fact that Isaac was born at the time God had told Abraham (vs. 2; cf. 17:21; 18:10). Abraham names his son Isaac (*yitschaq*, vs. 3) because his birth causes him and all who know about it to "laugh" (from the Hebrew root *ts-ch-q*, vs. 6; this same Hebrew wordplay on the words meaning "Isaac" and "laugh" also occurs in 17:17, 19; 18:12, 13). Abraham circumcises Isaac at eight days of age (vs. 4), as God had told him (17:12).

At Isaac's weaning, when he is two or three years old (2 Macc. 7:27-28) and Ishmael is sixteen or seventeen (cf. Gen. 16:16; 17:17), Sarah becomes jealous at the sight of Ishmael playing with Isaac as though he were his equal or superior (vs. 9). She urges Abraham to cast out Hagar and Ishmael so that Ishmael cannot be heir with Isaac (vs. 10). When Abraham hesitates to do this out of love for Ishmael, God tells him to do so (vss. 11-13), and he sends away Hagar and her son (vs. 14). They wander in the wilderness of Beer-sheba until they are exhausted. God hears Ishmael's crying, comes to Hagar, and tells her that he will make Ishmael "a great nation" (vss. 14-18). In order to indicate how God keeps his promises, the author of Genesis tells his readers of events that happened much later than the event being recorded here: Ishmael grew up and became an expert archer, lived in the wilderness of Paran, and married a woman from the land of Egypt (vss. 19-21).

[1] The OT speaks of the Lord "visiting" (Heb. *paqadh*) his people to punish them (Exod. 32:34) or to bless them (Exod. 3:16; 4:31; Ruth 1:6; Ps. 8:4). When he visits a woman, she conceives and gives birth to a child (1 Sam. 2:21). The meaning seems to be well expressed in the NEB: "the Lord showed favour to Sarah."

[2] A **son** born in a man's **old age** was regarded with special favor, as is indicated from the statements made about Joseph (37:3) and Benjamin (44:20).

[3] It was customary for the father to name a child (cf. 16:15), although this was not always the case (cf. 19:37, 38).

[6] The name Isaac, meaning "he laughed," is given in connection with different types of laughter. In 17:17 and 18:12-15, Abraham and Sarah laugh *in unbelief* when God tells them they will have a son in their old age; whereas in 21:6 Sarah and those who hear of Isaac's birth laugh *for joy* over the birth of a son in their waning years.

[7] Although Sarah bore only one **son** (Heb. *ben*), she refers to him by the generic word **children** (Heb. *banim*). Passages such as this show that a man with one child is suitable to serve as an elder of the church if his spiritual qualities are on a high godly plane (1 Tim. 3:4; Titus 1:6).

[8] When a child was **weaned**, apparently it was custom-

ary to have a family feast to celebrate the occasion (cf. 1 Sam. 1:22-24).

[9] Interpreters differ sharply over the nature of Ishmael's behavior described in this verse. (1) The LXX and the Vulgate (followed by the RSV) read: **But Sarah saw the son of Hagar . . . playing with her son Isaac.** If this is the original text (the words "with her son Isaac" do not occur in the MT), the thought is that Sarah became jealous when she saw the teenager Ishmael playing with her little two- or three-year-old son Isaac, possibly trying to amuse him, because Ishmael was acting as if he were Isaac's superior, or because she realized that the older son in the house ordinarily received the choice inheritance (a view that would fit nicely with vs. 10). (2) It has been suggested that Ishmael was abusing the innocent boy Isaac sexually, but there is nothing in the Hebrew word or the context to suggest this. (3) It seems best to retain the MT, which suggests that Ishmael mocked or made fun of the celebration of Isaac's weaning (KJV, ASV) or of Isaac on the day set aside to celebrate his weaning (NEB). This interpretation helps explain Paul's statement that Ishmael "persecuted" Isaac (Gal. 4:29). The Hebrew word translated **playing** in the RSV is *metsacheq,* which again is a wordplay on the name Isaac.

[11-12] Man is frequently **displeased** with what God does or expects him to do. David was angry because the Lord smote Uzzah for trying to keep the ark from tumbling off the cart to the ground (2 Sam. 6:8). And Abraham is displeased because Sarah asks that he send away Hagar and Ishmael (Gen. 21:11). Yet, God tells him to do just this (vs. 12). Morgenstern comments:

> Time and again we are confronted with conflicting duties and are forced to make our choice between them. A voice within keeps urging us to choose the easier and more agreeable duty. . . . But the other voice keeps insisting that this is the greater and more urgent duty, and it must be performed first at all costs. It is the hardest choice in life to make. . . . How shall we decide? There is but one way, the way which Abraham chose, to put aside all self-

ish considerations . . . and determine honestly and uncompromisingly which is the greater and more urgent duty, which is truly God's bidding.

Genesis, p. 139

That Abraham was displeased **on account of his son** (i.e., Ishmael, vs. 11) has led some scholars to infer that Abraham had no feeling for Hagar but was displeased only because of his love for Ishmael. However, the thought seems to be that Abraham loved both Ishmael and Isaac and would not wish to send either of them away.

The Lord's instruction to do what Sarah said (vs. 12) came to Abraham during the night (cf. vs. 14). One consolation that he gives Abraham in sending Hagar and Ishmael away is that **through Isaac shall your descendants be named**. This means that God has decreed that through Isaac, and not through Ishmael, his purposes for and promises to Abraham will become reality (cf. Rom. 9:7; Heb. 11:18). Once again, the Hebrew word translated **descendants** in the RSV and NEB is *zera'*, "seed" (KJV, ASV), which is singular in form but has a collective meaning. It is clear that the reference is to the Israelite people.

[13] Another consolation the Lord gives Abraham is that he will make Ishmael's descendants a great **nation**, just as he had promised (cf. 17:20). In this verse, the word "seed" (KJV, ASV) refers to Ishmael, and thus **offspring** (RSV) and "child" (NEB) are correct English equivalents.

[14-15] When Abraham was faced with a difficult task, he **rose early in the morning** to take care of it (cf. 19:27; 22:3); that is, he did not hesitate to do what God told him, but was resolute. As he sent Hagar away, he demonstrated his love and concern for her and Ishmael by giving her **bread and a skin of water**. It was customary to put water in dried animal skins. The word "bottle" (KJV, ASV) suggests to the modern English mind a container with a different shape, made out of a different kind of material.

Many scholars interpret verses 14-15 so as to find two earlier contradictory sources behind Genesis 17:24-25 and 21:8-21. At verse 14 they adopt the readings of the LXX and Syriac (cf. NEB), which state that Abraham put Ishmael on Hagar's shoulder, and understand the statement **she cast the child under one of the bushes** in verse 15 to mean that Hagar took Ishmael off her shoulder and put him under some bushes. These actions presuppose that Ishmael was an infant at the time, contradicting Genesis 17:24-25, which states that Ishmael was thirteen years old when he was circumcised. Abraham was ninety-nine at that time. This would make Ishmael about sixteen or seventeen when Abraham sent him and Hagar away, and it is hardly likely that Hagar could carry a seventeen-year-old boy on her shoulder or back!

However, this is not the only way to interpret the crucial lines in verses 14-15. The MT says: "and he [i.e., Abraham] took bread and a skin of water, and gave [them] unto Hagar, he put [them] upon her shoulder, and the child, and he sent her away." It is not clear whether **the child** is the direct object of **gave** or **put**. Speiser (*Genesis*, p. 155) acknowledges that "the various emendations that have been proposed merely substitute one set of problems for another. An acceptable solution has yet to be discovered."

If one acknowledges that those who collected and arranged narrative materials preserving records of historical events had enough common sense to recognize contradictions and knew that their readers could do the same, then in problem passages like the present, one must interpret on the side of consistency rather than on the side of discrepancy, where there is a genuine alternative. And in this case there is an alternative. Although the Hebrew syntax is awkward, it is quite possible that the MT means that Abraham **gave** the bread and waterskin to Hagar, putting these items on her shoulder, and then **gave** or committed his son Ishmael to her (cf. ASV), thus officially relinquishing his paternal control over and responsibility to him. After hard traveling in the **wilderness** for an unspecified length of time, Hagar and Ishmael drank all the water out of the skin; then Hagar, undoubtedly faced with Ishmael's foolhardy insistence that they continue and his teenage over-

GENESIS 21:16, 17 / *283*

confidence that he was up to any task, and realizing that
their only chance for survival was to conserve their energy,
took charge of the situation and **cast** (Heb. *shalakh*) him
under some bushes. "The word *cast* suits the exhausted
action of one who had half supported, half dragged her son
towards the shade of the bush" (Kidner, *Genesis*,
pp. 140–41).

As the book of Genesis is not altogether in chronological
order, the author uses the name **Beer-sheba** (which at the
time of the writing of the book was already well-known to
him and his readers), although it is not until later in the
book that he explains how this name originated (cf. 21:31;
26:33).

[16] Unwilling to watch her child die of starvation and
thirst, Hagar moves away **about the distance of a bowshot**
(KJV, ASV, RSV; NEB "about two bowshots away"), that
is, far enough away that she could not see him but close
enough that she could hear any of his cries for help.

On the basis of verse 17, many scholars follow the LXX
in reading **the child lifted up his voice and wept**. However,
this involves three emendations in the MT (not just one). It
seems preferable, therefore, to understand the last line in
verse 16 and the first line in verse 17 as describing two
separate events: first, Hagar wept over the prospect of her
son's death (so the KJV, ASV, and NEB); and second, God
heard the voice of Ishmael, who also presumably was
weeping or perhaps praying (although the text does not so
state).

[17] The Hebrew word translated **lad** (*na'ar*) covers a
broad range of ages. It is used of Moses at the age of three
months (Exod. 2:6; cf. vs. 2) and of Joseph at the age of
seventeen (Gen. 37:2).

Unlike the angels mentioned in 16:7 and 19:1, who operated on earth, **the angel** mentioned in the present verse
calls to Hagar **from heaven**, which calls to mind God's
speaking "from heaven" at Jesus' baptism (Matt. 3:17).

In the angel's statement **God has heard** [*shama' 'elohim*]
the voice of the lad, there is a wordplay on the name
Ishmael (Heb. *yishma'e'l*; cf. 16:11). It is not clear

whether the cryptic statement **where he is** refers to Ishmael's physical location under the bushes or to his emotional state in this distressing situation.

[18] The Hebrew phrase translated **hold him fast with your hand** (NEB "hold him in your arms") is *hachaziqi 'eth yadhekh bo*, which means literally "make firm your hand on him." This is a Hebrew idiom meaning "Give him your encouragement." The same expression occurs in Ezekiel 16:49, where the prophet says in condemnation of Sodom, "Neither did she *strengthen the hand* of the poor and needy"; (KJV, ASV; RSV "but did not *aid* the poor and needy"; and NEB "yet she never *helped* the poor and wretched"). A similar expression appears in Ezekiel 30:25, where Yahweh announces, "I will *strengthen the arms* of the king of Babylon" (KJV, RSV, cf. NEB; ASV "I will *hold up the arms* of the king of Babylon"). One is also reminded of a very similar phrase in 1 Samuel 23:16: "Jonathan . . . *strengthened his* [David's] *hand* in God" (KJV, ASV, RSV; NEB "Jonathan . . . *gave him fresh courage* in God's name"). The KJV, ASV, RSV, and NEB all fail to convey the significance of this idiom, and the KJV, ASV, and NEB leave the wrong impression that the angel was telling Hagar to hold Ishmael in her arms, which would have hardly been possible for her to do with a sixteen- or seventeen-year-old boy.

God's promise to make Ishmael's descendants **a great nation** indicates his concern for and care of nations outside Israel. As the creator of all mankind (1:26-27), God loves and is concerned about all mankind.

[19] God's guidance had brought Hagar and Ishmael to a well. However, Hagar had not seen the well because she was so preoccupied with her own exhaustion and the probable death of her son. God somehow intervened and **opened her eyes**, that is, caused her to look in the right direction and see the well that had been there all the time.

[20-21] The author of Genesis has now taken the story of Hagar and Ishmael as far as he deems necessary to convey his religious message to his readers. Thus, he covers a great period of time in a few lines in order to return to the story of Abraham. He tells how **God was with** Ishmael, how he **became an expert with the bow** as he grew up **in the wilderness of Paran**, and how **his mother took a wife for him from the land of Egypt**, which was her native land (cf. 16:1, 6-7; 21:9). Although it was customary for the father to secure a wife for his son (cf. Gen. 24), Hagar is forced to assume this responsibility due to the fact that Abraham had cast her out (vs. 10) or sent her away (vs. 14) from his home.

DISPUTE BETWEEN ABRAHAM AND ABIMELECH (21:22-34)

God had promised Abraham that he would give him and his descendants the land of Canaan (see the passages given at the beginning of this chapter). Abraham began to claim various portions of the land by building altars to Yahweh, and (in the present passage) by digging a well, planting a tamarisk tree, and calling on the name of the Lord. After his encounter with Abimelech over Sarah (Gen. 20), Abraham and his household move about twenty-five miles east-southeast of Gerar to Beer-sheba, apparently because there was good pasture land there. When he leaves Abimelech, Abraham swears to him that he will deal loyally with him and with his descendants (vss. 22-24). Later, Abimelech's servants seize a well of water that Abraham had dug to water his livestock, and Abraham complains to him. When Abimelech claims that he had no knowledge of this seizure, Abraham proposes that they make a covenant, testifying to the fact that Abraham had dug this well. Abimelech agrees; they make the covenant and separate from each other (vss. 25-34).

[22] It has been suggested that **Phicol the commander of** [Abimelech's] **army** (see also vs. 32; 26:26), was a Hurrian. Probably on the basis of Abraham's success and the earlier incident at Gerar (Gen. 20), Abimelech acknowledges that **God is with** Abraham.

[23] The present paragraph explains the origin of the name "Beer-sheba" (vs. 31). For one thing, it is connected

with the Hebrew word here translated **swear** (*hish-shabhe'ah*) and with the words translated "swore" (*nishbe'u*) and "oath" (*shabha'*) in verse 31 (cf. further vss. 28-30), indicating that Beer-sheba means "Well of the Oath." Abimelech appeals to Abraham to deal **loyally** with him, just as he had dealt loyally with Abraham by giving him rich gifts to show that he had no intention of taking another man's wife (20:14-16). At the same time, as a further incentive to Abraham to swear to him, Abimelech reminds Abraham that he is a sojourner in the land of Gerar and thus does not have the status of a native (cf. the statement of the men of Sodom concerning Lot in 19:9).

[25] The **well** mentioned here is apparently the same as that mentioned in verse 20. Genesis 26:15, 18 indicate that Abraham had dug several wells, and the LXX of 21:25 has the plural. However, verse 30 mentions only one well. Possibly this particular well was important because of its size or location.

[26] Instead of **know** (ASV, RSV, NEB), the KJV has the archaic form "wot," which is unintelligible to most modern English readers. *Wot* is the present first and third person singular from the Middle English verb *witen*, which in turn is based on the Anglo-Saxon verb *witan*, meaning "to know."

[27] Abraham apparently believes Abimelech when he states that he knew nothing about his servants seizing the well Abraham had dug. Accordingly, he gives Abimelech **sheep and oxen** to seal a **covenant** between the two men. In light of a similar covenant between God and Abraham described in 15:9-10, it seems likely that these animals were sacrificed as a sign or seal of the covenant.

[28-30] Abraham also gives Abimelech **seven ewe lambs** as a **witness** or validation that Abraham had dug the well over which the controversy had arisen (KJV, ASV, NEB; RSV reads *tihyeh* as a second person singular and translates **that you may be**, but it is preferable to take this verb form as a third feminine singular). The Hebrew word translated **seven** in these verses is *shebha'*, which provides a further explanation of the origin of the name Beer-sheba

(cf. vss. 23, 31), "Well of the Seven."

[33] Abraham planted a tamarisk tree in Beer-sheba, thus apparently claiming the territory concerning which he had made an agreement with Abimelech as rightfully his. Planting this tree had virtually the same meaning as erecting an altar (cf. 12:7, 8; 13:18). In calling **on the name of the Lord**, Abraham was claiming that this region belonged to the Lord (and to no other god), and the Lord had given it to Abraham as a special gift to guarantee that in due time he would give the land of Canaan to Abraham's descendants.

The special name of the God on whom Abraham calls is *'el 'olam*, **Everlasting God**, who has no beginning and no end. The context seems to suggest that God was invoked by this name as a confirmation of the continual validity of the covenant Abraham had made with Abimelech.

[34] The author of Genesis uses the phrase **land of the Philistines** in verses 32 and 34 because this territory was known by that name to him and to his readers. This does not mean that this was the name by which it was known to Abraham, Abimelech, and their contemporaries.

EXCURSUS

The Literary Problem of Similar Accounts

The two paragraphs in Genesis 21 (i.e., vss. 1-21 and vss. 22-34) contain accounts of events that are similar to passages elsewhere in the book of Genesis. Many scholars have concluded from this that the two accounts represent records of *the same event* originating in *two different sources*.

Genesis 21:1-21 is similar to 16:1-16. In both passages, (1) there is a conflict between Sarah and her Egyptian handmaid Hagar (16:4-6; 21:9-10); (2) Hagar flees from Abraham's home (16:6; 21:14); (3) Hagar flees toward her native land of Egypt (16:7; 21:14); (4) an angel of the Lord comes to Hagar and comforts her in misfortune (16:7-11; 21:17-18); (5) there is a wordplay on the name Ishmael and the Hebrew verb *shama'* meaning "to hear" (16:11; 21:17); (6) God promises Hagar that she will have a multitude of descendants (16:10; 21:18). Usually, most of chapter 16 is assigned to J and most of 21:8-21 to E.

However, this explanation does not adequately account for the many differences between these two accounts. (1) It assumes that Hagar would not have fled from Abraham's home twice, in spite of the fact that according to 16:6 Hagar flees voluntarily, while in 21:10, 12-14 Abraham officially releases her from his household. There is no reason why Hagar might not have left Abraham's household on two different occasions. (2) According to 16:4-6, a conflict arose between Sarah and Hagar over Hagar's disrespectful attitude toward Sarah, while 21:9 states that a conflict arose between them over Ishmael's arrogant treatment of Isaac. (3) Hagar fled to the wilderness of Shur in 16:7, whereas 21:14 states that she wandered in the wilderness of Beer-sheba. (4) Hagar returns to her mistress according to 16:9, 15-16, but she does not return according to chapter 21. (5) Genesis 16:15-16 relates the birth of Ishmael, while 21:8-9 tells of an event that occurred when Ishmael was a young man and Isaac was two or three years of age.

These differences are significant enough to indicate that the author of Genesis is relating two entirely different events in chapters 16 and 21. The similar order, words, and phrases in these two accounts are due to the fact that the same author related them and would be expected to use the same or similar terms in giving accounts of similar stories.

There are also similarities between Genesis 21:22-34 and 26:17-33. In both texts, (1) the patriarch deals with Abimelech and Phicol the commander of his army from Gerar (21:22, 32; 26:26); (2) Abimelech affirms that God is with the patriarch (21:22; 26:28); (3) Abimelech requests an oath that the patriarch will not deal falsely with him and his people (21:23; 26:28-29); (4) there is a dispute over the ownership of a well (21:25, 30; 26:19-20); and (5) an explanation of the origin of the name Beer-sheba is given (21:31; 26:33). Many scholars conclude from this that 21:22-34 and 26:17-33 are two accounts of the same event.

Again, however, there are a number of significant differences between these two stories: (1) Genesis 21:22-34 has to do with Abraham, while 26:17-33 has to do with Isaac; (2) Genesis 26:18 refers back to the account in 21:25, 30, indicating that the author of 26:17-33 knew the earlier account—indeed, that it was part and parcel of the *same* account that he was relating; (3) the oath between Abraham and Abimelech was sealed by offering sacrificial animals (21:27), but the oath between Isaac and Abimelech was sealed by a feast (26:30); (4) there are details in 26:17-33 which have no similarity whatsoever to details in 21:22-34—for example, Isaac's digging of three wells, the first two of which became objects of dispute but not the third (26:19-22), Yahweh's appearance to Isaac by night and Isaac's building of the altar at Beer-sheba (26:24-25), and Abimelech's expulsion of Isaac (26:27).

Furthermore, it seems typical for Isaac to frequent the same regions where his father had sojourned, to use the same wells his father had used (and evidently to which he had made claim) to water his livestock, to deal with the same king with whom his father dealt (and in the same way), and to use the same names for the wells that his father had used. The similarities in order, words, and expressions between 21:22-34 and 26:17-33 are due to the fact that the two events were similar and that the same author was relating them.

ABRAHAM AND ISAAC: THE TRANSFER OF THE BLESSING (22:1–25:18)

The author of Genesis relates very little concerning Isaac apart from his father Abraham on the one hand, and his son Jacob on the other. The present section records five events that are concerned directly or indirectly with the transfer of God's blessing from Abraham to Isaac: (1) God commands Abraham to sacrifice Isaac (22:1-19); (2) Abraham learns that his brother Nahor has a son Bethuel, who is the father of Rebekah (22:20-24); (3) Sarah dies and is buried (23); (4) Isaac marries Rebekah (24); (5) Abraham's children by Keturah and Hagar are blessed, but Isaac receives God's greatest blessings through Abraham (25:1-18).

God Commands Abraham to Sacrifice Isaac (22:1-19)

After God had given Abraham and Sarah the son he had promised them in their old age, and after Abraham had had a few years to enjoy him and to take for granted that finally Isaac was the child that God had promised, God tells Abraham to sacrifice Isaac (vss. 1-2). Without hesitation, Abraham obeys God's command (vss. 3-10). But just at the moment he is about to slaughter Isaac, God stays his hand and tells him to offer a ram in place of his son (vss. 11-14). Then God promises to bless Abraham as he had said, because Abraham had obeyed his voice (vss. 15-19).

Scholars have suggested various views as to the main intention of 22:1-19. Some believe that it is a polemic against child sacrifice. God tells Abraham to offer an animal instead of his son. However, this theory does not take into consideration the fact that it was God himself who told Abraham to offer up Isaac in the first place (vss. 1-2). Others think that the primary purpose is to emphasize the importance of obedience to God, and this is certainly a significant point in this paragraph (cf. vss. 3, 9, 18). As Morgenstern remarks:

> Dearer to God than even the richest animal sacrifice is the sacrifice of the heart, perfect faith in Him and willingness to obey His word, readiness to answer His call, even before its purpose be known, with the unfailing 'Here am I,' and to give up for Him what is best and dearest, even one's only, beloved child.
>
> *Genesis,* p. 145

It seems most likely, however, that God's primary goal in commanding Abraham to offer Isaac is to test his faith in God's promises and long-range purposes. When Abraham received his call in Haran, he had to give up his country, his kindred, and his father's house (12:1). In Gerar, he had to give up his concubine Hagar and his son Ishmael (21:10-14). Now God commands him to give up Isaac, his only son by Sarah:

> Abraham had to cut himself off from his entire past when he left his homeland and now is summoned to give up his entire future. The testing goes to the heart of his life, his hope for meaning, and his trust in Yahweh.
>
> Marks, "Book of Genesis," p. 18

Furthermore, Abraham had to project his faith far into the future:

> The process that Abraham set in motion was not to be accomplished in a single generation. It sprang from a vision that would have to be tested and validated over an incalculable span of time, a vision that could be pursued only with singlemindedness of purpose and absolute faith . . . . The object of the ordeal, then, was to discover how firm was the patriarch's faith in the ultimate divine purpose. It was one thing to start out resolutely for the Promised Land, but it was a very different thing to maintain confidence in the promise when all appeared lost.
>
> Speiser, *Genesis,* p. 166

[1] The Hebrew word *nissah*, translated **tested** (RSV) or "put to the test" (NEB), is not to be understood in the sense of "tempt" (KJV), as though God was trying to seduce or entice Abraham to sin. Such an idea of God's behavior toward man is flatly denied in James 1:13. This same Hebrew root is used in speaking of God's testing or proving Israel (cf. ASV; Exod. 15:25; 16:4; 20:20; Deut. 8:2, 16; 13:3 [Hebrew 4]), the tribe of Levi (Deut. 33:8), Hezekiah (2 Chron. 32:31), and the psalmist (Ps. 26:2). The suggestion in Deuteronomy 8:2, 2 Chronicles 32:31, and Psalm 26:2 is that the divine proving or testing of man is to bring out the real feelings and motivations of the heart. According to Genesis 22, God tested Abraham's faith to see if he really put God's will above what seemed to be logical, his love for Isaac, and the dreams of the future which God's promises had aroused in his breast (cf. Heb. 11:17-19).

> The real test is in the way we offer our sacrifice, the willingness with which we give up what is dear, the perfect faith in God which we still preserve, and which keeps us from doubting His wisdom and goodness.
>
> Morgenstern, *Genesis*, p. 148

[2] God's crescendo-like description of Isaac—**your son, your only son, Isaac, whom you love**—is intended to emphasize the magnitude of the sacrifice which he was commanding Abraham to make (cf. vss. 12, 16). Of course, Isaac was not Abraham's **only** son in the strict sense of the term (as Abraham had one son by Hagar [Ishmael], Gen. 16:15, and six by Keturah, Gen. 25:2-4), but he was his only son by Sarah.

Abraham was in Beer-sheba in the land of the Philistines when God told him to offer up Isaac (cf. Gen. 21:33-34). Scholars differ greatly over the location of **the land of Moriah**. Some identify it with the hill on which Solomon built the temple (2 Chron. 3:1), but this is a "mountain" and not a "land." By emending the text slightly, others have suggested that we read "land of Moreh" (cf. 12:6), "land of the Hamorites" (cf. 33:19; 34:2, 4, 6), or "land of the Amorites" (following the Syriac), which is a common term for the land of Canaan (cf. 15:16). The LXX reads "the high land," and the Vulgate has "the land of vision." As yet, no convincing location has been proposed.

[4] Abraham's heavy burden, which he had been carrying in his heart for three days, now suddenly becomes heavier as he catches sight of the place where God had charged him to slaughter Isaac.

[5] Because of God's promise, "through Isaac shall your descendants be named" (21:12), Abraham believed that somehow both he and Isaac would **come again** to the young men accompanying them, after they had worshiped. Hebrews 11:19 seems to suggest that one thought which crossed Abraham's mind is that after he had killed Isaac, God could raise him from the dead.

[6] **Fire** is used here by metonymy (see LWC-OT, vol. 1, ch. 1) for the equipment for making fire, which may have

been glowing embers of some sort.

[7] Again Abraham's heart must have been cut to the quick when his son asked him, **Where is the lamb for a burnt offering?**

[8] **God will provide himself** is a translation of the Hebrew *'elohim yir'eh lo*. This is the first of four word-plays, ending in verse 14 with *yahweh yir'eh*, "Jehovah-jireh" (KJV, ASV, NEB) or "The Lord will provide" (RSV). One also encounters *yere' 'elohim 'attah*, "you fear God," in verse 12 and *wayyar' wehinneh 'ayil*, "and looked, and behold, . . . a ram," in verse 13. The same God who had given Isaac to Abraham and Sarah in the first place could certainly provide a ram for a burnt offering as and when he pleased. It should be noted that Abraham deals most gently with Isaac throughout this delicate and tense experience, as is evidenced, among other things, by addressing him tenderly as **my son** (vss. 7, 8).

[9] Possibly to emphasize the great ordeal that Abraham was having to endure, this verse describes in great detail the preparations for the sacrifice: (1) Abraham **built an altar** (which he had done frequently elsewhere, cf. 12:7, 8; 13:4, 18), (2) **laid the wood** in the proper manner upon the altar, (3) **bound Isaac** (as he would have to have bound an animal), and (4) **laid him on the wood on the altar**. One can imagine Abraham's agony throughout this procedure.

[10] In radical obedience to God, Abraham raises the knife that he had brought (cf. vs. 6) to slay his son.

[11] The **angel of the Lord** is the Lord himself, as the context shows (cf. vss. 12, 14, 16-18; cf. 18:2, 22; 19:1). He speaks **from heaven** (vss. 11, 15), as the angel spoke to Hagar (21:17). His cry **Abraham, Abraham** expresses urgency (cf. "Jacob, Jacob," in 46:2; "Moses, Moses," in Exod. 3:4; and "Samuel, Samuel," in 1 Sam. 3:10).

[12] The statement **now I know that you fear God** should not be taken to mean that God does not know all things. Rather, this is an anthropomorphic statement (in which one speaks of God as if he were human). The whole context shows that the purpose of this entire ordeal was not to secure information for God but to probe the depths

of Abraham's faith. On previous occasions, Abraham had feared the Pharaoh of Egypt (12:11-13) and Abimelech of Gerar (20:2). But he also grew in his trust in God through these and other experiences. Now was the time for the supreme test, and Abraham boldly faced its challenge. This paragraph demonstrates graphically that in OT and NT times alike God wants first the man—his heart, his commitment, his trust—and then, and only then, his sacrifices or gifts (cf. 1 Sam. 15:22-23; Pss. 50:7-21; 51:20-21 [Hebrew 18-19]).

[13] Just as Hagar had seen a well at just the right moment in her crisis (21:19), now Abraham sees **a ram** at just the right moment in his crisis. In both cases, the Lord provided for human needs.

[14] It seems preferable to read a proper name here—"Yahweh [Jehovah]-jireh" (so KJV, ASV, NEB)—rather than to translate as **The Lord will provide**. Although this Hebrew verbal root can also mean "see" (cf. KJV), the context suggests that it should be translated **provide** here (cf. vs. 8). But even so, there is probably an intentional wordplay with the verb "see" in 21:19.

[16] The OT refers to God's swearing by himself also in Exodus 32:13 (referring back to this incident); Isaiah 45:23; Jeremiah 22:5; and 49:13. Furthermore, Hebrews 6:13-17 alludes to this passage. For Yahweh to swear by himself is to express his most solemn promise.

[17-18] God promises Abraham that he will **bless** him by doing three things for his **descendants**: (a) he will cause them to **multiply** in number **as the stars** and the grains of **sand**; (b) he will give them victory over their enemies; and (c) he will bless all the nations through them.

Once again, the Hebrew word *zera'*, which technically is singular and literally means "seed" (KJV, ASV), obviously has the collective meaning of **descendants** here.

In the statement **your descendants shall possess the gate of their enemies**, "gate" is a synecdoche (a speech form in which a part is used for the whole, or the whole for a part; see LWC-OT, vol. 1, ch. 1) for the whole city (cf. 24:60).

It is better to read the first phrase of verse 18 as a passive—**by your descendants shall all the nations of the earth** *be blessed* —in spite of the fact that the MT uses the hithpael (for a fuller discussion, cf. the note on 12:3).

God's statement to Abraham, **because you have obeyed my voice,** shows that God's warnings and promises are often dependent on the response of the hearers. This principle is clearly expressed in Jeremiah 18:7-10 and often illustrated in the OT. For example, Jonah told the people of Nineveh that forty days later they and their city would be overthrown (Jon. 3:4). However, they repented, and God did not destroy them as he had warned (Jon. 3:5-10).

[19] After his ordeal, Abraham returns to **Beer-sheba,** where God had told him to offer up Isaac (cf. 21:33).

News about Nahor's Family (22:20-24)

Abraham had two brothers, Haran (who died in Ur of the Chaldees before Terah's family left there, 11:28) and Nahor (11:27, 29). The author of Genesis picked up and carried on the story of Haran's son Lot in chapters 12–19, and now he returns to Nahor. His reason for doing so is to introduce Rebekah, who is the granddaughter of Nahor (cf. 28:5), in order to prepare his readers for the account of the marriage of Isaac and Rebekah in chapter 24. Like Ishmael (25:13-16), Esau (36:15-19), and Jacob (35:22-26), Nahor has twelve sons; and as in Jacob's case (35:22-26), eight of them are born to a wife and four to a concubine. It is obvious that what Abraham is told here covered a number of years and that the inspired author is omitting many details which might have been most interesting to a modern audience but apparently were irrelevant to his religious purposes to meet the needs of his readers.

[20] Nahor's wife, Milcah, was the daughter of Haran, and thus a (half-?)sister of Lot (cf. 11:29). Apparently, when Abraham and Nahor parted at Haran, neither had children. Genesis 21:2-3 related the birth of Isaac to Abraham and Sarah in their old age. Now Abraham learns that not only Sarah but also Milcah has borne children.

[21-22] Virtually nothing is known with certainty about

Nahor's sons or about tribes that may have descended from them. It is a mistake to view some of the people named as identical with others of the same name elsewhere. Uz, for example, is not the same person as the one named in 10:23. As often in ancient literature (including the Bible), the same name was given to a number of different individuals. (See the Excursus, "Key Figures in the Family of Terah," p. 315, below.)

Sarah Dies and Is Buried (Ch. 23)

The author of Genesis possibly skips as much as twenty-five years in the lives of Abraham and Sarah between the account of the offering of Isaac (22:1-19) and that of Sarah's death at the age of 127 (23:1), since Sarah was ninety when Isaac was born (17:17) and Isaac was still quite young when God commanded Abraham to sacrifice him. The modern reader would be intrigued by events in Abraham's life during these years, but the biblical writer selected certain events which had special significance for the needs of his audience and which conveyed his religious message, just as John did in writing his gospel (John 20:30-31; 21:25). What is at stake in Genesis 23 is God's promise to give the land of Canaan to Abraham and to his descendants. Abraham had begun to claim portions of this land by building altars to Yahweh at various places (12:7, 8; 13:18; 22:9) and by planting a tamarisk tree at Beer-sheba (21:33). Now, he makes a further claim by purchasing a field and cave in Machpelah as the family burial site. Before Joseph died in Egypt, he instructed the sons of Israel to carry his bones out of Egypt and to bury them in Canaan (50:24-25).

In the twenty-five year interval between the offering of Isaac and Sarah's death, Abraham and his household move from Beer-sheba (21:19) back to Hebron (23:2; cf. 13:18; 14:13). When Sarah dies, Abraham purchases a field and a cave in Machpelah (which is located east of Mamre, vss. 17, 19) from a certain Ephron for 400 shekels of silver (vss. 15-16).

The great antiquity of Genesis 23 is demonstrated by the detailed description of ancient bargaining customs, by the mention of the "Hittites," and by the nature and handling of money. Abraham is a stranger and a sojourner (vs. 4), and thus has no right to purchase property in a foreign land without special mediation. Before he speaks, he bows courteously to those with whom he is bargaining (vss. 7, 12). He does not deal with Ephron directly but asks the Hittites to mediate for him with Ephron (vss. 8-9). The whole transaction takes place very legally before all who are gathered at the gate of the city (note the expressions "in your presence," vs. 9; "among the Hittites," vs. 10; "in the presence of the sons of my people," vs. 11; "in the hearing of the people of the land," vs. 13; and "in the presence of the Hittites," vs. 18). Ephron offers to give the property to Abraham (vs. 11), which is not a serious offer but the ordinary way of initiating a bargaining. In customary style, Abraham insists on purchasing the field (vs. 13). Ephron then asks an exorbitant price (400 shekels of silver, vs. 15), which Abraham pays immediately and very legally (vs. 16).

[2] Although the Bible says very briefly, **Sarah died**, one must empathize with Abraham over the loss of God's greatest gift to him—his wife (cf. Prov. 18:22; 19:14). "All that is good and precious, even the love of dear ones, comes from God, is but lent to us for a time, and must be given back when He in His wisdom demands" (Morgenstern, *Genesis*, p. 155).

The name **Kiriath-arba** means "city of Arba." Arba was the father of Anak (Josh. 15:13; 21:11), from whom descended the Anakim (Num. 13:22, 28; Josh. 15:14; Judg. 1:20), who were living at Hebron when the Israelites began the conquest of Canaan under Joshua (Num. 13:22; Josh. 15:13-14). Anak and his descendants apparently gave this city this name in honor of their ancestor. Arba seems to be a non-Semitic name, which agrees with the fact that this city was inhabited by Hittites in the time of Abraham. Later, the Israelites changed this name to **Hebron** (cf. Josh. 15:13; 21:11). The author of Genesis and his readers were living after this change in name took place, and the name **Kiriath-arba** was no longer known. Therefore, he had to explain to them that **Kiriath-arba** was the ancient name for the more modern name **Hebron**. It should be noted that such explanations to later audiences help date the final form of a biblical book and must be taken into consideration in any biblical view of the inspiration of Scripture.

Abraham **went in** (so RSV, NEB; Heb. *yabho'*; not "came," KJV, ASV, which leaves the impression that Abraham was gone from home when Sarah died) to **mourn** and to **weep** for Sarah.

[3] After weeping bitterly over his loss of Sarah, **Abraham rose up.**

> Grief, indulged in too long, becomes base, ignoble and selfish . . . . We become self-centered; we think only of our own grief and our own sorrow, and indulge ourselves in them . . . . We refuse to believe that others have grief and sorrows, too, like ours, or even surpassing ours, and we cease to feel for them and to think of them . . . . We forget that God has created us for a purpose, and that this purpose is not to indulge outselves in grief, but like Abraham, after the first bitter pain of sorrow has passed, to rise up from before our dead, and resume the ordinary tasks and duties of life, to live in the world among our fellowmen, and bring unto them help and cheer and blessing. We are here on this earth, not to grieve too much, but to serve.
>
> Morgenstern, *Genesis*, p. 157

Scholars are divided over the identity of "the sons of Heth" or **the Hittites** in Genesis 23. (a) Speiser (*Genesis*, pp. 172–73) thinks they are the same as the Jebusites. (b) Source theorists suppose that "Hittite" was P's word for pre-Israelite inhabitants of Canaan, while J preferred "Canaanite," and E, "Amorite." (c) Some critics argue that the Hittites in this chapter are Hurrians. (d) It seems most likely that the Hittites actually swept into the Palestinian area prior to the conquest of Canaan and that some of them had settled at Hebron in patriarchal times (see I. J. Gelb, "Hittites," IDB, vol. 2, p. 613). Some of the details in this chapter are illuminated by Hittite legal documents discovered at modern Boghazköy in Turkey. Other passages in the book of Genesis attest to the presence of Hittites in southern Canaan in this period (cf. 26:34; 27:46; 36:2).

[4] As **a stranger and a sojourner** at Hebron, Abraham's legal position was that of a long-standing member of the community who had no land of his own. He had held a similar legal position in Egypt (12:10), as had Lot in Sodom (19:9). The verb **give** (Heb. *nathan*) in verses 4 and 9 means "sell," as the context shows.

[6] It is interesting to note that throughout the bargaining described in this chapter, when a speaker thinks he has a better suggestion than what has just been offered, he introduces it with the word **hear** (from the Hebrew root *sh-m-*'; cf. vss. 5, 11, 13, 15).

The first offer that the Hittites make to Abraham is to allow him to bury his dead in their sepulchres. They are happy to do this because of the high regard they have for Abraham. In their eyes he is **a mighty prince** (RSV, KJV, NEB). The Hebrew expression here is *neśi' 'elohim*, which means literally "a prince of God" (so ASV). However, *'elohim* can be a "noun of quality" meaning "divine," "awesome," "mighty." Apparently the expression here means **a mighty prince** (cf. the expression *ruach 'elohim* in Gen. 1:2, which probably means "a mighty wind"; see the comment on this verse).

[8] In keeping with ancient Oriental custom, Abraham does not wish to bargain with Ephron directly but asks the Hittites to **entreat for** him, that is, bargain in his behalf.

[9] **Machpelah** included not only the cave (it was customary to bury the dead in caves in ancient times), but a field in which the cave was located (cf. vss. 17, 19; 49:30; 50:13). This was east of Mamre (vss. 17, 19), where Abraham and his household had lived at an earlier time (13:18; 14:13; 18:1), and to which they apparently moved from Beer-sheba. Scholars generally agree that the cave of Machpelah lies below the modern Haram el-Khalil, east of Hebron (cf. V. R. Gold, "Machpelah," IDB, vol. 3, p. 218). Six members of Abraham's family were buried in this cave: Sarah (23:19), Abraham (25:9), Isaac, Rebekah

(49:29-32), Jacob, and Leah (49:29-32; 50:12-13).

Hittite law stated that if a person bought another's entire piece of property, he was bound to perform certain feudal services. This would explain why Abraham wanted to purchase only the area **at the end of** Ephron's **field**, and why Ephron refused to sell unless Abraham bought the whole field (vs. 11). Abraham offers to pay **the full price**, just as David did later when he purchased the threshing floor of Ornan (1 Chron. 21:22, 24). Some suggest that this is a customary bargaining maneuver in the Orient, but it may be that Abraham wants to make sure that later there can be no question that this property belonged to him and his household.

[10] Those **who went in at the gate of** Ephron's city (cf. also vs. 18) were his fellow Hittites who lived at Hebron (34:24 uses the expression "all who went out of the gate of his city" in the same sense; cf. 19:1) and thus had the legal right to serve as witnesses to legal transactions.

[11] Ephron's offer to give Abraham his field and cave is not a sincere offer but a commonly accepted bargaining maneuver in the Orient, designed to give the seller an advantage because of his apparent generosity.

[15] It seems preferable to translate the Hebrew word *'adhoni* by "sir" here (so NEB) rather than **lord** (so ASV, RSV, KJV), because of the usual connotation suggested by the word "lord" in modern English.

It is impossible to know the equivalent of **four hundred shekels of silver** at ancient Hebron in modern currency because the value of a silver shekel varied from time to time and from place to place in the ancient world. By way of general comparison, it may be noted that Omri purchased the hill of Samaria from a certain Shemer for two talents (i.e., 6,000 shekels) of silver (1 Kings 16:24), and Jeremiah bought a field in Anathoth from his cousin Hanamel for seventeen shekels of silver (Jer. 32:9). Accordingly, the price that Ephron states for his field and cave is quite exorbitant (see O. R. Sellers, "Weights and Measures," IDB, vol. 4, pp. 831–32).

[16] Weights current among the merchants served as a

standard for trading. A similar practice is attested in the Eshnunna and Old Babylonian Laws. In this way, neither the buyer nor the seller would feel that he was cheated. Abraham's silver was not counted but **weighed out.**

[17] Ancient man considered the east to be in front of him, thus explaining the Hebrew expression *liphne mamre'* (literally "before Mamre"—so KJV and ASV). For the modern mind, it is more meaningful to read **east of Mamre** (so RSV and NEB).

Whereas it might seem strange to modern man for the writer to mention **the field, the cave, the trees that were in the field,** and the **whole area,** this was widely done in ancient legal transactions. Hittite laws in particular mention trees in documents dealing with buying and selling.

Isaac Marries Rebekah (Ch. 24)

In his old age (vs. 1), Abraham's faith in God's promise is again tested. He must trust that the "God of heaven and of the earth" (vss. 3, 7) is in control of his world and works for the good of his people. In order that God's promises to give Abraham's descendants the land of Canaan and to bless all nations through them might be fulfilled, it is necessary that Isaac marry a woman from Abraham's "country and kindred" (vs. 4) to preserve the purity of Abraham's lineage and that Isaac live in Canaan and not in Mesopotamia (vss. 5-6).

The thread that holds this chapter together is the continued emphasis on God's activity in choosing just the right woman for Isaac. When Abraham dispatches his servant to seek a wife for Isaac, he assures him God will send his angel before him (vs. 7; see also vs. 40). After the servant arrives in the city of Nahor, he prays, "O Lord, God of my master Abraham, grant me success today" (vs. 12). When the maiden Rebekah comes to draw water for the servant's camels, he watches her closely "to learn whether the Lord had prospered his journey or not" (vs. 21). Once he is convinced that Rebekah is the girl God has chosen for Isaac, the servant praises God and says, "The Lord has led me in the way to the house of my master's kinsmen" (vs. 27; cf. vss. 48, 56). Laban and Bethuel agree and say, "The thing comes from the Lord" (vs. 50). Thus, the thing which distinguished Abraham and his servant from the world about them is that they saw and appreciated the work of God in all activities of life.

Genesis 24 is composed of six scenes, each of which describes a meeting and/or conversation between two major characters in the plot. The following discussion represents an attempt to follow this scheme of the inspired author.

Abraham instructs his servant to seek a wife for Isaac (vss. 1-9). Abraham makes his most respected servant (possibly Eliezer, cf. 15:2) swear that he will seek a wife for Isaac among his kinsmen in Mesopotamia and not among the Canaanites in the promised land (vss. 3-4). He specifically charges him to bring the maiden back to Canaan with him and not to take Isaac to Mesopotamia (vss. 5-8). Apparently Abraham did not take care of this matter in person because he was very old (i.e., 140—cf. 25:20 with 17:17).

[2] Abraham's **servant** is an inspiring example of ideal servanthood. He is unassuming but uses good common sense. He manifests great faith in God (vss. 12-14, 26-27, 52), and unwavering loyalty to his master (vss. 12, 14, 27; cf. Prov. 20:6). His first concern is to carry out the task his master has given him (vss. 33, 56). Morgenstern notes:

> Far too frequently the term, servant, is thought to be indicative of inferiority and degradation. We would all be masters; but few are willing to be servants. . . . God has created us, not to be masters, but to be servants, to serve Him and our fellowmen loyally and faithfully, like this servant of Abraham, without thought of reward, but with the consciousness of duty in our hearts and the fear of God upon us. Only by serving can we realize the purpose of existence.

> *Genesis,* p. 169

The precise significance of Abraham's command to his servant, **Put your hand under my thigh** (cf. vs. 9), is not known. Targum Jonathan, Jerome, and Rashi thought that the genital organs were intended, and that this was an appeal to the covenant of circumcision. Ibn Ezra suggested that it was an ancient symbol of subjection. Some more recent commentators think that since children are said to come forth from their father's thigh (cf. the Hebrew expression *yotse'e yerekho,* literally "those proceeding [going out] from the thigh [loins] of," RSV "[his own] offspring," in Gen. 46:26; Exod. 1:5; Judg. 8:30), an oath in which one placed his hand under another's thigh was a way of invoking sterility on himself or great curses (possibly extinction) on his descendants if he failed to carry out the oath. At least, it is clear that Abraham's intention was to bind his servant firmly to the oath because Abraham was not able to carry out the task himself. The same procedure is followed when Jacob (Israel) has his son Joseph swear to him that when he dies he will not bury him in Egypt but in the cave of Machpelah in Canaan (Gen. 47:29-31).

[3] The Hebrew root translated **swear** (vs. 3) and "oath"(vs. 8) is *sh-b-',* but the word translated "oath" in verse 41 is *'alah,* which indicates that Abraham put his servant under a curse if he failed faithfully to carry out his mission (see J. Scharbert, "*'alāh,*" TDOT, vol. 1, p. 263).

Abraham knows that God is not restricted to the region of Hebron in the land of Canaan where he is dwelling (cf. 23:19). After all, God had worked in his behalf in Ur of the Chaldees, Haran, Egypt, and other places in Canaan. Thus, he sends his servant to the distant land of Mesopotamia under an oath sworn by **the God of heaven and of the earth** (cf. vs. 7), that is, the Creator (Gen. 1:1; 2:4; 14:19, 22) and Sustainer (Gen. 14:20) of all that is.

Abraham's concern that Isaac not marry a Canaanite girl would seem to grow out of the more basic principle that a wife is intended to be a helper fit for her husband (cf. Gen. 2:18, 20). If she hinders him from deep commitment to God and his purposes (and a Canaanite worshiper of pagan gods would do just that to Isaac), he should seek a wife elsewhere. This principle is repeated often in both OT and NT (cf. Exod. 34:11-16; Deut. 7:1-4; 1 Kings 11:1-13; Ezra 9–10; Neh. 13:23-27; 1 Cor. 7:39; 2 Cor. 6:14).

[7] Abraham's confidence that God would help his servant find a wife for Isaac is based on what God had done for him in the past. He specifically mentions God's call in Ur of the Chaldees (Acts 7:2-3; Gen. 11:31) to leave his father's house and the land of his birth and his oath to give Abraham's descendants the land of Canaan (Gen. 13:14-15; 15:18-21). The idea that God would send his angel before Abraham's servant to assure his successful mission is paralleled by the many references to God's sending his angel to bring Israel out of Egypt (cf. Exod. 23:20, 23; 33:2; Num. 20:16).

The servant prays for guidance (vss. 10-14). In obedience to Abraham's command, the servant goes to Haran, where Nahor lives ("the city of Nahor," vs. 10; cf. 11:31). When he arrives at the well outside the city, he asks God to indicate to him the maiden he had chosen to be Isaac's wife by letting her be the one who would offer water to him and to his camels (vss. 12-14).

[10] Although camels were not used on a wide scale by seminomads or in military encounters until about 1200 B.C., surely they were used by individuals and families long before this for various domestic purposes. Bones of camels have been unearthed at Mari in houses (eighteenth century B.C.), perhaps indicating that they were considered part of the household there (see Thompson, "Camel," pp. 490–91). The servant takes **ten camels** as transportation for the chosen maiden and her attendants (cf. vs. 61) and **all sorts of choice gifts** as bridal gifts to the maiden (vss. 22, 53) and her relatives (vs. 53).

The Hebrew expression translated **Mesopotamia** is *'aram naharayim*, which means literally "Aram (Syria) of the two rivers." There is much discussion among scholars as to the exact area intended, and the present writer is not equipped to reach a conclusion. Some experts suggest that it refers to the area between the Tigris and the Euphrates. Others think it means those portions of Syria located on both sides of the Euphrates. The final statement in verse 10 would seem to suggest that this territory included the region of

Haran in northwest Mesopotamia. **The city of Nahor** does not mean the city called Nahor, but the city where Abraham's brother Nahor lived. This was Haran, as 11:31, 27:43, 28:10, and 29:4 confirm.

[11] Camels **kneel down** to allow their riders to mount or dismount and to rest. Just as Abraham's servant meets Isaac's bride for the first time at a well, so Jacob met Rachel (Gen. 29:2-12), and Moses met Zipporah (Exod. 2:15-21).

[13] The well (Heb. *be'er*) mentioned in verses 11 and 20 was fed by a **spring** (RSV, NEB) or "fountain" (ASV; Heb. *'ayin*; not a "well," KJV; cf. also vss. 29, 42, 43). The maidens filled their waterpots at the spring, then carried them to the watering trough, where they poured water out for the animals (vs. 20; see Gen. 30:38; Exod. 2:16).

[14] The servant's request for a sign from God is much like that of Gideon (Judg. 6:36-40) and that of Jonathan (1 Sam. 14:8-10).

The servant meets Rebekah (vss. 15-27). God gives the servant much more than he asks. Not only is the girl courteous and helpful, but she is Nahor's (Abraham's brother's) granddaughter (vs. 15) and very beautiful (vs. 16). Rebekah comes to the well, and when the servant asks her for water, she offers to feed the camels also—thus executing the sign which the servant had requested (vss. 15-21). The servant asks her if he may lodge at her family's home for the night, and she says that he may (vss. 22-27).

[15] The problem of Rebekah's genealogy is discussed in the Excursus, "Key Figures in the Family of Terah," page 315, below.

[16] The water of this particular well was apparently several feet below the surface of the ground. In order to reach it, the girls **went down** by a path or steps and then **came up**.

[18] Rebekah addresses the servant as *'adhoni*, which means literally **my lord** (RSV, KJV, ASV), but is roughly equivalent to the modern English term "sir" (NEB). The details in the story are striking. Rebekah lowers her water jar from her shoulder (vss. 15, 45, 46) to her hand (vs. 18), then tilts it slightly so the water can come out.

[22] Abraham's servant gives Rebekah a nose **ring** and **two** arm **bracelets** of gold to show his appreciation for her kindness to him and his camels. It is true that the Hebrew word *nezem* is used of an "earring" in Genesis 35:4 and Exodus 32:2, 3. However, it is also used of a "nose ring" in Isaiah 3:21 and Proverbs 11:2, and Genesis 24:47 shows it must have this meaning here. (So the KJV wrongly translates by "earring" here and in vs. 30. Note the strange reading in the KJV of verse 47: "and I put the earring upon her face.") The Samaritan Pentateuch adds "and he put it on her nose" in verse 22.

[25] The fact that Bethuel's household could accommodate Abraham's servant, the men who were traveling with him (cf. vss. 54, 59), and his camels on a moment's notice indicates its large size and wealth of possessions and calls to mind Abraham's own household.

[27] The LXX, Syriac, Vulgate, and Targum, as well as verse 48, read *'achi,* literally my master's "brother," instead of the MT *'ache,* literally my master's "brothers." But neither Bethuel nor Laban is Abraham's brother. Bethuel is his nephew, and Laban is his nephew's son. Hence, it is clear that the Hebrew word translated "brother" has a much wider connotation than simply "blood brother." One must determine its precise meaning from each context. In the present passage, the evidence favors the reading of the NEB, "my master's kinsman" (not "brethren," as in the KJV or ASV, or **kinsmen,** as in the RSV).

The servant relates his mission (vss. 28-49). Rebekah runs to her house and tells her family about the arrival of Abraham's servant. Her brother Laban goes out to invite the servant to spend the night, and the servant tells him about Abraham's charge to find a wife among his kindred (vss. 34-41) and about his encounter with Rebekah at the well (vss. 42-49). Much of verses 1-27 is repeated in verses 28-49, making only a minimum of comment necessary.

[28] Most scholars conclude from the reference to Rebekah's **mother's household** in the present verse, and

from the prominent role of Laban in verses 29, 50, 53, and 55, that Bethuel was no longer living. However, this necessitates interpreting the words "and Bethuel" in verse 50 as a late, incorrect interpolation. It seems more likely that Laban took the leading position in the household because his father was old and no longer able to shoulder the major responsibilities, just as Isaac was now taking a prominent role in Abraham's household (vs. 65) because his father was so old (vs. 1).

[30] The inspired author makes it clear to his readers from the very first that Laban was one who loved riches and who would stop at nothing to obtain them. Because **he saw the** [nose] **ring, and the bracelets on his sister's arms,** Laban was most courteous to Abraham's servant (cf. vss. 31-33), apparently hoping the servant would give him some of the riches he had brought along on the journey. Laban's attitude later, in his encounters with Jacob, reflects the same spirit (see chs. 29–31).

[32] The absence of a proper name in the MT of this verse makes it difficult to determine the subject of the verbs. It seems most likely that the author means that the servant **came into the house** in compliance with Laban's request (vs. 31), and that Laban **ungirded the camels** and **gave** the servant food for the camels and water to wash his feet. Here, once again, washing feet or providing for feet to be washed is assumed to be a sign of genuine hospitality (cf. 18:4; 19:2).

[35] Abraham's servant probably describes Abraham's wealth for two reasons: (1) he detects Laban's greedy disposition, and (2) he wishes to assure Rebekah's family that Abraham's son Isaac is quite capable of providing for a wife. It is most significant that the servant attributes Abraham's wealth to Yahweh (cf. 12:16; 13:2).

[36] The servant's passing allusion to Isaac's birth in Abraham's and Sarah's old age further confirms the accuracy of the accounts in 17:17; 21:2, 7. The statement that Abraham gave Isaac **all that he had** (cf. also 25:5) is not to be taken literally, because he gave certain gifts to Hagar and Ishmael (21:14) and to the sons of his concubines

(25:6) when he sent them away. The meaning seems to be that Abraham had turned over the bulk of his possessions to Isaac, and the Lord had transferred his promises to Abraham to him.

[37-41] By comparing the biblical record of the actual conversation between Abraham and his servant (vss. 3-8) and the servant's account of this conversation (vss. 37-41), it is clear that the biblical characters and authors do not feel it necessary to quote verbatim what is said. They feel free to state what was said in their own words. Accordingly, the doctrine of biblical inspiration does not demand that a biblical author quote the exact words (*ipsissima verba*) of any given speaker or that two accounts of the same event be told in exactly the same way (e.g., compare the accounts of the temptation of Jesus in Matt. 4:1-11; Mark 1:12-13; and Luke 4:1-13). Thus, the servant states that Abraham said, **The Lord, before whom I walk, will send his angel with you** (vs. 40). Abraham may have actually said, **before whom I walk**, although it is not recorded (vs. 7), or the servant may have attributed this to him because he knew Abraham's feeling that all that he did was before God. In either case, the thought is perfectly consistent with Abraham's attitude toward God (cf. 17:1).

[45] The Hebrew expression *ledhabber 'el libbi*, literally, "to speak unto my heart" (cf. the KJV, ASV, and RSV), must mean to speak silently ("*in* oneself," not "*to* oneself," because here Abraham is addressing God). The best reproduction of the Hebrew idiom into English idiom is that of the NEB: "before I had finished praying silently."

[48] Rebekah was the daughter of Bethuel son of Nahor (vss. 15, 24, 47), and thus the granddaughter of Nahor, Abraham's brother (cf. 11:27). Clearly, therefore, the Hebrew word *'achi* in the present verse cannot mean "brother" (KJV, ASV, and by implication NEB), but must mean a relative or **kinsman** (see the usage of the same word in 29:12, 15).

[49] Up to this point, it might appear that the servant was speaking to Laban alone. However, the use of the second person plural verbs in the present verse (**if you**

[masculine plural] **will deal loyally, tell** [masculine plural imperative] **me** [twice]) shows that he is speaking to Laban and Bethuel (cf. vs. 50) or to several members of Rebekah's family.

The expression **turn to the right hand or to the left** does not mean to turn elsewhere in search for a bride for Isaac (as the NEB would seem to imply) but to know where one stands or to know how to proceed.

Rebekah leaves with the servant (vss. 50-61). Having heard the servant's story, Laban and Bethuel agree that the Lord is at work in this matter and decide to let Rebekah return with him to marry Isaac (vss. 50-51). The servant gives Rebekah additional gifts and pays her brother and mother (Laban and Milcah) the bride price (vss. 52-53). The next morning, Rebekah's family requests that the servant wait at least ten days to depart with Rebekah (apparently realizing that they might never see her again because the distance back to Canaan was so long), but he insists that they go immediately (possibly because he wanted to return to Canaan before Abraham died, or because he was afraid the delay might give Rebekah and/or her family an opportunity to change her/their mind[s]; vss. 54-56). Rebekah and her family agree that she may leave immediately, and the servant departs with Rebekah and her attendants (vss. 57-61).

[50] Among the Hurrians (who lived in the region of Haran), it was customary for the bride's brother to act as the father's representative in making marriage arrangements. Accordingly, the marital contract was called a "sistership document." This may explain why Laban (and not Bethuel) took a leading role in the negotiations concerning Rebekah.

To speak **bad or good** is a Hebrew idiom meaning to "say anything" (cf. Gen. 31:24, 29; Num. 24:13). Since the events that happened to Abraham's servant show that Rebekah is God's choice as a wife for Isaac, it would be inappropriate for Laban or Bethuel to say anything, that is, they yield themselves to God's will.

[52] Here, for the third time, Abraham's servant prays to

God. The first time, he asked God to lead him to the divinely appointed bride for Isaac (vss. 12-14). The second time, he thanked God for doing so (vss. 26-27). Now, apparently, he thanks God for the willingness of Rebekah's family to let her go with him to Isaac.

[53] It was customary to give the bride's family a *mohar*, or bride price, as a token of good will or as a symbol of the groom's intention to care for the bride properly (cf. Gen. 34:12; Exod. 22:17 [Hebrew 16]; 1 Sam. 18:25).

[55] It seems most natural that Rebekah's family would want her to stay a few days longer before leaving for the distant land of southern Canaan:

> It was certainly startling that Rebekah's family should be asked to let her leave them at once, that very morning, for a distant land with a man whom none of them had ever seen till the previous evening, to marry a cousin whom they had never seen; especially as it was not very likely that they would ever see her again; and, as it turned out, they never did see her.
>
> Bennett, *Genesis*, pp. 254–55

[58] In keeping with Hurrian custom, the family seeks the bride's consent, and she agrees.

[59] In addition to **Abraham's servant and his men**, Rebekah was accompanied by "her maids" (vs. 61) and her own personal **nurse** (a woman named Deborah, cf. 35:8), who had suckled or nursed her in early childhood (this is the sense in which she is said to be her **nurse**). These women would stay with Rebekah to help her with her work as wife and mother in her new home.

[60] Before Rebekah departs, her brother Laban and her mother (and possibly also her father Bethuel, vs. 50) invoke a twofold bridal blessing upon her: (1) they wish her many descendants; (2) they wish that her **descendants** ("seed," KJV, ASV) might **possess the gate of those who hate them**. In this latter phrase, **gate** is a synecdoche for city ("cities," NEB; cf. 22:17).

Isaac and Rebekah meet and marry (vss. 62-67). Isaac and Rebekah encounter one another for the first time in a field in the Negeb in the evening. Abraham's servant tells Isaac all that had happened. In due time, Isaac and Rebekah marry, and Isaac is comforted after Sarah's death.

[62] After Sarah was buried at Hebron (23:19), apparently Abraham and Isaac and their household moved near the well **Beer-lahai-roi** in the Negeb (south), where the angel of the Lord had appeared to Hagar the first time she left Sarah's presence (16:14). It was near this well that Isaac met Rebekah for the first time.

[63] Scholars have attributed various meanings to the verb *śuach*. Some think it means that Isaac went out to "mourn" for his mother in the evening (cf. vs. 67); others, that he was "gathering brushwood"; others, that he went into the field to "relieve himself" (cf. the note in the NEB); others, that he went out each day in the evening "hoping to meet" the servant and his future bride (NEB); and others, that he went out to **meditate** (connecting *śuach* with *śiach*; so RSV, KJV, ASV) or pray.

[64] Alighting from a camel or a chariot when meeting another person was an ancient oriental custom for showing respect (cf. Josh. 15:18; Judg. 1:14; 1 Sam. 25:23; 2 Kings 5:21).

[65] Some critics interpret the servant's reference to Isaac as **my master** to mean that Abraham had died between the time he had sent his servant away and the time the servant returned with Rebekah. However, 25:20 states that Isaac was forty years old when he married Rebekah, which would mean that Abraham was 140, because he was 100 when Isaac was born (17:17). In other words, Abraham lived thirty-five years after Isaac's marriage to Rebekah. Perhaps the servant's statement may be interpreted in a different way. Abraham had given Isaac all that he had before he sent the servant to get Isaac a wife (vs. 36). In view of Isaac's approaching marriage and perhaps Abraham's own remarriage after Sarah's death (25:1), Abraham may have entrusted his servant to him. But even this supposition is not necessary, because to the servant both Abraham and Isaac were his masters.

Rebekah **covered herself** with her **veil** as a symbol that she was a chaste, unmarried maiden.

[67] The Hebrew syntax at the first of this verse is very difficult. Literally the text reads: "And Isaac brought her to the tent, Sarah his mother" (not "*of* Sarah his mother"). Many scholars delete "Sarah his mother" (cf. RSV, NEB) as a misplaced expression, perhaps originally belonging at the very end of the verse. However, based on the principle that the more difficult reading is probably the correct one (*lectio difficilior*), the meaning may be "And Isaac brought her into his mother Sarah's tent" (so KJV, ASV). It was customary in seminomadic society for the man and his wife or wives to have separate tents (cf. 31:33), and thus Sarah apparently had her own separate tent. Because of Isaac's deep love for his mother Sarah, he brought his bride Rebekah into her tent as a symbol of their marriage.

Many scholars think that the original text said "So Isaac was comforted after his father's death," not **after his mother's death**. But there is no textual evidence for this in the ancient Hebrew manuscripts or in the ancient versions. The thought is that Sarah's death (which occurred when Isaac was thirty-seven [Sarah was ninety when Isaac was born, 17:17, and 127 when she died, 23:1]) grieved Isaac tremendously, and he had still not recovered from it three years later. But after his marriage to Rebekah, it becomes easier for him to reconstruct his life and continue with a reasonable measure of happiness.

Blessings Given to Abraham's Children (25:1-18)

Genesis 25:1-18 stands at the end of the section dealing with Abraham. In a very brief and sweeping way, these verses tell how God blessed Abraham's descendants: the children of Keturah (vss. 1-6), Isaac (vss. 7-11), and Ishmael and his descendants (vss. 12-18).

[1] It is impossible to know whether Abraham married Keturah before or after Sarah died. That she is called a "concubine" (vs. 6; 1 Chron. 1:32) may favor the former view; that she is called Abraham's **wife** (vs. 1) may favor the latter. However, it could be that Abraham had two living wives, as Jacob did later in Rachel and Leah (32:22).

[2-4] Abraham's children by Keturah are also listed in 1 Chronicles 1:32-33. Little is known with certainty about any of these descendants. **Midian** (vs. 2) was the father of the Midianites, a seminomadic group that wandered far and wide in the regions around Canaan. Genesis 25:6; Judges 6:3, 33; and 7:12 suggest that, like the other descendants of Keturah, they lived primarily east of Canaan in the Arabian desert. In agreement with this, several OT passages locate them in Moab (Gen. 36:35; Num. 25:6-7; 31:2-3; Josh. 13:21; 1 Chron. 1:46). However, they also appear in the region around Mount Sinai (Num. 10:29; cf. vs. 12) south of the Dead Sea, and in the land of Canaan around Gaza (Judg. 6:3-4), the Valley of Jezreel (Judg. 6:33), and the hill of Moreh (Judg. 7:1). **Ephah** (vs. 4) was the father of the tribe of Ephah, which is mentioned along with Midian in Isaiah 60:6.

[5-6] Before his death, Abraham bequeaths all his possessions to Isaac as the son born of divine promise and sends the children of his **concubines** away from Isaac to the **east country**. Most scholars think the **concubines** intended here are Hagar and Keturah (cf. vss. 1, 12), but it may be that Abraham had other concubines not mentioned elsewhere in the Bible.

[8] There are at least three views as to the meaning of the phrase he **was gathered to his people** (see 15:15). (a) It refers to Abraham's having been buried in the family sepulchre (cf. 47:30) in the cave of Machpelah (cf. vs. 9), where Sarah had been buried some thirty-eight years earlier (cf. vs.10; 23:1, 19). (b) It means that Abraham went to Sheol (the realm of the dead), where human existence continues. (c) It is simply an idiomatic statement meaning "he died." The last explanation seems most likely (cf. vs. 17; Deut. 31:16).

[9] The death of Abraham temporarily brings **Isaac and Ishmael** back together for the burial, just as the death of Isaac later reunites Jacob and Esau for a brief time (35:29).

[11] After Abraham's death, God **blessed** Isaac in a special way as the son of Abraham through whom the divine promises were to be perpetuated. At this time, ironically,

Isaac was living at **Beer-lahai-roi**, the place where the angel had apprehended Hagar in her first flight from Abraham's house and had told her to return to her mistress (cf. 16:7-14).

[13] Esau married the daughters of Ishmael, Mahalath (28:9) and Basemath (36:3), both of whom are identified as sisters of **Nebaioth**. Scholars are not agreed as to whether **Nebaioth** is the ancestor of the Nabateans. **Nebaioth** and **Kedar** are mentioned together in Isaiah 60:7 as names of tribes, and **Kedar** is mentioned as a tribe in Isaiah 21:16-17; 42:11; Jeremiah 2:10; 49:28; and Psalm 120:5.

[15] **Tema** here is a person and is not to be confused with the city of Tema in Arabia. **Jetur** and **Naphish** are the ancestors of tribes by the same name, who settled east of the Jordan, and whom the tribes of Reuben, Gad, and the half-tribe of Manasseh defeated under the leadership of Moses (1 Chron. 5:18-20). In 1 Chronicles 5:19-20 they are called "Hagrites," apparently because they were descendants of Hagar.

[16] The Hebrew word *ṭirotham* means **their encampments** (RSV, ASV, NEB) rather than "their castles" (KJV).

[18] Scholars differ widely over the locations of **Havilah** and **Shur**. The only thing that is certain is that they are located east of Egypt. It is very improbable that **Assyria** in this verse is the great territory in the northern part of the Fertile Crescent. The context suggests a small region near Egypt and Palestine. The last line of verse 18 is very hard to interpret. Translated very literally, the Hebrew says: "in front of all his brothers he fell." But how are the expressions "in front of" and "he fell" to be understood? As Ishmael's death is already recorded in verse 17, the KJV "he died in the presence of all his brethren" is hardly correct. **He** does not refer to Ishmael the man but is a collective term for his descendants, the Ishmaelites, as the plural **they** of the first line shows. The ASV and RSV think the meaning is that **he** [i.e., Ishmael the people] **settled** [ASV "abode"] **over against all his people** (ASV "brethren"). In light of the meaning of *naphal* ("he fell") in Judges 7:12, Speiser (*Genesis*, p. 188) argues that the idea here is "each

[of the tribes mentioned in vss. 13-16] made forays against his various kinsmen." However, *naphal* may mean "settled" in Judges 7:12. Furthermore, *'al pene* is a Hebrew idiom often meaning "east of" in the OT (cf. BDB, pp. 818–19), as in Genesis 23:19; 25:9; 49:30; Joshua 13:3, 25; 17:7; etc. Accordingly, the NEB is probably correct in interpreting this phrase to mean "having settled to the east of his brothers" (yet see the note on 16:12).

EXCURSUS

Key Figures in the Family of Terah

The genealogical list at the end of Genesis 22 provides an opportunity to present a chart showing the main characters in the family of Terah (cf. Gen. 11:27-32; 22:20-24; 24:29, 47; 28:5; 29:5).

CHART VI

The Descendants of Terah

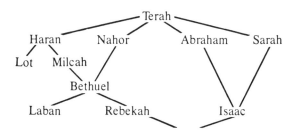

Genesis 29:5 states that Laban was "the son of Nahor," while 28:5 says he was "the son of Bethuel" (the son of Nahor) and "the brother of Rebekah." Actually, there is no contradiction here, because "son" often means grandson, great-grandson, great-great-grandson, etc., in the Bible (see Matt. 1:1 and p. 94, above).

V

The Life of Jacob
(25:19–36:43)

ISAAC AND HIS FAMILY (25:19–27:45)

Since Isaac is depicted almost entirely in relationship to his father Abraham (note 25:19) or to his son Jacob in the book of Genesis, it seems best to treat events in his life in conjunction with Abraham and Jacob respectively. The life of Jacob is filled with struggles with various individuals: Esau, Laban, Rachel and Leah, his own children, and God. These struggles are not neatly separated from one another in the text but are interwoven in the complex unfolding of Jacob's career. The intention of the comments that follow is to pursue the course of the biblical text as it stands and to emphasize the struggles that Jacob experienced. If there is a theme that holds 25:19–36:43 together, it is the problem of honesty or integrity in the life of Jacob or his antagonist.

The Birth of Jacob and Esau (25:19-26)

There are striking similarities between the births of Isaac and Jacob. (1) In both instances, the mother is barren (Sarah—11:30; Rebekah—25:21) and is able to have children only as a result of miraculous, divine intervention (18:14; 21:1-7; 25:21). (2) In both cases, the barrenness extends over a long period of time (for Abraham, from age seventy-five to age 100—12:4; 17:17; 21:5; and for Isaac, from age forty to age sixty—25:20, 26). (3) In both instances, the important child who is born is the younger of two brothers and yet is chosen to be recipient of his father's blessings and perpetuator of the divine promises (Isaac—17:19, 21; 25:5, 11; Jacob—25:23; 28:12-15). According to 25:19-26, the struggle between Jacob and Esau (which is a foreshadowing of the struggle between their descendants, the Israelites and the Edomites—vs. 23) begins in their mother's womb.

[20] **Paddan-aram** (28:2, 5, 6, 7; 31:18; 33:18; 35:9, 26; 46:15; called simply "Paddan" in 48:7) is another name for "Mesopotamia" (Heb. *'aram-naharayim*, 24:10) and refers to the region around Haran in the northern part of the Fertile Crescent. The people who lived here are called **Arameans** in 25:20 (twice); 31:24; Deuteronomy 26:5.

[21] Because of the frequency and quantity of births, it is commonly assumed that children are "natural" phenomena. The present account, however, emphasizes that conception is possible only if God supplies the power or the life. It was not until **Isaac prayed** and **the Lord granted his prayer** that **Rebekah conceived**. The Bible claims that children are God's gifts to parents. This cannot be proved or disproved but must be accepted or rejected by faith.

[22] It is difficult to understand Rebekah's statement in this verse. The Hebrew says literally, "If thus, why this I?" An incomplete utterance like this might be expected in view of the pain Rebekah was having to endure for the moment. The thought could be "Why did God enable me to conceive, only to cause me great pain by giving me twins in my womb who struggle with each other?" The Syriac reads, **If it is thus, why do I live?** (a reading adopted by the RSV and ASV, and frequently supported by 26:47). The NEB reads, "If this is how it is with me, what does it mean?" This would explain why Rebekah then went to inquire of the Lord, and also God's reply. However, it is a conjectural reading and has no support in any ancient version. The statement **she went to inquire of the Lord** suggests that she went to a nearby sanctuary (probably at Beer-lahai-roi, vs. 11, or Beer-sheba, 26:33) in search for divine information about the destiny of her children and their descendants.

[23] It is obvious that the statement **Two nations are in your womb** is not to be taken literally. By metonymy (the use of one word for a closely associated word—see LWC-OT, vol. 1, ch. 1), God envisions the nations of Israel and Edom in the persons of Jacob and Esau. Man is often too shortsighted to see the great potential in a child whom the Lord blesses.

God's choice of the Israelites above the Edomites (see Gen. 27:29, 40; Mal. 1:3-4) was not based on their respective moral qualities, because he chose Israel and rejected Edom before Jacob and Esau were ever born (Rom. 9:10-12). To the earthly, logical mind, such a choice seems arbitrary and unfair, like the election of believers in Christ and the rejection of unbelievers (Rom. 8:29-30; Eph. 1:3-5). However, man is not wise enough to comprehend the wisdom of God, nor is his knowledge vast enough to question God's decisions or actions (Isa. 40:13-14; Dan. 4:34-35; Rom. 11:33-36). It is worthy of note that according to Hurrian law, an older son was entitled to receive twice as much inheritance as a younger son, but the testator could designate his younger son in order of physical birth as his "elder son."

[25] The actual birth of twins is described in some detail in the OT only in the cases of Jacob and Esau (25:25-26) and of Perez and Zerah, the sons of Judah by his daughter-in-law Tamar (38:27-30). Two wordplays involving Esau appear in the Hebrew of verse 25. Neither represents an attempt to explain the etymology of the names of Isaac's oldest son. Instead, they both are based on similarities of sounds and letters. On the one hand, the word for **red**, *'adhmoni* (which apparently means "red-haired," and not "having a ruddy complexion"), looks and sounds much like *'edhom*, "Edom" (see the similar wordplay based on the "red [Heb. *'adhom*] pottage" in vs. 30). On the other hand, the word for **hairy** is *śe'ar*, which is reflected in the name *'eśaw*, **Esau**, the first two letters of which are the same as the first two letters in *śe'ar*, but in reverse order. A pun closely related to the latter appears in the connection made

between Esau and *śeʿir,* "Seir," the name of the land and of the hill country in which the Edomites lived (see Gen. 32:4 [Hebrew 3]; 36:8; Judg. 5:4).

[26] As in verse 25, the intention here is not to trace the etymology of the name **Jacob** but to portray a major facet of his character and life in a play on Hebrew words. The Hebrew word for **heel** is *ʿaqebh,* which looks and sounds very much like *yaʿaqobh,* **Jacob.** The writer is depicting Jacob as one who **had taken hold of Esau's heel**, which is a Hebrew idiom apparently meaning "one who had supplanted or replaced Esau" by trickery or treachery, thus foreshadowing the way in which Jacob was to obtain Esau's birthright and blessing.

The Struggle for the Birthright (25:27-34)

On one occasion Jacob found Esau in dire circumstances and took advantage of him in order to secure his birthright. This meant that at his father's death Jacob would become head of the household with authority over his brothers and sisters (27:29, 37; 49:3), receive his father's special blessing (27:33-36), inherit a double portion of his father's possessions (Deut. 21:17), and become perpetuator of the divine promises (28:13-14). Jacob obtained his brother's birthright by employing unloving and inconsiderate measures (Gen. 27:36; Jer. 9:3 [Hebrew 4]; Hos. 12:4 [Hebrew 3]). Esau manifested the unspiritual qualities of greed and concern only for the present, demonstrating that he was unworthy of the birthright, which had spiritual dimensions and contained far-reaching implications for the future. Hence, Hebrews 12:16-17 says he was "immoral" and "irreligious."

[27-28] These two verses briefly contrast Jacob and Esau. Esau is an outdoorsman who loves to hunt and eat wild game, and thus is Isaac's favorite. Jacob is **a quiet man**, a calm and retiring person who enjoys the simple things of life, and thus is Rebekah's favorite. The Hebrew word translated **quiet** here is *tam*, which literally means "perfect" (RSV "blameless;" cf. Job 1:1, 8; 2:3; 8:20; 9:20, 21, 22; Ps. 37:37). It is quite clear, however, that it cannot

mean "sinless." The context demands a contrast with the description of Esau as **a man of the field**, suggesting the idea that Jacob was a man of the tents, a quiet and home-loving man.

[**29**] "Sod" (KJV) is an obsolete form of the past tense of the verb "seethe," an archaic meaning of which was "to boil, to stew." As this word is no longer used in this sense, it is preferable to use **boiled** (RSV, ASV).

[**30**] That Esau is famished and craves frantically for something to eat is vividly portrayed in the Hebrew of this verse. The verb translated **eat** (RSV; "feed," KJV, ASV, and "swallow," NEB) is *la'at,* which actually means "to gulp down, to stuff oneself with." Also, Esau's words are intent and frenzied: "Let me gulp down, I pray, the red, this red!" By a wordplay, the name **Edom** is associated with the Hebrew word for **red** (*'adhom*) in "red pottage" (cf. vs. 34) here, just as it is associated with the word for **red** (*'adhmoni*) in "red (-haired)" in verse 25.

[**34**] By selling his **birthright** to Jacob (vs. 33), eating and drinking (gulping down) Jacob's food, and going his way without concern, Esau demonstrated that he was incapable of appreciating his birthright—he **despised** it, that is, "he showed how little he valued it" (NEB).

Isaac Lies about Rebekah (26:1-11)

This is the last of three accounts in which a patriarch lied about his relationship to his wife for fear that he might be killed by a foreign king in order to obtain her. Abraham lied about Sarah to the Pharaoh in Egypt (12:10-20) and to Abimelech in Gerar (20:1-18), and now Isaac lies about Rebekah to Abimelech in Gerar (26:1-11). Since there are striking similarities between the order, content, and vocabulary in these stories, most scholars think that a single account of a patriarch lying about his wife has been handed down in three different sources, which were later incorporated into the book of Genesis. However, certain significant considerations militate against this view. (1) In 26:1, the author of Genesis distinguishes between the famine that drove Abraham into Egypt (12:10) and the famine that

drove Isaac into Gerar. Since famines were frequent occurrences in ancient times in the area of Canaan, there is no
reason why the text could not refer to two different famines. (2) In 26:1-11, Abimelech does not take Rebekah into
his harem but is afraid that one of the men in his kingdom
might have sexual relations with her (cf. vs. 10). (3) Abimelech does not learn that Rebekah is Isaac's wife by a
miracle in which God causes a great sickness to come on
his household (as in 12:17), or closes the wombs of the
women in his harem (as in 20:17-18), but by seeing Isaac
fondle his wife (26:8). (4) While it is true that there are
several similarities in these three accounts, there are also
several details which are unique to each account, suggesting that the biblical writer is relating three separate events.
The similarities may be explained by the fact that the different incidents were actually alike in some ways and by
the fact that the same traditionist or author used the same
or similar words and expressions in telling or handing
down these stories. It is no less likely that Abraham lied
about his wife twice and that his son Isaac lied about his
wife once than that Peter denied three times that he knew
Christ (Luke 22:31-34, 54-62).

While Isaac is dwelling at Beer-lahai-roi in the Negeb
(south—cf. 25:11), a famine strikes and he goes to Gerar,
possibly intending to go to Egypt (as his father Abraham
had done some sixty-five years before, cf. 12:10, 4; 25:20).
But Yahweh instructs him to stay in Gerar and promises to
be with him, bless him, give his descendants all the land of
Canaan, multiply his descendants as the stars of heaven,
and bless all nations through them (vss. 1-5). When some
of the men of Gerar ask about Rebekah's identity, Isaac
says she is his sister, because he is afraid they might kill
him to get his beautiful wife. On one occasion, Abimelech
accidentally sees Isaac fondling his wife, rebukes him because he lied about her true identity, and warns his people
not to touch Isaac or his wife (vss. 6-11).

[1] It is hardly likely that **Abimelech** and Phicol (vs. 26)
are the same persons as those mentioned in 21:32. Possibly
one or both were official titles (like the Assyrian titles "the

Tartan, the Rabsaris, and the Rabshakeh," 2 Kings 18:17) in the royal court of Gerar or recurring names in the same family or closely related families. Most critics think that the mention of **the Philistines** here is anachronistic because these people did not come into Canaan until the twelfth century B.C. However, there is no reason why the masses of Philistine invaders into the Mediterranean area may not have been preceded by earlier less numerous and less aggressive ancestors.

[3] Isaac could not be a full citizen of Gerar but had the status of a sojourner, as was the case with Abraham earlier (20:1).

[4] The best translation of the last line of verse 4 is "in your [Isaac's] descendants [seed] all the nations of the earth shall be blessed" (KJV, ASV). The reading of the NEB, "all the nations of the earth will pray to be blessed as they are blessed," is not really a translation and hardly suggests the most likely interpretation, namely, that Israel was God's chosen people, whose task it was to bless the nations by their presence, example, and teaching (see the note on 12:3).

[5] God is willing and anxious to bestow his blessings on man. However, he does not force them on the ungrateful and disobedient but showers them on the appreciative and obedient.

[7] In all three accounts of a patriarch who lies about his wife, the patriarch says, **She is my sister** (cf. 12:13, 19; 20:5), because he is afraid that the people of the foreign land might **kill** him if he reveals that she is his **wife** (cf. 12:12; 20:11), in order to take her for themselves. In the stories of Abram's sojourn in Egypt (12:11) and of Isaac's sojourn in Gerar (26:7), the patriarch alludes to his wife's great beauty, but this does not seem to be a factor in Abraham's sojourn in Gerar (Gen. 20).

[8] Although Isaac stayed in Gerar **a long time**, neither the king nor any of the men of the land sought to have sexual relations with Rebekah. While Abimelech acknowledges that this was a constant potential danger (vs. 10), he demonstrates that his was a much higher moral standard

for his kingdom than Isaac envisioned. It is human to look for the bad in people (especially in those who are considered to be nonreligious), when frequently their values are admirably high.

In the Hebrew expression translated **Isaac fondling** (RSV), there is a wordplay on the name Isaac, *yitschaq metsacheq,* which is difficult to reproduce in English. "[Abimelech] saw Isaac and his wife Rebecca laughing together" (NEB) is about as close as one can get and retain some semblance of the meaning of this phrase. It immediately calls to mind the connection between "Isaac" and "laughing" which has been encountered several times previously (cf. 17:17, 19; 18:12, 15; 21:6, 9).

[10] The rhetorical question **What is this you have done to us?** or its equivalent occurs in all three accounts of a patriarch's lying about his wife (cf. 12:18; 20:10) and is designed to impress the patriarch with the seriousness of his lie. In this act, Isaac showed no concern for his fellowmen, whom God had charged him to bless. If one of the men of Gerar had had sexual relations with Rebekah, his **guilt** would have been due in part to Isaac's deliberate falsification of the facts. The word "lien" in the KJV is apparently an archaic spelling of the past participle of "lie."

Dispute between Isaac and Abimelech (26:12-33)

This paragraph is similar to 21:22-34 in some ways, and many scholars argue that the author of Genesis has used two accounts of the same incident. However, (1) there are several details in each of the two accounts that have no parallel in the other (one striking example is 26:12-16); (2) 26:15, 18 refer back to the record of Abraham's having dug wells in the region of Gerar, thus indicating that the author of Genesis regarded these as two separate, but related, incidents.

During his stay in Gerar, Isaac increases in wealth. This arouses the envy of Abimelech and his people, and the king sends Isaac away from the city of Gerar. Isaac moves into the valley of Gerar and digs once again the wells that Abraham had dug in order to get water for his flocks and herds. The herdsmen of Gerar claim the first two wells (Esek and Sitnah) as their own, because they are in the region claimed by Gerar. Just as Abraham gave in to Lot when strife arose between their respective herdsmen (13:5-9), Isaac yields to Abimelech's men to avoid conflict. When he digs a third well (Rehoboth), the herdsmen of Gerar do not contest his right to control it, and peace prevails (vss. 12-22).

> Peace is the greatest blessing of life . . . . The fundamental task of the servant of the Lord is to preserve and promote peace at all costs. And whoever does this is a true servant of the Lord. Yet more precious at times even than the safeguarding of rights and mere, mechanical justice is peace . . . . Doubtless it was not easy for Isaac to yield. It would have been far more natural, and possibly more agreeable, too, to say at the very commencement of the trouble, 'This well is mine, for I dug it, and I shall defend my rights at all costs.' Not improbably, too, he could have defended himself successfully, had the men of Gerar attacked him, for he had many servants and followers. But he was mindful of the teaching and example of his father and of his precious birthright of service.
>
> J. Morgenstern, *The Book of Genesis*, p. 178

In time, Isaac moves southeast from Gerar to Beersheba. Abimelech goes to him there and requests that they make a covenant of peace, which Isaac accepts. Isaac's men dig a fourth well (Shibah) to provide water for their flocks and herds in this new location (vss. 23-33).

[12] Ordinarily, seminomads did not have time for agricultural pursuits. But Isaac stayed in Gerar "a long time" (vs. 8), and the Lord "made room for" him (vs. 22), so he **sowed** a crop and **reaped a hundredfold** (cf. Mark 4:8). Seed was planted at the beginning of the year in the fall and reaped in the spring of that same year.

[14] Since man is concerned first and foremost with enhancing his own power and wealth, he easily becomes envious of those who have power and wealth. Later, Joseph's brothers become jealous at the thought of his ruling over them (37:9-11). One psalmist writes:

Fret not yourself because of the wicked,
be not envious of wrongdoers!

Psalm 37:1

Another confesses:

But as for me, my feet had almost stumbled,
my steps had well nigh slipped.
For I was envious of the arrogant,
when I saw the prosperity of the wicked.

Psalm 73:2-3

[15] The KJV, ASV, RSV, and NEB agree in reading verse 15 as a pluperfect: **the Philistines had stopped**. However, there is no distinction between the past and the pluperfect in Hebrew. Perhaps the people of Gerar became envious of Isaac because he had become so rich (vs. 14) and thus filled up the wells which his father had dug to show their spite toward him and to diminish his potential for continued success. The statements in verses 12-15 seem to cover a great deal of time.

[17] The Hebrew word translated **valley** is *nachal*, which really means "wadi," the bed of a stream or brook which is dry except in the rainy season.

[18] Because of the similarity of content, the NEB moves verse 18 immediately after verse 15. While this might seem logical to the modern Western mind, such a procedure runs the risk of obscuring the train of thought intended by the biblical writer.

[19] The Hebrew expression translated **springing water** in the KJV, ASV, and RSV is *mayim chayyim*, which means literally "living water." This is a common Hebrew idiom meaning "running water" (NEB; cf. Lev. 14:5, 6, 50, 51, 52; Song of Sol. 4:15; Jer. 2:13; 17:13; Zech. 14:8; cf. John 4:10, 11).

[20] This strife between the herdsmen of Gerar and the herdsmen of Isaac calls to mind similar strife between the herdsmen of Abraham and the herdsmen of Lot (13:5-7) and between the herdsmen of Abraham and the herdsmen of Abimelech (21:25). The Hebrew contains a wordplay

between *'eśeq*, **Esek**, and *hith'aśśequ*, **they contended**. In other words, the well was called **Esek** to commemorate the fact that the herdsmen of Gerar **contended** with the herdsmen of Isaac over control of it. Presumably the names given the wells mentioned in verses 20-22 are different from those given the same wells by Abraham, and by Isaac when he first dug them again (vs. 18).

[21] The second well is called **Sitnah**, that is, "enmity," because the herdsmen of Gerar quarreled with the herdsmen of Isaac over it, also.

[22] The name of the third well (like that of the first) is based on a wordplay in Hebrew. It is called **Rehoboth** (*rechobhoth*, "wide places") because the Lord had **made room** (*hirchibh*) for Isaac and his household in the land of Gerar. **Rehoboth** is probably the modern er-Ruhaibeh, which is about twenty miles southwest of Beer-sheba, where Isaac moves after an unspecified period (vs. 23).

[24] At Beer-sheba, the Lord gives Isaac four assurances intimately connected with the blessings that he had promised to Abraham and his descendants: (a) **I am the God of Abraham your father** (cf. vss. 3, 5); (b) **fear not, for I am with you** (cf. 15:1); (c) **I will bless you** (cf. 12:2; 22:17; 25:11; 26:3, 12); (d) **I will multiply your descendants** (cf. 17:2; 22:17; 26:4).

[25] Isaac responded much in the same way that Abraham responded on occasions when God blessed him. **He built an altar** (cf. 12:7; 13:18) and **called upon the name of the Lord** (cf. 12:8). By so doing, Isaac expresses his gratitude for God's gifts and claims the land as belonging to Yahweh.

[26] When Abimelech comes to Isaac, he is accompanied by two of his state officials: **Ahuzzath** "his friend" (KJV, ASV, NEB) and **Phicol the commander of his army** (RSV, NEB; cf. 21:22, 32). In the ancient Near East (including Israel and Judah), "the king's friend" was the title for the counselor (cf. 2 Sam. 15:37; 16:16; 1 Kings 4:5; 1 Chron. 27:33) or **adviser** of the king. (See T. N. D. Mettinger, *Solomonic State Officials*, [Lund: CWK Gleerup, 1971, pp. 63–69.)

[28] Abimelech sees that Isaac and his household are
blessed in spite of opposition and change of pasture
(cf. vss. 12-25) and concludes that this is because **the Lord
is with** him. He suggests a **covenant** with Isaac in order that
the divine blessings might flow over into the lives of his
people. "The king's recognition of Isaac's favored position
. . . is . . . an anticipated fulfillment of the promise that all
nations would be blessed in his descendants (cf. v. 4b)"
(E. H. Maly, "Genesis," JBC, vol. 1, p. 27).

[29] The end of this verse alludes back to Abimelech's
expulsion of Isaac from Gerar in verse 16. The point is that
Isaac and his household were not harmed when they were
sent away. It is difficult to understand how the last line fits
into the context. The reading of the KJV, ASV, and RSV,
You are now the blessed of the Lord, does not fit the situation. It seems preferable to read "Swear that you will do us
no harm, now that the Lord has blessed you" (NEB) or
"Henceforth, Yahweh's blessing upon you!" (E. A. Speiser,
Genesis, AB, pp. 200, 202).

[30] When two parties made a covenant, it was customary to share a common meal to solemnize the agreement
(cf. 31:46, 54).

[31] The word "betimes" (KJV, ASV) means **early** (RSV,
NEB) but is not used very widely in contemporary English.

[33] Isaac calls the well **Shibah** ("oath"), because of the
oath that he made with Abimelech there (cf. vs. 31), and
thus the city is called **Beer-sheba** (which means "well of the
oath"—cf. 21:31). The phrase **to this day** shows that the
author of this account related it to an audience a number of
years after the event took place; however, it is impossible
to know how many years had elapsed.

Jacob Steals Isaac's Blessing from Esau (26:34–27:45)

Apparently the event related here took place in Beer-
sheba (cf. 26:33; 28:10). In spite of the fact that Esau had
married two Hittite women, he is still Isaac's favorite son
(cf. 25:28). In his old age, Isaac tells Esau to get some

game for him to eat that he might bless him (26:34–27:4). Rebekah overhears this conversation and tells Jacob to go in to Isaac with savory food she prepares in order to get the blessing Isaac intended for Esau (27:5-17). Jacob does so and receives Isaac's blessing (vss. 18-29). Just after this, Esau comes in and Isaac realizes that he has been deceived and blessed the wrong son; he gives Esau a much inferior blessing (vss. 30-40). Esau purposes to kill Jacob for seizing his blessing, but Rebekah learns of this and tells Jacob that he must go to her brother Laban at Haran until Esau ceases to be angry (vss. 41–45).

According to Hurrian law, the father bestowed the birthright on whichever son he pleased without necessarily following the order of birth, and the son who received the birthright got a double portion of his father's inheritance. Apparently the "blessing" amounts to the official bestowal of the "birthright" in the father's old age. Thus, the content of the "blessing" and the "birthright" are the same.

All the participants in this event are guilty of the grossest sins. Isaac must have known that during Rebekah's pregnancy the Lord had told her that the elder (Esau) would serve the younger (Jacob), but he deliberately intended to reverse this in the blessing he thought he was pronouncing upon Esau (27:29). Esau had sworn to Jacob that he could have his birthright (25:33), but he accepts his father's offer of the blessing through which the birthright came (27:1-5, 30-31). Rebekah urges Jacob to deceive Isaac (vss. 6-10) and even accepts any curse that Isaac might speak against Jacob if he discovered his deceit (vs. 13). Jacob agrees to his mother's plan to deceive his father (vs. 14), participates with her in preparing himself to smell and feel like Esau (vss. 15-17), and lies to his father about his real identity (vss. 18-24). In spite of his unworthiness and obvious sins, God chose Jacob to receive his blessings and to perpetuate his promises to Abraham (cf. Mal. 1:2-3; Rom. 9:10-13). Genesis 26:34–27:45 may be divided into five scenes, each of which contains a discussion between two of the major characters.

Isaac offers Esau his blessing (26:34–27:4). Although Esau marries two Hittite women (26:34) who "made life bitter for Isaac and Rebekah"(26:35), Isaac instructs Esau to get him some savory food that he might bless him (27:1-4).

[34] Like Isaac his father (25:20), Esau marries when he is **forty years old**. He had four wives (and possibly five), all of whom were foreign women living in the land of Canaan: **Judith the daughter of Beeri the Hittite, Basemath the daughter of Elon the Hittite** (is she the same as Adah, 36:2?), Oholibamah the daughter of Anah the son of Zibeon the Hivite (36:2), and Basemath, Ishmael's daughter (36:3).

[27:4] Apparently the father's blessing on his favorite son is validated by their sharing in a common meal; otherwise, Isaac could have blessed Esau without the savory food. It is ironical that "just as Esau had sold his birthright in coming from the hunt (25:29-34), so would he lose his blessing in returning to the hunt" (Maly, "Genesis," pp. 27–28). The Hebrew term *naphshi*, literally "my soul" (KJV, ASV), is an idiom meaning simply I (RSV, NEB; cf. vss. 25, 31).

Rebekah persuades Jacob to seize Isaac's blessing (27:5-17). Having overheard Isaac offer his blessing to Esau, Rebekah commands (vs. 8) Jacob to fetch two kids from the flock that she might prepare them for Isaac so that Jacob might receive his father's blessing (vss. 5-11). When Jacob protests that his father might discover his deception because he was not hairy like Esau, Rebekah makes him coverings of goatskins so that he will feel like Esau to his father's touch.

[5] Like Sarah (18:10), Rebekah was eavesdropping on the conversation between Isaac and Esau.

[7] In repeating the statement that Isaac made to Esau (vss. 3-4), Rebekah adds the phrase **before the Lord**. It is impossible to know whether Isaac actually used this expression or not. The context would suggest it means that Isaac is depending on the Lord to carry out the paternal blessing and not that he and Esau went to a sanctuary or appeared before an image of Yahweh.

[9-10] Rebekah may have justified her suggestion that Jacob deceive Isaac by reasoning that:

> The promise made to her (25:23) and the sale of the birth-right (25:33) gave Jacob a right to the blessing; that Isaac was acting wrongly; and that she was justified in using any means to ensure a righteous end: as if God could not carry out His purposes without the aid of human fraud.
>
> W. H. Bennett, *Genesis,* CB, pp. 273–74

[11] As in 25:25, here again one encounters the wordplay based on the similarity of Hebrew letters in the words '*eśaw*, **Esau**, and *śe'ir,* **hairy** (cf. vs. 23).

[12] Jacob is not concerned with whether deceiving Isaac is right or wrong but with whether he will get caught (see Jer. 2:26).

[15] Even after a son married (cf. 26:34-35), it is possible that his **best garments** were kept in the house of his parents to be worn when his father officially pronounced the paternal blessing on him.

Jacob seizes Isaac's blessing by deceit (27:18-29). In order to get his father's blessing, Jacob deceives him in three ways: (1) he lies to him about his identity, affirming that he is Esau (vss. 18-19, 24); (2) he claims that he had gotten the game quickly because the Lord gave him success (vs. 20); (3) he wears the clothes of Esau and the skins of kids so that Isaac's touch and smell will lead him to think that Esau is before him (vss. 21-23, 26-27).

[29] This verse, compared with verse 40, shows that Isaac has in mind not merely Jacob the man but also his descendants, the Israelites, as in 25:23. The age in which this blessing was best realized was the reigns of David and Solomon.

Isaac gives Esau an inferior blessing (27:30-40). No sooner had Jacob left than Esau entered with the savory food he had prepared for Isaac. Quickly it becomes clear to Isaac and Esau that Jacob had taken away Esau's blessing by guile (vs. 35). Esau declares that Jacob is worthy of his name ("Jacob" means "supplanter," cf. 25:26), because he had "supplanted" him twice by seizing his "birthright" and his "blessing" (vs. 36). Esau begs Isaac for just one blessing. However, the only positive thing that his father has to say is that the time will come when he will break his brother's yoke from his neck (vs. 40).

[33] Once the paternal blessing had been pronounced, it could not be revoked, even if it was given to a person not intended by the patriarch and under false pretenses. It is ironic that later Laban deceives Jacob in a similar way by giving him Leah instead of Rachel (29:21-27).

[36] Esau's reflection on what Jacob had done contains two wordplays in Hebrew. He is called *ya'aqobh,* **Jacob,** because he **supplanted** (root *'-q-b*) or seized the rightful place of Esau. Also, he took away Esau's **birthright** (*bekhorathi*) and **blessing** (*birkhathi*).

[39] Unfortunately the translators of the KJV and ASV failed to capture the meaning of the Hebrew word *min* just preceding the words for **fatness** and **dew**. The RSV **away from** and the NEB "far from" convey the correct thought: Esau and his descendants will not have good land that can bear bumper crops.

[40] This verse (like vs. 29) clearly refers to Esau's descendants (the Edomites) and not to the man Esau. The Edomites will **live by** the **sword**, that is, they will raid neighboring peoples, plunder caravans, and the like. They will **serve** Esau's **brother**, meaning the Israelites, which refers to the period from David (2 Sam. 8:13-14) to Joram of Judah (2 Kings 8:20-22). Finally, they will succeed in **break**ing the Israelite **yoke from** their **neck**, which refers to the Edomite rebellion in the days of Joram (2 Kings 8:20-22) or of Ahaz (2 Kings 16:6).

Esau's threat and Jacob's flight (27:41-45). Esau hates Jacob because he seized Isaac's blessing with guile, so he resolves to kill him. Someone overhears his plan and tells Rebekah, who summons Jacob and urges him to flee to her brother Laban in Haran. She promises to send for him when Esau's anger is abated.

[41] Like Jesus (Matt. 5:21-24), the author of Genesis is concerned first with the attitude of the heart (hatred) and then with the act (murder). This recalls the account of Cain murdering Abel (4:5-8). Esau thinks Isaac will die very soon and he can kill Jacob during the period of mourning. It was customary to mourn for seven days (50:10).

[42] Whereas Rebekah had overheard Isaac's offer to give Esau his blessing (vs. 5), now she is **told** (by some anonymous bystander or eavesdropper) that Esau had declared he would kill Jacob. Possibly Esau had vocally threatened to avenge himself on his brother.

[44] When Rebekah suggests that Jacob flee to Haran, she expects him to be gone only **a while**. As things turn out, he is gone for twenty years (31:38, 41), and his mother never sees him again.

[45] Rebekah knows that if Esau kills Jacob, then he will be killed by a blood avenger, and she will lose both of her sons.

JACOB'S DEPARTURE FROM CANAAN
(27:46–28:22)

Isaac Sends Jacob to Haran to Seek a Wife (27:46–28:9)

There are two reasons why it was best for Jacob to leave Beer-sheba and go to Haran: (1) Esau had resolved to kill Jacob during the mourning period when Isaac died (27:41-45); (2) Esau's Hittite wives had made Isaac and Rebekah realize the importance of Jacob's not marrying Canaanite women (26:34-35; 27:46–28:2). At Rebekah's urging, Isaac sends Jacob to Haran to marry one of Laban's daughters. When Esau sees Isaac's attitude, he marries Mahalath the daughter of Ishmael.

[28:3] God Almighty (Heb. *'el shadday*) is one of several names used for the supreme deity in the OT (cf. Gen. 17:1; Exod. 6:3). Isaac's desire that God **make** Jacob **fruitful** and **multiply** him calls to mind the divine command to man in the beginning (Gen. 1:28) and to Noah and his sons after the flood (9:1, 7). The wish that Jacob become **a company of peoples** is similar to God's promise to Abraham that he would make of him a great nation (12:2); here the divine blessings originally given to Abraham are transmitted to his grandson Jacob.

[4] Isaac further prays that God's promise (**blessing**) to give Abraham and his descendants the **land** of Canaan in which Abraham, Isaac, and Jacob were not citizens, but sojourners (cf. 13:14-17; 17:8), might be perpetuated through Jacob.

[5] In this verse, the author jumps ahead in time to Jacob's arrival in Haran (29:1); then in verses 6-9 and 10-22 he relates two events that took place between Jacob's departure from Beer-sheba and his arrival in Haran.

[9] The opportunist Esau, seeing that Isaac blessed Jacob and instructed him not to marry a Canaanite woman, marries **Mahalath the daughter of Ishmael** (is she the same as Basemath in 36:3?). Apparently he thought that it would please his father to marry a granddaughter of Abraham.

God Reveals Himself to Jacob at Bethel (28:10-22)

On his way north from Beer-sheba to Haran, Jacob spends the night at Bethel. While he is asleep he dreams about a stairway leading up to heaven with angels ascending and descending on it. God reveals himself to Jacob and promises him that he will give the land of Canaan to him and his descendants, that he will have numerous descendants, and that in him and his descendants all the families of the earth will be blessed (vss. 10-15). When Jacob awakes the next morning, he realizes that God is present. In reponse, he sets up a stone as a pillar and consecrates it by pouring oil on top of it, calls the name of the place Bethel (meaning "house of God"), and vows that if God will protect him on his journey, he will serve him and give him a tenth of all God gives him (vss. 16-22).

[11] Like Moses at the burning bush (cf. Exod. 3:5), Jacob did not know at first that the **place** where he had stopped to spend the night was holy. He became aware of this only after God appeared to him in his dream (cf. vss. 16-17).

[12] The **ladder** which Jacob saw apparently was more like a solid stairway or a slanting pavement. The ziggurat at Ur in Mesopotamia has a flight of stairs leading up to its top, where it was thought that there was an opening connecting heaven and earth. In light of his experience, Jacob thinks of this place as "the gate of heaven" (vs. 17). The

description here recalls the tower of Babel "with its top in the heavens" (11:4). Jesus evidently has this scene in mind when he promises Nathanael that he "will see heaven opened, and the angels of God ascending and descending upon the Son of man" (John 1:51).

[18] Several scholars conclude from Jacob's setting up this stone at Bethel for a pillar (vss. 18, 22), rolling away the stone from the well's mouth at Haran (29:10), and struggling with the man at the Jabbok (32:25-26), that he had great strength. This may be, but one cannot know with certainty the size of the stone he set up for a pillar.

The Hebrew word translated **pillar** here is *matstsebhah*. The OT often condemns the use of "pillars" in worship because they are associated with pagan rites (cf. Lev. 26:1; Deut. 12:3; 16:22; 1 Kings 14:23; Hos. 10:1-2; Mic. 5:13 [Hebrew 12]). However, it also approves their use in a number of cases (Gen. 31:13, 45, 51, 52; 35:14; Exod. 24:4). The difference seems to be that pagans regarded pillars as objects of worship (cf. Exod. 23:24; 34:13-14; Lev. 26:1), while the Lord's people viewed them as symbols of God's presence (Gen. 28:16-18; 35:11-14; see G. A. Barrois, "Pillar," IDB, vol. 3, pp. 815–17).

[19] **Bethel** is the more recent name of the locale which in very ancient times was called **Luz**. A later writer naturally used the more modern name, as it was known to his readers (cf. 12:8), although at the time of the event being recorded it may have borne the ancient name. The statement **but the name of the city was Luz at the first** is not a part of the historical record but the author's explanation to his later audience (cf. Josh. 18:13; Judg. 1:23).

[20-22] Jacob vows that if God will (1) be with him on his journey to Haran, (2) supply his basic needs (**bread** and **clothing**), and (3) guide him safely back to his father's house (vss. 20-21a), then (a) the Lord would be his God, (b) the stone he had set up for a pillar would be God's house, and (c) he would give the Lord a tenth of all he received (vss. 21b-22). This sounds very much as if Jacob is bargaining with God. However, the inspired writer does not say whether Jacob's attitude was acceptable to God.

Jacob did arrive safely in Haran; he had sufficient food and clothing while he was there; and he returned safely to his father Isaac (31:18; 35:27). God gave Jacob and his family special protection from hostile cities on the way back to Isaac at Mamre in the land of Canaan (35:5), and when Jacob arrived at Bethel (35:6) he built an altar to the Lord "because there God revealed himself to him when he fled from his brother" (35:7).

Abraham had given a tenth of the spoil taken from Chedorlaomer's army to Melchizedek priest of God Most High (14:20), presumably as a gift of thanksgiving to God. Now Jacob offers to give the Lord a **tenth** of all the Lord gives him. As far as the Bible indicates, these were voluntary gifts, not acts of obedience to divine commands. Jacob recognizes that all he has is a gift from God and that whatever he gives is actually a giving back or returning of what God has given him. Some of the Pharisees of Jesus' day put great emphasis on tithing to the neglect of inner motives and godlike attitudes (Matt. 23:23). Paul calls for voluntary giving from the heart (2 Cor. 8:1-9), which accords nobly with the highest ideals of giving in the OT (cf. Deut. 15:7-11).

JACOB IN HARAN (CHS. 29–30)

After his encounter with God at Bethel, Jacob goes on northeastward until he arrives in Haran. Genesis 29–30 records three sets of events that occurred there: (1) Jacob marries Leah and Rachel (29:1-30); (2) Jacob's wives and concubines bear him eleven sons and one daughter (29:31–30:24); (3) Jacob becomes very wealthy (30:25-43).

Jacob Marries Leah and Rachel (29:1-30).

Jacob continues from Bethel toward Haran, his original destination. As he nears Haran, he meets Rachel, his uncle's (Laban's) daughter, and tells her who he is. She runs to tell Laban, who comes out to greet Jacob (vss. 1-14). After Jacob had spent a month with Laban

336 / GENESIS 29:1-8

(vs. 14), he agrees to serve his uncle seven years in order to marry Rachel. Laban agrees, but at the end of this period he gives Leah to Jacob instead. After the seven day marriage festival, Laban gives Rachel to Jacob, but Jacob has to work for her an additional seven years (vss. 15-30). Laban's deception seems to be the Lord's way of bringing retribution on Jacob for his similar deceptive treatment of Isaac and Esau.

[1] The land of the people of the east is northern Mesopotamia, where Haran is located.

[2] The **well** which Jacob approaches **in the field** outside Haran is probably the same well where Abraham's servant met Rebekah years earlier (cf. 24:11). Verses 2b-3 (beginning with the words **for out of that well the flocks were watered**) contain explanatory statements by the author of the book of Genesis for his audience, who apparently were unfamiliar with the well at Haran. The purpose of the large **stone** over the entrance down into the well was to keep out flocks and herds that did not have a right to its use (cf. 26:12-33).

[4] Verses 4, 12, and 15 show that the meaning of `ach` is not limited to "blood brother." In verse 4, apparently it means "friends" (so the NEB), and in verses 12 and 15, "kinsman" (RSV, NEB) or more accurately "nephew" (cf. 13:8, which uses this same word in speaking of the relationship between Abraham and Lot).

[5] This verse shows that the meaning of *ben* is not restricted to one's own fleshly son. Genesis 24:15, 24, 29 indicate that Laban was the son of Bethuel and the grandson of Nahor. Thus, **son** in 29:5 means "grandson" (so the NEB).

[7] When the shepherds point out Rachel approaching with Laban's sheep, Jacob suggests that they go ahead and water their sheep and take them back to pasture because the sun is still high in the sky, and it is not yet time to return them to their folds. Apparently he is anxious that they leave so that he can visit with Rachel privately.

[8] The MT reads *ha'adharim,* **flocks** (KJV, ASV, RSV), while the Samaritan Pentateuch and the LXX read

haro'im, "shepherds" or "herdsmen" (NEB). The latter
reading seems to fit the context better, but it is impossible
to know what the original text was at this point. The shepherds did not see how they could comply with Jacob's request, because they needed more men to roll away the
stone from the mouth of the well, and it was customary to
wait until all the flocks arrived. Presumably the shepherds
already at the well arrived early because those who came
first were allowed to water their sheep first.

[10] Having failed in his first attempt to arrange a situation in which he could talk to Rachel privately, Jacob
boldly bucks the local custom by rolling away the stone
from the mouth of the well and watering Rachel's flock.
Perhaps he felt he could accomplish this successfully before the remaining shepherds arrived with their flocks. His
ability to role away the stone by himself (cf. vss. 2-3, 8)
suggests that he had extraordinary strength (see the note
on 28:18).

[11-13] Since Jacob had never met his mother's family,
since he had anticipated meeting them for such a long time,
and since Laban had not heard from Rebekah and her family for many years, the first meeting of Jacob with Rachel
and Laban is filled with emotion. Jacob kissed Rachel and
wept for joy in the realization of his anxious anticipations.
When Rachel realized who Jacob was, she **ran** to tell
Laban. Laban **ran** to meet Jacob (as he earlier had run to
meet Abraham's servant, 24:29) and **embraced** him and
kissed him. Such emotional outbursts are typical of many
cultures and are not restriced to oriental customs.

[14] Laban's exclamation **Surely you are my bone and
my flesh** is his way of telling Jacob that he welcomed
him as a member of his sister's family. This expression
seems to be an idiom denoting intimate relationship
(cf. Gen. 2:23; 37:27; Judg. 9:2; 2 Sam. 5:1; 19:12-13
[Hebrew 13-14]).

[17] The statement **Leah's eyes were weak** is ambiguous.
It may mean that her eyes were not bright and appealing,
or it may mean that her only beauty lay in the softness of
her eyes, whereas Rachel was a beauty from head to toe.

[18] It was customary for a groom or his family to pay the bride's father a *mohar*, or bride price. Since Jacob did not have the money to do this, he offered himself as a servant, or employee, of Laban for seven years as a payment for Rachel to become his wife.

[20] When one has a goal in life, the work which he does to achieve that goal is a joy and passes quickly. Jacob's mind was filled with love for Rachel, and thus the work that he did for seven years to obtain her seemed to last only a few days.

[21-22] These verses seem to reflect the local custom of marriage at Haran in the patriarchal period. However, many details are missing. The text reveals the following: (1) The father of the bride held a **feast** involving the **men** of the city, which probably lasted seven days (cf. Judg. 14:12, 17; Tobit 11:19). (2) On the evening of the first day of the feast (cf. vs. 27), the father "brought" his daughter to the groom (this calls to mind the fact that God "brought" the woman he had created to the man, 2:22), and they slept together beginning that night (cf. 24:65), because Jacob did not know his wife was Leah until the next morning (vs. 25).

[23] It is ironic that just as Jacob had deliberately deceived his father Isaac by disguising himself as Esau (27:19, 24), so now Laban deceives him by bringing him Leah under the pretense that she is Rachel. Such poetic justice, which all men experience at one time or other, is powerfully capsuled in such biblical statements as "Be sure your sin will find you out" (Num. 32:23) and "Whatever a man sows, that he will also reap" (Gal. 6:7).

[24] One of the Nuzi Tablets (No. 67 in Harvard Semitic Studies, vol. 5) states that a certain Yalampa was assigned to a bride named Gilimninu at the marriage of the latter. This indicates that in the Hurrian culture around Haran in the patriarchal period, it was customary for a wealthy father to give his daughter a maid when she married. Thus, it was natural for Laban to give Zilpah to Leah and Bilhah to Rachel (vs. 29).

[25] Jacob's question **What is this you have done to me?** is rhetorical, intended to force Laban to see the seriousness of his deceitful actions toward him (cf. 3:13; 4:10; 12:18; 20:9; 26:10; 1 Sam. 13:11).

[26] One cannot help but wonder whether it was really mandatory in Haran to marry off one's firstborn daughter before the younger. To be sure, natural maturity and texts like Judges 15:1-2 and 1 Samuel 18:17 favor this as a general rule, but is doubtful that it can be shown that such was mandatory. Jacob's mother had come out of that society; why had she never mentioned such a practice to Jacob? Jacob had lived with Laban at Haran for seven years; why had he never heard of such a custom? It seems more likely from the context that Laban concocted this alleged rule on the spur of the moment to defend his actions to Jacob and that Jacob did not retaliate because he felt that it was useless to do so, or that it would be disrespectful to his new father-in-law, who seems to have used this feeling of Jacob to make him work for him and to stay with him for twenty years until Jacob could tolerate it no longer.

[27] We here may refer to Laban and his wife, or to Laban and his household, or it may be the use of the plural for the singular pronoun "I." Verses 27 and 30 taken together indicate that Jacob married Rachel one week after he married Leah, that is, as soon as the marriage feast for Leah and him had ended. Then he had to work an additional **seven years** to pay the bride price for Rachel.

Jacob has Eleven Sons and One Daughter (29:31–30:24)

Jacob loves Rachel more than Leah, and thus the Lord gives Leah children (29:31-35). Rachel envies Leah and demands that Jacob give her children, but Jacob does not have this power. So Rachel gives her maid Bilhah to Jacob, and she bears him two sons (30:1-8). Leah follows Rachel's lead and gives Zilpah to Jacob; she bears him two sons (30:9-13). Rachel trades her turn to have sexual relations with Jacob to Leah for some of Reuben's mandrakes, and Leah bears two more sons and a daughter (30:14-21). Finally, the Lord heeds Rachel's prayers for a child and gives her a son (30:22-24).

This section depicts the strong rivalry between Leah and Rachel, which calls to mind a similar rivalry between Peninnah and Hannah, the two wives of Elkanah (1 Sam. 1:2, 4-7). Later the Law forbade a man to marry sisters (Lev. 18:18).

The explanation of the names given to Jacob's children are not scholarly attempts to give etymological origins but wordplays on the various names. Therefore, the modern commentator is hardly justified in criticizing the lack of etymological connections in this paragraph.

[31] Hated (KJV, ASV, RSV) and even "was not loved" (NEB) are too strong to denote Jacob's attitude toward Leah. The thought is that he did not love and favor Leah as much as he did Rachel. Here, as elsewhere in the Bible, a woman is able to conceive and bear children because the Lord gives her that power (cf. 20:17–21:1; 1 Sam. 1:5, 6, 11, 19-20). Like Sarah (11:30) and Rebekah (25:21) before her, Rachel is barren.

[32] In 29:32–30:24, it is the mother who gives the child its name. The statements Leah makes when her first three children are born indicate she is hoping the fact she is bearing children to Jacob will cause him to love her more, perhaps even more than Rachel. When Leah's first son is born, she thinks, **Surely now my husband will love me.** Using a wordplay in Hebrew, she calls her son **Reuben** (*re'ubhen*), saying, **Because the Lord has looked upon** [*ra'ah be*] **my affliction.**

[33] Leah calls her second son **Simeon** (*shim'on*), saying, **Because the Lord has heard** [*shama'*] **that I am hated.**

[34] Leah calls her third son **Levi** (*lewi*), thinking, **Now this time my husband will be joined** [*yillaweh*] **to me**, that is, "we will be united to each other in true and full love."

[35] Leah calls her fourth son **Judah** (*yehudhah*), saying, **This time I will praise** [*'odheh*] **the Lord.**

[30:2] **Jacob's anger** at Rachel is a temporary loss of temper, which comes from his inability to make her pregnant. Ultimately it reflects the deep love he had for her (cf. 29:20, 30) and his sensitive feelings for her in her disappointment at not having borne a child. Jacob's response

Am I in the place of God, who has withheld from you the fruit of the womb? agrees with many statements made elsewhere in the Bible to the effect that God opens and closes wombs and that children are God's gifts to parents (cf. vs. 6; 4:1, 25; 16:2; 17:16; 18:10, 14; 20:17–21:2; 25:21; Ps. 127:3). The denial that man is **in the place of God** is used here to refute the idea that man has the power to make a woman pregnant without divine help; in 50:19, to oppose the view that a wronged man has the right to render vengeance on those who have wronged him; and in 2 Kings 5:7, to reject man's ability to heal the sick without divine intervention.

[3] Convinced that she cannot have children of her own, Rachel urges Jacob to go in to her maid. According to Hurrian law, a barren woman could give her maid to her husband, and any child born to that maid would be regarded as the wife's own child. Sarah had followed this procedure (16:2), and now Rachel does the same. As is now known from Hurrian and Hittite society, a newborn child was brought and laid on the knees of the person who had the prerogative of officially accepting that child as his own. So, the children of Machir, the son of Manasseh, the son of Joseph, are said to be "born upon Joseph's knees" (Gen. 50:23). Job, expressing the wish that he had already died, cries out in anguish, "Why did the [father's? mother's?] knees receive me?" (Job 3:12). And in the present passage, Rachel urges Jacob to have sexual relations with her maid Bilhah, **that she may bear upon my knees.**

[6] Rachel, regarding herself as the legal mother of Bilhah's children, seizes the prerogative of giving them names. Leah does the same in conjunction with Zilpah's children (vss. 9-13). Each name in this chapter emerges from a wordplay in Hebrew. It should be noted that Rachel gives God the glory for the birth of Bilhah's first son by declaring, **God has . . . given me a son** (see vs. 2). Rachel calls him **Dan,** saying, **God has judged me** (*dananni*). The verb "judge" can hardly mean "condemn" here, because Rachel is speaking very joyously and optimistically. It

probably means that God had decided in her favor by giving her a son through Bilhah.

[8] Rachel calls Bilhah's second child **Naphtali**, saying, **With mighty wrestlings** [*naphtule 'elohim*] **I have wrestled** [*naphtalti*] **with my sister, and have prevailed**. Rachel imagines herself in a great contest with Leah, the outcome of which is determined by the ability of each to bear children. There is a striking similarity between this and the contest between Jacob and the man at the Wadi Jabbok (32:24-30 [Hebrew 25-31]).

The literal meaning of the Hebrew expression translated **mighty wrestlings** (ASV, RSV), "great wrestlings" (KJV), or "a fine trick" (NEB) is "wrestlings of God." Apparently "God" here is a noun of quality and thus should be understood adjectivally in the sense of "mighty" or "great" (see the note on 1:2).

[11] Leah calls Zilpah's first son **Gad**, saying, **Good fortune** [*baghadh*]! The reading of the KJV, "A troop cometh," requires a different Hebrew text, *ba' ghedhudh*, for which there is no support in the ancient versions. However, there is a wordplay involving *gad* and *gedhudh* in 49:19, which could have influenced the translators of the KJV here.

[13] Leah calls Zilpah's second son **Asher**, saying, **Happy am I** [*be'asheri*]! **For the women will call me happy** ['ish-sheruni].

[14-15] Most commentators think that Rachel wanted some of Reuben's **mandrakes** because she believed they promoted conception. Two arguments may be adduced in support of this view: (1) Even in the modern world, some people in the East believe that mandrakes have aphrodisiac qualities. (2) Genesis 29:31–30:24 has to do with the birth of Jacob's children to his wives and concubines. If this is the correct interpretation, there is nothing to indicate that the author of the book of Genesis shared such a superstitious notion. As a matter of fact, he declares clearly that Rachel conceived when God "remembered" her, "hearkened to" her, and "opened her womb" (vss. 22-23). He is merely reporting Rachel's pagan concept—he does

not condone it, any more than the author of 2 Samuel 11 condones David's adultery with Bathsheba and murder of Uriah.

On the other hand, the context suggests an entirely different understanding. A mandrake is a somewhat poisonous plant of the potato family. It has wide, dark green leaves with purple flowers in the middle. Its large, brown root is shaped something like the human body, and its small, bright red fruit looks like a tomato. The present text suggests that mandrakes were a rarity in the region around Haran, and thus when Reuben brought them in from the field, Rachel wanted some very badly. There is no indication that she intended to eat the fruit, but if she did, they would have had a purgative or cathartic effect on her. The point is that Leah would not allow Rachel to have any of the mandrakes unless Rachel consented to give up her time to have sexual relations with Jacob. Rachel wanted the mandrakes so badly that she agreed to this bargain. The result was that Leah conceived again after a period of not bearing children and ultimately bore two more sons and a daughter. In principle, this account provides a striking parallel to Esau's relinquishing his birthright to Jacob for some red pottage (25:29-34).

[16-18] Leah calls her fifth son **Issachar**, saying (to Jacob), **I have hired you** [*śakhor śekhartikha*) **with my son's mandrakes** (vs. 16), and **God has given me my hire** [*śekhari*] **because I gave my maid to my husband** (vs. 18).

[20] Leah calls her sixth son **Zebulun**, which (like Issachar) is based on two wordplays: **God has endowed me** [*zebhadhani*] **with a good dowry** [*zebhedh*]; and **now my husband will** bring me presents (*yizbeleni*), an explanation supported by the cognate Akkadian word *zubullû*, "bridegroom's gift" (KJV and ASV—"now my husband will dwell with me"; RSV—**now my husband will honor me**; NEB—"now my husband will treat me in princely style").

[22] The statement **God hearkened to her** (Rachel) assumes that Rachel had been praying for a child (cf. NEB), as Isaac had earlier prayed for his barren wife Rebekah

(25:21). The claim that God **opened her** [Rachel's] **womb** again affirms the inspired biblical faith that God is personally and actively involved in human conception and birth and that this process is not merely a natural phenomenon.

[23-24] Rachel calls her first son **Joseph,** which again is founded on two wordplays: **God has taken away** [*'asaph*] **my reproach** (i.e., the reproach or humiliation of being a childless woman) and **May the Lord add** [*yoseph*] **to me another son,** which is correctly read as a wish (ASV, RSV, and NEB), rather than as a promise (KJV).

Jacob Becomes Wealthy (30:25-43)

After Jacob completes his seven years of service for Rachel, he asks Laban for permission to return to his home in Beer-sheba (vss. 25-26; cf. 26:33). Laban urges him to stay, declaring that he had learned by divination that God had blessed him because of Jacob and offering to give him any wage he might ask (vss. 27-30). Jacob agrees to stay if Laban will give him every speckled and spotted sheep, every black lamb, and every speckled and spotted goat. Since these types are rare, Laban gladly accepts Jacob's terms, and then promptly removes all the older speckled and spotted sheep and goats and the black lambs and sends them a three days' journey away under the care of his sons so that Jacob could not get what he had agreed to give him. But Jacob has the strong members of Laban's flocks breed before fresh rods of poplar, almond, and plane with peeled white streaks in them and practices selective breeding (vs. 40). The flocks produce large numbers of speckled and spotted sheep and goats and black lambs, so that Jacob's flocks increase and Laban's decrease. Over a period of seven years (cf. 31:38, 41), Jacob becomes very rich (vss. 31-43).

It should be noted that Laban (by divination, vs. 27) and Jacob (by magical power of suggestion, vss. 37-39) used pagan superstitions to accomplish their purposes. However, by reporting such practices, the biblical writer is not expressing his own belief in their validity, commending their use, or encouraging his readers to adopt them.

[27] The KJV "I have learned by experience" is not an adequate translation of *nichashti*, and the NEB "I have become prosperous" is based on a textual emendation. The preferable translation is **I have learned by divination** (ASV, RSV), which indicates that Laban had shaken arrows, consulted teraphim (cf. 31:30), looked at livers (Ezek. 21:21 [Hebrew 26]), or the like. Later, Joseph pretends to be angry because his brothers had stolen his silver cup, since he used it for divination (Gen. 44:5, 15).

[35] It is ironic that Laban removed the he-goats and she-goats that had **white** on them, as the word for **white** in Hebrew is *labhan* (the word for **Laban**).

[37] "Pilled" (KJV) is an archaic spelling of the modern word **peeled** (ASV, RSV, NEB).

[40] In addition to using peeled rods, Jacob also allows the ewes to run only with certain kinds of rams, thus increasing the number of striped, spotted, and speckled sheep and black lambs.

[43] This verse contains a summary description of Jacob's wealth, mentioning those things that he had acquired over a period of many years. Riches among semi-nomads were measured in terms of **flocks, maidservants and menservants, and camels and asses** (cf. 12:16; 24:35).

JACOB'S RETURN FROM HARAN TO CANAAN (CHS. 31–35)

After serving Laban for twenty years in Haran, Jacob resolves to return to his father's household at Hebron in southern Canaan (31:3, 17; 35:27). Out of the numerous events that undoubtedly occurred in the course of his journey, the inspired author of Genesis records nine: (1) Laban pursues Jacob, and they make a friendly agreement (ch. 31); (2) Jacob prepares to meet Esau (32:1-21 [Hebrew 2-22]); (3) Jacob wrestles with a man at the Jabbok River (32:22-32 [Hebrew 23-33]); (4) Jacob is reunited with Esau (33:1-17); (5) Shechem rapes Jacob's daughter Dinah, and her brothers Simeon and Levi kill him in revenge (33:18–34:31); (6) God promises Jacob that he will give his descendants the land of Canaan (35:1-15); (7) Rachel dies while giving birth to Benjamin (35:16-21); (8) Reuben commits adultery with Jacob's concubine Bilhah (35:22); (9) Jacob is reunited with his father Isaac, and later Isaac dies (35:23-29).

Jacob and Laban Separate (Ch. 31)

Six years earlier, Jacob had asked Laban to allow him to return to Isaac's household in Hebron (30:25), but Laban urged him to stay because he had been blessed by God so much while Jacob was at Haran and promised to give him any wages he asked (30:27-34); so Jacob remained. Now, however, a number of things indicate that it is time for him to leave Haran: (a) Laban's sons (cf. 30:35) harbor ill will against him because he has gained great wealth in Laban's employ (vs. 1); (b) due to Jacob's growing prosperity and Laban's losses, Laban has changed his mind about the advantage of having Jacob return to Canaan (vss. 3, 13). So Jacob summons Leah and Rachel and tells them that he feels it is time for them to leave Laban, and they agree (vss. 4-16).

Laban is occupied with shearing his sheep when Jacob and his family flee and thus does not learn of this for three days. He pursues Jacob, but God warns him in a dream not to harm or deter Jacob. Laban chides Jacob for leaving without allowing him to say goodbye to his daughters and for stealing his teraphim, or household gods. Jacob explains that he was afraid Laban would take away his wives by force and denies that he had stolen his gods. He challenges Laban to make a search throughout his household and (not knowing that Rachel had taken them) says that anyone in his family who has these gods will be put to death. Laban's search is futile, for Rachel had hidden them under her camel's saddle and had sat on it during the search of her tent (vss. 17-35).

Jacob sharply rebukes Laban for the way he had tried to cheat him and manipulate him for his own purposes over the past twenty years. Laban suggests that the two make a covenant not to harm each other from this time forward.

Jacob agrees, and they erect a heap of stones and a pillar as symbols of their mutual understanding, which they seal by sharing a sacrificial meal. Then, Laban kisses his daughters and grandchildren and returns home to Haran (vss. 36-55 [Hebrew 31:36–32:1]).

[1] The sons of Laban envy and despise Jacob, their brother-in-law, because he has taken possession of what had formerly belonged to Laban, which eventually was supposed to become their property. Just as Jacob had attained Esau's birthright (25:29-34), now he had obtained theirs. To cast disparagement on Jacob, they promote the rumor that he had taken what really belonged to Laban and that all his splendor was derived from him. The precise meaning of *kabhodh* in this verse is very difficult to determine. Texts like Isaiah 10:3 and Nahum 2:9 [Hebrew 10] seem to support the translation **wealth** (RSV, NEB). However, most OT passages that use this word in describing human beings place it after "riches," and apparently think of it as that which results from wealth (cf. Gen. 45:13; 1 Kings 3:13; 1 Chron. 29:12, 28; 2 Chron. 1:11, 12; 17:5; 18:1; 32:27; Esth. 5:11; Ps. 49:16-17 [Hebrew 17-18]; Prov. 3:16; 8:18; 22:4; Eccles. 6:2). Possibly, Laban's sons chafe at the "glory" (KJV, ASV) or magnificence which has come to surround Jacob as a result of his having acquired Laban's possessions.

[2] Many scholars interpret the reason given in this verse as a source variant (E) on the reason given in verse 1 (J). However, whereas verse 1 relates the jealousy and spite of *Laban's sons* toward Jacob, verse 2 records *Laban's own* changed attitude (cf. 30:27-28, 34) toward him (as vs. 5 further suggests).

[3] When God spoke to Jacob at Bethel in the dream above the stairway, he assured him that he was with him and that he would bring him back to the land of Canaan (28:15). Now, twenty years later, he repeats the same promises as he charges Jacob to return to Isaac in Hebron (vss. 3, 5, 13).

[7] If Jacob's claim that Laban had changed his wages **ten times** is taken literally, the biblical author has omitted a number of specific instances. However, it is likely that the phrase **ten times** is a Hebrew idiom meaning "several times" or "numerous times" (cf. vs. 41 and Num. 14:22). Jacob prospered in spite of Laban's attempts to cheat him, not because he was smarter than his father-in-law, but because God was protecting him (cf. also vs. 9).

[8] This verse helps clarify some of the obscure statements made in 30:31-43 and 31:7. Laban "changed Jacob's wages" by altering his agreement as to which kind of sheep and lambs would be given to Jacob. When the number of spotted animals seemed to be decreasing, he gave Jacob the spotted; then when the number of striped animals appeared to be diminishing, he gave Jacob the striped. Each time, God caused Jacob to get the larger number, and Jacob recognized that his prosperity was a gift of God (vs. 9).

[11] Verse 13 identifies **the angel of God** here with God himself (cf. 16:7-11 with 16:13).

[13] Jacob tells Leah and Rachel how that in the dream in which God told him to leave Laban and return to Isaac, God assured him that he was the same God who had appeared to him at Bethel when he saw the angels ascending and descending on the stairway (28:12-13, 19), where he had anointed a pillar (28:18) and made a vow (28:20-22).

[14-15] Leah and Rachel concur with Jacob's decision to leave Laban. This seems to have been legally necessary according to Hurrian laws or customs, because when Jacob desired to leave earlier, he had to ask Laban to "send him away" and to "give him" his wives and children (30:25-26). In other words, even though Leah and Rachel were Jacob's wives, they were regarded as members of Laban's house or household (cf. vss. 26, 29, 31, 43). Without Laban's consent, none of them could leave the household without sound legal reasons. Jacob's reasons were: (1) Laban did not regard him with favor as he once did (vs. 5), and (2) Laban cheated him and changed his wages ten times (vs. 6). Added to these are two reasons given by Leah and Rachel: (3) There is no longer any inheritance for them in Laban's house (vs. 14), possibly because this had been

given to Laban's sons (cf. 30:35; 31:1), and (4) Laban is treating them like **foreigners** instead of his own daughters, because he has kept and spent all that he had received from Jacob's twenty years of labor for him. Hurrian law specified that part of the dowry paid by the husband to the father was to be given to the wife (Exod. 22:17 [Hebrew 16] seems to reflect a similar law).

[19] Laban's sheepshearing time provided an excellent opportunity for Jacob to escape, because it was accompanied by a festival celebration that usually lasted several days (cf. Gen. 38:12-13; 1 Sam. 25:2-27; 2 Sam. 13:23-25).

The Hebrew word *teraphim* is used for various objects in the OT. First Samuel 19:13, 16 uses it of an object about the size and shape of a man, which Michal, the daughter of Saul, put in David's bed as a dummy so that he could escape from Saul's men. In Genesis 31:19, 34, 35, however, the *teraphim* are small, portable, and capable of being easily hidden under a camel's saddle. Apparently they are objects of worship here, since Laban and Jacob both speak of them as *'elohim,* **gods** (vss. 30, 32).

Commentators have suggested at least four reasons why Rachel took her **father's household gods**: (1) Some of the early rabbis suggested she thought that if she left them with Laban, they would expose the whereabouts of Jacob and his family. (2) Perhaps Rachel was an avid worshipper of these gods and felt that she must take them to protect Jacob's family. Later, Jacob has to command his household to put away their foreign gods and purify themselves so that they can worship the one true God at Bethel (35:2, 4). If this is the correct explanation, the author of Genesis is not approving or commending Rachel's actions but simply relating what she did. Other OT texts specifically condemn the worship of teraphim (cf. 1 Sam. 15:23; 2 Kings 23:24; Ezek. 21:21 [Hebrew 26]; Zech. 10:2). (3) It may be that Rachel took her father's gods to demonstrate that the God Jacob worshiped was superior to them because they could not even defend themselves against theft. If so, she would have considered them as prized booty, much like the Philistines looked upon the ark of the covenant as a prize of war and placed it in the temple of their god Dagon to symbolize his victory over Yahweh at Aphek (1 Sam. 4:11, 17, 19, 21, 22; 5:1-2). (4) One of the Nuzi tablets dealing with adoption shows that the head of a household could legally give his inheritance to his son-in-law or some member of the family other than his own son by entrusting that person with his images. This has led many scholars to think that Rachel took Laban's teraphim so that Jacob would become heir to his possessions rather than his sons. This fits the story very well and would explain why Laban was so upset over the theft (vs. 30) and why Jacob promised that if they were found in his household, the person that took them would be put to death (vs. 32).

[20] The phrase **Jacob outwitted Laban** reads literally "Jacob stole the heart of Laban" in the MT (see also vs. 26). Apparently this is a Hebrew idiom meaning "Jacob deceived Laban" (so the NEB). The same expression is used to describe Absalom's impact on the men of Israel (2 Sam. 15:6), which eventually led them to gather behind him at Hebron and to follow him in rebellion against David. The author of Genesis may have chosen this phrase to create a wordplay with verse 19: Rachel "stole" Laban's "gods," and Jacob "stole" his "heart." The reading "Jacob stole away unawares to Laban" (KJV, ASV) does not capture the precise meaning of the original.

Arameans settled in the northern Mesopotamian region around Haran at a very early period. It is significant that, among others, Bethuel (25:20), Laban (25:20; 31:20, 24), and Jacob (Deut. 26:5), all of whom lived in this region for many years, are designated as **Arameans** in the OT.

[22] Laban had separated his flocks from Jacob "a distance of three days' journey" (30:36) to make sure that Jacob could not cheat him by manipulating his animals to his own advantage. Ironically, this boomerangs on him when Jacob decides to flee, because it took a messenger three days to go from the place where Jacob had been living to Laban to tell him of Jacob's flight.

[23] The word "brethren" (KJV, ASV; Heb. *'ach*) here can hardly mean "blood brothers." The context suggests

that it denotes members of the household (cf. vss. 25, 37, 46, 54).

As the distance from Haran to the hill country of Gilead is approximately 350 miles, Jacob and his family with all the members of the household and flocks could not possibly have traveled this far in **seven days**. Thus, it is likely that this is an idiom denoting a great number of days (cf. 2 Kings 3:9; and Speiser, *Genesis*, p. 246).

[24] Just as God delivered Sarah from Abimelech by revealing her true identity to him *in a dream* (20:3), now he delivers Jacob from punishment at the hand of Laban by warning him *in a dream* not to do anything to try to change Jacob's decision.

God's charge **Take heed that you say not a word to Jacob, either good or bad** does not mean that he forbids Laban to say anything at all to Jacob or even to reprimand Jacob for departing in the way he did; at least, Laban did both of these things and still thought he was doing what God had told him (cf. vss. 26-30). The context suggests that God was instructing him to make no attempt to harm Jacob (cf. vs. 29) or to persuade him to return to Haran (vss. 43, 50).

[25] Some scholars take *har* in the sense of a single "mountain" here (cf. KJV, ASV) and then struggle to identify the mountain in the first line and to distinguish it from "the mountain of Gilead" in the second. It seems preferable to understand *har* as **hill country** (so RSV, NEB) and to take both lines to refer to the hill country of Gilead (cf. the previous reference in vs. 23).

[26] Laban's question **What have you done?** is rhetorical and has the goal of trying to get Jacob to see the seriousness of his actions (cf. the same question in 3:13; 4:10; 12:18; 20:9; 26:10; 29:25). In verses 26-30, Laban brings four charges against Jacob: (1) he took away his daughters like soldiers carry away captive women (vs. 26); (2) he fled secretly (vs. 27); (3) he did not give Laban an opportunity to say goodbye to his daughters and grandchildren (vss. 27-28); (4) he had stolen his household gods (vs. 30).

[27] Unless Laban is inventing a special situation to

make Jacob look bad, evidently the citizens of Haran followed certain customs when they parted from their loved
ones; they participated in some sort of festival accompanied by musical renderings (cf. the parting of Rebekah
from the family of Bethuel, 24:54, 59-60). The theoretical
scene bears striking similarities to the celebration accompanying the return of a member of the family after an extended absence (cf. Luke 15:22-25, 32).

[28] It is worthy of note that **sons** here and in verses 43
and 55 means "grandchildren." There is no linguistic justification for reading "my daughters and their children" in
verses 28 and 55 (contra NEB).

[32] As a biblical writer relates an earlier story unfamiliar to his readers, occasionally it is necessary for him to
explain something which they would not understand otherwise. So, in verse 32 he states, **Now Jacob did not know
that Rachel had stolen them**; again in verse 34 he writes,
**Now Rachel had taken the household go !s and put them in
the camel's saddle, and sat upon them.** Similar explanations
appear here and there throughout the Scriptures (see
1 Sam. 9:9; Matt. 1:23; John 2:21-22).

[33] Each of Jacob's wives and concubines had her own
separate tent where she lived with her children. In his
search for the household gods, apparently Laban

> went to Jacob's tent first, because the women's quarters,
> the harem, would only be entered in a case of necessity;
> he went next to the concubines' tent, because, if he had
> found the teraphim there, the wives would have been
> spared the annoyance of the search. For a similar reason
> he went *last* into the tent of the favourite wife, Rachel.
>
> Bennett, *Genesis*, pp. 304–5

[34] The *kar haggamal,* **camel's saddle** (RSV), is probably a basket-saddle, a palanquin, or litter strapped to the
saddle in some way (see BDB, p. 468).

It is most ironical that the household gods which Laban
worshiped were not only unable to prevent a woman from
taking them but also were rendered unclean when she **sat
upon them** in her menstruation period (cf. Lev. 15:19-20).

[35] Although it sounds strange to modern ears, it was common for wives (cf. Gen. 18:12; 1 Pet. 3:6) and daughters (as in the present verse) to call their husbands and fathers **my lord** (*'adhoni*) as an expression of respect.

[37] In verses 37-42, Jacob advances three arguments to show that he has acted toward Laban with all integrity. First, he challenges Laban to show one thing that Jacob carried with him when he left Haran that was not legally his. He is so confident of his right conduct that he tells Laban to place any item before legal witnesses from among his own kinsmen and Laban's kinsmen. Laban silently produces nothing.

[38] Second, Jacob declares that he has been **with** Laban (i.e., in his house. serving him, cf. vs. 41) twenty years and has faithfully served him both in extreme heat and in severe cold (cf. vs. 40).

[39] Third, although Jacob was not legally responsible for the loss of Laban's sheep that were killed by wild beasts (cf. the Code of Hammurabi, par. 266; Exod. 22:13 [Hebrew 12]; Amos 3:12), he bore the loss; and he faithfully recompensed Laban for any animal that was stolen (cf. Exod. 22:12 [Hebrew 11]).

[42] Among the many OT terms for God (as "God Almighty"—17:1; "the Mighty One of Jacob"—Ps. 132:2, 5; "the Shepherd"—Gen. 49:24; "the Rock of Israel"—Gen. 49:24; Deut. 32:4, 15; "the Lord of Hosts"—Isa. 1:9; "the Most High"—Ps. 91:9; etc.), verses 42 and 53 use **the Fear of Isaac.** Apparently, this means the God whom Isaac feared, that is, revered, respected, and worshiped (cf. Isa. 8:13).

[43] Although Laban feels that he has the legal right to punish Jacob and his household for fleeing from him, he cannot do so because God forbade him to harm Jacob (vss. 24, 29), and he cannot bring himself to render vengeance on his own daughters and grandchildren (vs. 43).

[44] Instead of bringing retribution on Jacob, Laban proposes that they make a **covenant.** The covenantal agreement consists of two promises: Jacob will not mistreat Leah or Rachel or take other wives besides them (vs. 50);

and neither Jacob nor Laban will come into the other's territory to harm him (vs. 52).

[45] As one sign of the mutual intention of Laban and Jacob to abide by the covenant, **Jacob** sets up a **stone** as a **pillar** (cf. 28:18, 22).

[46] As a second sign, **Jacob** has his kinsmen erect a **heap** of stones or "cairn" (NEB) and share a covenant meal. Several scholars want to read "Laban" instead of **Jacob** in verses 45 and 46 (the Old Latin reads "Laban" in vs. 46), because in verses 48 and 49 it is Laban who explains the significance of the cairn, and in verse 51 Laban claims to have set up both of them. This may be the best solution to the problem. However, it could be that Jacob (as the younger member of the household) actually had these two symbols erected physically, and then Laban (as the patriarch of the household) declared their significance. The present text seems to suggest that those entering a covenantal agreement participated in a common meal expressing goodwill and fidelity to the covenant both before (vs. 46; cf. 26:30) and after (vs. 54) the actual agreement was made.

[47] Laban calls the stone heap *yeghar-śahadhutha'*, **Jegar-sahadutha**, which is the Aramaic expression meaning "the heap of witness," and Jacob calls it *gal'edh*, **Galeed**, which is the Hebrew expression meaning "heap of witness," thus reflecting the two linguistic backgrounds represented here.

[49] Laban also calls the heap of stones *mitspah*, **Mizpah**, that is, "watchtower," as a wordplay in Hebrew on *yitseph*, "watch", in the statement, **The Lord watch between you and me, when we are absent one from the other**. Verse 50 indicates that Laban is threatening Jacob here. If Jacob should mistreat Leah or Rachel, or if he should marry other wives secretly and hide it from Laban and his household in Haran, he is to remember that God is watching as a witness between him and Laban and will punish him. Laban thus charges that Jacob is a clever and unscrupulous manipulator. Although the Samaritan Pentateuch reads *matstsebhah*, "pillar," instead of *mitspah*, **Mizpah**,

here, there is little real justification for reading **and** [Laban named] **the pillar Mizpah** (contra RSV).

[53] The meaning of this verse is very hard to determine. In the MT, the Hebrew word translated **judge** is plural (*yishpeṭu*), possibly suggesting that Laban is thinking of at least two gods. If so, one might translate: **The God of Abraham and the God of Nahor, the** [gods] **of their father** [i.e., Terah], **judge between us** (cf. Josh. 24:2, 14). Such a concept would be expected from one who maintained household gods (cf. vss. 19, 30, 32, 34, 35). At the same time, the Samaritan Pentateuch, LXX, Syriac, and Vulgate read the singular, in which case "the God of Abraham," "the God of Nahor," and "the God of their father (Terah)" would be the same God. This could be possible if Terah and Nahor (like Abraham) abandoned their Mesopotamian gods to worship Yahweh.

Jacob and Esau are Reunited (32:1–33:17)

(The Hebrew versification is 2-22; we follow the English numbering in the comments for the benefit of the English reader.) Having journeyed from Haran (31:18, 21) southwest to the hill country of Gilead east of the Jordan (31:21, 25), Jacob and his household now move farther south to Mahanaim on the Jabbok stream (32:2). Just as he had seen a host of angels at Bethel when he left southern Palestine to go to Haran (28:10-22), he now sees a host of angels as he prepares to reenter Palestine from Haran (vss. 1-2). Jacob sends word to his brother Esau in Edom south of Judah that he is returning to Canaan from Haran (vss. 3-5). His messengers return with news that Esau is coming with 400 men to meet him; Jacob is afraid that Esau still intends to kill him for seizing his father's blessing (27:41-45), and he divides his household into companies (32:6-8). Jacob reminds God that he had told him to leave Haran (31:3) and begs him to deliver him from Esau (32:9-12). Jacob then takes a large number of his goats, sheep, camels, cattle, and asses, divides them into several herds, and sends them in succession to Esau as a series of presents, hoping thereby to appease him (vss. 13-21).

[1-2] The present paragraph contains two wordplays on **Mahanaim**. (1) In verse 2, Jacob calls the place **Mahanaim** because angels met him and he exclaimed: **This is God's army!** (*machaneh 'elohim*), apparently for the purpose of giving him assurance of divine help in anticipation of the forthcoming encounter with Esau. (2) In verses 7, 8, and 10 he divides his household into "two companies" (*machanoth*), thinking, "If Esau comes to the one company (*machaneh*) and destroys it, then the company (*machaneh*) which is left will escape."

[4] In an attempt to establish a good relationship with his brother, Jacob tells his messengers to refer to Esau as Jacob's **lord** and to Jacob as Esau's **servant** (see vss. 18, 20).

[9] It is noteworthy that Jacob begins (vs. 9) and ends (vs. 12) his prayer by reminding God of his promise to make him prosperous if he left Haran, because Esau's approach seems to bring this promise into serious question. Between these two reminders, Jacob acknowledges his unworthiness of God's continual guidance and help (vs. 10) and asks him to deliver him from Esau (vs. 11). The (a) rehearsal of God's promises, (b) expression of one's own unworthiness, and (c) petition for help in time of crisis are fundamental elements of prayer.

[10] Jacob acknowledges his unworthiness of God's amazing gifts. When he left Canaan for Haran and **crossed the Jordan** (which flowed several miles west of Mahanaim), Jacob possessed **only** a **staff**, but in the intervening twenty years, God had increased his possessions to **two companies**.

[11] The Hebrew phrase *'em 'al banim*, literally "mother upon (over) children," is apparently an idiom meaning "everyone." It has been suggested that this figure was derived from a mother hen hovering over her chicks to protect them from danger (cf. Deut. 22:6), but there is not enough evidence to be certain of this.

[13] The word for **present** is *minchah*, which forms still another wordplay with "Mahanaim" (cf. vss. 2, 7, 8, 10).

[20] In verses 16, 17, 20, 21, and 30, the Hebrew word *panim*, literally **face**, occurs nine times (once each in vss. 16, 17, and 21 [before me; "before you;" "before him"]; four times in vs. 20 [**I may appease him**; **before me; his face; he will accept me**], and twice in vs. 30 ["face to face"],where it forms a wordplay with *peni'el*, "Peniel," or *penu'el*, "Penuel" (vs. 31), which means literally "face of God"). The expression **I may appease him** is literally "I may cover his face," while the phrase **he will accept me** is literally "he will lift up my face" (cf. 19:21).

Jacob wrestles with an assailant at the Jabbok River (32:22-32). After sending away his servants with his livestock, part of which were to be given to Esau, Jacob sends his wives and children across the Jabbok River a few miles west of Mahanaim at Peniel or Penuel and stays behind alone for the rest of the night. A man wrestles with him until dawn. He puts Jacob's thigh out of joint but does not prevail against him. Jacob refuses to let him go until he blesses him. The man changes Jacob's name to "Israel," and Jacob calls that place "Peniel," "the face of God," saying, "I have seen God face to face, and yet my life is preserved." This calls to mind Hagar's encounter with God at Beer-lahai-roi and her query, "Have I really seen God and remained alive after seeing him?" (16:13-14).

In this difficult paragraph, the biblical author is not relating a vision, dream, or fantasy; nor is he using well-known external phenomena to symbolize an inner struggle (like prayer) anticipating a critical situation (here, the encounter with Esau); rather, he is relating a real, hand-to-hand combat. Verses 28 and 30 show that Jacob was actually wrestling with God himself, but apparently God had assumed a human form, for Jacob's assailant is called a "man" in verses 24 and 25 (cf. also vs. 28). Although the plain meaning of the text is very hard for modern man to comprehend and rationalize, there is no justification for forcing it to say something it does not say.

[22] Although *yeladhim* often means **children** in the OT (ASV, RSV), the context demands that it mean "sons" here (KJV, NEB), because at this time Jacob had twelve

children—**eleven** sons and one daughter (cf. 30:21). The
Jabbok River is the modern Nahr-ez-Zerka, which flows
into the Jordan from the east, about twenty-five miles
north of the Dead Sea.

[24] The Hebrew word for **wrestled** is *'abhaq,* which
forms a wordplay with *yabboq,* **Jabbok,** in verse 22.

[26] God calls for the combat to cease at dawn to protect
Jacob from death, for otherwise he would have actually
seen God face to face (see the note on vs. 30).

[28] God changes **Jacob's** name to **Israel** (*yiśra'el*), which
forms a wordplay with his explanation: **for you have striven
[*śaritha*] with God and with men, and have prevailed.** As in
the case of Abraham (17:5) and Sarah (17:15), this divine
change of name symbolizes a change in the character of
Jacob (cf. Jesus' changing Simon's name to Cephas, or
Peter, John 1:42). "The cunning Jacob becomes the
divinely commissioned Israel" (Maly, "Genesis," p. 34).
Again:

> The man who could be a party to the cruel hoax that was
> played on his father and brother, and who fought Laban's
> treachery with crafty schemes of his own, will soon con-
> demn the vengeful deed by Simeon and Levi (xxxiv) by
> invoking a higher concept of morality (xlix 5–7).
>
> Speiser, *Genesis*, p. 257

"As a prince hast thou power" (KJV) translates one
word in the MT (*śaritha*) and assumes that it is a
denominative verb from *śar,* meaning "prince." This interpretation is unfounded and is rightly rejected by other
modern English versions.

[30] Jacob calls the place **Peniel** or "Penuel" (vs. 31),
"the face of God," which provides a wordplay with his
explanation: **I have seen God face to face [***panim 'el panim***],
and yet my life is preserved.** Surely the author of Genesis
does not mean that Jacob actually saw God as he really is.
Instead, the thought is that his personal experiences made
it vividly clear to him that he had been dealing with God
himself and not with a mere man or even an angel. "No
one has ever seen God" (John 1:18), that is, no one has

seen God with the physical eye as he really is.

[32] In this verse, the author of Genesis interrupts his record of events involving Jacob to explain to his audience why **Israelites do not eat the sinew of the hip which is upon the hollow of the thigh**, namely, because God had put Jacob's thigh out of joint when he wrestled with him. This is the only place in the OT where this eating custom is mentioned.

From the struggle with God,

> Jacob emerged broken, named and blessed. His limping would be a lasting proof of the reality of the struggle: it had been no dream, and there was sharp judgment in it. The new name would attest his new standing: it was both a mark of grace, wiping out an old reproach (27:36), and an accolade to live up to.
>
> D. Kidner, *Genesis*, TOTC, p. 169

Jacob is reunited with Esau (33:1-17). The biblical writer does not indicate how much time elapsed between Jacob's struggle with God at the Jabbok River and his encounter with Esau. It is significant that in both meetings Jacob's life is apparently in jeopardy, and in both incidents he emerges the better for the trial. Fearful of Esau and his 400 men, Jacob goes out first to meet them and arranges his family behind him so that the least loved would be nearest Esau and the best loved farthest from him for the sake of protection (vss. 1-3).

The reunion of Jacob and Esau provides a striking picture of reconciliation. Jacob, who had seized Esau's blessing over twenty years before, approaches his brother with several tokens of submissiveness and humility: (a) he bows before him seven times (vs. 3); (b) he refers to himself as Esau's "servant" (vss. 5, 14) and to Esau as his "lord" (vss. 8, 13, 14 [twice], 15); (c) he insists that Esau take a large amount of his possessions as a present (vss. 8-11); (d) he declares that seeing Esau's face is like seeing the face of God (vs. 10). In response, like the father of the prodigal son (Luke 15:20; cf. *Enuma elish* I, lines 53ff.; Gen. 45:14; 46:29), Esau "ran to meet" Jacob, "embraced him, fell on his neck, and kissed him" (vs. 4). He lovingly addressed him as "my brother" (vs. 9) and accepted his present only under protest (vs. 9) and after great insistence (vs. 11).

Once the reconciliation is complete, Esau suggests that he and his men escort Jacob and his household to Esau's homeland of Seir. Jacob declines, with the argument that his children and flocks and herds could not travel very rapidly. Esau suggests that he leave some of his men to help Jacob, but again Jacob declines. Esau and his men leave for Seir, and Jacob and his household spend a great deal of time at Succoth east of the Jordan (vss. 12-17).

[3] The Tell el-Amarna Tablets (fourteenth century B.C.) include communications from vassal rulers in Palestine to their overlord, the Pharaoh of Egypt, in which they write: "At the feet of my lord, my Sun, I fall down seven and seven times." Similarly, Jacob bows before Esau **seven times**, although not to subject himself to Esau as a vassal or slave, but to convey the air of humility.

[5] Jacob acknowledges that his children (vs. 5) and his possessions (vs. 11) are gifts that God had **graciously given** to him. Many think of their children as merely natural products of sexual intercourse. The Bible repeatedly claims that God works actively in conception and birth (cf. 4:1, 25; 17:16; 18:10, 14; 20:17–21:1; 25:21; 29:31, 33; 30:1-2, 6, 22). Just because a phenomenon like childbirth occurs often does not prove that God is not causing it to happen or providing the life for the newborn babe. It cannot be proved or disproved scientifically that God works actively in conception and birth. One must accept or reject this by faith. But to reject it is to reject clear biblical claims. (In addition to the above-mentioned passages in Genesis, see also Job 1:21; Pss. 104:30; 127:3; and the general statement in James 1:17.)

[10] When Jacob says to Esau, **to see your face is like seeing the face of God**, apparently he is drawing a parallel between God's blessing him when he wrestled with him at the Jabbok River (32:26-29) and Esau's receiving him with forgiveness and brotherly love on the present occasion.

The expression **face of God** (*pene 'elohim*) is virtually the same as *peni'el,* "Peniel," or *penu'el,* "Penuel" (32:30-31). It was common to compare someone with God or one of his angels if one wished to express great respect for him (cf. 1 Sam. 29:9; 2 Sam. 14:17, 20; 19:27 [Hebrew 28]).

[11] The Hebrew word translated **gift** in the ASV, RSV, and NEB is *berakhah,* which often means "blessing" (KJV) in the OT. However, it also means "gift" or "present" in a number of passages (Josh. 15:19; Judg. 1:15; 1 Sam. 25:27; 30:26; 2 Kings 5:15), and the context shows that this is the meaning here (cf. BDB, p. 139).

[14] In spite of the apparent reconciliation, Jacob apparently still feels very uneasy around, and very suspicious of, Esau. Not only does he decline Esau's offers to lead his household to Edom (vs. 12) and to leave some of his men behind to escort his household there (vs. 15), he also indicates to Esau that he is planning to come to **Seir** (i.e., Edom, cf. vs. 16), knowing all the while that he had made a vow to go to Bethel (cf. 28:20-22; 31:13; 35:1).

[17] After persuading Esau to go back to his country of Seir or Edom, Jacob continues west from Peniel to **Succoth** (cf. Judg. 8:4-9; also Josh. 13:27), where he apparently stays for several years. The flow of the narrative in Genesis 30:21-43 coupled with 31:41 would seem to suggest that Dinah was approximately seven years old when Jacob's household left Haran, but 34:1-2 indicates that she was a grown young woman when Jacob's family lived in Shechem. Of course, it may be that Jacob's household lived in Shechem several years before Shechem raped Dinah, but the fact that Jacob **built himself a house, and made booths for his cattle** at Succoth makes it probable that he lived there for several years. Verse 17 contains another wordplay in Hebrew. The place was called **Succoth** because Jacob made **booths** (*sukkoth*) for his cattle there.

Jacob Back in Canaan (33:18–35:29)

Shechem rapes Dinah; Simeon and Levi kill him (33:18–34:31). After staying several years in Succoth,

Jacob's household crosses the Jordan westward to Shechem, where Jacob pitches his tent and builds an altar
(33:18-20). Shechem, the son of Hamor, the prince of Shechem, rapes Dinah, Jacob's daughter by Leah (cf. 30:21).
Later Shechem and Hamor ask Jacob and his sons to give
Dinah to Shechem for a wife and suggest that Jacob's family intermarry with the people of Shechem (34:1-12).
Jacob's sons agree to these proposals on the condition that
all the males at Shechem be circumcised. Hamor and Shechem meet with the men of the city at the city gate, and
they decide to submit to circumcision (vss. 13-24). On the
third day after circumcision, when the men of Shechem are
sore, two of Dinah's older brothers (by Leah), Simeon and
Levi, come upon the city unawares and kill all the males
including Hamor and Shechem. Jacob's sons seize all the
spoil of the city. Jacob reprimands them for putting him in
jeopardy with the Canaanites and Perizzites, the inhabitants of the land of Canaan, but they reply that Shechem
should not have treated Dinah like a harlot (vss. 25-31).

As elsewhere in the book of Genesis (cf. 3:6; 4:3-8;
13:10-13; 14:12; 19:1-16) and throughout the Bible (Josh.
7:21;   2 Sam. 11:2-4;   Pss. 1:1;   7:14;   James 1:14-15),
the present paragraph vividly describes man's slow but
sure, progressive entanglement in sin: (1) Jacob "came
safely to" Shechem (33:18); (2) he "camped" or "pitched
his tent" before the city (vss. 18, 19); (3) he "bought the
piece of land" on which he was encamped (vs. 19);
(4) "Dinah went out to visit the women of the land" (34:1);
(5) Shechem "saw her" (vs. 2); (6) he "seized her" (vs. 2);
and (7) he "lay with her and humbled her" (vs. 2).

[18] The Hebrew word *shalem* may be interpreted in one
of three ways with almost equal linguistic and contextual
justification. First, it can be understood as a proper name,
"Shalem" (KJV; so also the LXX, Syriac, and Vulgate).
The subsequent context gives no help, because it simply
refers to the place as **the city** (33:18; 34:25, 27, 28), "their
[i.e., Hamor's and Shechem's] city" (34:20 [twice]), or "his
[i.e., Hamor's] city" (34:24 [twice]). In this case, **the city of**

Shechem could mean the city belonging to the man Shechem (the son of Hamor), or a hamlet belonging to the
city-state of Shechem, which some scholars have identified
with the modern village of Salim located about four miles
east of the modern Nablus (ancient Shechem). The main
objection to the latter view is that there is no other instance in the OT where a hamlet is called "the city of" the
neighboring city-state. Second, it may mean "in peace"
(ASV), especially in light of 34:21, which indicates that the
people of Shechem welcomed Jacob's household to their
territory in a friendly manner. Third, it can mean **safely**
(RSV, NEB), in which case the biblical author would be
emphasizing that Jacob successfully separated from Esau
and moved westward without encountering hostile opposition or danger. Although *shalem* itself does not have this
meaning anywhere else in the OT, its noun (Gen. 28:21;
43:27) and verb (Job 9:4) cognates do.

The phrase **before the city** (RSV, KJV, ASV; Heb. *'eth
pene ha'ir*) is an idiom meaning "to the east of" the city
(NEB; see the notes on 23:17 and 25:18).

[19] The Hebrew word translated **pieces of money** is
qeśiṭah, which occurs elsewhere only in Joshua 24:32
(which refers back to the present incident) and Job 42:11.
Since archeologists have not yet found an ancient coin or
weight inscribed as a *qeśiṭah*, it is impossible to know the
value of 100 qesitahs. The NEB follows the LXX, Vulgate,
and Targum Onkelos in reading "sheep."

[20] Since the Hebrew verb translated **erected** is
yatstsebh, which is cognate with *matstsebhah,* "pillar," and
which is not used anywhere else in the OT in connection
with an altar, some scholars want to emend the text from
mizbeach, "altar," to *matstsebhah,* "pillar." However, there
is no support for this in the ancient versions, and the KJV,
ASV, RSV, and NEB agree in following the MT by reading
altar. That Jacob would erect an **altar** is in keeping with the
practices of Abraham (12:7, 8; 13:4, 18) and Isaac (26:25).
Jacob named the altar **El-Elohe-Israel**, that is, "God, the
God of Israel," at this point evidently referring to himself
(cf. 32:28) and not to the nation of Israel.

[34:2] Although **Hivites** are mentioned several times in the OT (cf. Exod. 3:8, 17; 13:5; 23:23; etc.), no extrabiblical evidence of their existence has yet been discovered. The LXX reads "Horite[s]" instead of **Hivite**[s] in Genesis 34:2 and Joshua 9:7. Some scholars think that the Horites were the pre-Edomitic inhabitants of Seir (cf. Gen. 36:2, 20) and that those who handed down the biblical stories sometimes confused them with the Hurrians who lived in Canaan. It seems wiser, however, to wait for new archeological discoveries, which may well open up now unsuspected information on the Hivites, just as has been done with regard to the Hittites (cf. E. A. Speiser, "Hivite," IDB, vol. 2, p. 615).

It is difficult to determine the political position intended by the term **prince** (Heb. *naśi'*). Evidently Shechem was held in high respect at Shechem (cf. vs. 19) and could make certain authoritative decisions. At the same time, it was necessary for Hamor and Shechem to get the consent of "the men of their city" (vs. 20) or "all who went out of the gate of his city" (vs. 24) before entering into an agreement with Jacob's household to intermarry and to have the men of Shechem circumcised. Perhaps the best translation of *naśi'* is "sheik" (cf. R. de Vaux, *Ancient Israel*, 2d ed. [London: Darton, Longman and Todd, 1968], p. 8).

In spite of certain implications to the contrary, the whole drift of the chapter indicates that Shechem raped Dinah against her will and forced her to live in his house. This is suggested by the verbs **humbled** (Heb. *'innah*; vs. 2), "defiled" (*timme'*; vss. 5, 13, 27), and "treat as a harlot" (*khezonah ya'aśeh*; vs. 31). Verse 2 states that Shechem **seized** or "took" (Heb. *laqach*) Dinah; later, verses 17 and 26 declare that Jacob's sons "took" (Heb. *laqach*) her out of Shechem's house, apparently meaning that they had to rescue her. Jacob's sons conclude that in raping Dinah, Shechem "had wrought folly in Israel" by doing "a thing" that "ought not to be done" (vs. 7). This entire chapter shows the great concern the biblical writers had for chastity and purity prior to marriage. Both premarital sexual intercourse and rape are strictly condemned.

[3] The word **soul** here and in verse 8 means simply "he." The expression **spoke tenderly to her** is literally "spoke upon/to the heart of the girl." This *can* be taken to mean that Shechem comforted her (cf. 50:21; Ruth 2:13; Isa. 40:2) when he saw that she was greatly upset because he had raped her, by trying to show that he really loved her. However, it seems more likely that it means that he persuaded her that she should stay with him because he loved her (cf. Judg. 19:3; Hos. 2:14 [Hebrew 16]).

[7] Rape (Gen. 34:7; Judg. 19:23; 20:6, 10; 2 Sam. 13:12-13), fornication (Deut. 22:21), and adultery (Jer. 29:23) were all regarded as **folly** in Israel. The word **folly** (Heb. *nebhalah*) is not simply childish foolishness, but disgraceful behavior—**such a thing ought not to be done.**

[9] Numerous passages throughout the Bible emphasize the strong temptation to marry one who is not a true worshiper of God and the religious dangers confronting one who enters into such a marriage (in particular, the danger of renouncing a genuine lifetime commitment to God in deference to one's earthly mate; cf. Gen. 34:9, 16, 21; Exod. 34:11-16; Deut. 7:1-5; Josh. 23:11-13; 1 Kings 11:1-10; 16:31-33; Ezra 9–10; Neh. 13:23-27; 2 Cor. 6:14–7:1).

[10] Hamor points out that if Jacob's family agrees to marry the people of Shechem, they will come to be regarded as full-fledged citizens of Shechem and no longer as sojourners.

[12] Shechem seems to be offering both a **marriage present** (*mohar*) to the parents (cf. Exod. 22:16-17; 1 Sam. 18:25) and a **gift** (*mattan*) to the bride, which is similar to the gifts that Abraham's servant gave Rebekah and her parents (Gen. 24:53), although Speiser finds a case of hendiadys (see LWC-OT, vol. 1, ch. 1) here and reads "a bridal payment" (*Genesis*, p. 265).

[14] God had commanded Abraham and his descendants to be circumcised (17:1-14), so Jacob's family regarded it a **disgrace** to marry those who were **uncircumcised.**

[16] The suggestion made that the Israelites and the

Shechemites become **one people** (cf. vs. 22) indicates only that their intermarriages would eventually result in obscuring any differences between them and carries no hint that by submitting to circumcision the Shechemites were accepting Israel's religion or Israel's God. Jacob's sons here are saying what they know the Shechemites want to hear— they are speaking "deceitfully" (vs. 13).

[17] It is curious that Jacob's sons would refer to their "sister" as **our daughter**. Perhaps they are intentionally maintaining the same general language that they had just used in speaking of potential intermarriages between Israelites and Shechemites: "we will give our daughters to you."

[19] The translation of the KJV, "he [Shechem] was more honorable than all the house of his father," suggests to the modern mind that because Shechem was willing to do anything to marry Dinah and thereby to try to correct the fault of raping her, he did the honorable thing. But this is not the thought of the Hebrew text, which means instead **he was the most honored of all his family** (so the RSV; cf. the ASV and NEB), that is, he was the most respected member of his family.

[20] Neither Hamor nor Shechem had the authority to demand that all the male citizens of Shechem submit to circumcision. They had to come **to the gate of their city,** where public business was normally transacted and decisions involving the whole community were made (cf. 23:10, 18; Ruth 4:1, 11; Amos 5:10, 15), and meet with **the men** of the city.

[25] In view of the fact that the population of Shechem was probably very small, and that an adult male who is circumcised is very sore on the third day after the operation (and this would have been true especially in ancient times when crude instruments and operational methods were used—cf. Josh. 5:8), it would have been very easy for two men to slip into the city and kill all the men. **Simeon and Levi** were the second and third oldest sons of Jacob by Leah (29:33-34) and thus were **Dinah's** full blood **brothers** (cf. 30:21).

[27] Some scholars think that after Simeon and Levi had killed the males at Shechem, the other **sons of Jacob** came and plundered the city. However, the context does not demand this. If one reads verse 27 in conjunction with verses 25 and 30, he gets the impression that **the sons of Jacob** here are Simeon and Levi.

[30] Although Jacob had nothing to do with the murders of the men of Shechem, the hostile act of his sons put him and his entire household in jeopardy. Such a reputation would normally lead to severe reprisals from the full-fledged citizens of the land, **the Canaanites and the Perizzites** (cf. 12:6; 13:7), especially against those who were only sojourners and who had acted in a hostile way against settled citizens of the land. When he says **my numbers are few**, Jacob reflects a sensitivity and concern for his family which Simeon and Levi ignored or despised. Before acting, a child of God should weigh carefully the effect his actions will have on others (cf. Col. 4:5-6).

God renews his promise to Jacob (35:1-15). God commands Jacob to leave Shechem, return to Bethel (where he had seen the angels descending and ascending on the stairway in his dream as he was going from Beer-sheba to Haran perhaps thirty-five years earlier, 28:10-22), and build an altar to him there. Jacob has his entire household give him their foreign gods, and he hides them under the oak near Shechem. They go to Bethel, and Jacob builds the altar. Rebekah's nurse, Deborah, dies and is buried (vss. 1-8). For sake of emphasis, God repeats the change of Jacob's name to Israel (cf. 32:28) and promises him that a company of nations and kings will come from him and that he will give his descendants the land he had given to Abraham and Isaac. Jacob sets up a pillar of stone to express gratitude for God's blessings and to worship him and for emphasis reaffirms that the name of the city is changed from Luz to Bethel (vss. 9-15). It is significant that as Jacob returns through Bethel on his way from Haran to Hebron (cf. vs. 27), he does many of the same things that he had done on his way from Beer-sheba to Haran several years before and that God promises him many of the same things that he had promised him on his earlier sojourn there (the similarities are pointed out in the following notes). Apparently God selected Bethel as the place where he would appear to Jacob in a most meaningful way and declare what he had in mind especially for him and his descendants.

[1] God's command to **go up** is geographically accurate, as Bethel is about one thousand feet higher than Shechem.

[2] In order to prepare to worship God, Jacob felt it necessary for all those with him to: (a) **put away** their **foreign gods** (evidently including the household gods that Rachel had stolen from Laban, 31:19, 30, 32-35, but not limited to them); (b) **purify themselves** (the text does not specify how this was to be done [unless the next phrase explains it], implying that Jacob's household already knew); and (c) **change** their garments (cf. Exod. 19:10; Zech. 3:3-5). In the OT, holiness

> is least of all a special quality which can belong to men or things, but rather simply the state of belonging to God. This state is made possible at all only by God's preceding choice or call and therefore it requires of men a kind of confessional renunciation of everything 'unholy' and a cultic, symbolic demonstration of his desire for purification and clarification of his relation to God.
>
> G. von Rad, *Genesis*, OTL, p. 331

The present passage emphasizes the importance of making proper preparation for worship, and the inseparable relationship that exists between one's daily life and public profession of worship (cf. Isa. 29:13-14; Matt. 15:7-9; Titus 1:16).

[3] The **distress** to which Jacob refers is his anguish in having to leave his father's household (cf. 27:46–28:5, 10) because Esau had planned to kill him (cf. 27:41-45). He expresses gratitude that God had been **with** him wherever he went, just as he had promised (28:15) and just as Jacob had desired (28:20).

[4] Evidently many members of Jacob's household believed that **earrings** had magical or supernatural powers,

possibly to ward off evil spirits. Exodus 32:1-4 and Judges 8:24-27 indicate that they were used to make images. All these texts show the intimate connection between earrings and foreign gods.

[5] The Hebrew phrase *chittath 'elohim* can have one of two meanings: (1) If *'elohim* is a proper noun (God), it means "a [the] terror of God" (KJV, ASV), that is, **a terror from God** (RSV), a terror that God sends, an idea that corresponds closely with that of Exodus 23:27; Joshua 10:10; 2 Chronicles 14:14 (Hebrew 13); (2) If *'elohim* is a noun of quality, as it seems to be in Genesis 1:2 and 30:8, it means "a great terror." Apparently it was the massacre of Shechem (34:25-29) that struck panic in the hearts of the surrounding inhabitants of the land.

[6] The little parenthetical note **that is, Bethel** comes from a period later than the event itself and its initial oral or written preservation, when the Israelites for whom the book of Genesis was intended no longer knew that the ancient name for **Bethel** was **Luz**. It is similar to New Testament passages written for people who did not know Hebrew or Aramaic (as Matt. 1:23; Mark 5:41; 15:34; John 1:41, 42), or who did not know some detail in an event that had occurred several years earlier than the time of the writing of the book (as John 2:21, 22; 4:2).

[7] Since the word *'elohim* is plural, when it occurs with a singular verb or adjective or is associated with a singular pronoun, it means **God**, and when it occurs with a plural verb or adjective or pronoun, it means "gods." In the present verse, the verb (*nighlu*) is plural. Therefore, *'elohim* apparently means "divine beings" or "angels," probably referring to the angels that Jacob saw in his dream ascending and descending on the stairway (28:12; Heb. 2:7 interprets the *'elohim* of Ps. 8:5 [Hebrew 6] in the same way).

[8] **Rebekah's nurse** is also mentioned in 24:59, although not by name as here. This was the woman that had nursed Rebekah in Bethuel's home for the first two years of her life (cf. 24:15, 24, 50, and the note on 24:59). **Below Bethel** apparently means south of Bethel. The **oak** was called

Allon-bacuth, that is, "oak of weeping," to signify the mourning of Rebekah and her family over the death of the loyal **Deborah.**

[9] When Jacob's family put away their foreign gods and Jacob built an altar at Luz (cf. vs. 6), **God appeared to Jacob again, when he came from Paddan-aram,** that is, the region around Haran, just as he had appeared to him many years earlier at Bethel on his way toward Paddan-aram (28:10-22).

[10] God gave or changed individuals' names to symbolize a change of life he expected from them or a new mission or destiny that he had in mind for them. It is not inappropriate at all, therefore, for God to repeat this, since the person involved might not yet have made the transition that God required or might need further divine encouragement or a strong reminder to continue on the way which he had already begun. When Andrew first brought his brother Simon to Jesus, the Lord changed his name to Cephas or Peter (John 1:42), but he repeated this later when Simon confessed that he was the Christ (Matt. 16:17-18), and Peter continued to wear the name Simon even after his name was changed (Acts 10:5, 18; 11:13). Similarly, God changed Jacob's name to Israel when he wrestled with him at the Jabbok River (Gen. 32:28), but Jacob still dealt deceitfully with his brother Esau (33:13-14) and allowed foreign gods to be kept and worshiped in his own household (35:1-3). Thus, God reminds him that his name is no longer Jacob, but Israel.

[11] God reveals himself to Jacob as **God Almighty** (Heb. *'el shadday*), the same name he wore when he revealed himself to Abraham to make a covenant with him through circumcision (17:1), and the same name his father Isaac had used in his prayer that Jacob be blessed when Jacob left Beer-sheba for Haran (28:3). In fact, God's command to Jacob, **be fruitful and multiply,** and his promise to him, **a nation and a company of nations shall come from you,** are strikingly similar to Isaac's prayer for his younger son (28:3). Also, God's promise to Jacob, **kings shall spring from you,** calls to mind his earlier promise to Abraham

(17:6) and Sarah (17:16) that kings would come from them. The command **be fruitful and multiply** apparently does not refer to Jacob the individual (for at this time he already had eleven sons and a daughter), but to his children and descendants.

[12] The word "seed" (KJV, ASV; Heb. *zera'*) is a collective singular meaning **descendants** (RSV, NEB), as is normal in the Bible.

[13] When God finished talking with a person, he **went up** from him (cf. 17:22).

[14] When Jacob was at Bethel many years earlier, he had erected **a pillar of stone** and had **poured oil on it** (cf. 28:18). Here he repeats that ceremony and also **pours out a drink offering** on the pillar. It is difficult to know the precise significance of these acts, but the context here and in chapter 28 would seem to suggest that Jacob is expressing appreciation to God for blessing him so richly and thanking him for his abundant promises.

[15] It is not inappropriate for Jacob to call Luz **Bethel** a second time (cf. 28:19). Because it had been over thirty years since he had been there, the inhabitants of that place would not have known of and/or accepted such a name change. Also, Jacob's wives and children were not present when he first changed its name, so this would be entirely new to them. Furthermore, such a name change had important religious implications and overtones, since **Bethel** means "house of God." Jacob seems to be confessing or proclaiming that it was at this place that God revealed himself most graciously and powerfully in Jacob's checkered career for the ultimate benefit of Jacob and his descendants.

Rachel dies giving birth to Benjamin (35:16-21). Jacob's family journeys on southward toward Ephrath or Bethlehem. Rachel gives birth to Benjamin, dies, and is buried between Bethel and Bethlehem. Afterwards Jacob's household moves on south beyond the tower of Eder.

[16] The present verse and others (Gen. 48:7, 1 Sam. 10:2; Jer. 31:15) indicate that Rachel died and was buried in the territory that later belonged to the tribe of Ben-

jamin, approximately twelve miles north of Bethlehem, for they were still some distance from Ephrath (the KJV "there was but a little way to come to Ephrath" gives the wrong impression of the meaning of the Hebrew phrase here).

[17] As Rachel was having her hardest pains and was nearing death, the household midwife tried to encourage her with the assurance that she was about to give birth to another son, for whom she had prayed when her first son Joseph was born (cf. 30:24).

[18] The expression as her soul was departing is not a highly religious affirmation meaning "as her eternal spirit was leaving her body to begin eternity in heaven or hell" or the like; it simply means "as she was breathing her last few breaths."

Because of the severe suffering accompanying the birth of her second son, Rachel calls him Ben-oni, that is, "the son of my sorrow (or affliction)." However, Jacob calls him Benjamin, literally, "the son of the right (hand, side)," which should be interpreted as a contrast to Ben-oni. Since "right" is south in Hebrew thought, some scholars have suggested that Benjamin means "son of the south," either because the tribe of Benjamin is the southernmost of the ten northern tribes geographically or because Jacob's family was on its southern journey toward Hebron when Benjamin was born. However, as a contrast to Ben-oni, it is preferable to understand Benjamin as the son on whom the father depends for comfort and support or the son whose birth is a symbol of good fortune for the future of the family. The right hand was a symbol of honor and strength in Hebrew thought (cf. Exod. 15:6 [twice], 12; Deut. 33:2; Judg. 5:26; 1 Kings 2:19; Pss. 16:8; 17:7; 18:35 [Hebrew 36]; 20:6 [Hebrew 7]; 21:8 [Hebrew 9]; 44:3 [Hebrew 4]; 48:10 [Hebrew 11]; 60:5 [Hebrew 7]; 63:8 [Hebrew 9]; 78:54; 80:17 [Hebrew 18]; 89:13, 25, 42 [Hebrew 14, 26, 43]; 98:1; 108:6 [Hebrew 7]; 110:1, 5; 118:15, 16 [twice]; 138:7; 139:10; Eccles. 10:2; Isa. 62:8; Jer. 22:24; Lam. 2:4).

[20] The pillar of Rachel's tomb still existed and could be viewed by travelers at the time that the book of Genesis

was written. The author's expression **to this day** suggests that a great deal of time had elapsed between the setting up of this pillar and the writing of the book.

[21] The Hebrew phrase *mighdal 'edher* can mean "tower of the flock," "tower of Eder," or "Migdal-eder." It occurs elsewhere only in Micah 4:8, where it stands in synonymous parallelism with "hill of the daughter of Zion." In other words, Migdal-eder is a section or portion of Jerusalem. As Jerusalem lies between Rachel's tomb in Benjamin and Bethlehem in Judah, the most natural meaning of verse 21 is that after Jacob buried Rachel, he and his household moved south beyond Migdal-eder at Jerusalem.

Reuben's adultery with Bilhah (35:22a-b). The flow of the text would seem to suggest that Rachel's death made her maid Bilhah (cf. 29:29) vulnerable, perhaps because she was no longer subject to her mistress. Reuben, the oldest son of Jacob (by Leah, cf. 29:32), took advantage of the situation and committed adultery with her. As a result of this immoral act, Reuben (and through him his tribal descendants) lost the birthright that otherwise would have been inherited by the oldest son (cf. 49:3-4; 1 Chron. 5:1).

Jacob and Isaac reunited; Isaac dies (35:22c-29). Verses 23-26 give a list of the twelve sons of Jacob by his two wives and two concubines. Jacob returns to his father Isaac, who had moved from Beer-sheba (cf. 28:10) to Hebron (vs. 27) during the years that Jacob was in Haran and other places. Isaac later dies at the age of 180, and Jacob and Esau bury him (vss. 27-29).

[22c] Like Nahor (22:20-24) and Ishmael (25:12-18), Jacob has **twelve** sons, who are the ancestors of the twelve tribes of Israel.

[26] The statement that Jacob's twelve sons were born **in Paddan-aram** must be taken generally, because Benjamin was born between Bethel and Ephrath in the land of Canaan (cf. vss. 16-18). The author of Genesis would hardly have stated this in the way he did in such close approximation to verses 16-18 if he thought the two statements were mutually contradictory.

[27] Apparently Isaac moved from Beer-sheba to **Hebron** (i.e., **Mamre** or **Kiriath-arba**) after Jacob went to Hebron, possibly because it was here that his father Abraham had lived so long (cf. 13:18; 14:13; 18:1), and it was here that his mother Sarah (23:2) and Abraham (25:9-10) were buried in the cave of Machpelah.

[28] When Jacob left Isaac at Beer-sheba to go to Haran, he was forty years old (since he was Esau's twin, and Esau was forty, cf. 26:34), which means that Isaac was 100 (since he was sixty when Jacob and Esau were born, cf. 25:26). When Jacob left, Isaac was old and said, "I do not know the day of my death" (27:1-2). But now in 35:28 we learn that Isaac did not die until he was 180. Many scholars find a great discrepancy between 27:1-2 and 35:28. However, Abraham considered himself to be an old man at 100 (17:17), and yet he did not die until he was 175 (25:7). The life expectancy in the patriarchal period was much higher than it is in the modern world, and biblical writers cover a long time period in a few verses.

[29] The statement **Isaac . . . was gathered to his people** is simply a Hebrew idiom meaning "he died" (see the note on 25:8). Just as the previously hostile brothers Ishmael and Isaac had reunited to bury their father Abraham in the cave of Machpelah (25:9), so now the previously hostile brothers Jacob and Esau reunite to bury their father Isaac in the same cave (cf. 49:31). The death of a common loved one often breaks down human walls of hate, jealousy, and disharmony.

ESAU'S DESCENDANTS (Ch.36)

There are major characters and minor characters in the book of Genesis. The author gives a great deal of space to the former but treats the latter only as they have a significant bearing on events pertaining to the major characters, or (briefly) after finishing a lengthy section on another. Thus, he discusses Ishmael in certain passages in the section on Abraham and Isaac and ends that section with a brief list of Ishmael's descendants, their movements, and their leaders (25:12-18). Now, in a similar way, having dealt with Esau in certain passages in the section on Jacob, he ends that section with a brief list of Esau's descendants, their movements, and their leaders (ch. 36). It is worthy of note that this same material is found in a somewhat abbreviated form in 1 Chronicles 1:35-54. Since Genesis 36 primarily consists of a list of Esau's descendants and of chiefs and kings of his descendants, the Edomites, the phrase "These are . . . " occurs thirty-one times in this chapter (vss. 1, 5, 9, 10, 12, 13 [twice], 14, 15, 16 [twice], 17 [3 times], 18 [twice], 19 [twice], 20, 21, 23, 24, 25, 26, 27, 28, 29, 30, 31, 40, 43). Accordingly, the smaller sections of the chapter must be determined by content. It seems best to divide these into three groups: (1) the descendants of Esau, including the chiefs of the Edomites (vss. 1-19 [**cf. vss. 40-43**]); (2) the descendants of Seir (who inhabited the land of Edom before the Edomites took it and who intermarried with them; vss. 20-30); (3) the kings of Edom (vss. 31-39).

The descendants of Esau (vss. 1-19, 40-43). Some scholars have tried to find twelve sons and grandsons of Esau in this chapter, but actually it lists five sons (by three wives) and ten grandsons. *Chart VII* gives their names and relationships. (See p. 377; beside each name is the verse [or verses] in which it appears.)

Esau's sons were born in Canaan before Jacob returned from Haran (vs. 5). After Jacob returns, Esau and his household move south to the hill country of Seir because the land of Canaan cannot support both households (vss. 6-8). Here Esau's grandsons are born, and over a long period of time the Edomite nation emerges with its chiefs (vss. 9-19).

[**2-3**] The names of Esau's wives here do not correspond to those given in 26:34 and 28:9; the following comparison indicates the differences:

ESAU'S WIVES

1. Adah the daughter of Elon the Hittite (36:2)

1. Basemath the daughter of Elon the Hittite (26:34)

2. Oholibamah the daughter of Anah the son of Zibeon the Hivite (36:2)
2. Judith the daughter of Berri the Hittite (26:34)

3. Basemath, Ishmael's daughter, the sister of Nebaioth (36:3)
3. Mahalath the daughter of Ishmael, the sister of Nebaioth (28:9)

There are at least three possible explanations for these apparent discrepancies. (1) Scribal copyists may have accidentally miscopied the text in any one of the passages concerned; for example, the Samaritan Pentateuch reads "Mahalath" instead of "Basemath" in 36:3, 4, 10, 13, 17. (2) Some of Esau's wives may have had more than one name (after all, this was the case with many biblical characters, including Jacob [Israel] and Esau [Edom]). (3) Esau may have married four women. This seems quite possible in view of the complete differences in the identifications of Oholibamah and Judith.

Verse 24 makes it clear that "Anah" was the "son of Zibeon" (so the RSV and NEB, following the Samaritan Pentateuch, LXX, and Syriac) and not his "daughter" (as the KJV and ASV, following the MT). In Hebrew *ben*, "son," and *bath*, "daughter," are frequently confused.

Whereas verse 2 identifies "Zibeon" as "the Hivite," verse 20 describes him as the son of Seir "the Horite." It seems that the OT uses Hivite and Horite indiscriminately to refer to the Hurrians, who had migrated into Syria and Palestine from the Mesopotamian region around Haran early in the second millennium B.C. (see the note on 34:2).

[6] The description of the departure of Esau's household from Canaan to Seir is very similar to that of the departure of Abraham's household from Haran to Canaan (12:5). The Hebrew word translated **members** in the RSV is *naphshoth*, literally "souls" (so the ASV; the KJV reads "persons"). Unlike the modern English word "soul," the Hebrew word ordinarily means the whole person, not the eternal part of a human being.

The MT and the ancient versions vary considerably on the last sentence in verse 6. The KJV, ASV, and RSV

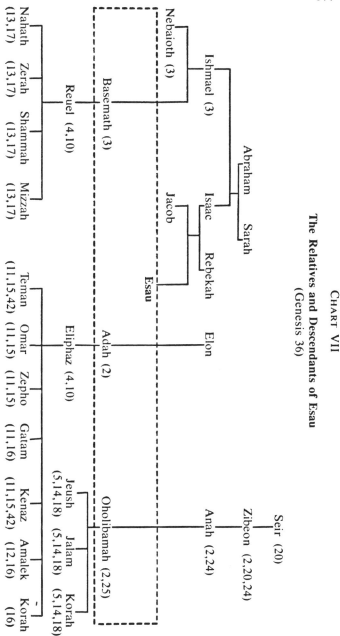

CHART VII

The Relatives and Descendants of Esau
(Genesis 36)

378 / GENESIS 36:7-24

represent attempts to render the sense of the MT: **he** [i.e., Esau] **went into a land** [the country] **away from** [from the face of] **his brother Jacob**. However, the context seems to call for a more specific designation. The Targums Onkelos and Pseudo-Jonathan and the Vulgate read "he went into another land," while the Samaritan Pentateuch and the LXX read "he went from the land of Canaan." The NEB follows the Syriac Peshitta in reading "he went to the district [land] of Seir," which receives some support from verse 8.

[7] The large households of Esau and Jacob separate because the land around Hebron is not able to support them both, recalling the separation of the households of Abraham and Lot, which also arose over the inability of the land near Bethel and Ai to support both of them (13:6).

[8] The main territory taken over by the Edomites lay due south of the Dead Sea almost as far as the Gulf of Aqabah, although it extended westward to Kadesh-barnea, at least during part of the period in which it was controlled by the Edomites (cf. Num. 20:16).

[15] In time, the grandsons of Esau became the **chiefs** (Heb. *'alluphim*) or ancestors or namesakes of the clans of Edom after they settled in their new territory in the hill country of Seir. The KJV reads "dukes," which is an Anglicized form of the Latin *dux* of the Vulgate. **Chiefs**, however, is the preferable reading.

The descendants of Seir (vss. 20-30). This brief paragraph apparently contains important names of ancestors of the pre-Edomite inhabitants of the region south of the Dead Sea, "the Horites." These people descended from "Seir." When the Edomites moved into their territory, evidently they overran the Horites (see Deut. 2:12, 22) and intermarried with them (cf. Gen. 36:2, 14, 24). It seems likely that the Horites were Hurrians who migrated into this district from Mesopotamia over a period of several years.

[24] The ASV and RSV follow the Vulgate in reading **hot springs** here. This would fit nicely in the region south of the Dead Sea. The Samaritan Pentateuch reads "the Emim" (the pre-Moabite inhabitants of the region east of

the Dead Sea, cf. Deut. 2:10), while the Targum Onkelos reads "the giants." The KJV and NEB follow the Arabic version by reading "the mules." If this is correct, it calls to mind Saul searching for his father's asses (1 Sam. 9:3-5). Some scholars think that the first two letters of the Hebrew word *yemim* in the MT have been reversed in the process of scribal copying and suggest that the original reading was *mayim*, "water." In a desert region, the discovery of water would have been a notable event. Nevertheless, there is not enough information in this text to determine the original reading or the occurrence being described.

The kings of Edom (vss. 31-39). This passage names eight kings who reigned over Edom before any king reigned over Israel. These kings were not members of a dynasty; in fact, no two of them were related. Each came from a different city or city-state in Edom and resembles the OT judges much more than the OT kings.

The statement "before any king reigned over the Israelites" (vs. 31) shows that this verse was written after Saul had taken the throne. If it refers to a time after an Israelite king ruled over Edom, it cannot be earlier than the time of David (cf. 2 Sam. 8:13-14; 1 Kings 11:14-17). This date for the writing of the book of Genesis in its final form finds further confirmation in the allusion to the second "Hadad" (cf. 1 Chron. 1:50; the MT of Gen. 36:39 has "Hadar," but "Hadad" is undoubtedly the correct spelling, as 1 Chron. 1:50 indicates; the Hebrew letters *daleth* [d] and *resh* [r] are almost identical and are often confused in transmission), as he is probably the same person who fled before David as a child (1 Kings 11:17) and later rebelled against Solomon (1 Kings 11:14). Assuming that each Edomite king reigned over the entire nation approximately twenty years (unfortunately the length of the reigns is not given anywhere), the Edomites had a monarchy approximately one hundred fifty years before the Israelites. The elders of Israel may well have had them (as well as others) in mind when they said to Samuel, "Appoint for us a king to govern us like all the nations" (1 Sam. 8:5, 20).

[33-34] Bozrah toward the north (cf. Amos 1:12; Isa. 34:6; 63:1; Jer. 49:13, 22) and **Teman** toward the south (cf. Amos 1:12; Jer. 49:7; Obad. 9; Ezek. 25:13) are important cities of Edom.

[35] There is not enough information to determine the exact military encounter mentioned in this verse. Some scholars have suggested that it may belong to the period when the judge Gideon fought against the Midianites (Judg. 6:1–8:32), but this is by no means certain.

VI

THE STORY OF JOSEPH

(Chapters 37–50)

The last section in the book of Genesis deals with Joseph and his brothers. It describes eleven major events: (1) Joseph's brothers sell him to Midianite (Ishmaelite) merchants, who later sell him to Potiphar in Egypt (ch. 37). (2) Judah commits adultery with his daughter-in-law Tamar, and she bears twins (ch. 38). (3) Potiphar's wife accuses Joseph of trying to commit adultery with her, and Potiphar casts Joseph into prison (ch. 39). (4) In prison, Joseph interprets the dreams of the Pharaoh's chief butler and chief baker (ch. 40). (5) Joseph interprets the Pharaoh's dreams, announces a great famine, and is put in charge of preparing for it (41:1-52). (6) When the famine comes, Joseph's brothers make two trips to Egypt to get grain for Jacob's household (41:53–44:34). (7) Joseph reveals his identity to his brothers, and they bring the news to Jacob (ch. 45). (8) Jacob's family moves to Egypt (chs. 46–47). (9) Jacob blesses Joseph's two sons, Ephraim and Manasseh (ch. 48). (10) Jacob forecasts future events concerning his sons and their descendants and then dies (ch. 49). (11) Joseph and his brothers bury Jacob; Joseph makes peace with his brothers, dies, and is embalmed (ch. 50).

These chapters contain evidences of historical accuracy and authenticity sprinkled throughout. Officials of the Egyptian court wear correct titles. Egyptian life and customs are faithfully represented. The names of the various Egyptian characters are Egyptian, as Potiphar (37:36; 39:1), Zaphenath-paneah (41:45), Asenath (41:45, 50), and

Potiphera (41:45, 50). The Tell el-Amarna Tablets (ca. 1377–1360 B.C.) mention a certain Yanhamu, who had the responsibility of supervising the storing of grain for the national stockpile of food, a striking parallel to Joseph's task under the Pharaoh. Further, the Egyptian "Tale of the Two Brothers" (which is at least as old as the thirteenth century B.C.) bears certain similarities to the famous story of the attempt of Potiphar's wife to seduce Joseph (ch. 39). Details of these matters are included in the comments. It is impossible to date the migration of Jacob's household into Egypt with absolute certainty. However, the Hyksos invasion of Egypt about 1720 B.C. fits many of the circumstances suggested by the Joseph narrative and has the advantage of placing this migration 430 years before the exodus (cf. Exod. 12:40-41; Gen. 15:13), which many scholars date about 1290 B.C. (see LWC-OT, vol. 1, ch. 4).

It is all but universally agreed that the religious emphasis in the story of Joseph is on the idea that "God was with Joseph" in all of his trials and in spite of his own sins and failings (cf. 39:2, 3, 5, 21, 23; 40:8; 41:16, 25, 28, 32, 38, 39, 51, 52; 45:4-9; 46:1-4; 48:9, 15-16, 21; 49:24-26; 50:18-20):

> Throughout the story we shall see God's providence and divine purpose running, like a thread of gold through a web of silver, and God somehow, in a way which we can not fully comprehend, but still can realize and believe in, out of all the evil of Joseph and his brothers, at last bringing greater good for them and all about them, keeping alive many people, and enabling Joseph to fulfill the birthright of Israel, to be a blessing unto mankind. Even as the beautiful rose blossoms forth from out the dirt and dung, in accordance with God's law, so, likewise in accordance with God's law, out of men's evil deeds greater good and blessing must in time spring forth for later generations. Men may mean it for evil, but God means it for good. God has not merely created the world and set it going, and since then sits back in passive idleness; God is still in the world, guiding the destinies of men and nations aright in accordance with his wise and beneficent laws, changing evil to good, and bringing mankind steadily forward upon the path of truth and progress, which leads to the goal of

human existence which He has appointed.

J. Morgenstern, *The Book of Genesis*, pp. 267, 272

JOSEPH BECOMES A SLAVE IN EGYPT (Ch. 37)

After Isaac's death, Jacob's family continues to live in Canaan around Hebron (cf. 35:27). Joseph, Jacob's seventeen-year-old son, comes to be hated by his brothers because: (1) he brings an evil report of his half-brothers Dan and Naphtali (the sons of Bilhah, cf. 30:5-8), Gad and Asher (the sons of Zilpah, cf. 30:9-13), to his father (vs. 2); (2) his father shows him partiality by giving him a long robe with sleeves (vss. 3-4); (3) he has two dreams (of the eleven sheaves, and of the sun, moon, and eleven stars) which suggest that he is to be exalted above the rest of his family (vss. 5-11).

Joseph's brothers go north from Hebron (cf. vs. 14) to Shechem to find pastureland for Jacob's flock. After some time, Jacob sends Joseph to make sure his brothers are all right. By the time Joseph gets to Shechem, his brothers have moved even farther north to Dothan, and Joseph finally finds them there (vss. 12-17). As Joseph approaches, his brothers, still filled with jealousy and hatred, entertain the possibility of killing him. However, Reuben intervenes and persuades them not to kill him but to cast him into a dry pit or cistern (vss. 18-24). Reuben leaves (possibly to pasture some of Jacob's flock), and while he is gone some Ishmaelite or Midianite merchants come by on their way south from Gilead to Egypt. Judah suggests that Joseph be sold to these merchants, and his brothers agree (vss. 25-28). When Reuben returns and finds Joseph gone, he is very anxious. Joseph's brothers dip his robe in goat blood and bring it back to Jacob, who concludes that Joseph had been killed by a wild beast. But in reality, the Midianite merchants sell him to Potiphar, an officer of the Egyptian Pharaoh (vss. 29-36). (Many scholars argue that Gen. 37 contains the strongest evidence in the book that two distinct, contradictory documents lie behind this work. This issue is treated in the Introduction.

[1] Once again the author of Genesis emphasizes that the patriarchs (in this case, Isaac) were sojourners in the land of Canaan, and not full-fledged citizens, although their descendants were destined to possess this land (cf. 12:10; 20:1; 21:23, 34; 23:4; 26:3). The author of Hebrews (Heb. 11:8-16) and Paul (Phil. 3:17-21) use this imagery to describe the Christian's walk on earth as a citizen of heaven.

[2] Genesis 37–50 tells **the history of the family of Jacob,** that is, of Jacob and his sons, with a special interest in Joseph.

By bringing **an ill report** to his father Jacob about the actions of some of his half-brothers (**the sons of Bilhah** [Dan and Naphtali, 30:5-8] **and Zilpah** [Gad and Asher, 30:9-13]), Joseph naturally aroused their hatred. God commands: "You shall not go up and down as a slanderer among your people" (Lev. 19:16). Further:

> He who goes about gossiping reveals secrets;
> therefore do not associate with one who speaks
> foolishly.
>
> Proverbs 20:19

And Morgenstern contributes this story:

> Rabban Simon ben Gamaliel once ordered his servant to bring from the market the best thing to be found there. To the good rabbi's surprise he brought a tongue. At another time the rabbi commanded him to bring the worst thing the market could offer. To his still greater surprise the servant again brought a tongue. "How is this?" the master asked. "When I bade thee bring the best thing the market provided, thou didst bring a tongue. And now that I have ordered the worst thing, thou dost still bring a tongue?" "Good master," answered the wise servant, "dost thou not know that a tongue may be either the best or the worst thing in this world accordingly as its owner uses it?" . . . Had Joseph been inspired by sincere love for his brothers, and by the desire to help them correct their faults, his motives might have been commendable. But he seems merely to have delighted in telling all the evil things about

his brothers he could, and in representing himself thereby as better than they . . . . It has been said, that the worth of a man depends upon his two smallest organs, his heart and his tongue.

Genesis, pp. 263–64

[3] Jacob also aroused hatred against Joseph because he **loved Joseph more than any other of his children.** One would think that Jacob might have learned better than to play favorites among his children from the bitter experiences that he had known because his father Isaac had loved Esau and his mother Rebekah had loved him (cf. 25:28), but the sins of parents have a way of repeating themselves in their children. Jacob was partial to Joseph because Joseph **was the son of his old age.** Since Joseph was seventeen when his brothers sold him into Egypt (vs. 2) and thirty when he became second-in-command to the Pharaoh (41:46); since it was nine years after this that Jacob's family moved to Egypt (seven good years [41:53] plus two years into the famine [45:10-11]); and since Jacob was 130 at that time (47:9), presumably he was ninety-one when Joseph was born. Accordingly, he must have been 108 when Joseph was sold into Egypt. (Jacob died at the age of 147 [47:28].) Since Jacob thought Joseph was dead and his brothers assumed he would never return, it is not surprising that Benjamin also was called "the child of his [Jacob's] old age" (44:20).

The KJV and ASV follow the LXX and Vulgate in interpreting the Hebrew phrase *kethoneth passim* as "a coat of many colors." However, most scholars agree with the RSV and NEB that the Hebrew expression really means **a long robe with sleeves.** This is usually taken to mean that Jacob gave Joseph a royal robe, because the only other time this expression occurs is with reference to the garment worn by Tamar when she was raped by Amnon (2 Sam. 13:18-19; but this hardly fits the seminomadic setting in which Jacob and Joseph lived), or a robe with long sleeves which symbolized that his father did not require him to work like the other sons, because laborers wore short garments with short sleeves in order that their hands and arms might be free to labor (but vss. 2, 12-14 give the impression that Joseph worked along with his brothers as long as they were near Jacob's dwellingplace but stayed with his father when they went far away because of his youth). On the basis of the Akkadian expression *kitû* (or *kutinnū*) *pišannu* (which is very similar to the Hebrew phrase here) found in cuneiform inventories, E. A. Speiser argues that this means "an ornamented tunic" (*Genesis,* AB, pp. 289–90). The context indicates that Jacob gave Joseph a special kind of garment to indicate that he loved him best of all among his children. Beyond this it is difficult to go with certainty.

[4-11] Joseph further intensifies the antagonism of his brothers against him (cf. vss. 4, 5, 8, 11) by relating two dreams in which he is exalted. In the first, he tells how the sheaves of his brothers bowed down to his sheaf, and his brothers strongly deny that he will **reign** or **have dominion over** them (vss. 6-8). In the second, he relates how the sun, the moon, and eleven stars bowed down to him, and his father rebukes him (vss. 9-10).

[9] Joseph's allusion to **eleven stars** indicates that Benjamin was born before he was sold into Egypt. When only ten of his brothers come to him in Egypt seeking grain, he asks if they have another brother (43:7) to conceal his true identity and not because he does not know of Benjamin's birth, as some scholars have suggested.

[10] Since Rachel had died when she gave birth to Benjamin between Bethel and Ephrath (cf. 35:16-21), it is difficult to explain Jacob's allusion to Joseph's **mother** here. It seems very unlikely that the events recorded in 37:1-11 occurred before the birth of Benjamin, because of the apparent chronological sequence in 35:16-29 plus 37:1-11 (note especially the references to Hebron in 35:27 and 37:14), and because Joseph's leading question in 43:7 indicates that he was not sold to the Midianite merchants until after Benjamin was born. It may be that Leah, or Rachel's maid Bilhah (cf. 29:29; 30:3), was regarded as Joseph's mother after Rachel died.

[11] Whereas Joseph's brothers were jealous of him, like the mother of Jesus (Luke 2:19, 51), Jacob **kept the saying in mind**. He decided to wait to see whether Joseph's dreams had any validity.

[13] Jacob's sending Joseph to make sure all is well with his older brothers calls to mind Jesse's sending David to make sure all was well with three of his older brothers in Saul's army (cf. 1 Sam. 17:17-18, 28).

[17] **Dothan** is the modern Tell Dothan, located about fifteen miles north of Shechem and sixty miles north of Hebron. The dangers that lurked behind crag and tree over such a long distance would help Joseph's brothers convince their father that Joseph had been killed by a wild beast (cf. vss. 31-35).

[19] The Hebrew phrase translated **dreamer** is *ba'al hachalomoth,* literally "master of dreams." It is common in Hebrew to use a genitive phrase "to represent a person (poetically even a thing) as possessing some object or quality, or being in some condition" (GHG, par. 128s), often with *ba'al* (singular or plural) in the genitive. For example, "masters of arrows" (Gen. 49:23) are archers, "a master of the lending of his hand" (Deut. 15:2) is a creditor, "a master of the tongue" (Eccles. 10:11) is a charmer, "a master of two wings" (Eccles. 10:20) is a bird, etc.

[20] The Hebrew adjective *ra'*, which is translated "evil" in the KJV and ASV, means "sinful" or "wicked" in some contexts and "harmful" or "punishing" in others. In Genesis 37:20, 33, it clearly means "harmful," so **wild** (RSV, NEB).

[22] The author of the book of Genesis tells his readers why Reuben tried to dissuade his brothers from killing Joseph—**that he might rescue him out of their hand, to restore him to his father**. It has been suggested that he did this to try to regain the favor of Jacob which he had lost by committing adultery with Bilhah (cf. 35:22), but it is just as possible that he believed it was wrong to kill (cf. 9:5-6), in spite of his hatred and jealousy of Joseph (see vss. 4, 5, 8, 11).

[24] A **pit** was a cistern that held water during the rainy

season but went dry toward the end of summer (see Jer. 2:13; 38:6).

[25] After Joseph's brothers cast him into the pit, apparently Reuben left for awhile, possibly to attend to some of the sheep, evidently assuming that his brothers would leave Joseph in the pit (cf. vss. 29-30) and that he could return later to rescue him and restore him to Jacob (cf. vs. 22). The other brothers **sat down to eat**, as if they could kill their own brother without any qualms of conscience. Their attitude is similar to that of the adulteress:

> she eats, and wipes her mouth,
> and says, "I have done no wrong."
>
> Proverbs 30:20

It is also similar to that of the soldiers who divided Jesus' garments among them by casting lots while he was dying on the cross (Matt. 27:35-36). The trade route from **Gilead** (east of the Jordan and south of the Sea of Galilee) passed westward through Dothan toward the Mediterranean Sea and then turned south toward **Egypt**. Merchants used **camels** to transport items that were in great demand in Egypt, namely, **gum** (possibly "gum tragacanth"; so the NEB), **balm** (possibly a resin that exudes from the mastic tree, which was used as medicine; cf. Jer. 8:22; 46:11; 51:8; Ezek. 27:17), **and myrrh** (a sweet-smelling resin; cf. Gen. 43:11).

[26] For some strange reason, man continues to think that he can commit a sin and then cover it up so that neither God nor man will ever discover it. Cain attempted this in vain (4:10), and now Joseph's brothers contemplate the same possibility. The Bible repeatedly attests to God's ability to expose the blood that man has attempted to hide by covering it with dirt (cf. Job 16:18; Isa. 26:21; Ezek. 24:7). Motivated by self-concern, Judah suggests to his brothers that they take advantage of their opportunity, use Joseph to make some extra money, and at the same time avoid slaying their own flesh.

[28] Verses 28, 36, and Judges 8:22-26 show that **Midianites** and **Ishmaelites** are overlapping terms often used for

the same people. The idea suggested by the NEB that Midianite merchants came by the pit (now abandoned by Joseph's brothers!), drew up Joseph out of it, and sold him to Ishmaelite merchants does not make sense in light of verse 36, which states that Midianites sold Joseph to Potiphar in Egypt. It was Joseph's brothers that drew him out of the pit, not the Midianites—the Hebrew has simply **they**, and thus the subject must be determined from the context.

Twenty shekels of silver was the price of slaves in the ancient Near East in the second millennium B.C. It was the redemption price for a male between five and twenty who was consecrated to Yahweh (Lev. 27:5).

[30] The Hebrew word *yeledh* is used here of a seventeen-year-old boy (cf. vs. 2) and thus should be translated **lad** (RSV) or "boy" (NEB) rather than "child" (KJV, ASV). Accordingly, that Ishmael is called a *yeledh* in Genesis 21:14 does not indicate that he is a babe in arms (see the note on that verse).

[32] When Joseph's brothers bring the blood-stained robe to their father, they do not describe it as "Joseph's robe" or "our brother's robe," but as **your** [i.e., Jacob's] **son's robe**. This calls to mind the way that the elder brother spoke to his father of the prodigal ("this son of yours," Luke 15:30) and indicates that Joseph's brothers still felt strong hatred and jealousy toward him.

[34] It was quite common in ancient times to rend one's garments (cf. vs. 29; 2 Sam. 1:2, 11; 13:31; Job 1:20) and to put on sackcloth (cf. 2 Sam. 3:31; 2 Kings 6:30; 19:1; Isa. 37:1; Neh. 9:1; Esth. 4:1; Jer. 4:8; 6:26; 48:37; 49:3; Lam. 2:10; Ezek. 7:18; 27:31; Dan. 9:3; Joel 1:8, 13; Amos 8:10; Jon. 3:5, 6, 8) as symbolic expressions of mourning.

[35] The reference to Jacob's **daughters** may be explained in several ways. (1) It may be that "sons and daughters" is simply an idiom for "children." (2) It may be that "daughters" here includes Jacob's "daughters-in-law" (see Ruth 1:11, 13). (3) It is possible (though not probable) that Jacob had more than one daughter, even though the

OT mentions only Dinah (cf. 30:21). (4) The plural word "daughters" is used in 46:15, where Dinah alone can be intended. Like "sons," "children," etc., this is a generic word and can mean one person or several, depending on the passage. This seems to be the most natural explanation in the present passage.

Jacob's statement **I shall go down to Sheol to my son, mourning** has been interpreted in various ways. (a) Some assume there was an ancient belief that a person appeared in Sheol (the realm of the dead) just as he was when he left the earth and that Jacob intends to wear his mourning garments until he dies so that when he arrives in Sheol, Joseph will know how greatly he had grieved over him. (b) Comparing 2 Samuel 12:23, others think that Jacob intends to mourn for the rest of his life so that he will still be mourning when he is reunited with Joseph in Sheol, and from this Joseph will know the depth of his grief. (c) However, it seems most likely that Jacob means that his loss of Joseph is so great that he will mourn for him until he dies (without suggesting any idea of a reunion of the two in Sheol). Verses 34-35 provide a good illustration of a man who believed a lie and acted on the basis of that faith.

[36] The RSV, KJV, ASV, and NEB follow the ancient versions in reading **Midianites** instead of the MT "Medanites." Medan and Midian are listed in 25:2 as sons of Abraham's wife Keturah; thus, the tribes that descended from them were probably very closely related. The context of Genesis 37 suggests that **Midianites** are intended (cf. vs. 28).

Potiphar is a Hebrew transliteration of a common ancient Egyptian name which means "he whom [the sun god] Re has given." Joseph's father-in-law wore virtually the same name, Potiphera (cf. 41:45, 50). But these two Egyptians are not to be confused: Potiphar was the captain of the guard, while Potiphera was priest of On.

The Hebrew word translated **officer** in the RSV, KJV, and ASV is *saris*, which literally means "eunuch" (cf. the NEB). Apparently, however, this word had a broader official connotation, because Potiphar was married (cf. 39:7).

As his duties were connected with the royal court, perhaps "courtier" would be the most precise correct translation.

The exact meaning of the phrase translated **captain of the guard** (Heb. *šar haṭṭabbachim*) is uncertain. (1) Some scholars think it means "chief of the executioners," which would fit his role as custodian of the prison (40:3). One might imagine that he was responsible for the hanging of the chief baker (cf. 40:16-19, 22). (2) Others argue that it means "chief of the butchers" (cf. the LXX; somewhat parallel to the "chief butler" and the "chief baker," cf. 40:2, 9, 16, 20-23) and suggest that he may have been superintendent of the royal kitchen. (3) The context of Genesis 39–40 would suggest that this man was the official over the prison where "the king's prisoners were confined" (39:20).

Judah's Adultery with Tamar (Ch. 38)

After Joseph is sold to the Midianite merchants, Judah leaves his brothers at Dothan and goes south to Adullam, where he lives with a certain Hirah. In time, he marries a Canaanite woman named Shua, and they have three sons: Er, Onan, and Shelah. When Er is grown, he marries a certain Tamar, but Yahweh slays Er because he is wicked. Judah tells Onan to perform his duty as Tamar's brother-in-law and have sexual relations with her that she might bear a child (which would legally be regarded as Er's child). Knowing that the child would not be his, Onan spills his semen on the ground, and Yahweh slays him also. Judah requires that Tamar remain a widow in her father's house, promising to give Shelah to her when he grows up (but actually Judah is afraid that Yahweh will slay him also; vss. 1-11).

As Shelah is growing up, Judah's wife dies. After Shelah is grown, Judah does not send him to Tamar. Tamar, realizing that Judah does not intend to send Shelah to her, dresses like a harlot and positions herself on the road between Adullam and Timnah where she knows Judah will go. Not knowing her identity because she is veiled, Judah

asks that he might have sexual relations with her, for which
he offers her a kid. She requires a pledge that he will send
her the kid, namely, his signet and cord and his staff. He
complies, they have intercourse, Tamar becomes pregnant,
and she again clothes herself in her garments of widow-
hood. When Judah sends Hirah with the kid he had promised Tamar, she is nowhere to be found (vss. 12-23).

About three months later, someone tells Judah that Tamar is pregnant. He decrees that she is to be burned, but
she produces Judah's signet and cord and staff, thus revealing that he was the one who made her pregnant. In due
time, Tamar gives birth to twins. As the hand of the first
child seems to be emerging from his mother's womb, the
midwife binds a scarlet thread around it. But the child
withdraws his hand, and his brother is born first. Accordingly, the first child that is born is called Perez, which
forms a Hebrew wordplay with *parats,* "to make a
breach"; and the second is called Zerah, a name for which
there is no explanation or Hebrew wordplay in the context
(vss. 24-30).

Many scholars contend that there is no connection between chapter 38 and its surrounding chapters, and that
this chapter is an intrusion into the story of Joseph. However, there are several factors which suggest coherence between chapter 38 and the material around it.

(1) Although Joseph is the chief character in Genesis 37–50, these chapters deal with "the history of the family of *Jacob*" (37:2). Their ultimate purpose is to describe
how Jacob and his descendants came to live in Egypt (especially since God had promised them the land of Canaan).
Joseph is the focal point only because of the unique role he
played in this migration. Chapters 38 and 46–50 show
clearly that Joseph is by no means the only important character in this series of events.

(2) According to 37:26-27, Judah was responsible for
saving Joseph's life in Reuben's absence (cf. 37:29). It may
well be that Judah "went down from his brothers" (38:1)
because he felt uncomfortable around them, since they
had wanted to kill Joseph (which he thought was

going too far) and had deliberately deceived their aging father. While Judah felt hatred and jealousy toward Joseph, he does not seem to wish to react violently toward him.

(3) Judah is destined to receive his father's birthright and blessing (cf. 49:8-12), which are forfeited by his three older brothers when they sin (by Reuben, when he commits adultery with Bilhah, 35:22; 49:3-4; and by Simeon and Levi, when they kill the men of Shechem while they are sore from circumcision, 34:25-31; 49:5-7). In view of this, Judah's activities naturally have a special interest to the author of Genesis, and it is to be expected that a good deal of space should be devoted to him in "the history of the family of Jacob."

(4) There is a striking contrast between Judah's yielding to the temptation to go in to the harlot sitting beside the road (ch. 38) and Joseph's resisting the temptation to commit adultery with Potiphar's wife (ch. 39).

(5) Before continuing the story of Joseph in Egypt, it is logical for the author to relate a significant event in the life of another of Jacob's sons which occurred shortly after Joseph was carried off by the Midianite merchants (cf. 38:1).

[1] When Judah leaves his brothers in Dothan (cf. 37:17), he goes south to **Adullam**, the modern Tell esh-Sheikh Madhkur, about twelve miles southwest of Bethlehem.

[2] Judah makes the sad mistake of marrying a **Canaanite** woman named Bath-shua (1 Chron. 2:3), the daughter of **Shua** (cf. Gen. 38:12), which calls to mind Esau's marriages to Hittite women (cf. Gen. 26:34-35; 36:2-3).

[3] In the OT, sometimes the father names the child (cf. 5:29), and sometimes the mother does (cf. 29:32). Here the MT (adopted by the RSV, KJV, and ASV) reads **he** [i.e., Judah] **called his name Er**. However, the mother names the second and third sons (vss. 4-5). Thus, it seems preferable to follow some Hebrew manuscripts, the Targum Pseudo-Jonathan, and the Samaritan Pentateuch in reading "she called" in the present passage (so the NEB). Still, this matter cannot be settled with certainty.

[5] The MT says that "he [Judah] was in Chezib when

she [Bath-shua] gave birth" to Shelah (so the KJV and ASV), implying that he was not with his wife when their youngest son was born; the LXX says **she** (RSV) was in Chezib when Shelah was born, possibly also implying the two were not together at that time. Could this have caused Judah to have had a special love in his heart for his youngest son, as Jacob did for Joseph and later Benjamin, thus partly explaining his hesitancy to give Shelah to Tamar after the deaths of Er and Onan (cf. vs. 14)? **Chezib** seems to be the same as Achzib (cf. Josh. 15:44; Mic. 1:14), the modern Tell el-Beida, located three miles west of Adullam.

[6] In the patriarchal age in the ancient Near East, it was common for the father to make proper negotiations to secure a wife for his son (cf. 24:3; 34:4).

[7] That the Lord kills people because of their wickedness is taught in both the OT (cf. vs. 10; Num. 16:35; 2 Sam. 6:7) and the NT (Acts 5:1-11; 1 Cor. 11:27-30). Man is forbidden to take life (Exod. 20:13) unless he is specifically commanded by God to do so (Deut. 22:22; 1 Sam. 15:3), because killing is God's prerogative (Ps. 104:29; Heb. 10:30-31).

[8] This verse describes the ancient custom of levirate marriage. If a man dies childless, his brother must marry his widow. The first male child that is born to this marriage is considered to be the son of the deceased husband. In this way the deceased brother's name is perpetuated. According to the later law given through Moses, a man could refuse to perform this duty only with great disgrace (Deut. 25:5-10). Boaz performed something similar to this by marrying the Moabitess Ruth (Ruth 3–4), although he was not Mahlon's brother (cf. 4:10).

[9-10] These verses assume that the Lord originated or at least wholly sanctioned the law of levirate marriage, even though its origin is not specified in the Scriptures. The Lord kills Onan for not discharging this responsibility.

[11] Many scholars think that the story of the deaths of Er and Onan is based on a mythical motif of a goddess (Ishtar) who killed her lovers and cite the apocryphal story

of Tobias and Sarah (Tobit 3:8; 8:12) as a parallel. However, in that story it was the wicked demon Asmodeus that had killed Sarah's seven husbands, and the text in Genesis 38 makes no allusion to such a demon but declares that Yahweh slew Er and Onan because of their wickedness. The author of Genesis does not explain goddess (Ishtar) who killed her lovers and cite the apocryphal sbrothers if he went to Tamar.

[12] There are at least two places called **Timnah** in the OT. The one mentioned in this verse is probably identical with the "Timnah" of Joshua 15:57, which is the modern Tibne, located ten miles west of Bethlehem and four miles northeast of Adullam. From Adullam to Timnah, one **went up** topographically.

[14] The Bible does not state why Tamar dressed as a harlot and planted herself on the road where she knew Judah would be traveling so she could have sexual relations with him. Two reasons seem most likely: either (a) she sincerely wanted to bear a son that could perpetuate the name of her first husband Er, and since his brothers did not or would not perform the duty of a brother-in-law, it seemed to her that the next best thing was to try to bear a son by her husband's father; or (b) when she realized that Judah did not intend to let Shelah come to her that she might bear a son by him, she decided that she would get back at him by seducing him to come in to her so that she might have a son by him (see vs. 26).

Judah's sin of adultery is inexcusable, but there are a number of factors that made him vulnerable to Tamar. (1) His wife had died (vs. 12). (2) It was sheepshearing time (vss. 12-13), when there was great joy over the anticipated wealth to be accumulated from the sale of the wool (cf. 1 Sam. 25:2, 4, 7-8, 11, 36-37). (3) The inhabitants of the land practiced prostitution as an act of worship to promote fertility. In verses 21-22, Tamar is called a *qedheshah,* which apparently means "cult prostitute," as the only other places where this word occurs in the OT (Deut. 23:17 [Hebrew 18]; Hos. 4:14) use it in this sense. According to Assyrian law, only a cult prostitute was to wear a veil. Tamar may have tried to persuade Judah that he would be aiding fertility if he committed adultery with her, although he apparently viewed her as a common "harlot" (*zonah,* vs. 15).

As long as a woman was a widow, she wore **widow's garments** (cf. 2 Sam. 14:2), but the Bible does not make clear what these were. For **garments,** the NEB reads "weeds" (cf. also vs. 19), which is a legitimate, though archaic, word based on the Anglo-Saxon *wáede,* meaning "garment."

Instead of **wrapping herself up, and sat at the entrance to Enaim, which is on the road to Timnah,** the NEB has "perfumed herself and sat where the road forks in two directions on the way to Timnath." This reading requires several textual emendations, and thus it seems preferable to follow the RSV, KJV, and ASV in adopting the MT.

[15] The NEB reads "although" for *ki,* which gives this verse the opposite meaning that it has in the KJV, ASV, and RSV. Such an interpretation flies in the face of the context (even vs. 14 of the NEB) which suggests that Tamar veiled herself so that she would be taken as a harlot. Also, the most natural meaning of *ki* is **for** or "because."

[16-18] Apparently it was commonly understood that a man would have to **give** a woman something for having sexual relations with her. As he is engaged in sheepshearing, the first thing that comes to Judah's mind is **a kid from the flock.** Tamar agrees to this but requires a **pledge** (Heb. *'erabhon,* which is cognate to the Greek *arrabon* [appearing in the NT in 2 Cor. 1:22; 5:5; and Eph. 1:14, always with reference to the Holy Spirit] and a loanword from Akkadian) or guaranty that Judah will bring her a kid. At her request, Judah gives her his **signet** and **cord** and his **staff.** The **signet** (Heb. *chotham*) is apparently a cylinder seal made of wood, ivory, stone, or metal, with the owner's design on it, which could be pressed into damp clay, leaving the owner's insignia when the clay dried. The **cord** (Heb. *pethil;* "bracelets" in the KJV is incorrect) was run through a hole in the **signet** and tied around the owner's neck; thus, the **signet** and **cord** form one piece. Judah also gives Tamar his shepherd's **staff** (Heb. *maṭṭeh*).

[20] A pledge was given back to the owner when he gave the gift he had promised. Judah is anxious to get his pledge back because it is valuable to him, so he sends his friend Hirah the Adullamite to take the kid to Tamar and to get the pledge he had given her.

[24] Judah manifests no conscience about having committed adultery with the harlot beside the road, but he is very angry when he learns that his daughter-in-law Tamar has committed adultery. David reflects a similar spirit in his attitude toward his own actions against Uriah and toward the rich man in Nathan's parable of the little ewe lamb (cf. 2 Sam. 12:5-6). It is so much easier to see and condemn the sins of others than to see one's own.

Since Tamar was betrothed to Judah's son Shelah, Judah had legal jurisdiction over her. Betrothal was as binding as marriage (cf. Matt. 1:18-19), and therefore Tamar's act was viewed as adultery. The penalty for adultery in Judah's time in Canaan was burning to death. The Code of Hammurabi (par. 157) prescribes burning as a punishment for incest with one's mother, and Leviticus 21:10 decrees that a priest's daughter who commits adultery is to be burned with fire. Other men and women who commit adultery are to be stoned to death (cf. Deut. 22:23-24; Ezek. 16:40; John 8:5).

[26] Just because Judah says of Tamar, **She is more righteous than I**, this does not mean that the author of Genesis is praising her for her actions. Adultery is sin under all circumstances; no situation justifies it (cf. Prov. 7:6-27). Two wrongs (Judah's deception of Tamar and Tamar's seduction of Judah) do not make a right.

[27-30] The births of Perez and Zerah call to mind those of Jacob and Esau (25:21-26).

[29] Since the first son to appear at the opening of the womb puts forth his hand (which the midwife binds with a scarlet thread) and then withdraws it, and the second son to appear is actually born first, the latter is called **Perez**, which means **breach**, and the midwife says, **What a breach you have made for yourself!** (Heb. *mah paratsta 'aleykha parets*). Again, the child's name involves a wordplay.

[30] For some inexplicable reason, no wordplay is connected with the giving of the name Zerah to the other son.

GOD RAISES JOSEPH FROM SLAVE TO RULER
(39:1–41:52)

Joseph Accused and Imprisoned (Ch. 39)

After relating Judah's adultery with his own daughter-in-
law Tamar (ch. 38), the author of Genesis resumes the
story of Joseph in Potiphar's house in Egypt (cf. 37:36).
Because of Joseph's success and prosperity, Potiphar puts
him in charge of all his possessions. Yahweh blesses
Potiphar's house because of Joseph, thus partially fulfilling
his promise to Abraham (22:18), Isaac (26:4), and Jacob
(28:14) that in their descendants all the families of the earth
would be blessed (39:1-6).

After some time, Potiphar's wife begins trying to seduce
Joseph, but each time she makes advances to him, he
boldly resists. One day she is alone with him in the house,
seizes his garment in an attempt to get him to commit
adultery with her, and he flees, leaving the garment behind.
She tells the men of her household, and later Potiphar, that
Joseph had tried to rape her and uses his garment as proof
(vss. 7-18).

Angered by his wife's report, Potiphar puts Joseph in the
king's prison. But in time the keeper of the prison puts all
the prisoners under Joseph's care, and Joseph prospers in
all that he does (vss. 19-23).

The secret to Joseph's success and prosperity when he is
living in Potiphar's house, when Potiphar's wife is tempting
him, and when he is a prisoner, is that the Lord is with him
(vss. 2, 3, 5, 21, 23). God did not stop working in his world
when he finished his initial work of creation (cf. John 5:17)
but continues to work throughout human history in keeping
with his nature as the living God and with his promises
(cf. Matt. 28:20).

There are some similarities between the story of Joseph

and Potiphar's wife and the Egyptian "Tale of the Two Brothers," copied by a student as a writing exercise about 1210 B.C., which is found on Papyrus 10183 (the D'Orbiney papyrus) in the British Museum. This Egyptian tale tells about two brothers who worked together in a field. The elder (Anupu) was married, and the younger (Bata) was living with him. Once Anupu sent Bata to get some grain, and Anupu's wife tried to seduce him. Bata became very angry at her because of his fidelity to his brother. When Anupu came home that evening, his wife was feigning illness, claiming that Bata had tried to rape her when he came in from the field to get the grain. Anupu was filled with anger against his brother and hid behind a door, where the cows were driven, to kill him. However, two of his cows walking ahead of him called out and warned him that Anupu was behind the door, and Bata fled. Later, Bata was able to convince Anupu that his wife had tried to seduce him, and Anupu returned home and killed her.

Now, the few similarities in these two stories hardly support the hypothesis that the biblical writer borrowed his account from this Egyptian tale. "It would require much greater similarity of detail between the Egyptian and the Hebrew stories to justify the oft-made suggestion that the Egyptian story is the origin of the incident described in Genesis" (J. M. Plumley, "The Tale of the Two Brothers," *Documents from Old Testament Times*, ed. D. Winton Thomas [New York: Harper and Row, 1961], p. 168). "In spite of the striking similarity in the treacherous activity of the woman in each instance one cannot speak of a direct dependence of our Joseph narrative on that tale" (G. von Rad, *Genesis*, OTL, p. 361).

[6] The renderings "he knew not ought he had" (KJV) and "he knew not aught that was with him" (ASV) are very literal (see also vs. 8) and suggest to the modern mind that Potiphar was not aware of the possessions that belonged to him. This interpretation misses the point of the Hebrew phrase, which means that Potiphar **had no concern for anything** (RSV) or "concerned himself with

nothing" (NEB). The context shows this to be the meaning. Joseph was so dependable and trustworthy that
Potiphar did not have to worry about anything in his
household **but the food which he ate,** which may mean that
his greatest problem was planning and eating his meals or
seeing to it that the food eaten by his household was properly prepared according to Egyptian rituals (which a foreigner would not know or could not legally perform).

[7] As elsewhere in the book of Genesis (cf. 3:6), the
author delineates the slow, progressive nature of temptation in his description of the approaches of Potiphar's wife
to Joseph: (a) she **cast her eyes upon** him (vs. 7); (b) "spoke
to" him "day after day" (vs. 10); (c) "caught him by his
garment, saying, 'Lie with me' " (vs. 12).

[8] Joseph's resistance to sin is more resolute than the
advances of Potiphar's wife: (a) **he refused** (vs. 8); (b) "he
would not listen to her" (vs. 10); (c) when she caught him
by his garment and tried to force him to commit adultery
with her, "he left his garment in her hand, and fled"
(vss. 12, 13), the real meaning of which she turns into a lie
(vss. 15, 18).

Two great spiritual principles arm Joseph against yielding
to the temptation of sexual impurity. First, his master or
employer trusted him completely, and he felt that it was
absolutely necessary to honor that trust with unswerving
fidelity to him (vss. 8-9; cf. Prov. 20:6; Eph. 6:5-8; Col.
3:22-25; 1 Tim. 6:1-2). Second, he was keenly aware of the
fact that God was with him even in a foreign land like
Egypt (vs. 9; cf. vss. 2, 3, 5, 21, 23), and he had no intention of showing blatant ingratitude to him by doing something that was abominable to him. There is no indication in
the book of Genesis prior to this event that God had given
a command that man should not commit adultery, and thus
what is involved here is much more than simply disobeying
a divine law. Man and woman were created in the image of
God (cf. 1:26-27). Therefore, to show any disrespect or
dishonor to man (as by killing him, 9:6) or woman (as by
committing adultery with her) is to "sin against God"
(20:6; 39:9; 2 Sam. 12:13; cf. Pss. 41:4 [Hebrew 5]; 51:4

[Hebrew 6]), in whose image they are made.

The verb "wotteth" (KJV; concern, RSV) is the third person singular of the present tense of *wit*, which is derived ultimately from the Anglo-Saxon verb *witan*, meaning "to know." Since this word is archaic, it is better to use a term that makes sense to modern readers.

[12] Sometimes the only way to avoid sin is to "flee" from temptation (cf. Prov. 4:14-17; 5:8; 7:7-8, 25; 1 Cor. 6:18; 2 Tim. 2:22). This is not cowardice but realistic acknowledgment of the power of sin (cf. 1 Cor. 10:14; 1 Tim. 6:11) and of one's need for God's help in time of trial and temptation (Acts 26:22; 1 Cor. 10:12-13; Heb. 13:5-6).

[14] It is clear from the context that Potiphar's wife uses the word Hebrew to refer to Joseph (vss. 14, 17) because it had derogatory connotations in Egypt at the time. Hebrew may be related to Ḥapiru, a term that was used widely throughout the ancient Near East for peoples who migrated across national boundaries and stood socially between free citizens and slaves. Possibly the Hebrews of the OT were a part of a larger ethnic or social group called the Hapiru, who migrated from the Mesopotamian area into Palestine and Egypt (see the note on 14:13).

[20] The Hebrew expression translated prison in the RSV, KJV, and ASV, of 39:20 (twice), 21, 22, 23; 40:3, 5 is *beth hassohar*, which means literally "house of roundness," that is, Round House (NEB "Round Tower"). It may be that the king's prisoners were kept in a tower or fortress where they were put to forced labor, or it may be that *sohar* is the Hebrew spelling of an Egyptian word for a certain kind of prison. This place is also called *mishmar* (which the RSV translates "custody" in 40:3, 4, 7; 41:10; and "prison" in 42:17, 19) and *bor* (which the RSV translates "dungeon" in 40:15; 41:14), which are common Hebrew words for places of confinement.

[21-23] The Lord was with Joseph in prison just as he had been with him when Potiphar bought him as a servant (vss. 21, 23; cf. vss. 2, 3, 5). The Lord gave him favor in the sight of the keeper of the prison (vs. 21; cf. vs. 4). The

keeper of the prison put Joseph in charge of the prisoners (vs. 22; cf. vss. 4-5). He was not concerned about anything that was in Joseph's care (vs. 23; cf. vs. 6). The Lord caused all that Joseph did to prosper (vs. 23; cf. vs. 3). The parallels between verses 2-6 and 21-23 are too numerous and striking to be accidental. Here the author of Genesis emphasizes one of his great theological tenets: God is alive and at work in the life of Joseph, and this alone explains his success and prosperity.

Joseph Interprets the Dreams of the Chief Butler and the Chief Baker (Ch. 40)

Some time after Joseph is cast into prison, the Pharaoh becomes angry with his chief butler and chief baker and has them thrown into the same prison. Like the other prisoners (cf. 39:22), they are put under Joseph's care (vss. 1-4). One night, the chief butler and chief baker have dreams. Since they cannot go to a trained Egyptian interpreter, they relate their dreams to Joseph, who declares that interpretations of dreams belong to God. The chief butler tells how he had seen three branches that produced clusters of grapes, from which he got wine to give to the Pharaoh. Joseph declares that the three branches represent three days, and that in three days the Pharaoh will restore him to his former role; Joseph asks that he mention him to the Pharaoh when he is restored. The chief baker tells how he had seen three cake baskets on his head with all sorts of baked food for the Pharaoh, but the birds were eating it out of the top basket. Joseph declares that the three baskets are three days, and that in three days the Pharaoh will have him hanged. These interpretations prove to be correct, but the chief butler forgets to mention Joseph to the Pharaoh (vss. 5-23).

With the same emphasis reflected in the previous chapter (i.e., God was with Joseph) and in the following chapter (i.e., God alone gives and interprets dreams, 41:16, 25, 28, 32, 38), in the present chapter attention is called to the fact that God alone can interpret dreams (40:8) and see to it that his interpretations come true (vss. 20-22).

This chapter contains an interesting wordplay on the phrase "lift up the head" (Heb. *naśa' ro'sh*; vss. 13, 19, 20). In verse 20, apparently it means "to review the cases of" the chief butler and the chief baker, which corresponds to the meaning of the cognate Akkadian phrase *rēšam našûm*. In verse 13, it means "to release from prison and pardon" the chief butler (as in 2 Kings 25:27; Jer. 52:31). And in verse 19, it means "to behead or decapitate" the chief baker, after which his body was hung on a tree (possibly as a public example of what happens to a subject that angers the Pharaoh).

[1] The chief **butler** (or cupbearer) was an Egyptian official (vss. 2, 7, 13, 21) who prepared the royal wine, filled the king's cup, and "placed the cup in Pharaoh's hand" (vss. 11, 13, 21). The chief **baker** was also an Egyptian official (vss. 2, 7) who prepared all sorts of baked goods for the royal house (vss. 16-17).

[3] **The captain of the guard** is apparently Potiphar (cf. 37:36; 39:1), who is to be distinguished from his subordinate, "the keeper of the prison" (39:21-23). Potiphar is called Joseph's "master" consistently in this material (cf. 39:2, 3, 7, 8 [twice], 16, 19, 20; 40:7); especially striking is the repetition of the phrase *beth 'adhonayw*, "his master's house," in 39:2 and 40:7.

[8] If the chief butler and the chief baker had not been in prison, they would have consulted a professional Egyptian interpreter of dreams. Against such a superstitious practice, Joseph declares that **interpretations** [of dreams] **belong to God.**

[9-11] W. H. Bennett comments:

> In his dream the chief butler sees the whole process of wine-making pass before his eyes in a few seconds. The buds appear upon the vine branches, they unfold into blossoms, and ripen into grapes. He gathers them; presses them forthwith into Pharaoh's cup; they become wine; and, as the royal cupbearer, he serves the wine to Pharaoh.

Genesis, CB, p. 351

[15] If the Hebrew verb *ganabh* should be translated literally as **stolen** (as in the KJV, ASV, RSV), then Joseph may be referring to the cheap price that the Midianite merchants paid for him (twenty shekels of silver, 37:28). But if it should be translated more generally as "carried off" (as in the NEB), then Joseph is simply referring to the events described in 37:25-28. The phrase **land of the Hebrews** is an enigma. If the author of Genesis used "Hebrews" here as identical with "Israelites," then he was substituting a later term for an earlier one, because in the time of Joseph, Canaan was not in Israelite hands. But if he used "Hebrews" for peoples migrating into the Palestinian area from northern Mesopotamia and intended "land of the Hebrews" in a loose sense, this could fit the period of Joseph.

[16] The Hebrew expression *sheloshah salle chori* is very difficult to interpret. The KJV reads "three white baskets." The ASV and NEB read "three baskets of white bread," but this is hard to harmonize with the statement in verse 17, "in the uppermost basket there were all sorts of baked food." The RSV reads **three cake baskets**, which accords well with verse 17 and may agree with the reading of the LXX and Syriac. Symmachus reads "three baskets of palm branches," which seems to rest on an Aramaic rather than Hebrew word. Some modern scholars (Rashi and Ehrlich) prefer to read "three wicker baskets," following an Arabic cognate. Then the birds could peck at the baked goods both from above and at the sides of the baskets. The precise meaning is uncertain.

[17] It is not clear whether the two lower baskets contained the same thing as the topmost basket, or inferior baked goods, or nothing at all. The thing which is so disconcerting to the baker is his inability to drive away the **birds**, who come to eat the baked goods he had prepared for the Pharaoh. As often happens in dreams, he is unable to cope with this problem, which he could easily have handled when he was awake (cf. 15:11).

[19] The birds eating the baked food out of the topmost basket carried by the baker (vs. 17) symbolizes the fact that birds will eat the flesh of the baker (vs. 22) after he is

beheaded (vs. 19). The Egyptians placed such great emphasis on preserving the body after death by embalming (cf. 50:2, 26) that the destruction of a decaying, impaled corpse by birds must have been regarded as a horrible abomination. The OT often refers to birds feeding on dead human corpses in connection with terrible catastrophes (cf. Deut. 28:26; 1 Sam. 17:44, 46; 2 Sam. 21:9-10; 1 Kings 14:11; 16:4; 21:24; Ps. 79:2; Jer. 7:33; 15:3; 16:4; 19:7; 34:20; Ezek. 29:5; 31:13; 32:4).

[20] The present account and the story of Herod Antipas' beheading John the Baptist on Herod's birthday (Mark 6:21) suggest that birthdays of kings or great rulers in the ancient world were national holidays and were used by rulers as times for showing special kindness to certain prisoners and for doling out severe penalties to others.

[23] It is typical of human beings to forget people who do good things for them in times of need, after their problem has been solved (cf. Eccles. 9:13-16; Luke 17:11-19).

Joseph Becomes a High Official in Egypt (41:1-52)

Two whole years after Joseph had interpreted the dreams of the chief butler and chief baker, the Pharaoh has two dreams. In the first, he sees seven fat cows coming up out of the Nile, then seven thin cows coming up out of the Nile and eating the fat ones. In the second, he sees seven plump ears of grain growing on one stalk, then seven thin ears swallowing them. These dreams trouble him; he summons the magicians and wise men of Egypt to interpret them, but they cannot (vss. 1-8).

The chief butler suddenly remembers that Joseph had interpreted his dream and the dream of the chief baker in prison and tells the Pharaoh about Joseph. The Pharaoh sends for Joseph, tells him his dreams, and Joseph interprets them. He states that the seven fat cows and the seven plump ears of grain represent seven years of abundance. On the other hand, the seven thin cows and seven thin ears represent seven years of famine, which will immediately follow the seven years of abundance (vss. 9-32).

Joseph advises the Pharaoh to select a man discreet and

wise and to set him over the land to prepare for the famine. The Pharaoh decides to set Joseph over the land because God had shown him what he was about to do. He gives him the name of Zaphenath-paneah and gives him in marriage to Asenath, the daughter of Potiphera, priest of On. During the seven years of abundance, Joseph stores up vast amounts of grain in the store cities of Egypt. During this time also, his wife Asenath gives birth to two sons, Manasseh and Ephraim (vss. 33-52).

The primary religious emphasis in this lengthy paragraph is that God is in control of history and human life, even in the strange and foreign land of Egypt. It is he who gives the seven years of abundance and the seven years of famine (vss. 28, 32), reveals the meaning of the Pharaoh's dream to Joseph (vss. 16, 25, 39), elevates Joseph from the dungeon (vs.14) to the position of vizier in Egypt (vss. 32-33, 38-40, 44), guides Joseph in proper preparation for the famine (vss. 32-36, 46-49), and gives him his two sons (vss. 50-52). As elsewhere in Genesis 37–50, the inspired writer stresses the fact that God is with his people and that he is at work constantly in his world, even when men are unaware of his activities.

[1] The **Pharaoh** under whom Joseph was elevated to second position in the kingdom was probably one of the Hyksos rulers shortly after 1720 B.C. The "river" (KJV, ASV) of Egypt is the **Nile** (RSV, NEB; Heb. *ye'or,* an Egyptian loanword).

[2] The Hebrew word for **reed grass** (RSV, ASV; cf. "reeds" in the NEB; "meadow" [KJV] is an incorrect rendering) is *'achu,* an Egyptian loanword referring to the papyrus plants that grow abundantly in the marches of the Nile (cf. vs. 18; Job 8:11).

[6] The **east wind** is the Hamsin or sirocco, which blows from the southeast in Egypt from February to June each year and destroys many plants because of the extreme heat and drought it produces.

[8] Magicians (Heb. *chartummim,* which apparently is an Egyptian loanword) and **wise men** were groups of professional experts in Egypt who knew how to manipulate ritual books of magic and priestcraft. In the present situation, they must have consulted volumes of books on dreams in an attempt to determine the meaning of the Pharaoh's dreams. On these two groups, see also Exodus 7:11.

[10-13] These verses contain a brief summary of the events recorded in chapter 40 and show the intimate coherence between chapters 40 and 41.

[14] Egyptian custom demanded that one appear before the Pharaoh properly shaved and attired. Egyptian documents would seem to suggest that Joseph was required to shave both his head and his beard.

[15] Either the Pharaoh uses the word **dream** in a collective sense meaning "dreams," or he thinks of his two dreams as being one.

[32] Joseph declares that the reason the Pharaoh had two dreams which meant the same thing is that God had determined to bring seven years of abundance on Egypt followed by seven years of famine, and he would shortly cause it to happen.

[33-35] Joseph's recommendation as to the best way to prepare for the famine is that the Pharaoh select a discreet and wise man to organize the gathering and storing of grain during the years of abundance and that he appoint overseers to work under this leader. Speiser (*Genesis*, p. 313) argues that the Hebrew verb *chimmesh* comes from a root meaning "to organize" (vs. 34), but it seems preferable to adopt the traditional view that it means to **take the fifth part of** [the produce of] (so the RSV, KJV, ASV, NEB; cf. 47:24, 26). The Hebrew noun *bar* means "wheat" (vs. 35). "Corn" (KJV, NEB; cf. vss. 49, 57 in the KJV and vss. 56, 57 in the NEB) is actually a neutral word denoting the leading cereal crop in any given region. In Scotland and Ireland, corn would be oats; in the United States, Canada, and Australia, it would be Indian corn or maize; and in England, it would be wheat. **Grain** (RSV, ASV) is the more commonly used generic term in America.

[38] It is virtually impossible to know the meaning of the Hebrew expression *ruach 'elohim* (cf. the note on 1:2). The RSV and KJV translate **the Spirit of God,** which could

mean "the Spirit who is God" or "the Holy Spirit." The
ASV reads "the spirit of God," which apparently means
"the spirit who is God." The NEB renders "the spirit of a
god," evidently because the speaker here is the Pharaoh.

[41] The position to which the Pharaoh elevated Joseph
is that of *T'ate* or Grand Vizier. This individual was the
authorized representative of the Pharaoh, director of the
royal palace, and second-in-command in the empire.

[42] Verses 42-45 describe six official acts performed by
the Pharaoh to signify to the people of Egypt that he was
making Joseph the Grand Vizier. First, the Pharaoh gives
Joseph his **signet ring**, which was used for sealing official
documents (cf. 1 Kings 21:8; Esth. 3:12; 8:8 [twice]) and
was given to denote bestowal of authority (cf. Esth. 3:10;
8:2). As early as the third millennium B.C., the Grand Vizier of Egypt wore the title of "Sealbearer of the King of
Lower Egypt." Second, the Pharaoh arrays Joseph in royal
Egyptian **garments of fine linen**. Third, he places a gold
chain around Joseph's neck. This possibly refers to the
so-called "Reward of the Gold," which the Pharaoh con-
ferred on his subjects as a recognition of outstanding service rendered to the crown.

[43] Fourth, the Pharaoh has Joseph ride in his **second
chariot**, which indicates Joseph is second-in-command in
Egypt (cf. 1 Sam. 23:17; 2 Chron. 28:7; 35:24; Esth. 10:3).
Prior to the eighteenth century B.C., Egyptian dignitaries
were transported from place to place in sedan chairs borne
on the shoulders of servants. Then the Hyksos invaders
introduced horses and chariots into Egyptian life. Well-
built chariots have been found by archeologists in the
grave of the Pharaoh Tut-ankh-Amon (1352–1344 B.C.);
they have two wheels and a platform on which the chario-
teer and the official dignitary of the kingdom stood while
traveling.

When Joseph arrives at any given place in Egypt riding
in his chariot, his servants cry out before him, *'abhrekh*,
which most likely is an Egyptian loanword with a Hebrew
spelling. Scholars differ on the precise meaning of this
term. (1) Some want to equate it with *abarakku*, which is

one Akkadian title for a high official. Then the meaning would be "The Abrek [is here, is coming, has arrived]!" (2) Noted Egyptologists connect it with the Egyptian expression '*b r-k,* which means literally "Your heart to you!" and understand it in the sense of "Attention!" or "Look out!" or "Make way!" (so the NEB). (3) Others link it with the Hebrew verb *barakh,* "to kneel," and translate **Bow the knee!** (so the RSV, KJV, ASV). All of these explanations are conjectural.

[45] Fifth, the Pharaoh changes Joseph's name to **Zaphenath-paneah,** which has been variously interpreted to mean "Ruler of the Nome Place of Life," "Savior of the World," "Revealer of Secrets," and "The god speaks and he lives." It was common in ancient times to give new names to individuals when they were elevated to official governmental positions, as when Pharaoh Neco changed Eliakim's name to Jehoiakim (2 Kings 23:34).

Sixth, the Pharaoh arranges for Joseph to marry **Asenath,** the daughter of one of his leading officials, **Potiphera priest of On.** On (cf. vs. 50; 46:20; Ezek. 30:17) is the ancient biblical name for Heliopolis (cf. Jer. 43:13), which is located seven miles northeast of modern Cairo; in ancient times it was a worship center of the sun-god Re.

[46] Joseph was seventeen years old when his brothers sold him to the Midianite merchants (37:2) and thirty when he became second-in-command to the Pharaoh. God is able to move rapidly in mysterious ways to carry out his purposes among men. (For further chronological data connected with this verse, see the notes on 37:3, 10.)

[51-52] The names Joseph gives his two sons are based on wordplays in Hebrew. He calls the first **Manasseh** (Heb. *menashsheh*), saying, **God has made me forget** [*nashshani*] **all my hardship and all my father's house**—that is, God has enabled me to learn to live with and to rise above the afflictions that my brothers brought upon me. He calls the second **Ephraim** (Heb. *'ephrayim*), saying, **God has made me fruitful** [*hiphrani*] **in the land of my affliction**—that is, God has made me prosper and has elevated me to a high position in Egypt.

FAMINE, CONFLICT, AND FAMILY REUNION (41:53–45:28)

The Famine Comes and Joseph's Brothers Make Two Trips to Egypt (41:53–44:34)

After seven years of abundant harvests, a great famine strikes Egypt and surrounding lands. The Egyptians and peoples from other lands come to Pharaoh for relief, and he sends them to Joseph, who supplies their needs out of the grain in the storehouses (41:53-57). Jacob learns that Egypt has grain for sale during the famine and sends ten of his sons (all but Benjamin) to buy grain so that his household can survive. When they come to Joseph, he recognizes them, but they do not recognize him. Joseph accuses them of being spies, and when they deny it, he declares that in order to prove this, they must leave one of their number behind in Egypt as a prisoner, go back to their father, and bring their youngest brother to Egypt with them. They agree to this, leave Simeon in prison, and conclude that this affliction had come upon them because of the way they had treated Joseph. Joseph has the money they spent for the grain returned to their sacks, and when they discover it on their way home, they are greatly troubled. When Jacob learns what had happened to his ten sons in Egypt, at first he refuses to allow Benjamin to return to Egypt with them, even when Reuben promises to bring Benjamin back to him (ch. 42). Apparently, Jacob assumes that the famine will end before the grain runs out, and he is more willing to give up Simeon (who had caused him much trouble at Shechem, 34:30) than Benjamin, who (after Joseph's loss) is his favorite son (42:38; 43:14; 44:22, 27-30, 34), "the child of his old age" (44:20). But the famine persists.

After their grain is gone, Jacob tells his sons to return to Egypt for more. However, Judah insists that they must not go without Benjamin, because Joseph had told them that he would not give them another audience unless they brought Benjamin with them. Jacob reluctantly agrees and does everything he can to gain Joseph's good will: he sends him choice gifts from Canaan, twice as much money as he had sent before, and Benjamin. When Joseph sees Benjamin with his brothers, he has a meal prepared for them. During the meal, Joseph is so filled with joy at seeing his brothers and at hearing his father is still alive that he has to leave and weep (ch. 43).

When Joseph's brothers prepare to return to Canaan, Joseph has each one's sack filled with food, their money returned, and his silver cup put in Benjamin's sack. Shortly after they leave, he sends his servants after them to accuse them of stealing from him and to bring them back to the city. Joseph declares that he has decided to release all the men except Benjamin, whom he would keep as his slave in Egypt. Judah carefully reviews for Joseph the events that had transpired and pleads with him to let him stay as Joseph's slave in place of Benjamin, because he had become a surety for him, promising his father that Benjamin would return safely from Egypt (ch. 44).

Two important religious emphases stand out in this section. On the one hand, the various characters are keenly aware that God is at work in the affairs of history and in their own personal lives. When Joseph tells his brothers that they must leave Simeon in prison until they return with Benjamin, he assures them that he will keep his part of the agreement by saying, "I fear God" (42:18). When one of his brothers discovers that his money has been returned to his sack, he says fearfully, "What is this that God has done to us?" (42:28). Upon finally deciding to allow Benjamin to go to Egypt with his brothers, Jacob prays, "May God Almighty grant you mercy before the man [i.e., Joseph—43:14]." As Joseph's brothers try to explain to the steward of Joseph's house that the money which they had paid for their grain on the first trip was restored to their sacks, he replies, "Rest assured, do not be afraid; your God and the God of your father must have put treasure in your sacks for you" (43:23). When Joseph first sees Benjamin after their many years apart, he exclaims: "God be gracious to you, my son!" (43:29). In trying to defend himself and his brothers against the implication that they had stolen Joseph's cup and the money paid for the grain on their second trip to Egypt, Judah (undoubtedly referring to their treatment of Joseph) affirms: "God has found out the guilt of your servants" (44:16).

On the other hand, these chapters stress that Joseph's brothers had to suffer the consequences of their hateful treatment of him. They bow themselves before Joseph as ruler of Egypt (42:6; 43:26, 28) and refer to themselves as his "servants" (42:10, 11, 13), just as he had told them when he related the dreams of the sheaves and the sun, moon, and stars (42:9; cf. 37:5-11). Joseph keeps them in prison three days (42:17), which is an ironic reversal of the circumstance in which they kept him in the pit while trying to decide what to do with him (37:24). Joseph's brothers view their distress in Egypt as retribution for the distress that they had brought on him when they cast him into the pit and later sold him to Midianite merchants (42:21-22). After Joseph's cup is found in Benjamin's sack when the brothers begin the return from their second journey to buy grain in Egypt, and it appears that Joseph is not going to allow Benjamin to return to Canaan with them, Judah concludes that God was punishing them for the way they had treated Joseph (44:16).

All the while, Joseph feels great love for his brothers and does not hold any grudge against them, although for a while he pretends to be harsh with them in his role as second-in-command to the Pharaoh. When he learns that Reuben had intended to rescue him from the pit and restore him to his father (cf. 37:22, 29-30), he goes away from his brothers and weeps (42:22-24). He restores the money that his brothers had paid for the grain on two occasions (42:25, 35; 44:1-2). Joseph is greatly concerned about his father Jacob and his younger brother Benjamin (43:7, 27, 29; 44:19-21, 23). When his brothers return a second time for grain, Joseph prepares a banquet for them (43:16) and charges his servants to show them the utmost hospitality (43:24-25). Upon seeing Benjamin for the first time in twenty-two years, Joseph goes into his chamber and weeps (43:29-31). He has his silver cup planted in Benjamin's sack as an excuse to keep him with him in Egypt (44:2, 4-5, 15, 17).

[42:1] For **grain** (RSV), others read "corn" (vss. 1, 2, 5, 6, 19, 26 of the KJV and NEB, and vss. 3, 25 of the KJV). The word "corn" means the the main cereal grain of a country, here of Egypt. (See the note on 41:35.)

[6] Here Joseph is given the title of **governor** (Hebrew *shalliṭ*) over the land of Egypt (cf. vss. 30, 33). Joseph's brothers **bowed themselves before him** as was customary when foreigners came to Egypt on a peaceful mission. An Egyptian grave relief dating from about 1330 B.C. depicts a group of Asiatics bowing before the Egyptian general Haremhab.

[9] Joseph accuses his brothers of coming to Egypt as **spies . . . come to see the weakness of the land.** The KJV and ASV have "nakedness" for the Hebrew *'erwah* (cf. vs. 12). The context and a cognate Arabic root indicate that the strange word "nakedness" has reference not to the dry and unfruitful land in Egypt during the famine but to the unoccupied and undefended regions on the northeastern frontier, "things that are meant to be hidden from potential enemies" (Speiser, *Genesis*, p. 321). In ancient times, the Egyptians were constantly plagued with spies and invaders from the northeast, and thus Joseph's accusations reflect a true situation in Egyptian life at the time. The translations of the RSV and the NEB ("to spy out the weak points in our defenses") are not rigidly literal renderings of the Hebrew but accurately convey the meaning of the original to modern English-speaking minds.

[11] Joseph's brothers contend that they are **honest** (KJV, ASV "true") or genuine **men,** who are what they appear to be, and not **spies** pretending to be in Egypt to buy grain, as Joseph accuses (see also vss. 16, 19, 31, 33, 34).

[15] **By the life of Pharaoh** (vss. 15, 16) translates the Hebrew phrase *che phar'oh*, which has the same form as *che yhwh*, "As Yahweh [the Lord] lives," which is used often in the OT as a solemn oath followed by a statement

that cannot be broken under any circumstances (see Judg. 8:19; Ruth 3:13; 1 Sam. 14:39, 45; 19:6; 26:10, 16; 28:10; 29:6; 2 Sam. 2:27; 4:9; etc.). In ancient Egypt, the Pharaoh was regarded as a god, and an inscription from the Twentieth Dynasty contains an oath by the life of the Pharaoh. Perhaps a preferable translation of the Hebrew phrase in 42:15, 16 would be "As the Pharaoh lives."

[16, 19] At first, Joseph decrees that only one of his brothers return to Canaan to get Benjamin (vs. 16). But after his brothers stay in prison three days, he allows all of them to return except one, possibly in an attempt to show enough human kindness to encourage their speedy return. However, they seem not to have returned for a year or more (cf. 45:6), perhaps because Jacob thought that the famine would come to an end shortly (after all, he knew nothing of the Pharaoh's dreams or of Joseph's interpretation) and that he could endure the loss of Simeon (who had caused him great trouble at Shechem, 34:25-31) more easily than he could the loss of his youngest son by his favorite wife, who had died while giving birth to him (cf. 35:16-20).

[20] Here and in 29:28, the Hebrew phrase 'aśah khen, literally **they [he] did so**, means "they [he] agreed" (i.e., in each case, to the proposition just stated).

[21] After agreeing to accept Joseph's test of their honesty and leave one of their number in Egypt, the brothers speak to one another in their native language, assuming that Joseph cannot understand what they are saying. They state clearly and concisely the OT principle of retribution, namely, this **distress** has come upon us (and we cannot avoid it), just as we refused to listen to Joseph's pleas that we release him when he was in **distress** (and unable to defend himself). The statement **when he** [i.e., Joseph] **besought us** supplies a detail of the story which is not mentioned in chapter 37.

[22] Reuben reminds his brothers that he had tried to dissuade them from dealing so severely with Joseph (cf. 37:22). Now he thinks that God is punishing them for Joseph's death. (The reference to Joseph's **blood** would seem to suggest that Reuben believes that Joseph must

have been killed after they sold him to the Midianite merchants, and thus they are responsible for his death, cf. 4:10-11.)

[24] Apparently Joseph **wept** because he had just learned for the first time that Reuben had tried to rescue him from his brothers. This may explain why he kept **Simeon** (the second-oldest son of Jacob by Leah) with him in Egypt rather than Reuben.

[28] The Hebrew phrase *yetse' libbam,* literally "their heart went out," is a Hebrew idiom meaning "they were afraid" (cf. vs. 35). This was due to two things: (1) they interpreted the return of the money as a sign that God was punishing them for the way they had treated Joseph (vs. 28); (2) they realized that they might be apprehended by Egyptian authorities and accused of stealing the money (cf. 43:18).

[30] In verses 30 and 33, Joseph's brothers refer to him as **the lord** [Heb. *'adhone*] **of the land** of Egypt (cf. vs. 6).

[36-37] Jacob, filled with emotional distress, complains that his sons had brought grief on him with regard to his **children**: they had brought the evidence that Joseph was dead, they had brought the bad news that the Egyptians were keeping Simeon under custody, and now they wanted him to let **Benjamin** return with them to Egypt, which might certainly lead to his loss or death. Reuben appropriately rejoins that if he does not bring Benjamin back to his father safely from Egypt, his father may slay his **two sons** (possibly Hanoch and Pallu, cf. 46:9).

[38] However, with plenty of grain on hand and Benjamin alive and well, Jacob sternly refuses to allow his sons to return to Egypt immediately with Benjamin. His grief over Joseph's loss was so great (cf. 37:35) that he felt he simply could not survive the loss of Benjamin also.

The events related at the end of chapter 42 and the beginning of chapter 43 are true to life and fit the character of Jacob as it is depicted in chapters 25–36, making it difficult to accept the view of some scholars that two disparate sources lie behind the present material. When Jacob learns that his sons left Simeon in prison in Egypt and that the

ruler of Egypt had told them he would not see them again
unless Benjamin came with them, it is quite understandable
for Jacob to refuse to allow them to return immediately and
to take Benjamin with them. Undoubtedly he reasoned that
the famine would end before their newly purchased grain
ran out and that it would be better to have ten living sons
than nine or possibly none. (The actions of the ruler of
Egypt and a general feeling that Egyptians were hostile to
outsiders like his family would certainly have made him
very hesitant about sending his sons back there;
cf. 42:29-38.) But when the famine grew worse and the
grain ran out, one can understand why Jacob would change
his mind. If he did not send for grain, his whole household
would perish (43:8). But his sons insist that Joseph will not
give them an audience to buy additional grain unless Benjamin goes along. Thus, he yields to what seems to be the
lesser of two evils and reverts to his old trading spirit. He
sends the ruler of Egypt some of the finest products of
Canaan that he can find under such trying circumstances,
hoping that Benjamin and Simeon will be released and preparing his mind as best he can for the worst (43:1-15).

[43:2] As in the previous chapters, "corn" (KJV, NEB;
here the Hebrew word is *shebher*) represents the main cereal grain in Egypt, that is, wheat (see the notes on 41:35
and 42:1).

[3] To **see** [Joseph's] **face** is court language meaning "to
get an audience with Joseph" or "to be permitted into his
presence" (cf. the NEB; vss. 5; 44:23, 26; Exod. 10:28
[twice], 29; 2 Sam. 3:13 [twice]; 14:24, 28, 32). The same
expression is used in the sense of "seeing Joseph (physically)" in Genesis 46:30 and 48:11, where Jacob tells
Joseph how happy he is to see him alive after having believed for a number of years that he was dead.

[8] The word **lad** (Heb. *na'ar*) does not necessarily indicate that Benjamin was a young boy at this time. The same
word is used to describe Joseph at age seventeen (37:2).
Benjamin was born before Joseph's brothers sold him to
the Midianite merchants (35:16-20), and Joseph had been in
Egypt twenty-two years before his brothers made their sec-

ond trip there to buy grain (thirteen years before he became second-in-command to the Pharaoh, 41:46; seven years of abundance, 41:47-48, 53; and two years of famine, 45:6). Thus, Benjamin was probably between twenty-two and twenty-five at this time. Judah refers to him as a **lad** because he was so much older than he and as a term of endearment undoubtedly used frequently of Benjamin by his father and older brothers.

[9] The Hebrew verb translated **be surety for** is *'arabh*, a cognate of the noun *'erabhon*, "pledge," in 38:17, 18. Judah, who had offered his signet and cord and his staff to Tamar as a "pledge" that he would give her a kid for the privilege of having sexual relations with her, now offers himself as "surety" to his father that he would bring Benjamin back alive. He vows that if he fails to do this, he will accept the blame as long as he lives. The Hebrew expression translated **for ever** (RSV, KJV, ASV) is *kol hayyamim*, which means literally "all the days" (cf. NEB, "all my life"). The Hebrew phrase usually rendered "for ever" is *'adh 'olam* or *le'olam*.

[10] Unaware that Joseph was the ruler in Egypt and that God was working out his plan to transport Jacob's whole household to Egypt, Jacob persists in his original decision not to allow his sons to return to Egypt as long as he could. His sons' impatience with their father's unbending determination is reflected in Judah's outburst: **if we had not delayed, we would now have returned twice**, that is, if you had not forced us to stay here, we could have made two round trips to Egypt since we returned the first time and would not be in the difficulty in which we now find ourselves.

[11] In ancient times, it was customary to send a **present** to a person in high position (1 Sam. 16:20; 17:18). Some of the items Jacob sends to Egypt are the same as those which the Midianite merchants carried there (37:25). Apparently, it was commonly known in Mesopotamia and Canaan that the Egyptians were especially fond of these products. **Honey** is the honey of the wild bee, and **gum** is "gum tragacanth" (so the NEB).

[18] Without knowing all the facts, Joseph's brothers assume that he has brought them to his home to accuse them of stealing Egyptian grain on their first visit in order that he might enslave them and seize their asses for his own use or for use by the Egyptians. The truth is that Joseph wants them to share a meal with him (vs. 16). Man is often suspicious of the pure motives of his fellows.

[21] Payments were made by **weight** until coins began to be used about the middle of the first millennium B.C.

[24] It was a common courtesy in ancient times throughout the ancient Near East to provide guests with **water** that they might wash **their feet**. The OT specifies that this was done by various people in different localities: Abraham at Hebron (18:4), Lot at Sodom (19:2), Laban at Nahor in Mesopotamia (24:32), Joseph's steward in Egypt (43:24), and an old man sojourning in Gibeah of Benjamin (Judg. 19:21; cf. also 2 Sam. 11:8; Song of Sol. 5:3; Luke 7:44; John 13:1-20; 1 Tim. 5:10).

[25] The RSV **they made ready the present for Joseph's coming** is to be preferred over the awkward and archaic KJV "they made ready the present against Joseph came at noon."

[26] In keeping with Joseph's dreams (37:7, 10), his brothers **bowed** before him on their first (42:6) and second journeys (43:26, 28) to Egypt.

[30] "Bowels" (KJV) is not the best translation of the Hebrew word *rachamim* to convey the thought of the original to the modern English mind. The RSV **heart** and the NEB "his feelings for his brother mastered him" are much better renderings.

[32] Joseph and the Egyptians did not sit at the same table with the Hebrews because it was **an abomination to the Egyptians** to **eat bread with the Hebrews**. Apparently the reason for this is that the Hebrews raised (46:31-34) and sacrificed (Exod. 8:26 [Hebrew 22]) animals that were sacred to the Egyptians. There is no indication that Joseph ate at a different table because of his rank or because he had married into an Egyptian priestly family (cf. 41:45).

[34] "Mess" (KJV, ASV) is a little used word in modern

America. It came into English from the Latin *missus* through the Old French *mes*, meaning "course at a meal," and means dish or **portion** (RSV, NEB) of food.

Joseph sent **five times as much** food to Benjamin as he sent to his other brothers, not because he would actually eat five times as much as they, or with the intention of depriving them of a goodly amount of food, but because this was an accepted means of showing special honor or respect (cf. 1 Sam. 1:4-5; 9:24). Joseph probably did this because Benjamin was his only full brother (cf. vs. 29), but his eleven brothers probably understood it to mean that the ruler of Egypt was acknowledging their honesty in harmony with the agreement they had made on the first trip (cf. 42:19-20, 33-34) and that he gave five portions to Benjamin because he was the brother that he demanded to see before he would give them a second audience, and now that they had indeed brought him, he reaffirmed his intention to keep his end of the bargain by supplying him extra food. His gestures were given and received as gestures of good will.

The last phrase means "they drank and got drunk [Heb. *shakhar*] with him." Whereas at first they were afraid (vs. 18), now they feel relaxed. (This is not to say that the author of Genesis commends the actions of Joseph and his brethren here.)

[44:1] During the night after Joseph held the banquet for his brothers (cf. 43:25, 32-34; 44:3), he told his **steward** his plan to put money in his brothers' sacks and the silver cup in Benjamin's sack and to apprehend them and accuse them of theft. The following story shows how completely the steward cooperated with Joseph in his plan (cf. especially vss. 6, 10). But even at this, the steward had no idea that Joseph intended to test his brothers to see if they would abandon their youngest brother Benjamin to save their own lives as they had sold him to Midianite merchants out of their jealousy and hatred of him (cf. 37:4, 11, 25-28).

[2] (For **grain** [RSV] or "corn" [KJV, NEB], see the note on 41:35.)

[4] Unfortunately it is impossible to know what **city** in

Egypt is intended here (see also vs. 13). This is one of many details deleted or not included by the author of Genesis in selecting events that would be most effective in conveying his religious message to his readers. He may have omitted this detail because his readers already knew what city was meant, or because it offered nothing really significant to his message, or for some other reason. But the modern reader would like to know the city in which these interesting events took place.

Joseph's steward charges Joseph's brothers with returning **evil for good**, that is, with stealing money and Joseph's silver cup when Joseph had sold them a large amount of grain (vs. 1) and had treated them to a sumptuous banquet (43:34). The OT frequently emphasizes the sin of returning evil for good (1 Sam. 25:21; Pss. 35:12; 38:20 [Hebrew 21]; 109:5; Prov. 17:13) and extols the virtue of returning good for evil (Exod. 23:4-5; 1 Sam. 24:17 [Hebrew 18]; Job 16:4-5; Prov. 25:21-22).

The RSV and NEB follow the LXX in reading **Why have you stolen my silver cup** [the silver goblet]? This line is not in the MT, and it is impossible to determine with certainty whether it is original and was accidentally overlooked by a later copyist or whether the translator(s) of the LXX added it because he (they) felt the context demanded it. The argument that the word "this" (Heb. *zeh*, masculine singular) in verse 5 requires "cup" as its antecedent is not conclusive because "the text as it stands [in the MT—JTW] is effective by indirection: the steward pretends that the brothers know what he is talking about" (Speiser, *Genesis*, p. 333).

[5] It is difficult to know what kind of divination was practiced in Egypt at this time. Mesopotamian sources indicate that oil was poured into water in a bowl, or water was poured into oil, or fragments of silver and gold were dropped into water or oil, and a priest or diviner derived a message from the way in which the globules or fragments arranged themselves. It is difficult to determine from verses 5 and 15 whether Joseph really practiced divination or whether he was trying to make his brothers believe that he could practice it, perhaps as a temporary means of chid-

ing them indirectly for not taking his dreams seriously years before (cf. 37:5-11).

[9-10] Joseph's brothers are so certain the silver cup will not be found in any of their sacks that they state that the man in whose sack it is found will die and the rest will become Joseph's slaves. However, knowing that the cup will be found in Benjamin's sack, the steward declares that the man in whose sack it is found will become Joseph's slave and that the rest will go free. He knows that this alternative suggestion will make Joseph appear more humane in the eyes of his brothers and that their grief will not be as severe when the cup is discovered in Benjamin's sack as it would have been if he had agreed with their proposal to put him to death and to enslave the rest.

[13] In ancient times, people **rent their clothes** to show their grief (Gen. 37:34; Judg. 11:35; 2 Sam. 1:11; 3:31; 13:19, 31 [twice]; 15:32; 2 Kings 2:12; 6:30; 18:37; 19:1; Esth. 4:1; Isa. 36:22; 37:1; Jer. 41:5), to demonstrate their penitent spirit (1 Kings 21:27; 2 Kings 22:11, 19; 2 Chron. 34:19, 27; Jer. 36:24; Joel 2:13), or to express their displeasure or regret that something had happened (Gen. 37:29; Num. 14:6; Josh. 7:6; 2 Kings 5:7, 8 [twice], 11:14; 2 Chron. 23:13; Ezra 9:3, 5). The context in Genesis 44 seems to indicate that Joseph's brothers rent their garments to show that they genuinely regretted what had happened and were grief-stricken over what might happen to Benjamin as a result of it.

[14] Joseph's brothers were brought back to the city so early in the morning (cf. vs. 3) that Joseph was still at his house (cf. 43:16, 17, 18, 24, 26; 44:1) and had not yet gone to the palace (cf. 43:15), where he did his work as the Egyptian vizier each day. Again, the brothers fell down before Joseph, just as he had said they would do when he related his two dreams to them (cf. 37:7, 10).

[15] Joseph already knows what his brothers had done when he asks the rhetorical question, **What deed is this that you have done?** But he says this to impress on their minds the seriousness of stealing his silver cup (cf. the similar question in 3:13; 4:10; 12:18; 20:9; 26:10; 29:25; 31:26).

[16] Judah's statement **God has found out the guilt of your servants** is difficult to interpret precisely. Surely he is not making a confession that he and/or his brothers had deliberately stolen the silver cup (cf. vss. 8-9). This sentence may carry a double meaning: (1) Unable to deny the fact that the cup was in Benjamin's sack, and yet knowing that he and his brothers had not stolen it, the only conclusion which Judah can draw is that God was somehow responsible for it and that he was punishing them for something they had done wrong years before; (2) Judah had been burdened for many years with the guilt of what he and his brothers had done to Joseph, and now he feels that God is punishing them for this. If this latter idea was in Judah's mind, he would not have thought that Joseph understood what he meant. How ironical his statement would have sounded to Joseph, who knew much more about the incident than Judah could ever have imagined!

[17] It seems clear from the unravelling of Joseph's plot that he decrees Benjamin alone is to remain as his slave in order to test his brothers to see if they will abandon Benjamin to save themselves, as they had sold Joseph to the Midianite merchants because they despised him.

[21] The expression **that I may set my eyes upon him** must be taken literally here and should not be understood as court language meaning "to take care of" or "to show favor to," which does not fit the general pattern of the story.

[27-29, 31] Verse 27 presupposes 30:22-25; 35:16-19; verse 28 recalls 37:33; and verses 29 and 31 call to mind 37:35; 42:38.

[30] His [Jacob's] **life is bound up in the lad's** [Benjamin's] **life** means that Jacob deeply loves Benjamin (see 1 Sam. 18:1, 3). Since he has poured out his whole being for Benjamin, he cannot continue to live if Benjamin does not return with his brothers. The word **lad** (vss. 30 [twice], 31, 32, 33 [twice], 34) does not suggest that Benjamin was a young boy at this time. Judah uses this term as a word of endearment and naturally, because Judah is several years older than Benjamin.

[32] "For ever" (KJV, ASV) is too strong a translation
of the Hebrew phrase *kol hayyamim* (which means literally "all the days") for the modern American mind, which
understands "for ever" in the sense of "endless time."
It is preferable to read **all my life** (so the RSV, NEB; see
the note on 43:9).

[33] Just as Judah had saved Joseph's life by persuading
his brothers to sell him to the Midianite merchants
(37:26-27), now he offers to take Benjamin's place as
Joseph's slave in order that his younger brother might return to his father.

[34] **Evil** (Heb. *ra'*) obviously does not mean "sin" here,
but "misery" (NEB), grief, or sorrow. It is worthy of note
that the cognate word *ra'ah* is translated "sorrow" in verse
29 in the RSV, KJV, and ASV (where the NEB reads
"trouble," and then "sorrow" for *yaghon* in vs. 31).

Joseph Reveals His Identity (Ch. 45)

Deeply moved by Judah's concern for his aged father
Jacob and by his willingness to become Joseph's slave in
place of his young half-brother Benjamin, Joseph has
everyone leave the room except his brothers and reveals to
them his true identity. He urges them to return quickly to
Jacob and tell him that Joseph is still alive and has become
vizier in Egypt and to bring his entire household to Egypt
for the remaining five years of the famine in order that they
might survive. At first, his brothers are shocked and afraid,
but when Joseph states that he holds no animosity toward
them for their actions because God was at work to carry
out his purposes, and weeps upon their necks, they begin
to talk with him (vss. 1-15). When the Pharaoh learns that
Joseph's brothers have come from Canaan, he sends word
that they are to go back to Canaan, bring the whole household, and settle in Egypt (vss. 16-20). Joseph sends his
brothers back to Jacob with ample provisions, they tell
their father that Joseph is alive and ruler in Egypt, and
Jacob prepares to carry his household there (vss. 21-28).

This chapter strongly emphasizes that God is working in
nations and in the lives of individuals to carry out his pur-

poses. When the brothers sold Joseph to Midianite merchants, they intended for him to suffer for his apparent arrogance, but God was sending Joseph to Egypt ahead of them so that when the famine came, the entire household of Jacob might be spared (vss. 5, 7, 8). Accordingly, God made Joseph lord over all Egypt (vs. 9). The Pharaoh's positive attitude toward Joseph and his brothers, and Jacob's ability and willingness to go to Egypt, further suggest God's activity in human affairs.

[1] Joseph had had difficulty in holding back the tears in the presence of his brothers the night before, when he saw Benjamin and shared his food with his brothers (cf. 43:30-31). After what was undoubtedly a sleepless night, when his brothers are brought back to his house, he can no longer **control himself**; he commands all his servants to leave and amid sobs and tears reveals his true identity to them.

[5] It is worthy of note that Joseph "recognizes the hand of God, not merely in miraculous interventions, but in the working out of divine ends through human agency and what we call secondary causes" (Skinner, *Genesis,* p. 487).

[6] For **plowing** (RSV, ASV, NEB), the KJV has "earing," an archaic English word, which came into English from the Latin verb *arare* (meaning "to plow") through the Anglo-Saxon *erian.* It appears in the KJV also in Exodus 34:21; Deuteronomy 21:4; 1 Samuel 8:12; and Isaiah 30:24.

[7] A comparison of the use of the word **remnant** (RSV, ASV; Heb. *she'erith*) in 2 Samuel 14:7 and Jeremiah 44:7 suggests that it means "posterity" (KJV) or "descendants" (NEB) here. It is possible that this particular word was chosen to convey the idea that God "rescued" Jacob and his household from apparent destruction from the famine, just as he rescued Noah and his family from the flood and Abraham and his household from the confusion of men whom God confounded and scattered over the face of the earth.

[8] As early as approximately 2350 B.C., the Egyptian vizier Ptah-hotep wore the title "Father of God" (that is, of

the Pharaoh, whom the Egyptians regarded as a god). The term **father** (Heb. *'abh*) was used throughout the ancient Near East as a title for a king or a high official of state (cf. in the OT 1 Sam. 24:11 [Hebrew 12]; 2 Kings 5:13; Isa. 9:6 [Hebrew 5]; 22:21). The continued reference to Jacob as the **father** (cf. vss. 3, 9, 13 [twice], 18, 19, 23) of Joseph (who is **a father to Pharaoh**) and of Joseph's brothers (vss. 25, 27) puts an interesting perspective on the relationship between Jacob, the bearer of the divine promise handed down to him from Abraham through Isaac (cf. 12:1-3; 13:14-18; 18:17-19; 22:17-19 [Abraham]; 26:2-5 [Isaac]; 28:13-15; 35:11-12 [Jacob]), and the Pharaoh. This theme of "fatherhood" is carried one step further when God demands that the Pharaoh let Israel, his "son," go out into the wilderness to worship him (Exod. 4:22-23; Deut. 1:30-31).

[9] Frequently in the ancient Near East, a king or a high state official or some individual sent a messenger (or messengers) to convey a specific message orally to some recipient (or recipients). It was customary to begin such messages with the words "Thus says. . . ." So, when Jacob sends messengers to Esau, he instructs them to begin his message with the words "Thus says your servant Jacob" (33:3-4). Similarly, in the present text, Joseph sends his brothers to his father Jacob with the instruction to begin his message with the words **Thus says your son Joseph**. The same formula is used by Ben-hadad king of Syria (1 Kings 20:2, 5) and by Sennacherib king of Assyria (2 Kings 18:19, 29). In light of this practice, it was natural for OT prophets and other spokesmen for God to introduce their oral messages from the Lord with the words "Thus says the Lord."

[10] **The land of Goshen** (cf. also 46:28 [twice], 29, 34; 47:1, 4, 6, 27; Exod. 8:22 [Hebrew 16]; 9:26) is that region of northeastern Egypt between Port Said and Suez known in modern times as the Wadi Tumilat. It is called "the land of Rameses" in 47:11 (possibly because Rameses was the leading city, or one of the leading cities, of that area; cf. Exod. 1:11; 12:37; Num. 33:5). About 1220 B.C. the

Pharaoh Merneptah allowed seminomadic Edomites to settle in this region to pasture their flocks and herds (Papyrus Anastasi VI, 4, 14). This territory was not very suitable for agriculture but was ideal for grazing livestock, which explains why Joseph wanted his father's household to live there. It is impossible to know how **near** this was to the "city" in which Joseph lived (cf. 44:4, 13), but it was certainly much closer than was the land of Canaan. Instead of **Goshen**, the LXX reads "Gesem of [in] Arabia." "Arabia" in this translation probably refers to one of the districts in the delta region of Egypt.

[16] **Report** (RSV, ASV, NEB) is the preferable rendering of the word translated "fame" in the KJV. It does not mean "lofty reputation," as the context makes clear. "Fame" is an archaic word from the Latin *fama*, meaning "public report or rumor."

[19] At the beginning of this verse, the MT reads: "And you [singular] are commanded, This do [plural subject], take for yourselves [plural] from the land of Egypt wagons," etc. (cf. the KJV and ASV). In order to make sense of this, several words must be added (at least in one's mind)—perhaps: "And you [Joseph] are commanded [to say to your brothers], This do," etc. The LXX and Vulgate have a slightly different text, namely, "And you [Joseph] commend them [i.e., your brothers]," etc. (cf. the RSV and NEB). It is impossible to know beyond question what the original text was.

[22] Joseph gave Benjamin **three hundred shekels of silver**, that is, the price of ten slaves (as a slave was valued at thirty shekels of silver, Exod. 21:32). Just as he had given Benjamin five times as much food as his brothers (43:34), now he gives him **five festal garments** to their one.

[24] Knowing the nature of his brothers and their usual interaction with each other, and perhaps remembering Reuben's chastisement of his brothers for treating Joseph as they did (42:22), Joseph admonishes them not to **quarrel** (RSV, NEB) or "fall out" with one another (KJV, ASV), as they travelled back to their father in Canaan. Having just learned that Joseph was still alive, there would have been a

strong tendency to chide each other and to cast blame on each other for the way they had treated Joseph, still fearful of what he might do to them by way of retaliation (cf. 45:5, 8, 15; 50:15-21).

[26] When Joseph's brothers brought his bloodstained robe to Jacob, he believed that a wild beast had killed him, and thus he mourned for many days (37:22-24). Now, when they tell him that Joseph is still alive, he does **not believe them** at first but thinks they are unnecessarily opening an old wound. In both instances, Jacob was honest but believed a lie and acted on that faith.

[27] **Spirit** (Heb. *ruach*) here does not mean "the eternal part of man," but the whole man. The thought is that the unexpected good news gave Jacob a new vitality and reason to live and to rejoice (cf. Prov. 15:30; 25:25).

[28] The reason Jacob is so happy is not that Joseph is rich and has a high political position in Egypt but that he is alive (cf. 46:30; Lk. 15:24, 32).

JACOB'S FAMILY IN EGYPT (CHS. 46–50)

Jacob's Family Migrates to Egypt (Chs. 46–47)

Jacob and his family depart from Hebron (cf. 37:14) to go to Egypt. On their way south, they come to Beer-sheba, where God appears to Jacob and tells him not to be afraid to go into Egypt, because he will be with him and will bring him up again. Jacob's household moves on into Egypt (46:1-7).

The biblical author interrupts the flow of the story to list the seventy members of Jacob's family who came into Egypt (including Joseph and his two sons; vss. 8-27). Jacob sends Judah ahead to tell Joseph that the household has arrived and to escort him to Goshen, where they are staying. Jacob and Joseph embrace emotionally (vss. 28-30).

Joseph tells his father and brothers that he will inform the Pharaoh of their arrival and that when they appear before him they are to tell him they are shepherds, so that he will allow them to live in the land of Goshen away from the heart of the land of Egypt (since shepherds were an abomination to Egyptians, vss. 31-34). Joseph brings five of his brothers before the Pharaoh and tells them to settle in the land of Goshen (47:1-6). Then Joseph brings his father Jacob before the Pharaoh, and Jacob blesses him (vss. 7-10).

Joseph settles his father's household in the land of Goshen. As the famine continues, Joseph first receives money from the Egyptians for grain. When this runs out, he receives their livestock in payment for grain. When this is gone, he takes their fields and makes them slaves of the government as remuneration for grain. Joseph decrees that when the famine is over, the people must give one-fifth of their produce to the Pharaoh; only the priests are exempt from this (vss. 11-26). Seventeen years later, when Jacob is about to die (at the age of 147), he calls Joseph to him and makes him swear that he will not bury him in Egypt but in the family sepulchre in Canaan (vss. 27-31).

Four significant religious truths stand out in these two chapters. First, God is at work in the affairs of nations and individuals to accomplish his purposes and to carry out his promises. When he appears to Jacob at Beer-sheba, he tells him not to be afraid to go to Egypt, because he will make of him a great nation (vs. 3), go down with him to Egypt, and bring him up again to Canaan (vs. 4). The sequence of these promises shows that God is here announcing the exodus of Jacob's descendants from Egypt at a much later time (cf. Exod. 3:8; 6:8) and is not speaking primarily of the return of Jacob's bones to Canaan. That Yahweh can guide human affairs equally well in Canaan and in Egypt is a further indication of his universal sovereignty, a truth that is taught throughout the OT (and the NT as well).

Second, even though Joseph is now a very wealthy man in a high governmental position, he is not ashamed of his past or of the family that had so much to do with making him the kind of man he was (46:31–47:6). Morgenstern comments that Joseph

was not ashamed of his origin, lowly and mean though it

might seem to some, who were animated by false standards of cheap and superficial culture. On the contrary, he gloried in this origin, for he realized full well that to it he owed all the spiritual knowledge, insight and strength which he possessed, which had alone enabled him to endure all trials, and to rise to his exalted and honorable station, and which now prompted him to use all the powers and privileges of his high office, not for his own selfish advantage, but for the benefit and blessing of his fellowmen. . . . There is a powerful temptation when success, prosperity, and social advancement come, to leave poor or unprogressive relatives and friends behind, to feel that we have outgrown them, and that circumstances compel new associations. . . . Loyalty declares that we may not rise at the expense or to the neglect of others. Love and friendship which have been tried and tested, may not be cheaply cast aside. If we rise, we must carry our loved ones with us, to whatever station we may attain.

Genesis, pp. 293–94

Third, when Jacob comes into the Egyptian court, it is he and not the Pharaoh that proves to be master of the situation. "Jacob blessed Pharaoh" (47:7, 10) and:

This incident symbolizes . . . the triumph of the spiritual over the temporal and the material, of eternal truth over evanescent might and power. Before the dignity of old age, knowledge and experience, and the wisdom which comes from God alone, even the king upon his throne must bow.

Morgenstern, *Genesis,* pp. 296–97

Fourth, Joseph acts in the best interest of all the citizens of Egypt in the steps he takes to carry them through the increasingly severe days of the famine. Some scholars suggest that he was inhumane in taking first the peoples' money for grain, then their livestock, then their lands and themselves as slaves (47:13–26). However, just the reverse is true. Egypt was apparently in a condition of unsettled disorganization during much of the period of Hyksos domination. The Egyptian people would have welcomed a stronger, more secure central government, especially in a national crisis like a famine, even if this meant infringements on individual rights or privileges.

[1] Jacob's household leaves Hebron (cf. 37:14) for Egypt and passes through **Beer-sheba** on the way. Jacob, probably in order to express his deep gratitude to God for sparing his family thus far in the famine and for keeping Joseph alive through all the years that he thought he was dead, offers **sacrifices**, perhaps on the altar that Isaac had built there (cf. 26:23-25). Jacob was accustomed to worshiping the God of his father Isaac (cf. 31:53).

[2] God's decrees differ according to the wide variety of circumstances in which man finds himself, because God always does what is best for man, and requires what is best from him. Accordingly, when a famine came in the days of Isaac, God forbade him to go to Egypt (26:1-2), but now he instructs Jacob to go to Egypt:

> The land was promised to Abraham and Isaac; might Jacob leave it? . . . This step, which was decisive for the subsequent history of the growing nation of Israel, did not proceed from human arbitrariness, even the most humanly comprehensible, but . . . God . . . directed the steps of Israel's ancestors by a command.
>
> von Rad, *Genesis,* p. 397

Long before this time, God had promised Abraham that he would make of him "a great nation" (12:2; 18:18; cf. the divine assurances to Abraham [13:16; 22:17], Isaac [26:4], and Jacob [28:14; 35:11] that their descendants would be as the sand on the seashore and as the stars of heaven). Now God specifies to Abraham's grandson Jacob that this great increase in population will take place in Egypt.

[4] Just as God had promised to be **with** Jacob and to **bring** him back to Canaan when he sent him to Mesopotamia (28:15), he now makes the same promises as he sends him to Egypt. The reference to the "nation" in verse 3 suggests that when God says he will bring Jacob (**you** here is singular) back up again (cf. also 48:21; 50:24), he is announcing the exodus of the nation of Israel from Egypt, although it is not impossible that he is also declaring that Jacob's children will bring his bones out of Egypt after his

death (cf. 50:1-14). This may help explain why Jacob was so anxious for Joseph to swear to him that he would not bury him in Egypt but in the land of Canaan (cf. 47:29-31). Whereas Jacob had thought that he would go down to Sheol to Joseph mourning (37:35), God promises him that Joseph **shall close your eyes**, which apparently was a customary practice at the time.

[6] Although the word translated "seed" (vss. 6, 7) in the KJV and ASV is singular (Heb. *zera'*), the context shows that it has a collective meaning and thus means **offspring** (in the plural sense, RSV) or "descendants" (NEB), as is usually the case throughout the Bible.

[7] The word **daughters** here and in verse 15 (Heb. *banoth*) is plural but has a singular meaning, since Dinah was the only daughter Jacob had (cf. the note on 37:35). The argument that a man is not qualified to be an elder if he has only one child because the Bible refers to an elder having "children" (cf. 1 Tim. 3:4; Titus 1:6), has no support whatever in the biblical use of the terms "sons," "daughters," and "children." Note that "sons" refers to one son in Genesis 46:23, where the NEB has no justification for emending the Hebrew text so as to read "son".

[8-27] The list of members of Jacob's household who came into Egypt also appears in whole or in part in Exodus 1:1-5; 6:14-16; Numbers 26:5-51; and 1 Chronicles 2-8. The names do not always coincide (see the notes below). The way in which the family is divided in the present section is interesting. The author lists thirty-three descendants through Leah (vs. 15) and sixteen through her handmaid Zilpah (vs. 18), then fourteen descendants through Rachel (vs. 22) and seven through her handmaid Bilhah (vs. 25).

The Bible gives three different total numbers for the members of Jacob's family who came into Egypt: sixty-six (vs. 26), seventy (vs. 27; Exod. 1:5), and seventy-five (Acts 7:14-15). It is impossible to explain the reasons for these differences with certainty. It may be that the number sixty-six excludes Er and Onan, the sons of Judah, because they died in the land of Canaan (cf. vs. 12), and Ephraim

and Manasseh (cf. vss. 20, 27), because they were born in
Egypt and were already there when Jacob's household
came. The number seventy may also exclude Er and Onan
but include Ephraim and Manasseh, Jacob (vs. 8), and
Dinah (vs. 15). Finally the number seventy-five in
Acts 7:14-15 follows the LXX, which lists three grandsons
and two great-grandsons of Jacob in Genesis 46:20 who do
not appear in the MT.

[8] The wording of this verse is almost identical with that
of Exodus 1:1.

[10] Numbers 26:12 and 1 Chronicles 4:24 read "Nem-
uel" instead of **Jemuel**, which appears here and in Exodus 6:15; **Ohad** occurs here and in Exodus 6:15, but is not
mentioned in the lists in Numbers and 1 Chronicles;
1 Chronicles 4:24 reads "Jarib" in place of **Jachin** here, in
Exodus 6:15, and in Numbers 26:12; Numbers 26:13 and
1 Chronicles 4:24 have "Zerah" instead of **Zohar**, which is
found here and in Exodus 6:15. Genesis 46:10 indicates
that Simeon was a polygamist and that one of his wives
was a **Canaanite** woman.

[11] First Chronicles 6:16 [Hebrew 1] reads "Gershom"
in place of **Gershon**, which appears here, in Exodus 6:16,
and in Numbers 26:57.

[13] First Chronicles 7:1 has "Puah" instead of **Puvah**,
which occurs here and in Numbers 26:23; at the same time,
Numbers 26:24 and 1 Chronicles 7:1 read "Jashub" in
place of **Iob** here.

[14] **The sons of Zebulun** are not enumerated in
1 Chronicles.

[15] The Hebrew word translated "soul" (*nephesh*) in the
KJV and ASV of verses 15, 18, 22, 25, 26 (twice), and 27
(twice) does not mean the eternal part of man, as does the
modern English word "soul," but the whole "person" (so
correctly the RSV). The number **thirty-three** apparently includes Jacob (vs. 8) and **Dinah**.

[16] The list of **the sons of Gad** in 1 Chronicles 5:11-17
differs widely from the list given here and allows for no
significant comparison. Numbers 26:15 reads "Zephon" instead of **Ziphion**; Numbers 26:16 has "Ozni" in place of

Ezbon; and Numbers 26:17 reads "Arod" instead of **Arodi**.

[17] **Ishvi** does not occur in the parallel list found in Numbers 26.

[20] Joseph's marriage to **Asenath** and the births of **Manasseh** and **Ephraim** are recorded in Genesis 41:50-52.

[21] **The sons of Benjamin** pose a very difficult problem for students of the book of Genesis. Benjamin seems to have been approximately twenty-five years of age when the household of Jacob moved to Egypt (cf. 35:16-19; 41:46, 53; 45:6), and it would appear very unlikely that he would have had ten sons by this time unless he had several wives. At the same time, Numbers 26:38-41 and 1 Chronicles 8:1-5 list some of the names found in our passage as grandsons of Benjamin. Perhaps the author of Genesis includes children or grandchildren born in Egypt to attain the number seventy, as might be indicated by the inclusion of Joseph and his two sons, who were in Egypt before Jacob's family arrived, but this is not certain, and our text remains an enigma. Numbers 26:38 reads "Ahiram" instead of **Ehi**; **Rosh** does not occur in Numbers 26 or 1 Chronicles 8; Numbers 26:39 has "Shephuphim," whereas 1 Chronicles 7:12 has "Shuppim," in place of **Muppim**; Numbers 26:39 reads "Hupham" instead of **Huppim**, which appears here and in 1 Chronicles 7:12; and 1 Chronicles 8:3 has "Addar" in place of **Ard**, which is found here and in Numbers 26:40 (where he is the son of **Bela**, and thus the grandson of **Benjamin**).

[23] First Chronicles 2-8 does not contain a list of **the sons of Dan**. Numbers 26:42 reads "Shuham" instead of **Hushim**.

[24] 1 Chronicles 7:13 has "Jahziel" in place of **Jahzeel** here and in Numbers 26:48; 1 Chronicles 7:13 reads "Shallum" instead of **Shillem** here and in Numbers 26:49.

[28] This verse contains a different textual problem with regard to the phrase rendered **to appear before him**. The MT says that he [i.e., Jacob] sent Judah before him to Joseph "to show [point out] the way [Heb. *lehoroth*] before him to Goshen" (so the ASV; the KJV "to direct his face" perhaps suggests the same thought, but its meaning

is very obscure). This implies that Jacob and Judah had agreed on a rendezvous somewhere in the land of Goshen and that Judah's task was to inform Joseph of its whereabouts and to escort him there. The LXX has *sunantēsia kath' Herōōn polin eis gēn Hramessē*, "to meet [him] at Heroopolis in the land of Rameses" (cf. 47:11), which suggests an original *lehiqqaroth*, "to meet [him]." The Samaritan Pentateuch and the Syriac read *lehera'oth*, **to appear** (before him in Goshen), evidently in order to tell him that Jacob's household had safely arrived in Goshen (so the RSV and NEB). Although it is impossible to know with certainty what the original text was at this point, the surrounding context would seem to support the MT (so the KJV and ASV). Joseph had instructed his brothers to go back to Canaan and to bring Jacob's family to Goshen (45:10). After Jacob sends Judah to Joseph (46:28), Joseph goes up to meet Jacob in Goshen (46:29). It would be most logical to believe that Judah's role between these two events was to inform Joseph of the arrival and whereabouts of Jacob's household and to escort him to meet them.

[29] Horses and **chariots** were introduced into Egypt for the first time by the Hyksos invaders (1720–1580 B.C.).

[34] It is very difficult to understand the statement **every shepherd is an abomination to the Egyptians**, because the Egyptians themselves raised livestock, and the Pharaoh even told Joseph that he could put his brothers in charge of his "cattle" (47:6; Heb. *miqneh*, a comprehensive term including cattle, sheep, goats, and the like). Some scholars have suggested that the Egyptian antipathy for shepherds was due to their experiences with Hyksos rulers, so-called "shepherd kings." However, Joseph apparently lived in Egypt during the Hyksos period (ca. 1720–1580 B.C.). Exodus 8:26-28 (Hebrew 22-24) would seem to suggest that the Egyptians despised shepherds who sacrificed animals that they considered to be sacred (cf. the note on 43:32).

There were at least three advantages to the Hebrews in living in the land of Goshen: (a) this was the best grazing land for their flocks and herds, even in the time of famine;

(b) they would not be tempted to marry Egyptians and to adopt their religious and social practices; (c) they would be in an ideal location to escape from Egypt when Yahweh was ready to take them back to the land of Canaan, as he had promised (vs. 4). But in order to ensure that the Pharaoh would allow them to live there, Joseph tried to show him the advantages that the Egyptians would incur if the Hebrews settled there. First, the Egyptians would not have to fear being contaminated by them if they lived apart from the main population areas. Second, since Goshen was a frontier area through which enemy armies and vagabonds had to pass on their way to invade Egypt, the Hebrews, by their presence in this region, would function as a natural protection for the Egyptians.

[47:4] The patriarchs repeatedly were made aware that their lot on earth was **to sojourn** (Heb. *gur*; cf. vs. 9 [twice]; 12:10; 19:9; 20:1; 21:23, 34; 26:3; 32:4 [Hebrew 5]; 35:27; Heb. 11:9-10, 13-16):

> Sojourning was indeed the characteristic of the entire road of life which God had pointed out to the patriarchs. Sojourning meant renunciation of settlement and land ownership: . . . it meant a life which was oriented toward future fulfillment, namely, toward the promise of land which was often renewed to the patriarchs."
>
> von Rad, *Genesis*, pp. 402–3

[5] The LXX of verses 5-6 is quite different from the MT. For one thing, the order varies (the LXX has 5a, 6b, 5b, 6a); and for another, the LXX inserts a whole verse after 6b which does not occur in the MT. The reading of the LXX is as follows:

> (5a) Then Pharaoh said to Joseph, (6b) Let them dwell among them, put them in charge of my cattle. [Additional verse: And Jacob and his sons came into Egypt to Joseph. And Pharaoh the king of Egypt heard.] (5b) Then Pharaoh said to Joseph, your father and your brothers have come to you. (6a) The land of Egypt is before you; settle your father and your brothers in the best of the land.

Most scholars think that the LXX text was original and

explain the missing line in the MT as an instance of homoioteleuton, that is, an eye skip from the phrase "Then Pharaoh said to Joseph" in one line to the same words in another.

[7] Chapters 47–49 describe occasions on which Jacob **blessed** (Heb. *barakh*) certain individuals: the Pharaoh (47:7, 10), Joseph (48:15; 49:26), Manasseh and Ephraim (48:9, 16, 20), and his twelve sons (49:28). The order of these chapters is interesting and seems to be intentional. First Jacob blesses the Pharaoh, whose heredity lies completely outside the genealogy of Abraham; then he blesses Joseph and his sons (the former having married an Egyptian woman and the latter having an Egyptian mother), who were born away from Jacob's household; and finally he blesses his own sons, who had been with him all along (except, of course, for Joseph, 49:22-26) and had traveled with him into Egypt.

[9] Jacob's days were **few** in comparison with the antediluvians (5:4-32; 11:10-26), Abraham (who died at 175, 25:7), and Isaac (who died at 180, 35:28), even though he was 130 when he said this and was to live to be 147 (47:28). They were **evil** (which does not mean "sinful" here) because of the hardships that he had to endure, such as his struggles with Esau and Laban; his griefs over the sinful actions of his sons Reuben, Simeon, and Levi; his deep sorrow upon learning that Joseph had been killed by a wild beast (or so he had been led to believe); and his anxiety over Benjamin's going with his brothers into Egypt.

[11] The land of Goshen is called **the land of Rameses** only here in the OT (this term also appears in the LXX of 46:28). Evidently it refers to the district or region in which the city of Rameses was located (cf. Exod. 1:11; 12:37; Num. 33:3, 5). Unfortunately, one cannot be certain about the exact location of Rameses. Some archeologists locate it in the Wadi Tumilat, possibly at the modern Tell el-Maskhutah or Tell er-Retaba a few miles northeast of Cairo. Others identify it with Pelusium to the northeast on the Mediterranean Sea east of Lake Menzaleh or with Tanis south of Lake Menzaleh. Still others equate it with

Qantir about fifteen miles south of Tanis. (For a fuller discussion, see J. A. Wilson, "Rameses [City]," IDB, vol. 4, p. 9.) Egyptian sources indicate that the Pharaoh Ramses II (1290–1224 B.C.) named Rameses after himself, which suggests that in Genesis 47:11 the biblical author is using a later name for this city and region because the earlier name "Goshen" was no longer understood by his readers and needed to be explained to them.

[17] It does not seem likely that the Egyptians actually turned over all their livestock to Joseph but rather that they bound them over to the Egyptian government as security, so that these animals became the property of the government but were still used by the people. Extant evidence suggests that horses and chariots were introduced into Egypt for the first time by the Hyksos invaders (1720–1580 B.C.).

[18] The two **years** mentioned here are not the first two years of the famine, for these had already passed by this time (cf. 45:6). On the contrary, the severity of the situation described here points toward the end of the famine.

[19] It is apparently in the seventh year of the famine that the Egyptians ask for (vs. 19) and receive (vs. 23) **seed** to be sown the following year with the expectation of having a good crop.

[21] The MT reads *he'ebhir 'otho le'arim*, "he removed them to the cities" (so the KJV and ASV), and this reading is followed by the Syriac and the Targums Onkelos and Pseudo-Jonathan. However, it makes little sense to believe that Joseph would move the people into the cities and then give them seed to sow the land (vs. 23). Most scholars, therefore, adopt the reading suggested by the Samaritan Pentateuch, the LXX, and (more loosely) the Vulgate, namely, *he'ebhidh 'otho la'abhadhim*, **he made slaves of them** (RSV), or "set them to work as slaves" (NEB). The Hebrew letters for *d* (daleth) and *r* (resh) are so similar that they are often confused in copying, which seems to be the case here. The people had suggested that Joseph make them "slaves" of the Pharaoh (vs. 19), and after he gave them seed (vs. 23), they expressed their desire to continue

to be his "slaves" (vs. 25), apparently in thankful response
to his generous help and wise guidance through the famine.
Thus, it makes more sense to believe that the original reading of verse 21 was: **he made slaves of them.**

[22] Religious personnel, including **priests,** were highly
respected in ancient Egypt. Inscriptions on Egyptian
monuments show that the priests had large estates (see
also vs. 26). It was common for the Pharaohs to make
massive donations of wheat to the temples.

[24] The decree to give a **fifth** of the harvest to the
Pharaoh (cf. also vs. 26) may be due (at least in part) to the
terrible experience through which Egypt had just come.
Joseph had advised the Pharaoh to store up a fifth of the
produce during the seven plenteous years in preparation
for the famine (cf. 41:34), and this had saved the people
from destruction. Now, during good years following the
famine, it would seem advisable to store up wheat for the
future, not knowing when another famine might occur.
(Other famines in the region of Canaan and Egypt are mentioned in 12:10; 26:1; Ruth 1:1; 2 Sam. 21:1; 1 Kings 18:2;
2 Kings 4:38; 7:4; 8:1; 25:3; Neh. 5:3; and the prophets in
particular often announced the coming of a famine as divine punishment on Israel or Judah for their sins,
cf. Isa. 51:19; Jer. 11:22; 14:12, 13, 15, 16, 18; 15:2; 16:4;
18:21; etc.; Ezek. 5:12, 16, 17; 7:15; 12:16; etc.) It was not
uncommon in ancient times to assess a tax of 20 percent on
the citizens of a country.

[26] By telling his readers that Joseph's **statute** that the
Egyptians give the Pharaoh a fifth of their produce still
stands to this day, the author leaves a slight clue indicating
that he is writing the book of Genesis long after the event
recorded here. Of course, the same thing would be indicated by the fact that he describes the deaths of Jacob
(47:28; 49:33) and Joseph (50:22, 26) as historical facts of
the past and that he alludes to the establishment of the
Israelite monarchy as a past event (36:31; see the note on
this verse).

[27] The book of Genesis often notes that mankind, and
especially God's chosen people, **were fruitful and multi-**

plied (cf. 1:22, 28; 8:17; 9:1, 7; 17:20; 28:3; 35:11; 48:4). At a later period, Israel's population growth in Goshen was destined to arouse fear in the Egyptians that they might take over the country and to lead to severe persecution of the Israelites (Exod. 1:7-14).

[28] Jacob and his family had come to Egypt when Jacob was 130 (vs. 9). Now we learn that he lived there seventeen years and died at the age of 147. The literary style of the author of Genesis should be noted here. He relates the death of Jacob and tells his readers how old Jacob was when he died, only then to relate several other events in Jacob's life (47:29–49:32). Thus, 47:27-28 are comprehensive verses that anticipate events which have not yet been depicted and should not be pressed as evidence of two (or more) sources lying behind this material. The author of Judges describes the whole period of the Judges in a brief paragraph (Judg. 2:11-23) before dealing with events connected with specific Judges; the author of 2 Samuel notes the birth of Solomon (2 Sam. 5:14) several chapters before he records that birth in its historical setting (2 Sam. 12:24-25). The OT is replete with examples of this literary means of relating history.

[29] On the significance of putting the **hand under** [the] **thigh,** see the note on 24:2.

[30] To **lie with** [one's] **fathers** is an idiomatic expression in Hebrew, apparently meaning to be buried at the same place as one's ancestors (**in their burying place**), near their graves. Jacob wants Joseph to see to it that he is not buried in Egypt but in the cave of Machpelah, where Abraham (25:9; 49:31) and Isaac (35:29; 49:31) had been buried (cf. 49:29-32).

[31] The statement **Israel bowed himself upon the head of his bed** is problematic (a similar expression appears in 1 Kings 1:47). It could mean that Jacob thanked God for Joseph's oath that he would bury him at the cave of Machpelah, and in order to do this he felt it necessary to assume a position of reverence but was so feeble in his old age that he had to support himself on the head of the bed. (Note that when Joseph comes to Jacob, he feels it necessary to

sit up in bed, yet to do this he must summon all his strength, 48:2.) Instead of *miṭṭah,* **bed,** in 47:31, the LXX, Syriac, and Old Latin have words which suggest an original *maṭṭeh,* "staff" (a reading which requires no change in the Hebrew consonants; the translators of these early versions did their work before the Massoretes added vowel points to the text between A.D. 500 and 900). When the author of the book of Hebrews alludes to Jacob's blessing Joseph's sons (apparently referring to 48:2), he writes: "By faith Jacob, when dying, blessed each of the sons of Joseph, bowing in worship over the head of his staff [Greek *hrábdos*]" (Heb. 11:21). But actually this last line is a verbatim quote of the LXX of 47:31. The LXX of 48:2 has *klinē,* **bed,** in harmony with the MT. One cannot be absolutely sure about the original text of 47:31.

Jacob Blesses Ephraim and Manasseh (Ch. 48)

In his waning years, Jacob becomes ill and to some extent bedridden. Joseph, apparently anticipating his father's death in the comparatively near future, brings his two sons, Ephraim and Manasseh, to receive Jacob's blessing. The patriarchal blessing was a very solemn, formal, and serious affair. Jacob had received Isaac's blessing above Esau by disguising himself at Rebekah's urging when Isaac was an old man with poor eyesight (27:1-40). Now it is his turn to bless his grandsons as an old man with poor eyesight. He tells Joseph that God had appeared to him at Luz (Bethel) as he returned from Paddan-aram and had promised him that his descendants would be many and that they would inherit the land of Canaan (cf. 35:11-12). He declares that Ephraim and Manasseh would be regarded as his own sons, since Joseph's mother (Rachel) had died when Benjamin was born, making it impossible for Joseph to have additional brothers like the first two sons of Leah (vss. 1-7).

Jacob blesses Joseph and his two sons, Ephraim and Manasseh (vss. 8-22). If a man's blessing was inspired of God, when he uttered that blessing divine power was released which guaranteed that his promises would be carried out. Furthermore, after the blessing was uttered, it could not be revoked (as Isaac's blessing of Jacob above Esau clearly indicated; cf. 27:35). Accordingly, it was important to include certain formal elements in the blessing. Genesis 48:8-22 includes some of these elements: (1) the patriarch (Jacob) asks the identity of those to be blessed and is told (vss. 8-9a); (2) the patriarch invites those to be blessed to come forward (vs. 9b); (3) he kisses and embraces them (vs. 10); (4) Joseph removes his sons from Jacob's knees and bows to the earth (vs. 12); (5) the patriarch places his right hand on the son who is to receive the greater blessing and his left hand on the other (vss. 13-19); (6) he pronounces the blessing (vss. 20-22).

Ephraim and Manasseh must have been approximately twenty years of age when Jacob blessed them. They were born before the famine came (41:50), and Jacob and his family had moved to Egypt when Jacob was 130 (47:9), after the famine had been going two full years (45:6). Jacob died seventeen years later at the age of 147 (47:28). The blessing of Ephraim and Manasseh apparently occurred in the last part of his life (cf. 48:21).

[3] The divine name under which the deity appeared to Jacob at Luz when he returned from Paddan-aram was **God Almighty** (Heb. *'el shadday*, cf. 35:11; God is called by the same name in 17:1; 28:3; 43:14; 49:25; Exod. 6:3; and often elsewhere in the OT). **Luz** was the ancient name of Bethel (cf. 28:19; 35:6). Because God had **blessed** Jacob, he could bless his descendants.

[4] On the idea of being fruitful and multiplying, see the brief note on 47:27. The word "seed" (Heb. *zera'*) here and in verses 11 and 19 (KJV, ASV) is singular but clearly has a collective meaning, as is usually the case throughout the Bible. Thus, **descendants** (vss. 4 and 19 in the RSV and NEB), "children" (vs. 11 in the RSV), and "sons" (vs. 11 in the NEB) are all excellent translations. The word **everlasting** (RSV, KJV, ASV) or "perpetual" (NEB; Heb. *'olam*) does not denote "endless time," but "a long period of time" in contrast to a brief period. This is often the meaning of this term throughout the Bible; its precise

meaning must be determined in each context.

[5] Jacob officially recognizes Joseph's two sons, Ephraim and Manasseh, as his own children, holding the same status in his eyes as his two oldest sons by Leah, **Reuben and Simeon**. This recognition is necessary because Ephraim and Manasseh were sons of an Egyptian woman (Asenath; cf. 41:50-52; 46:20) and were born in Egypt away from Joseph's household in Canaan. It is significant because Rachel's death at Benjamin's birth made it impossible for Jacob to have any additional children by her (cf. vs.7) and because the tribes who issued from Joseph's two sons are now destined to become leading tribes in Israel. First Chronicles 5:1-2 supplies an interesting commentary on this verse:

> He [Reuben] was the first-born; but because he polluted his father's couch, *his birthright was given to the sons of Joseph* the son of Israel, so that he is not enrolled in the genealogy according to the birthright; though Judah became strong among his brothers and a prince was from him, yet *the birthright belonged to Joseph*.

[6] Jacob claims Ephraim and Manasseh as his own two sons (vs. 5) but states that any sons born to Joseph after them shall be regarded as his sons and shall be considered members of the tribes of Ephraim and Manasseh.

[7] Here Jacob recalls Rachel's death and burial between Bethel and Ephrath (cf. 35:16-20). Strangely, many scholars do not see any connection between this verse and the surrounding context. However, Jacob is simply explaining why he was officially adopting Joseph's sons as his own: Rachel died when Benjamin was born, making it impossible for him to have any additional sons by her; in place of others sons, he recognizes his grandsons through Joseph, the oldest son of Rachel. The parenthetical phrase **that is, Bethlehem** is the author's explanation to a group of readers who did not know that **Bethlehem** was called **Ephrath** at an earlier period.

[8] Jacob's question **Who are these?** does not seem to be a question seeking information, but the first step in the

formal ritual connected with a patriarchal blessing.

[9] Joseph acknowledges that his children are God's gifts to him, and not simply the product of natural human sexual relations (see the note on 33:50).

[10] In the first line of verse 10, the author interrupts the flow of the narrative to explain to his readers that in Jacob's old age he could not see very well, in order that they might understand why Joseph guided Ephraim and Manasseh to his father, to the hands to which he thought each belonged for his blessing because of age. Jacob himself had been able to disguise himself as Esau because his aged father Isaac could not see well (cf. 27:1).

[12] By receiving a child on his **knees**, the father of the family officially accepted that child into his household (cf. 30:3; 50:23; Job 3:12). That **Joseph removed** [Ephraim and Manasseh] **from his** [Jacob's] **knees** presupposes that Jacob had taken them on his knees a few minutes prior to this. The NEB interprets the phrase "that I may bless them" in verse 9 as "that I may take them on my knees." The Hebrew word for **bless** is *barakh*, and the word for **knee** is *berekh*, which would lend some support to this view.

[14] The NT practice of "laying on hands" (Matt. 19:13, 15; Mark 5:23; 6:5; 10:16; 16:18; Luke 4:40; 13:13; Acts 6:6; 8:18-19; 9:12, 17; 13:3; 19:6; 1 Tim. 4:14; 5:22; 2 Tim. 1:6) seems to be rooted in the patriarchal blessing of the OT, where the father of the family imparted blessings which God had bestowed upon him to his children and descendants. (See H. H. Shepherd, Jr., "Hands, Laying on of," IDB, vol. 2, pp. 521–22.)

[15-16] Speaking of Joseph, Jacob prays that God will **bless** Ephraim and Manasseh in two ways: (1) by letting (causing) the names of Abraham, Isaac, and Jacob (to) be called upon (over) them, and (2) by letting (causing) them (to) grow into a multitude in the midst of the earth (vs. 16). To "let (cause) one's name (to) be called on someone" (Heb. *yiqqare' bhahem shemi*) is a very specialized technical term meaning "to consider that person as one's own," in this case as one's son (cf. vs. 5). A husband's name is

called upon his wife (Isa. 4:1), and God's name is called upon the city of Jerusalem (Jer. 25:29; Dan. 9:18), the temple (Jer. 7:10, 11, 14, 30; 32:34; 34:15), his people (Deut. 28:10; Isa. 43:7; 63:19; 65:1; Jer. 14:9; 15:16; Dan. 9:19), and the nations (Amos 9:12). In the NT, Christians are designated as those upon whom God's honorable name is called (James 2:7), that is, God's children.

In this blessing, Jacob uses three interesting phrases to describe God. First, he calls him **the God before whom my fathers Abraham and Isaac walked** (vs. 15; cf. 17:1; 24:40). The patriarchs were constantly aware that they were living their lives in God's presence; he knew their words, deeds, and intentions. The same is true of every man in every generation (cf. Prov. 15:3; Isa. 38:3; Jer. 23:23-24), a truth which assumes that God is alive and working in his world at all times. Second, he describes him as **the God who has led me all my life long to this day** (vs. 15). The Hebrew word translated **led** is *ro'eh*, which means literally "was shepherding," thus explaining the translations "fed" (KJV, ASV) and "has been my shepherd" (NEB). As Jacob was a "shepherd" by occupation, it is most appropriate that he use this term to describe God's relationship to him. This word frequently occurs in the Bible in speaking of God (cf. 49:24; Pss. 23:1-4; 28:9; 80:1; Isa. 40:11; Ezek. 34:11-16; Luke 15:3-7; John 10:11, 14). Third, he refers to him as **the angel who has redeemed me from all evil** (vs. 16). The word **angel** is often used for "God" in the OT (cf. e.g., 16:7-13; 18:1-20; 19:1-23; 21:15-20; 31:11-13). The **evil** (i.e., danger or affliction, not sin) from which God had **redeemed** him apparently includes such things as Esau's threat to kill him (cf. 27:41), the deceit of Laban (29:15-30; 31:36-41), the encounter with the men of Shechem (33:18–34:31), the apparent death of Joseph (37:25-36; 45:25-28), and the danger of losing Benjamin when he went with his ten brothers to Egypt (42:29–43:15).

[21] It is important to note that the word **you** in this verse (twice) is plural and thus refers (not to Joseph alone, but) to Joseph's descendants, or more specifically, the descendants of Ephraim and Manasseh (cf. vs. 19). Through-

out the book of Genesis, emphasis has been placed on God's being **with** his people (cf. 26:3, 24; 28:15; 35:3; 39:2, 3, 21, 23; 46:4). God had promised Joseph that he would make of him a great nation and bring him (i.e., his descendants = that nation) out of Egypt (46:4). Now, apparently under divine inspiration, Jacob makes the same promise to Joseph concerning his descendants through Ephraim and Manasseh (see also 50:24).

[22] Jacob's statements in verse 22 continue to anticipate the conquest of Canaan by his descendants, the Israelites, with particular emphasis on the territory to be received by the Joseph tribes, Ephraim and Manasseh. The word translated **mountain slope** in the RSV and "ridge of land" in the NEB is *shekhem,* literally "shoulder," which can also be interpreted as a proper name—"Shechem." In either case, Jacob promises Joseph that his descendants will dwell in the very desirable region of Shechem. Eventually this region became a part of the territory controlled by the tribe of Manasseh. The last line of verse 22 either refers to the rout of Shechem by Simeon and Levi, perhaps as a symbolic microcosm of the later conquest (34:25-29; however, Jacob disapproved of his sons' action at the time, 34:30-31) or to some overthrow of Shechem to which there is no allusion elsewhere in the OT.

Jacob's Declarations Concerning His Descendants and Death (Ch. 49)

In many ways, Genesis 49 is one of the most difficult chapters in the entire OT. For one thing, almost every line in the poem of Jacob (vss. 2-27) is fraught with textual difficulties of all sorts. Also, the poem contains a number of words whose meaning is obscure, the ancient versions often do not agree on the original reading, the poetic symmetry is frequently broken, and comparisons with the appropriate verses in the similar poem in Deuteronomy 33 pose difficulties. In this commentary it will be possible to deal with only a few of the textual difficulties, and even then in a very elementary way. The serious student is urged to consult scholarly commentaries, journal articles, word studies, and the like for more detailed exegesis.

Further, although verse 28 describes Jacob's words as a "blessing," many of the tribes are actually "cursed," and in fact the word "cursed" (Heb. *'arur*) is used in verse 7. Perhaps "bless" (Heb. *barakh*) is to be interpreted as a polar word here, meaning both "bless" and "curse" as the individual case demands, or at least is to be taken as a relative term depending on the character of the father of the tribe and/or that of the tribe itself.

Furthermore, even a cursory reading of Genesis 49 makes it clear that Jacob is not speaking primarily of his sons as individuals but of the tribes that came from them, and verse 28 makes this explicit. Most critical modern scholars, therefore, view this poem as historical statements composed *after* the various tribes had settled in the land of Canaan, and date the various units between the period of the Judges and the reigns of David and Solomon. However, verse 1 claims that Jacob is speaking of *future* events; Jacob's statements in verses 29-32 can hardly refer to tribes; verse 33 explicitly states that his charge in verses 29-32 was addressed to his sons; and verses 1 and 28, and the positive assurance with which he speaks, indicate that he was able to predict what would happen to the tribes that were to descend from his sons because he was speaking under divine inspiration. Jacob's knowledge of Canaan was intimate and comprehensive, because he had traveled widely therein.

> To those who cannot accept prediction the oracles of this chapter are *vaticinia ex eventibus*, prophecies fabricated from the events they appear to foresee; and because the events are widely separated the speech then must be broken down into a string of sayings uttered over the centuries. But taken as a genuine vision of Jacob, its variable range presents no difficulty: there is no reason why the curtain should fall at the same point for all the tribes, every reason why it should not.
>
> D. Kidner, *Genesis*, TOTC, p. 215

The general assumption of this chapter is that God is in

control of human history and is able to announce and execute the plans and purposes that he has for his people and for all mankind. When God speaks, things begin to happen, just as they did when he created the world by uttering his powerful word (cf. Gen. 1; Heb. 11:3). Viewing Jacob as God's spokesman, in Genesis 49:2-27

> all the various destinies of the tribes are to be understood only as the outcome of the prophetic statements of the ancestor. As later in the case of the prophets, so here Jacob created history by the authority of his creative word, either of blessing or of curse.
>
> von Rad, *Genesis*, p. 417

After sketching the destinies of the tribes which were to descend from his twelve sons (vss. 1-28), Jacob instructs his sons to bury him in the cave of Mach-pelah in the land of Canaan and then dies (vss. 29-33). The order in which the twelve sons appear in verses 2-27 does not correspond to the order of their births as presented in Genesis 29:31–30:24 and 35:16-18, or to the order of the tribes presented in Deuteronomy 33. Instead, the arrangement is: Reuben, Simeon, Levi, Judah (the first four sons of Leah, 29:31-35), Zebulun, Issachar (the fifth and sixth sons of Leah, but in the reverse order of their births, 30:17-20), Dan (the first son of Bilhah, Rachel's concubine, 30:5-6), Gad and Asher (the two sons of Zilpah, Leah's concubine, 30:9-13), Naphtali (the second son of Bilhah, 30:7-8), Joseph, and Benjamin (the two sons of Rachel, 30:22-24; 35:16-18). In Deuteronomy 33, Simeon and Issachar are omitted, and the order is: Reuben, Judah, Levi, Benjamin, Joseph, Zebulun, Gad, Dan, Naphtali, and Asher.

[1] In days to come translates the Hebrew expression *be'acharith hayyamim*, literally "in the end of the days." This phrase occurs thirteen times in the OT (Gen. 49:1; Num. 24:14; Deut. 4:30; 31:29; Isa. 2:2=Mic. 4:1; Jer. 23:20=30:24; 48:47; 49:39; Ezek. 38:16; Hos. 3:5; Dan. 10:14), and its Aramaic equivalent, *be'acharith yomayya'*, appears once (Dan. 2:28). As a careful examination of these passages shows, the meaning of this phrase varies and thus must be determined in each place by the context. Here, it would be a serious mistake to interpret it as a technical phrase for "the end time" or "the Christian era" or "the final age," as some are inclined to construe the rendering "in the last days" (KJV) or "in the latter days" (ASV). Rather, it means "in the remote or distant future," as in Numbers 24:14; Deuteronomy 4:30; 31:29; Jeremiah 23:20=30:24; 48:47; 49:39; and like the equivalent Akkadian expression *ina arkāt ūmī*. Accordingly, the translation **in days to come** (RSV, NEB) is preferable.

[4] The MT has **unstable** [uncontrollable] **as water** (so the KJV and RSV) and probably means that Reuben lost control of himself over his lust for Bilhah and committed adultery with her (cf. 35:22). The rendering "turbulent as a flood" (NEB) approaches the thought. The translation "boiling over as water" (ASV) is based on Symmachus and the LXX.

Until the last line in verse 4, Jacob has been addressing Reuben in the second person singular (you, thou). Then— if one follows the MT—he suddenly changes to the third person singular, "he went up [Heb. *'alah*] to my couch" (so the KJV and ASV). The same shift occurs in verse 9. The LXX, Syriac, and Targum Onkelos have the second person singular throughout and provide support for the reading **you went up to my couch** (RSV). The rendering "then you defiled his concubine's couch" (NEB) requires a more radical textual emendation than is justified. Either we should retain the second person singular throughout with the RSV or imagine that suddenly Jacob turned to his other sons and (possibly with a gesture of the hand) said concerning Reuben, "He went up to my couch."

Because Reuben committed adultery with his father's concubine Bilhah (35:22), Jacob wrested from him the privileges and blessings that would normally go to a patriarch's first-born. Therefore, not only he but also his tribe is destined to suffer the consequences of being relegated to an inferior position among Jacob's sons and in the tribes of Israel.

[5] **Simeon and Levi** are described as **brothers** here, not

because they were both the sons of Leah (29:33-34), since the same thing was true of Reuben and Judah (see 29:32, 35), but because they conspired together to kill the men of Shechem while they were sore from having been circumcised (cf. 34:25-26).

[6] **My soul** (Heb. *naphshi*) and **my spirit** ("glory," ASV; Heb. *kebhodhi*) stand in parallel synonymous lines and thus mean the same thing, that is, "I." The word **soul** does not refer to the "eternal part of man" as it does in modern American thought in many circles. For **my spirit**, the LXX reads "my liver," which seems to point to the Hebrew *kebhedhi* and requires no change in the consonantal text. In this case, the "liver" would be viewed as the seat of man's life or emotions. The renderings **my spirit** (RSV) or "my heart" (NEB) are simply attempts to accommodate a strange Hebrew expression to modern English terminology.

Genesis 34:26 states that Simeon and Levi slew men at Shechem, but not that they "hamstrung oxen" (although 34:28-29 does mention that they captured their livestock); thus, this verse provides a detail omitted in the earlier story. Biblical writers frequently omitted material which was at their disposal because it did not fit their religious message at the time that they wrote their books (cf. John 20:30-31; 21:25). Frequently in ancient warfare, soldiers would disable horses or other animals belonging to the enemy by cutting the tendons or sinews on their hind legs (cf. Josh. 11:6, 9; 2 Sam. 8:4), thus making it impossible for their foes to escape on the backs of the animals or use them in fighting by riding on them or having them pull chariots, or to employ them in some other way. In reading "they digged down a wall," the KJV follows Aquila, Symmachus, the Vulgate, the Syriac, and Targum Onkelos, rather than the MT.

[7] Simeon and Levi, the second and third sons of Jacob, also lost their father's birthright and blessing, because they slew the men of Shechem to avenge the rape of their sister Dinah. Jacob severely opposed such violent retaliation (cf. 34:30). As divine punishment for their sins, Jacob declares that the descendants of Simeon and Levi will be

divided and scattered in Israel. The tribe of Simeon was absorbed into the tribe of Judah at a very early period, and the descendants of Levi had to live in certain specified cities in each of the territories allotted to the other tribes, where they served as priests and Levites.

[8] After Reuben, Simeon, and Levi, **Judah** stands next in line for his father's birthright and blessing. He is the first son of Jacob that is blessed in this poem. Verse 8 contains the same Hebrew wordplay on **Judah** (Heb. *yehudhah*) and **praise** (Heb. *yadhah*) as does 29:35 (see the note there). The idea of Judah's **hand** being **on the neck of his enemies** seems to suggest the figure of Judean soldiers seizing their enemies by the neck as they fled and dashing them in pieces to the ground (cf. Job 16:12), which points to the conquests of Judah in the period of the Judges (Judg. 1:1-21) and to Israel's battles under the Judean, David (cf. 2 Sam. 5:6-8; 8:1-14). By acknowledging the kingship of David and Solomon over all Israel (see 2 Sam. 5:1-3), the other tribes were destined to **bow down before** Judah.

[9] **Judah** will attack his enemies with the ferocity of a **lion,** devour **the prey,** and then go back up to the safety and security of his den. The last two lines of this verse are almost identical (in Hebrew) with the first two lines of Numbers 24:9, which compares the ferocity of Israel with a lion. It should be noted that there is a shift from the second person singular in verses 8-9a to the third person singular in verse 9b, which corresponds to that which appears at the end of verse 4. The retention of the second person singular by the NEB has no support in the MT or the ancient versions and appears to be based on a modern desire for rigid literary symmetry.

[10] **The scepter** and **the ruler's staff** are symbols of kingship in the ancient Near East, including Israel (on this use of **scepter,** cf. Ps. 45:6 [Hebrew 7; twice] =Heb. 1:8; Isa. 14:5; Ezek. 19:11, 14; Amos 1:5, 8; Zech. 10:11). The Hebrew word *mechoqeq* is interpreted as "law-giver" by the LXX, Vulgate, and Targums Onkelos and Pseudo-Jonathan (so the KJV), and it does mean

"commander" in Judges 5:14. But the synonymous parallelism in the present verse shows that here it means **ruler's staff**, as it does in Numbers 21:18 and Psalm 60:7 (Hebrew 9) = 108:8 (Hebrew 9). Ancient drawings picture kings sitting on their thrones holding a staff in front of them **between their feet.**

The Hebrew phrase which the RSV translates **until he comes to whom it belongs** is very hard to interpret. The text itself is fraught with difficulties, and the ancient versions differ widely on the sense. Only a few interpretations can be mentioned here.

(1) The MT can be translated "until Shiloh come" (so the KJV and ASV), but what does this mean? Targum Onkelos apparently understood "Shiloh" as a title for the Messiah, and this understanding has been adopted in some circles in modern times. However, it should be kept in mind that the NT nowhere appeals or alludes to this passage as relating to Jesus Christ.

(2) The MT can also be rendered "until he (Judah) comes to Shiloh." Then the thought would be that Judah will rule over or be leader of the other tribes until he comes to Shiloh (where the ark was kept during a portion of the period of the Judges, cf. 1 Sam. 3:3; 4:3-11, and which seems to have been the central sanctuary of all the Israelite tribes). However, there is no historical evidence that might support or illuminate such a view.

(3) An ancient midrash and certain medieval Jewish rabbis read *shay lo*, that is, "to the end that tribute be brought him" or "so long as tribute is brought him" (so the NEB), a reading that finds some support in Isaiah 18:7.

(4) The Samaritan Pentateuch, LXX, Syriac, and Targum Onkelos seem to have read an original *shello(h)*, which can mean either "until he [Judah] comes into his own" or **until he comes to whom it** [the scepter, the ruler's staff, and thus the kingship] **belongs** (so the RSV). If this line is taken in connection with **and to him shall be the obedience of the peoples,** which follows, and with verses 11-12, "the thought seems to be that Judah will exercise tribal authority

(cf. Judg. 1:1-2) until the monarchy is established with a Judahite on the throne, at which time peace and prosperity will become proverbial" (J. H. Marks, "The Book of Genesis," IOVC, p. 31). Jacob, under divine inspiration, announces the coming of David, who will unite the loosely organized tribes into a nation under a king and will defeat the enemies around them so that God's people can live in peace in the land which God had promised them. This theme fits in beautifully with the strong emphasis on God's promise of the land of Canaan to the descendants of Abraham (13:14-17; 15:18-21; 22:17), Isaac (25:3), and Jacob (28:13, 15; 35:12).

[13] The tribal territory of **Zebulun** did not border on the Mediterranean Sea (cf. Josh. 19:10-16). Taking into consideration the close connection between Zebulun and Issachar both here (vss. 13-15) and in Deuteronomy 33 (vss. 18-19), the present verse may mean that the tribe of Zebulun profited from trading on the high seas because of her geographical proximity to Phoenicia (represented here by **Sidon**), a view that finds support in the statement "they [i.e., Zebulun and Issachar] suck the affluence of the seas" (Deut. 33:19). Or it may mean that Zebulunites served as slaves at forced labor in Phoenician ports (cf. the last statement concerning Issachar in Gen. 49:15).

[14-15] The section concerning **Issachar** lends itself to two possible interpretations. The RSV, ASV, and NEB interpret *mishpethayim* as **sheepfolds** and then understand verses 14-15a as a description of the ideal location of the territory of Issachar in a fertile and peaceful region and verse 15b as an indication that this tribe would be subjected to forced labor by their Canaanite neighbors. On the other hand, the KJV, J. Skinner (*Genesis*, ICC, p. 526), and Speiser (*Genesis*, p. 367) take *mishpethayim* in the sense of "burdens," "panniers," or "saddlebags" (respectively), and thus apparently see an *a b a b* structure in verses 14 and 15, with the *a* portions depicting Issachar's advantageous geographical position and the *b* portions portraying the subjection of his tribesmen to Canaanite taskmasters.

[16] **Dan** was one of the weakest tribes of Israel, and the last tribe to conquer a territory successfully—at the end of the period of the Judges! (Cf. Josh. 19:47; Judg. 18:27-29.) But with all this impotence and timidity, Jacob declares that still **Dan shall judge his people as** [any] **one of the tribes of Israel.** Here, as in 30:6 (cf. note there), there is a Hebrew wordplay on **Dan** (Heb. *dan*) and **judge** (Heb. *din*).

[17] Because the tribe of Dan will be small in number and weak in military strength, it must resort to guerilla tactics to defeat its enemies. But it will be successful, just as a **serpent** or a **viper** (a "horned snake" [*cerastes cornutus*]—so correctly the NEB) throws the rider by striking his horse's heels.

[18] Viewing in his mind's eye the precarious condition which the descendants of Dan will have in the promised land, Jacob turns to the Lord, who had stood by him in times of severe trial and affliction and declares that he is trusting in his **salvation** (deliverance) to spare the tribe of Dan in its plight.

[19] This entire verse consists of a Hebrew wordplay on **Gad**: *gadh gedhudh yeghudhennu wehu' yaghudh 'aqebh*, which the RSV and NEB capture reasonably well by using variations on the word **raid** (cf. another Hebrew wordplay on the word **Gad** in 30:11). In its location east of the Jordan, the tribe of Gad was more vulnerable to attacks by marauding bands, particularly its Ammonite neighbors (cf. Judg. 10:6–11:40; 1 Sam. 11:1; 1 Chron. 5:18-26; Jer. 49:1). But Jacob declares that Gad's descendants will be able to retaliate successfully for a long period of time.

[20] Jacob announces the same abundant prosperity for the descendants of Asher that is celebrated in Deuteronomy 33:24-25.

[21] This verse concerning the descendants of **Naphtali** is very difficult and has been interpreted in at least three ways. (1) Apparently for the purpose of making the first line correspond to the second, "who gives goodly [beautiful] words," the Syriac and Targum Pseudo-Jonathan render the first line "Naphtali is a swift messenger." (2) The LXX and Targum Onkelos seem to have pointed the sec-

ond Hebrew word in the first line as *'elah* (which requires no change in the consonantal text), which gives the meaning "Naphtali is a spreading terebinth putting forth lovely boughs" (so the NEB). (3) If one follows the Massoretic pointing and reads *'ayyalah*, **hind**, in the first line and then interprets *'imre* as a shortened form of *'immare*, **fawns**, in the second, he can read **Naphtali is a hind let loose, that bears comely fawns** (so the RSV). The reading adopted in the KJV and ASV does not preserve a good metaphor.

[22] Jacob announces that Joseph's descendants (i.e., the tribes of Ephraim and Manasseh) will be well-populated and prosperous in the land of Canaan. His comparison of Joseph with a tree contains two interesting Hebrew idioms. The expression translated **fruitful bough** (RSV) is *ben porath,* literally "son of a fruit-bearer." The Hebrew (and Aramaic) expression "son of" is used to call attention to the excellence of that which is named. So, for example, Joseph's name is changed to Barnabas, that is, *"son of* exhortation" (Acts 4:36), and James and John are called Boanerges, that is, *"sons of* thunder" (Mark 3:17). Again, the Hebrew word for **branches** is *banoth*, literally "daughters." The "daughters" of a tree are its branches. These two items again demonstrate that it is not always best to translate a text literally in order to convey the meaning that the writer had in mind.

[24] There is a slight textual problem in the last line. The MT reads *mishsham,* "from thence" (so the KJV and ASV), but this does not make sense in the context. The Syriac and Targum Onkelos read **by the name of** (RSV), which requires no change in the consonantal text but simply a change of pointing to read *mishshem*. Be this as it may, the point of verses 23 and 24 is clear: the descendants of Joseph will be severely attacked by enemies, but they will survive because God will be with them and protect them.

In four synonymous parallel lines in verses 24b-25a, Jacob uses five different terms for God: (1) **the Mighty One of Jacob**—see Psalm 132:2, 5; Isaiah 49:26; 60:16; (2) **the Shepherd**—see Psalms 23:1; 80:1; Ezekiel 34:11-16 (cf. the note on the verb "led" in 48:15); (3) **the Rock of Israel**—although the Hebrew words are different, virtually the same title occurs in Deuteronomy 32:4, 15, 18, 30-31, 37; 1 Samuel 2:2; 2 Samuel 22:3=Psalm 18:2 (Hebrew 4); 23:3; Isaiah 30:29; (4) "the God of your father"—see Exodus 3:15; and (5) "God Almighty" (Heb. *'el shadday*)—see 17:1; 28:3; 35:11; 43:14; 48:3; Exodus 6:3.

[26] The MT (*horay 'adh*), Vulgate, Syriac, and Targums Onkelos and Pseudo-Jonathan have "of my progenitors unto" in the second line (so the KJV and ASV). However, the LXX and the parallel passage in Deuteronomy 33:15 (cf. Hab. 3:6) favor a slight emendation to *harare 'adh*, **the eternal mountains** (so the RSV), which affords an excellent synonymous parallelism with the next line.

The reading "prince" (NEB) interprets the Hebrew word *nazir* as a derivative of *nezer*, "crowned one" (see Lam. 4:7). It seems more likely, however, to be associated with Nazirite in the sense of one **separate from his brothers** or consecrated to God (so the RSV, KJV, and ASV). Jacob is referring not to the abuse and punishment that Joseph's brothers heaped upon him because of their hatred and jealousy (37:18-28; in other words, the idea is not that Joseph's brothers left him out of their activities) but to the role of leadership that the tribes of Ephraim and Manasseh would have during the period of the Judges (cf. Judg. 1:22-29).

[27] Jacob announces that the descendants of **Benjamin** will be a ferocious warlike tribe, **a ravenous wolf**. Several passages bring out the accuracy of this description (see, e.g., Judg. 3:15-30; 5:14; chs. 19–20; 1 Chron. 8:40; 12:1-2; 2 Chron. 14:8 [Hebrew 7]; 17:17-18).

[29-32] Previously Jacob had instructed Joseph *as a great authority in Egypt* to see that he be buried at the family sepulchre in Canaan (cf. 47:29-30), probably to make sure that this would be done in keeping with Egyptian burial laws or customs. This would help explain why he had Joseph "swear" to him that this would be carried out after his death (cf. 47:31). Now, he tells all of his sons *as members of his family* and recipients of God's blessings and purposes through him to bury him in **the cave of Mach-**

pelah, which his grandfather Abraham had purchased from the **Hittites**. Jacob's rehearsal of events which are recorded in much greater detail in Genesis 23:3-20 indicates that **the cave** of **Machpelah** was regarded with great respect by Abraham and his descendants and that it was customary in ancient times to preserve much earlier events orally for long periods of time. This is the only place in the OT where one learns that **Isaac, Rebekah,** and **Leah** were buried in this cave. Undoubtedly, at one time the accounts of their deaths and burials were related orally or in writing (as was the case with Sarah, 23:1-2, 19; and Abraham, 25:7-10), but the author of the book of Genesis has deleted these records because they did not fit his message to his audience or meet their present needs (this is the same principle as that explicitly stated by John in John 20:30-31). Genesis 35:28-29 briefly relates the death and burial of Isaac but does not state where he was buried, while the deaths and burials of Rebekah and Leah have not been previously mentioned. The absence of Leah's name among those of Jacob's household who went down into Egypt (46:8-27) may indicate that she had already died by this time.

[33] A patriarch's official pronouncement concerning the future of his descendants was considered to be so important that the patriarch felt he must at least sit up in bed to deliver it (cf. Jacob's posture when he blessed Ephraim and Manasseh, 48:2), even though he was very weak and nearing death. Thus, after he had finished forecasting what would become of his tribal descendants, Jacob **drew up his feet into the bed**.

The last two lines of verse 33 do not necessarily mean that Jacob died a few moments or hours after he had spoken to his sons; the writer may be covering several days or even months with a few words here.

Jacob's Burial and Joseph's Death (Ch. 50)

Joseph has experienced Egyptian physicians embalm his father, and the Egyptians mourn for Jacob seventy days. Then Joseph asks the Pharaoh to allow him to go to Canaan to bury his father, and permission is granted. Joseph is accompanied by the adult members of Jacob's household, the elders of his own household in Egypt, and the elders of Egypt. When they come to the threshing floor of Atad east of the Jordan, they mourn for Jacob seven days. Joseph and his brothers bury Jacob in the cave of Machpelah at Hebron, then return to Egypt (vss. 1-14).

Joseph's brothers fear that, now that their father is dead, Joseph will take revenge on them for the way they treated him when they sold him to the Midianite merchants. They send to him and tell him that Jacob had told them before his death to tell Joseph to forgive them. Later, when they come before him, Joseph tells them not to fear, because he has no intention of retaliating (vss. 15-21).

Joseph lives to the good old age of 110 and gets to see his great-grandchildren. Before his death, he reiterates to his brothers the promise which Jacob had made that Jacob's descendants would come out of Egypt and possess the land of Canaan. He has his brothers swear that they will carry his bones with them when they leave Egypt for Canaan. In time, Joseph dies, is embalmed, and his remains are put in a coffin in Egypt (vss. 22-26).

This chapter contains two powerful illustrations of God's rule over men's lives. On the one hand, God uses the evil intended by Joseph's brothers to see to it that proper preparations are made for the famine. So, when Joseph's brothers reveal that they fear Joseph's vengeance, he replies: "You meant evil against me; but God meant it for good, to bring it about that many people should be kept alive, as they are today" (vs. 20). On the other hand, God's work in behalf of his people continues after the death of his great servants. The book of Genesis does not end with a period, but with a comma, as it were, for before his death, Joseph optimistically points his brothers to the bright future that God has in store for them when he brings them out of Egypt and gives them the promised land (vss. 24-25).

[2] Joseph does not use professional embalmers to embalm his father but **physicians** who were members of his household as the vizier of the land, perhaps in order to

avoid the pagan magical rites that were normally associated with the process of embalming in Egypt.

[3] Embalming in ancient Egypt took **forty days**, and the
Egyptians customarily mourned **seventy**[-two] **days** for high
officials of state. It is not clear whether the forty days is
included in the seventy or whether the seventy days followed the forty. At a later period, the Israelites mourned
for Aaron (Num. 20:29) and Moses (Deut. 34:8) thirty
days.

[4] It would have been contrary to proper Egyptian eti-
quette for Joseph to appear before the Pharaoh in person
during the period of mourning over his father, because during this time Joseph probably did not cut his beard and hair
and wore mourning clothes. One had to be shaved and
clothed in clean garments before being allowed to come
into the Pharaoh's presence (cf. 41:14). Therefore, Joseph
asks certain members of the Pharaoh's household to carry
his message to the Pharaoh.

[5] Many scholars see a contradiction between this verse
and 47:29-30; 49:29-32; 50:12-13. They contend that 50:5
refers to some tomb other than one in the cave of Machpelah. However, this understanding is not necessary, and the
problem arises from a lack of more detailed information. If
karithi is from the root *karath* and means **I hewed out**
(RSV) or "I have digged" (KJV, ASV), the thought may be
that Jacob had his **tomb** inside the cave of Machpelah
hewed out before he and his family went into Egypt that it
might be ready for his burial when his sons brought him
back. If it is from *karah* and means "I bought" (NEB;
cf. the same root with this sense in Deut. 2:6; Hos. 3:2),
the idea may be that, even though Abraham had bought the
field and cave of Machpelah from the Hittites (cf. 23:3-20),
Jacob had to pay the local inhabitants of a later generation
to retain possession of the land, as he was regarded as a
sojourner. Even if it could be proved that verses 5 and
12-13 were from two originally separate sources (the former from J and the latter from P), it seems highly unlikely
that the author of the book of Genesis would incorporate
both of them into his work if he thought they were inhar-

monious. Note especially the statement "Thus his sons did for him as he had commanded them" (vs. 12), which demands a prior command—and this is found only in 47:29-30; 49:29-32; and 50:5.

[7-9] The description of the **very great company** that went to Canaan to bury Jacob calls to mind pictures on Egyptian tombs depicting elaborate funeral processions for Pharaohs and high state officials. The **chariots** would have added color to and protection for the caravan.

[10] The location of **the threshing floor of Atad** is unknown. Nor is it clear why Joseph and his companions took the long route to the region east of the Jordan on their way from Egypt to Hebron, since it would have been much shorter to come into Canaan directly from the south. The time in which Joseph lived was filled with alternating periods of peace and unrest between Egypt and the peoples in the territory of Canaan. Perhaps Egyptian travelers were not welcome in the southern area, or all caravans were in constant danger of being raided by warlike inhabitants living in this region.

The phrase **which is beyond the Jordan** (vss. 10, 11) is the author's explanatory note to his readers, who did not know the location of the threshing floor of Atad; this indicates that he is writing many years after the event he is describing. A few scholars have proposed that *be'ebher hayyarden* means "in the region of the Jordan" rather than **beyond** [i.e., east of] **the Jordan**. However, the use of this phrase elsewhere in the OT makes this view doubtful. At the same time, it is probably true that the threshing floor of Atad is not very far east of the Jordan, because Canaanites observed the mourning of the travelers (vs. 11). Just upon entering the land which God had promised to the descendants of Jacob, Joseph and his entourage stop to mourn over Jacob **seven days**; at a later time, the men of Jabesh-gilead fast seven days after they bury the bones of Saul and his sons, whom the Philistines had killed at Mount Gilboa (1 Sam. 31:13).

[11] When the Canaanites living in the area see the intensity of the Egyptians' **mourning** (Heb. *'ebhel*), they name

the place **Abel-mizraim** (Heb. *'abhel mitsrayim*), that is, "meadow (or mourning) of Egypt," which once again contains a Hebrew wordplay.

[15] Even before Joseph revealed his true identity to his brothers (45:1-15), the heavy weight of their guilt over having treated him so harshly (cf. 37:18-28) caused them to think that their misfortunes might be divine punishments for their heinous crime (cf. 42:21, 28; 44:16). And after he told them, they feared that he might avenge himself on them (cf. 45:3). Now that their father Jacob is dead, they again fear that Joseph will use his powerful position in the Egyptian government to get even with them.

[16-17] Fearing what Joseph might do to them, his brothers do not go to him personally but send him a message. They claim that before his death, Jacob told them to **command** Joseph to forgive the evil they had inflicted on him. The statement assumes that Jacob met with (at least one of) his sons when he knew Joseph would be absent, that he shared their fear that Joseph might retaliate against them after his death, and that the most dynamic way to avert this was to tell Joseph his father's command after he had died. All of this looks very suspicious, and it is difficult to avoid the conclusion that Joseph's brothers invented this story in a desperate effort to assure their own safety. Joseph, who loved his brothers sincerely (cf. 42:24; 43:30-31; 45:1-15), is deeply hurt that they would think he held any animosity against them, and so he weeps when he hears the message from his brothers.

[18] When Joseph's brothers come in person to him, they again (cf. 42:6; 43:26, 28; 44:14) fall **down before him**, just as his dreams had indicated they would (cf. 37:7-10), and declare, **we are your servants** (cf. 44:16). This thought ties the end of the story of Jacob and Joseph to its beginning.

[19-21] Joseph's threefold response to his brothers reflects some of the highest and most noble attitudes in the Bible. (1) He declares that if there are any wrongs to be righted, God must take care of them (vs. 19; cf. Rom. 12:19; 1 Pet. 4:19). Here, Joseph's question **Am I in the**

place of God? means "Is it my prerogative to judge men and to punish them for their injustices to others?" When Jacob asked Rachel this same question (30:2), he meant "Do I have the power to enable you to conceive and give birth to a child?" The answer in both instances, of course, is no! (2) He affirms that God is able to work good in the very acts that men intend for evil (vs. 20; cf. 45:5, 7, 8; Rom. 8:28). The clearest illustration of this principle appears in Christ's death on the cross. Here, God opens a door of salvation to ungrateful, sinful, rebellious men, who cry out for and obtain the death of his Son because of their hatred and ignorance. (3) Not only does Joseph forgive his brothers, but he also cares for them in a practical way, returning good for evil (vs. 21; cf. Prov. 25:21-22=Rom. 12:20 [cf. vs. 21]; Matt. 5:38-48; Luke 6:27-36).

The Hebrew phrase *dibber 'al lebh,* literally "speak to the heart," is an idiom meaning "to comfort" (so the RSV), "to reassure" or to "set one's mind at rest" (so the NEB; cf. 34:3; Judg. 19:3; Ruth 2:13; 2 Sam. 19:8; 2 Chron. 30:22; 32:6; Isa. 40:2; Hos. 2:14 [Hebrew 16]).

[22] Several ancient Egyptian sources state that **a hundred and ten years** (cf. vs. 26) is an ideal lifetime.

[23] Although **Ephraim's children of the third generation** can mean Joseph's great-great-grandchildren through Ephraim, the similarity with the following statement concerning Joseph's great-grandchildren through Manasseh and the reading of the Samaritan Pentateuch strongly suggest that the author means Joseph's great-grandchildren through Ephraim.

The descendants of Manasseh's son **Machir** became the most powerful clan in the tribe of Manasseh (see Judg. 5:14).

The statement that **the children . . . of Machir . . . were born upon Joseph's knees** is an idiomatic Hebrew way of saying that Joseph officially made them members of his own household and looked on them as if they were his own children (cf. 30:3), just as Jacob had viewed Joseph's sons, Ephraim and Manasseh (cf. 48:5, 12).

[24] Like Jacob earlier (cf. 48:4, 21), Joseph assures his

brothers that God will bring up their descendants out of Egypt and give them the land of Canaan.

[25] Again like Jacob (cf. 47:29-31; 49:29-32), Joseph has his brothers take an oath that they will see to it that his bones are carried out of Egypt by their descendants when they begin their trek toward Canaan. Moses does what Joseph had commanded and even quotes this verse as authority for his action (Exod. 13:19). At approximately the beginning of the period of the Judges, the Israelites buried Joseph's bones at Shechem in Canaan in the portion of ground that Jacob purchased from the sons of Hamor for 100 pieces of money (Josh. 24:32; cf. Gen. 33:19). That Joseph would give such specific instructions concerning his bones before his death shows his great faith that God would give his people the land of Canaan as he had promised (cf. Heb. 11:22). Stephen states that Jacob was buried at Shechem (Acts 7:16), but apparently he means Jacob's son Joseph. (Jacob was buried at Hebron in the cave of Machpelah, Gen. 50:13.)

[26] The **coffin** was a wooden mummy case. After the embalmed body was placed in it, the coffin was usually set in a stone sarcophagus. The effectiveness of Egyptian embalming techniques in ancient times is attested by the mummified body of Pharaoh Rameses II (who lived about the time of Moses) on display in the Cairo Museum.

In the period covered by the book of Genesis, man traveled a long way from the garden of Eden to a coffin in Egypt, and God's chosen people covered a great distance from Ur of the Chaldees to the sojourn in Egypt. But God has promises to keep, and future generations can look forward to a brighter day.